LANDMARK ESSAYS ON SPEECH AND WRITING

Classical rhetoric was originally all about speech; then as the new technology emerged, it took an interest in writing. We are at a kind of mirror moment now. The present field of composition and rhetoric has been preoccupied with writing for the last fifty or more years, but scholars are looking once again at speech and how it relates to writing.

At this moment, then, we are inheritors of research showing that writing can be thought of as different and yet not different from speech. In this Landmark Essays volume, Peter Elbow, a leading expert on speech and writing, gathers a selection of classic essays that show the main streams of thinking that scholars have published about speech and writing. Through the interdisciplinary essays included, he invites readers to think critically about the relationship between speech, writing, and our notion of literacy.

Peter Elbow is Professor of English, Emeritus, at the University of Massachusetts at Amherst and former director of its Writing Program.

THE LANDMARK ESSAYS SERIES

Landmark Essays is a series of anthologies providing ready access to key rhetorical studies in a wide variety of fields. The classic articles and chapters that are fundamental to every subject are often the most difficult to obtain, and almost impossible to find arranged together for research or for classroom use. This series solves that problem.

Each book encompasses a dozen or more of the most significant published studies in a particular field, and includes an index and bibliography for further study.

Series Editors:
James J. Murphy
Krista Radcliffe

Landmark Essays on Rhetoric and Feminism: 1973-2000
Edited by Cheryl Glenn, Andrea Lunsford

Landmark Essays on Speech and Writing
Edited by Peter Elbow

Landmark Essays on Basic Writing
Edited by Kay Halasek, Nels P. Highberg

Landmark Essays on ESL Writing
Edited by Tony Silva, Paul Kei Matsuda

Landmark Essays on Rhetoric and Literature
Edited by Craig Kallendorf

Landmark Essays on Contemporary Rhetoric
Edited by Thomas B. Farrell

Landmark Essays on Aristotelian Rhetoric
Edited by Richard L. Enos, Lois P. Agnew

Landmark Essays on Bakhtin, Rhetoric, and Writing
Edited by Frank Farmer

Landmark Essays on Rhetoric and the Environment
Edited by Craig Waddell

Landmark Essays on Rhetoric of Science: Case Studies
Edited by Randy Allen Harris

Landmark Essays on Advanced Composition
Edited by Gary A. Olson, Julie Drew

Landmark Essays on Writing Centers
Edited by Christina Murphy, Joe Law

Landmark Essays on Rhetorical Invention in Writing
Edited by Richard E. Young, Yameng Liu

Landmark Essays on Writing Process
Edited by Sondra Perl

Landmark Essays on Writing Across the Curriculum
Edited by Charles Bazerman, David R. Russell

Landmark Essays on Rhetorical Criticism
Edited by Thomas W. Benson

Landmark Essays on Voice and Writing
Edited by Peter Elbow

Landmark Essays on Classical Greek Rhetoric
Edited by A. Edward Schiappa

Landmark Essays on Kenneth Burke
Edited by Barry Brummett

Landmark Essays on American Public Address
Edited by Martin Medhurst

LANDMARK
ESSAYS ON SPEECH AND WRITING

Edited by
PETER ELBOW

Routledge
Taylor & Francis Group
NEW YORK AND LONDON

First published 2015
by Routledge
711 Third Avenue, New York, NY 10017

and by Routledge
2 Park Square, Milton Park, Abingdon, Oxon, OX14 4RN

Routledge is an imprint of the Taylor & Francis Group, an informa business

© 2015 Taylor & Francis

The right of Peter Elbow to be identified as the author of the editorial material, and of the authors for their individual chapters, has been asserted in accordance with sections 77 and 78 of the Copyright, Designs and Patents Act 1988.

All rights reserved. No part of this book may be reprinted or reproduced or utilised in any form or by any electronic, mechanical, or other means, now known or hereafter invented, including photocopying and recording, or in any information storage or retrieval system, without permission in writing from the publishers.

Trademark notice: Product or corporate names may be trademarks or registered trademarks, and are used only for identification and explanation without intent to infringe.

Library of Congress Cataloging in Publication Data
Landmark essays on speech and writing / edited by Peter Elbow.
    pages cm.—(Landmark essays series)
  Includes bibliographical references and index.
  1. Rhetoric. 2. Written communication. I. Elbow, Peter, editor.
  P301.L293 2014
  808—dc23
                                                          2014018260

ISBN: [978-0-415-64168-5] (hbk)
ISBN: [978-0-415-64169-2] (pbk)

Typeset in Minion
by Keystroke, Station Road, Codsall, Wolverhampton

Printed and bound in the United States of America by Publishers Graphics, LLC on sustainably sourced paper.

*To Hettie, coming into speech—and Izzy,
coming into writing*

CONTENTS

INTRODUCTION   1

SECTION 1
HISTORICAL STORIES ABOUT THE DEVELOPMENT AND EFFECTS OF ALPHABETIC LITERACY   17

1. Denise Schmandt-Besserat and Michael Erard, Origins and Forms of Writing (2007)   19
2. Richard Leo Enos, The Emergence of a Literate Rhetoric in Greece (2006)   34
3. Jack Goody and Ian Watt, The Consequences of Literacy (1963)   46
4. Walter J. Ong, Writing is a Technology that Restructures Thought (1986/2001)   83
5. Beth Daniell, Narratives of Literacy (1999)   97
6. Lee Honeycutt, Literacy and the Writing Voice: The Intersection of Culture and Technology in Dictation (2004)   113

SECTION 2
ANALYSES OF HOW SPEECH AND WRITING RELATE TO EACH OTHER   139

7. Douglas Biber and Camilla Vásquez, Writing and Speaking (2007)   141
8. M.A.K. Halliday, Spoken and Written Modes of Meaning (1987)   157
9. Peter Elbow, The Shifting Relationships Between Speech and Writing (1985)   181
10. Wallace Chafe, Punctuation and the Prosody of Written Language (1988)   201
11. Deborah Tannen, Relative Focus on Involvement in Oral and Written Discourse (1985)   228
12. Geneva Smitherman, "The Blacker the Berry, the Sweeter the Juice": African American Student Writers and the NAEP (1999)   246

SECTION 3
EXPLORATIONS OF SOME FEATURES OF SPEECH WITH A SPECIAL RELEVANCE TO WRITING   255

13. Jim Milroy, Historical Description and the Ideology of the Standard Language (2000)   257
14. Peter Elbow, Intonation: A Virtue for Writing at the Root of Everyday Speech (2012)   268

APPENDIX
WRITERS TRYING TO CREATE THE ILLUSION OF SPEECH:
A SELECTION OF BRIEF PASSAGES   286

Introduction *286*
Robert Burns, from "To A Mouse. On Turning Her Up in Her Nest
  with the Plough" (1785) *287*
Mark Twain, from *Adventures of Huckleberry Finn* (1885) *288*
Robert Frost, from "The Death of the Hired Man" (1917) *288*
Zora Neale Hurston, from *Their Eyes Were Watching God* (1937) *289*
Jozuf Hadley (bradajo), "chaloookyu eensai" (1972/2002) *290*
Juliet Kono, from "A Scolding from My Father" (1995) *292*
David Mamet, a link to a passage from *Glengarry Glen Ross* (1984) *294*
Louise Bennett, from "Aunt Roachy Seh" (1993) *294*
James Kelman, from *How Late It Was, How Late* (1998) *295*
Alan Bennett, from *Talking Heads* (2008) *296*
Laura Wright, from "Medieval Business English" (2001) *297*

Index   300

ACKNOWLEDGMENTS

I've enjoyed help from myriad people I've worked with on these issues for more than a decade. I send gratitude to them all—even those I've forgotten.

But I send special thanks to Jerry Murphy for generous encouragement from his place of deep learning; and to Ross Wagenhofer at Routledge for gracious and deft help in making this book happen.

Peter Elbow

INTRODUCTION
Peter Elbow

> It should be observed that each kind of rhetoric has its own appropriate style. The style of written prose is not that of spoken oratory.
> — Aristotle, *Rhetoric*, Book III, Chapter 12

> [W]riting makes speaking precise and speaking makes writing easy.
> — Quintillian, *Institutes*, X, 7, 29[1]

The essays collected here concern the relationships between speech and writing: about the many ways in which speech and writing can be compared, can interact, and can each be looked at through the lens of the other. But even using this limiting lens, I had to reject lots of good work that is pertinent, and so I recognize that good readers may question some of my choices. In particular I have probably been influenced by having spent my career focused on writing; I'm a newcomer to the field of speech and my forays into linguistics are relatively new. (It would have been impossible to consider the vast array of brilliant essays about speech or writing themselves, not in relationship to each other.)

The two epigraphs above represent the tradition we have been living with for two thousand years. That "common sense" is valid in many ways, but the essays here show that things are not so simple.

I will begin with a very brief word about each of the essays collected here. Afterwards, I'll go on to use most of the Introduction to lay out some background information and thinking that will better prepare readers for the essays that follow.

1. Schmandt-Besserat and Erard, "Origins and Forms of Writing." A detailed account of the development of writing; more attention to the Middle East and the alphabet than to other sites of origin.
2. Enos, "The Emergence of a Literate Rhetoric in Greece." An account of how the earliest writing in Greece was not just a matter of using alphabetic letters but also, almost concurrently, a matter of using a root structural principal—the paragraph—and how that early form reached almost all the way to what we think of the paragraph.
3. Goody and Watt, "The Consequences of Literacy." An argument that the development of alphabetic literacy in Greece led to profound changes in human thinking and ways of looking at the world.
4. Ong, "Writing is a Technology that Restructures Thought." The title accurately summarizes the argument.
5. Daniell, "Narratives of Literacy." A survey that looks at competing theories of how the development of literacy affected thinking and culture.
6. Honeycutt, "Literacy and the Writing Voice: The Intersection of Culture and Technology in Dictation." An exploration of the nature and effects of

dictation—from the dawn of Greek literacy to the modern office and recent uses of voice-activated software.
7. Biber and Vásquez, "Writing and Speaking." A comprehensive survey of masses of research about the nature of written and spoken language.
8. Halliday, "Spoken and Written Modes of Meaning." A detailed exploration of the grammar of spoken and written language with, among other things, attention to the complexity and intricacy of spoken modes as opposed to written modes.
9. Elbow, "The Shifting Relationships Between Speech and Writing." A paradoxical argument that speech and writing are profoundly different and profoundly similar.
10. Chafe, "Punctuation and the Prosody of Written Language." An argument that good punctuation can more accurately be described as largely reflecting the actual prosody of spoken language than purely grammar-based rules of punctuation.
11. Tannen, "Relative Focus on Involvement in Oral and Written Discourse." An argument that the distinction between spoken and written language breaks down, and that the more accurate and productive distinction is between language with involvement features versus language with distancing features.
12. Smitherman, "'The Blacker the Berry, the Sweeter the Juice': African American Student Writers and the NAEP." An analysis of data showing that while Black grammar correlated with low scores by NAEP raters, Black discourse or rhetoric actually correlated with high scores.
13. Milroy, "Historical Description and the Ideology of the Standard Language." An exploration of the ideological implications of a larger argument: that early modern English was not the dialect spoken in London—the new economic and political capital of England—but rather an idealized, abstract invented dialect that had never been spoken by anybody.
14. Elbow, "Intonation: A Virtue for Writing at the Root of Everyday Speech." An argument for the centrality of audible spoken intonation or prosody for silent writing.

Appendix. A collection of short passages to illustrate the highly diverse ways in which writers have tried to create the illusion of speech on the silent page.

Starting with a Counter Claim: That Speech and Writing have Nothing to Do with Each Other

All the essays in the volume (and my attempt in this introduction to define speech and writing) rest on an assumption that's almost universally held: that writing and speech are deeply and inherently related. But Roy Harris makes this intriguing counter argument: that our pervasive linking of speech and writing represents a basic conceptual confusion. He makes a clump of interesting arguments. He says that it's only through a kind of historical accident that writing has so often been used to represent speech.

Introduction

He insists that this accident masks the *essential nature* of writing—a modality that has nothing to do speech; and that humans only developed writing by creatively *moving away from speech* to an entirely different realm—moving from the temporal/audible realm to the visual/spatial realm.

He points out, for example, that we can *speak* the words "three thousand and forty-eight," but that it was only by leaping away from the temporal/audible realm of speech that humans figured out what can be done by exploiting the *spatial* representations of meaning, namely "3,048:"

> If mathematics had to rely on speech as its cognitive mode, we should still be living in a primitive agricultural society.
>
> (*Origin* 144)

> The mathematicians were the first thinkers who realized the enormous potential of writing as writing.... The alphabet itself was a blind alley for mathematics, as it was for music. In Greek and Roman mathematics, alphabetically based numerical systems were a hindrance rather than a help [because they treated written numerical symbols as nothing more than abbreviations for words].
>
> (Ibid. 135–137)

> [The Sumerian invention of zero as "place-holder"] represents not a development of but a complete break away from any notion that written signs should conform to or mirror the structures of spoken language.
>
> (Ibid. 136)

In his two books about writing and how it differs from speech, Harris points out an important general principle: Space is a poor medium for representing events in time (see the section below, on the rebus). For example, it's not easy to represent complex rhythms of music on a paper score (especially in the case of jazz). Yes, the score is an accurate representation of the rhythms (though skilled players often "bend" these paper rhythms). Yet these visual sequences of notes and rests on paper are extraordinarily intricate and difficult to read, while in fact most of these complex rhythms come naturally to the body! We can scarcely keep from moving our fingers or our whole bodies in time with rhythms that only skilled musicians can read. Yes, these "natural" rhythms depend on our lives in this culture, but that experience does not make it any easier to read those complex visually coded messages.

What Harris celebrates about writing is how well it represents *information*, not audible, temporal speech—which is why the medium of space is ideal for mathematics and diagrams. Harris shows how well space can represent electrical circuits and other complex logical diagrams. He focuses on these as paradigms for writing. He insists that a true understanding of the nature of writing only comes clear when we free it from the link with speech—free it as a spatial entity from the shackles of time.

I don't see any way to refute many of Harris's claims and examples, nor his larger argument about the limitations of writing as an attempt to represent speech as a temporal phenomenon. Yet of course nothing he says can help me—or probably most of you—to escape from the inevitable linking of speech and writing. So the rest of this book will leave Harris's intriguing argument behind.

Defining Speech and Writing in Relationship to Each Other

To prepare the ground for these essays about the relationships between speech and writing, it is necessary to explore the complexities in these very words, *speech* and *writing*. To open the door, consider this example: Remember or imagine a time when you were dictating a letter or memo—or perhaps using voice-activated software to produce a written text. So were you speaking or writing? Not an easy question; but the answer will come clear as I work out clearer definitions of the two terms.

There are actually four different meanings for the relationship between speaking and writing:

(1) Speaking and writing as verbs for different **outward physical actions**

We mostly don't get confused as to whether we are using our mouths or our fingers to produce words. There are some borderline perplexities, as with dictation, but this perplexity will resolve as I move to the next way of contrasting the two terms.

(2) Speaking and writing as verbs for different **inward mental actions**

The prominent linguist M. A. K. Halliday focuses not so much on the physical differences between using the mouth or the fingers, but rather on the following inner differences between two ways of using the mind—two ways of generating language: spontaneously allowing words to arrive without planning them versus choosing them with care. He emphasizes how casual speech usually leads to unplanned or "spontaneous" language; and how careful writing usually leads to language that is "self-monitor[ed]," "controlled," and "self-conscious" (his words, from his essay in this volume). But he explicitly recognizes exceptions: We can use our mouths to produce carefully planned language—for instance during a job interview or a dangerous argument. And we can use our fingers to produce spontaneous unplanned language—for instance during freewriting and in some emails or letters or journal entries. (Perversely, perhaps, he even uses the word "speak" for the act of writing spontaneously [see p. 167])

It's this distinction between physical writing and mental writing that helps us resolve the puzzle about dictation. On the one hand, when people dictate, they are often *mentally* creating written sentences or written lines of a poem. They think about where the sentences begin and end; sometimes they even speak the punctuation aloud (as voice-activated software invites you to do). When Milton was dictating *Paradise Lost* to his daughter, he surely thought about where to end each line and probably also about the punctuation. But on the other hand, people often enough *mentally speak* when they dictate. The difference was borne home to me on occasions when I was trying to dictate careful writing but became tangled up and self-conscious. I gave up the struggle and changed mental gears and let myself "just talk"—putting out careless unplanned language in order to "get down" as many words and thoughts as possible without any worries about wording and organization.[2]

We now move on to (3) and (4), a comparison between which gives helpful perspective. I will start now with (3); its story can be quickly told. When we get to (4), however, the story becomes complicated.

(3) Speech and writing as nouns—for different **physical products**—*one audible, one visible*

Speech in this third sense is a noun for audible sounds for the ear; writing is a noun for marks for the eye. Sounds are nothing but compressed air molecules, so speech in this sense dissipates the moment it is uttered. The words are gone forever unless they have been recorded. Spoken words exist in the medium of *time*, a medium that traps us in the *now* and sweeps us implacably toward the future. We can't experience the past or the future—only thoughts *about* the past or future.

In contrast, writing in this third sense means marks for the eye. These visible marks can persist through time—on the page or the screen or the billboard—as long as we want (or longer!). We can examine written words at whatever time or pace we want—for example skimming or re-reading. And visible words exist in *space*, a medium of remarkable freedom. We can look back in space to where we came from and forward to where we're headed—look left and right, up and down, often for great distances. In time, however, we can't look forward, and we can't trust our attempts to look back. We can compare two or three versions of a visible text almost simultaneously, whereas it's extremely difficult to compare multiple spoken stretches of language. (Technology now lets us record audible words and thus "check the record," yet it's very hard to compare recorded texts.)

In short, speech and writing as nouns for contrasting physical sensory products are just as distinct from each other as speech and writing as verbs for contrasting bodily activities. And here too we have an intriguing borderline example: sign language. It's a kind of speaking, and thus temporal and ephemeral, yet it's like writing for being visual and spatial.

(4) Speech and writing as nouns for different **linguistic products**—*that is, different kinds of language*

This is the realm of greatest confusion and dispute. Linguists do a dance with two surprising steps:

(i) Even though most people assume that the language that comes from our fingers is different and more formal than the language that comes from our mouths, linguists have worked to demonstrate that the difference disappears if we look more carefully. When they examine a full range of spoken and written language produced in a full range of human contexts and purposes, the dividing line between spoken and written language pretty much disappears. In a 2007 survey of all the research on speech and writing (included in this volume), Biber and Vásquez conclude as follows: "[T]here are few, if any, absolute linguistic differences between the [language that is produced in the] written and spoken modes. . . ." (Biber and Vásquez, see 143, see also Biber *Variation*). For example, they show that some *written* language is more informal and "speech-like" than most speech. (Consider much email and many diaries and personal letters.) And some *spoken* language is more formal and "writing-like" than much writing. (Consider the formality of some spoken lectures, announcements, and interviews.) Another linguist, Wallace Chafe, makes the same point: "Nothing consistently differentiates all varieties of speaking [spoken language] from all varieties of writing [written language]" (*Consciousness* 48).

(ii) But after linguists are done demolishing the distinction between spoken and written language, they turn around and reinstate it. They manage this by using the terms in a more restricted way, making a distinction between what they call "*typical spoken language*" and "*typical written language.*" In short, they focus on two common *kinds* or *genres* or *registers* of language: everyday conversational *spoken language* versus careful informational or expository prose or "essayist" *written language*.

In fact, I cut Biber and Vásquez off when they were saying that there's no difference between spoken and written language. They finish by saying: "However, there are strong and systematic linguistic differences between stereotypical speech and stereotypical writing." (143). And so, interestingly, the latest and most careful linguistic analysis supports the common naive assumption: that speech is more informal than writing—as long as we add the word "typical." (We see the greatest contrast between typical speech and writing if we look at the case of speakers of nonsanctioned vernaculars. See Nero and Ahmad.)

But what *is* typical writing? To define it, Biber and Vásquez use the somewhat vague phrase "careful written informational prose." This creates a large umbrella that covers many kinds of writing used in many different fields at different educational levels and in many nonschool settings—but it's a useable umbrella nevertheless and one that most people recognize. (See Olson "From Utterance to Text," where he uses the term "essayist prose" as a rough equivalent for "careful written informational prose.")

And what is *typical speech*? It's the everyday conversational language that children start to master and produce and internalize from toddlerhood. Linguists permit themselves the linguistic shortcut of referring to this language as "spoken language." This complex language comes out of our mouths without planning, when we have a thought or feeling to share. It's also the language we usually use when we talk to ourselves inside our heads. Halliday is at pains to show that spoken language has a more complex and intricate grammar than what is specified as "correct grammar"—the "edited written

English." He gives this striking example of a spontaneously spoken sentence: "They'd been going to've been paying me all this time" (*Complementarities* 127). He goes on to analyze the amazingly complex syntactical rules the speaker followed without trying. Another linguist, Stephen Pinker, remarks that "A preschooler's tacit knowledge of grammar is more sophisticated than the thickest style manual or the most state-of-the-art computer language system...."(*Instinct*, 6).

Of course when people don't feel comfortable or safe, they may plan their words slowly and carefully. Some literate people even manage to internalize the rules for "correct writing" and become, as it were, native speakers of writing who can fluently speak careful language that linguists call "*untypical* speech."

But we mustn't forget the larger picture: These terms, spoken and written language, are shorthand for restricted registers. In fact, there's no kind of language that humans don't create with their hands or mouths. I find it helpful to add the terms "easy" or "unplanned" or "uncareful" to distinguish typical everyday unplanned speech from the wide range of language that *can* be spoken.

When people get into arguments about speech and writing or about orality and literacy, their conflicts will often dissolve if they stop to untangle these four dimensions of speech and writing. One disputant might often unconsciously assume one meaning of the terms, while the other assumes a contrasting meaning. No wonder they can't agree.

A note on methodology. When I analyze the binary opposition between speech and writing by breaking it down into four different oppositions, I am making a kind of Aristotelian move. He loved to increase clarity and precision by dividing entities into species or sorts or parts; "in a sense" was one of his favorite phrases. What's important here is that thinking often becomes confused or arguments become fruitless because people silently slide between different senses of a term.[3]

Readers of this volume would do well to know some other complexities in the meanings of our two central terms, speech and writing, as they have been used across history.

—During the Middle Ages, when few could write at all, speaking and writing were often simultaneous activities. That is, many monks who copied manuscripts in monasteries would speak or mutter the words as they wrote them. This speaking-while-writing was particularly helpful if the monk were weak in his knowledge of the original language. In fact, many monks didn't know Latin very well—or could speak it but not read it easily. Speaking words aloud often reveals meanings that the eye cannot understand, and it cuts down errors. (Many modern inexperienced readers of Chaucer find his language understandable if they sound out the words.) Chaytor argues that Medieval scriptoria in monasteries had cubicles because of the noise of scribes all speaking or muttering at the same time (19).

Sometimes monks wrote (copied) texts in a language completely unfamiliar to them. It's widely known that the Western world got access to many Greek and Latin texts only because they were translated into Arabic and thus preserved. Relatively few monks knew Arabic, so when they copied these manuscripts, there were no sounds or meanings involved: It's as though they were copying a picture.

And for yet another wrinkle in the Medieval relationship between speech and writing, people who were entirely unable to write nevertheless dictated books and letters. Charlemagne was a case in point and "wrote" a book with Alcuin. And often enough it was the other way around. Many scribes who could write something out from dictation were not able to "compose": to conceive of meanings and words that were considered worthy to write out.

There was a comparable intertwining between speaking and *reading* throughout the entire Classical and Medieval periods, and often somewhat later. That is, people who knew how to read almost never engaged in the process without speaking the words aloud. It was very common for Greeks and especially Romans to have someone else read aloud for them—even if they happened to be able to read themselves. In an interesting link between literacy and slavery throughout this long period, slaves in Greek and Roman societies were often more literate than their masters and were used for both jobs of reading and writing. (Compare this to how U.S. slave owners tried to prevent slaves from learning to read and write.)

Historical Perspective on How We Got from Speech to Writing

Early Bridges Across the Gulf Between Speech and Writing

"Art preceded writing by some 25,000 years"! (Schmandt-Besserat and Erard, on the first page of the first essay in this volume). So it was a long wait till the first small step toward writing—a step that was itself merely an offshoot of art: drawing little pictures of generic objects like a sun, moon, human, and tree. This happened first in the Middle East—and much later in China and later still in Middle America. These were pictures for the eye, but they served as symbols telling the mouth how to *say* "sun," "moon," "human," and "tree." Was this writing? It depends on definitions that historians and linguists argue about (for example, is it writing if it doesn't have syntax?). We might call it proto-writing. This first bridge between speech and writing—between the realms of seeing and hearing, space and time—involved only nouns. Nouns are spoken and heard, but they are fairly static and thus not so far from the visual/spatial realm. There were no verbs, no syntax.

Then something happened around 7500 BCE. Some clerks in Mesopotamia learned to make little clay tokens, like monopoly pieces, to stand for commodities like beer, grain, and oil (see Schmandt-Besserat and Erard). The tokens didn't *resemble* beer, grain, and oil, but they were easy to remember, and so they did the job of bringing the right sound to "readers'" lips with nothing but a visual cue. With this form of three-dimensional proto-writing-*plus*, they could keep fairly complex financial records. Note how art from the earliest times was used to convey large artistic and sometimes spiritual meanings, while writing was born from financial needs: for recording the most concrete and down-to-earth transactions.

And then well before 3500 BCE, some administrator or scribe in a Sumerian city state came up against the real hurdle that lay between humans and genuine writing. He needed visual representations for the names of individuals who had bought or sold commodities, and also for the tombs of kings, but there were too many names to remember with visual tokens.

Whoever first solved this problem was a genius. He (a group? a woman?) came up with one of the biggest conceptual breakthroughs in human history: the *rebus*. We have trouble seeing the brilliance here because we've come to see the rebus as nothing but a simple children's game. What could be simpler for us than drawing a visual sketch of a bee and a leaf and using those pictures to stand for our spoken/audible word "belief"? Schmandt-Besserat and Erard give an early example from the region of the breakthrough: Someone wrote a man's name, *Luka*, by drawing a schematic picture of man's body (prounounced "lu") followed a picture of a mouth (pronounced "ka").

It's worth pausing to note that this story involves immense gaps of time: Art began who knows when; then after 25,000 years we get to 7500 BCE and proto-writing; then sometime before 3500 BCE we get the invention of rebus as a way to represent names that cannot be pictured.

And there's an interesting paradox buried in these glacial expanses of time. The story of writing up to this point involved moving *away* from resemblance or mimesis and toward abstraction, for example by using nonrepresentational tokens, (e.g., a cone for a small measure of grain and a sphere for a large measure.) And then came an even larger step toward abstraction: The cone came to stand not for a *small measure of grain* but for the *numeral one*; and the sphere not for a *large measure of grain* but for the *numeral ten*! Thus the cone and sphere became abstractions that could represent one and ten of *anything*. With the invention of the rebus, the path toward writing swerves back toward picturing—yet the goal was to achieve greater abstraction; that is, to represent what cannot be pictured.

We don't see rebuses or pictures of bees or mouths in our alphabet, with its completely abstract nonrepresentational letters. But the pictures were once there. The Hebrew word *aleph* (source for the first letter of our alphabet) means "ox," and the visual Hebrew letter *aleph* derived from a schematic picture of an ox's head. This was a kind of rebus: They used a picture to represent a *sound*—in this case the sound of the glottal stop used for saying *aleph*. The same goes for the second letter of the alphabet, *beta*, meaning "house": A schematized picture of a house was used to represent the "buh" sound that begins *beta/house*. Almost all our letters carry the same buried representational history, but when this Hebrew alphabet got to Greece, the letter names were kept, although the "pictures" evolved and lost any representational quality. We can no longer see how the rebus gave us our alphabet, but it did.

Three Superhighways Between Speech and Writing

Because speech is rooted in biology, it has some similar features across languages: "linguistic universals." Writing has no biological roots, however; it's an invented artifact, and different cultures invented completely different forms of writing.

There were evidently only three occasions when humans were brilliant and creative enough to invent written language. Around 3500 BCE the Canaanites or Semites in the Middle East came up with the alphabet that led to ours, and then around

1200 BCE the Chinese evolved their non-alphabetic character-based system. And around 200 CE the Maya in Central America invented their hieroglyphic writing system. (Egyptian hieroglyphs? Schmandt-Besserat and Erard suggest they were derived from Mesopotamian symbols.)

As writing evolved from these three sources and spread around the world over the centuries, we ended up with three different *kinds* of writing symbols:

- *Alphabetic* symbols are the ones you are looking at. Compared with the other two systems, alphabetic letters represent the *smallest* units of meaning (phonemes). A phoneme like the letter like "b" has no meaning at all; it stands only for the sound *buh*. It gets meaning only when combined with other phonemes or letters, as in *bat* or *bet* or *but*.
- At the opposite extreme are *logographic* symbols—like Chinese characters or Egyptian or Mayan hieroglyphs. They carry the *most* meaning. They represent entire words or concepts. Yet a logographic symbol gives no clue about sound—about how to pronounce a word. Notice that English uses a few logographic symbols too, such as "&" and "3"—and indeed all our borrowed Arabic numerals. That is, we use a kind of picture—"3"—but this picture bears no relationship at all to what we call it in English, "three"—nor to the German "drei" or the French "trois."
- The *syllabic* system lies in the middle. Syllabic symbols or "letters" carry more meaning than alphabetic letters but less meaning than Chinese characters or Egyptian hieroglyphs (or "3"). As syllables, they obviously relate to the sounds of the spoken language. In our English alphabetic system we also have a few traces of a syllabic system—as when we use the letter "a" to mean *not*, as in "amoral" or "asymmetrical." In this case, "a" functions not as a meaning-free letter but as a syllabic symbol that actually does carry its own meaning. Japan uses two complete syllabic systems for writing—along with a logographic one.

It is common and handy to label entire writing systems as alphabetic, logographic, or syllabic, but in fact no actual writing system is wholly consistent. We just saw that English mixes in some logographic and syllabic symbols.

> [A]ll writing systems use a mixture of phonetic and semantic signs. What differs [from one written language to another] . . . is the *proportion* of phonetic to semantic signs. The higher the proportion [of phonetic signs], the easier it is to guess the pronunciation of a word. In English the proportion is high, in Chinese it is low.
>
> (Robinson 14)

Robinson makes a continuum of languages that run from maximum phonography to maximum logography. Here is the sequence:

> At one extreme is the pure phonography of the International Phonetic Alphabet; then Finnish/French/leading to the midpoint of English; then Korean/Japanese/Chinese leading to the other extreme, the pure logography of mathematical symbols.
>
> (17)

Despite the differing degrees of phonography and logography shown in this continuum, Robinson insists that *every* writing system is linked to speech:

> Writing and reading are intimately and inextricably bound to speech, whether or not we move our lips. Chinese characters do *not* speak directly to the mind without the intervention of sound, despite centuries of claims to the contrary by the Chinese and by many Western scholars. Nor do Egyptian hieroglyphs, notwithstanding the beauty of their symbols and the fact that we can recognize people, animals, objects and the natural world depicted in them.
>
> (17)

Therefore, even though Chinese characters and Egyptian and Mayan hieroglyphs tend to picture a thing (sometimes faintly or in a very stylized way), occasionally those symbols function rebus-wise and do *not* mean what they picture. That is, sometimes an extra mark is added: It says to the reader, "This little picture of a spear doesn't stand for *spear*, it stands for the initial *sound* of *spear*; that is, the sound *sp*."

The three writing systems each have advantages and disadvantages. In Western culture, we like to brag about how easy literacy is with an alphabetic system. The alphabet works particularly well for Finns and Spaniards because they have made their spelling fit consistently with the pronunciation of written words. English speakers and writers are at a disadvantage because there are so many anomalies in spelling. Still, alphabet users can write and read every word in the language by learning to use only twenty-five to forty letters—depending on the alphabet.

In contrast, Chinese readers, using their logographic writing system, cannot sound out their visible writing into speech—nor speakers sound out their audible speech into writing. Yet because of this very fact, Chinese writing can be read by people who can't speak to each other. This is a big help for speakers of the four or five mutually unintelligible spoken forms of Chinese. Because of this convenience and because the characters are so ancient and beautiful, most literate Chinese feel enormous pride in their writing system and have a big psychic investment in it—despite the fact that Mao Tse Tung came very close to imposing the Roman alphabet on the huge nation in order to make literacy more available to the masses. (He was dissuaded at the last minute; see *Vernacular Eloquence*, 336–39). Literacy in Chinese puts an immense burden on rote memory. There are something like eighty thousand Chinese characters; however, ten thousand will render ninety-eight percent of the writing, and one thousand will render ninety percent of the writing. Still, it's a daunting task for Chinese children to attain literacy—even for only ninety percent of their writing.

Despite the pride of both Chinese and Westerners in their writing systems, the *syllabic* writing system is probably the most practical and efficient. Syllabic "letters" denote sound—providing a bridge between visual writing and sounded speech. Reading and writing are far easier with a syllabary than with an alphabet. True, a syllabary requires learning a couple of hundred symbols compared to a mere twenty-six or more alphabetic letters, but when you learn the syllabic symbols, reading and writing come much more quickly. In 1820 in Arkansas, Sequoya, a Cree Native American, singlehandedly invented a syllabary for the spoken Cree Indian language. It was astoundingly successful at producing widespread literacy—and in only a matter of months for most learners (see Cushman; Lepore).

Historical Sketch of How Scholars Have *Looked at* Speech and Writing

Early Greek rhetoricians could study only speech; there simply was no writing yet available to them. When rhetors composed celebratory or courtroom speeches or poems, composition was always in speech. Thus all insights about language depended on careful listening, and the insights were framed in terms of speech—and in particular about what made a good speech.

When the technology of writing was devised in the Silicon Valley of the day, rhetoric gradually came to focus on writing as well. Insights about language could shed light on what makes a good text. Speaking and writing were entwined in ways that might surprise modern readers. For example, rhetors often composed language by speaking it while someone else transcribed the words into writing; or they might write a text for someone else to deliver as a speech.

Starting in late antiquity and on through the Middle Ages and Renaissance, and even up through much of the nineteenth century, scholars of language (latterly called philologists) tended to see writing as the genuine form or manifestation of language—and spoken language as only an imperfect distorted form. To study language was to study *writing*—almost invariably in the form of canonical texts in Greek, Latin, Hebrew, or Arabic.

But then—partly but not entirely because electronic technology enabled us to record speech and examine our "winged words" more carefully—attitudes gradually swung the other way. The newer breed of scholars who studied language (calling themselves linguists now, rather than philologists) came to insist that the *spoken* version of a language is the real version and a truer picture of that language. Writing came to be seen as second hand—an artificial and unreliable picture of the actual language. As this development took place, linguists gradually came to see the intricate rule governed grammatical patterns in spoken language—no longer seeing spoken grammar as a debased departure from "real grammar" (i.e., Latin-based grammar). In the twentieth century there grew up a large industry of linguists (and a few scholars in composition and other fields) who wrote extensively about the *relationship* between speech and writing. (Biber and Vásquez, Halliday, and Tannen give us examples in this volume.) Still, it should be noted that the bias toward writing as the *standard* or best version of a language dies hard. Milroy, in this volume, complains as follows:

> [D]espite the prominent insistence of Henry Cecil Wyld that our aim must be to write histories of spoken English, the canonical account of the history of English is—arguably—still not as far removed as it ought to be from a history of written English.
>
> (p. 260 [14 in the original])

Halliday in his essay here, and especially in his longer works, is notable for his devotion to analyzing the grammar of spoken English on the hoof.

The present field of composition and rhetoric got started in the mid twentieth century with a focus on writing, but conditions are now encouraging those of us in the field to think more about speech and how it relates to writing. This development is partly fueled by many colleges and universities starting to insist that students develop some effectiveness giving speeches or taking part in discussions. I recently heard this paradoxical locution: "To be literate, students now need skill in speaking." When institutions have speech departments, they usually take on this job, but often the job has fallen to the composition (writing) faculty—few of whom have any training in speech.

Not so many years ago, I audited a course from a prominent Chomskean linguist here at UMass, Tom Roeper, and I remarked to him one day: "Isn't it sad that the field of English used to take speech as one of its main interests. Speech was one of the 'three legs' of the stool called English. But now speech has disappeared from our field." "We wouldn't be caught dead with English," he replied. "Linguistics is a science." Not every linguist would agree, but surely it's time for people in English and composition to study spoken language again and to learn from linguistics—whether or not defined as science. I've tried to take on some of that job in my *Vernacular Eloquence: What Speech Can Bring to Writing*.

Two Recent Scholarly Tangles about Speech and Writing

Both arose in the second half of the twentieth century. Both involve speech and writing, yet few of the participating scholars had much of a foundation in speech studies.

The first tangle has come to be referred to as the "orality/literacy wars." There was no sense of war in the beginning, when one of the most respected classicists of our times, Eric Havelock, made ambitious claims about the effects of alphabetic literacy in Ancient Greece—effects even on how humans came to think, see the world, and interact with each other. Others followed, notably Walter Ong, Jack Goody, Ian Watt, and even Marshall McLuhan. Their work, however, gave rise to a chorus of vociferous skeptics accusing these scholars of denigrating oral cultures, of being seduced by technological determinism, and of succumbing to the myth of constant progress. Participants in this tangle came from an amazingly wide array of disciplines: classics, history, sociology, cultural studies, and of course composition and literature. On both sides there was a temptation to overstatement. The essays in this volume by Goody and Watt, Ong, and Daniell give some sense of an important scholarly tangle, but the heat has gone out of it by now.

The second scholarly tangle was about *voice*, and it involved participants from a smaller array of fields: mostly composition, cultural studies, and literature (and Derrida as a philosopher). In the beginning the discussion was about voice *in texts*. Thus, the term is necessarily a metaphor, since it refers to a literally silent feature in a literally silent text. I was an early proponent for the importance of voice as a feature of texts that often has a big effect on how readers experience a text, sometimes without awareness of that textual voice and its effect. Among other virtues, the voice lens functions as a useful alternative to the style lens: Each lens brings to light features of a text that the other leaves in shadow. For example, the style lens might yield the following critique of student writing: "This passage is too heavily nominalized and uses too many passives and the verb *to be*." In contrast, the voice lens might yield this: "The passage sounds a bit pompous or bureaucratic." The style lens yields something more precise and even quantifiable, yet I find that the voice lens helps more students get rid of the problem.

The interest in voice started in the seventies, and before long garnered enthusiasm— and also overstatement: e.g., if a text "had voice" it must be good writing. (Despite my arguments for the importance of voice as a dimension of texts, I took care to avoid this claim.) The dangerous terms "authenticity" and "sincerity" came into use. It was understandable, then, that all this talk about voice led to some focus on the connection between and writing and *self*. Skeptics about voice talked about the irrelevance of an alleged self to the quality of writing, about sincerity as a red herring, and about importance of conscious craft. (On the difference between craft and sincerity, see the brilliant Auden poem, "The Truest Poetry is the Most Feigning.") Discussion moved on into the postmodern era, with arguments actually denying the existence of a self— arguments widely taken up. During a heated public discussion about self, I recall this pungent remark: "As soon as we women started insisting on having strong voices and selves, prominent theorists concluded that there is no such thing as a self."

So what started out as a discussion among writing teachers about how to encourage certain desirable strengths in student writing, gradually turned into an argument centered mostly on theory. But as with the orality/literacy war, this scholarly debate about voice has died down. The strongest theoretical arguments left on the table probably belong to the skeptics about voice. And yet actual writers and even prominent literary critics seem oblivious to these arguments that so deeply preoccupied the fields of composition and cultural studies. Writers of all stripes, and literary critics high and low, cannot seem to resist talking unselfconsciously about voice—frequently even using a locution that was particularly offensive to theorists: about a writer "finding her own voice."[4]

I didn't put an essay about voice in this volume, mostly because I edited *Landmark Essays about Voice* in 1994.

Conclusion

I started this introduction with Harris' intriguing argument that writing has nothing to do with speech. As I maintain in "The Believing Game," counter-intuitive views are always helpful: When someone has a view that looks crazy, it means she can see something that we "sane" people cannot see. If we make the effort to try to see what she sees, we almost always get good insights. In this case, by taking Harris seriously, we can see past some common assumptions about spoken language and writing—and in particular about the relationships between symbolic systems like mathematics and writing. Further pursuit of his argument will no doubt yield more insights.

Still, it's irresistible to see speech and writing as deeply related. The essays in this volume explore this relationship in diverse and fruitful ways. I hope more people in my field of composition will look beyond metaphorical voice in texts and turn more of their attention to *literal speech* and the field of linguistics: spoken language and the act of speaking. When we do that, we'll see myriad interesting ways in which speech and spoken language can throw useful light on writing.

Notes

1 See Murphy.
2 Dictation by serious writers is more common than we often hear about. Here are some notable writers who dictated important parts of their work: Adam Smith, Johann Goethe, Walter Scott, Henry James, Fyodor Dostoevsky, Leo Tolstoy, James Thurber, Eugene Ionesco, Bertrand Russell, and Richard Feynmann. The successful contemporary novelist Richard Powers makes this statement in a column in the *New York Times Book Review*: "Except for brief moments of duress, I haven't touched a keyboard for years. No fingers were tortured in producing these words—or the last half a million words of my published fiction." (For more about writers who have dictated, see my *Vernacular Eloquence*, 178 ff.)
3 I applied this approach to the vexed concept of *voice in writing* in order to reduce confusion and dispute in that realm. I posited five different kinds of voice that can exist in a text: audible voice or intonation (the illusion of sound in a text); dramatic voice (the sense of a person or character or implied author); recognizable or distinctive voice (a voice that's characteristic of a particular person); voice with authority; and resonant voice or presence (see my "Voice"). For another example, I applied this same methodological approach to *academic discourse*, arguing that we can reduce confusion and needless dispute if we notice differences between different species of academic discourse in different disciplines (for example, what counts as evidence or how an essay ought to be structured). Even between subdisciplines, the conventions can vary: For most literary criticism, naive students are told not to write "Virginia" when they mean "Woolf," but biographical scholarship accepts the first name (Elbow, "Reflections on Academic Discourse").

When I take this approach, I think of Derrida, who was also trying to undermine the binary opposition between speech and writing. But his goal was far more ambitious than my Aristotelian approach. He was trying to undermine the very ontology at the heart of Western thinking. I'm simply trying for clearer thinking to help us avoid drifting unaware between different meanings for unstable multivalent terms.

By the way, for an extraordinarily rich summary of linguistic research about the differences between speech and writing, see Chafe and Tannen.
4 Two examples:

T. S. Eliot: "The kind of poetry that I needed, to teach me the use of my own voice, did not exist in English at all; it was only to be found in French [referring to poetry of Gautier and Laforgue]. (Quoted in A. Alvarez, 30.)

The distinguished critic, novelist, and biographer, Colm Tóibín writes this about Tennessee Williams: "It is strange how out of all this mostly inchoate and random writing, a sense of a personal vision emerges that would make its way into the very core of Williams's main character and scenes. These entries capture an authentic voice, an artist alone and deeply fearful and unusually selfish. Many of his most whining entries were written on the very days when he was producing his most glittering work. His whining was not a game or done for effect; it seems, indeed, a rare example of a whining both sincere and heartfelt." (38)

Works Cited

Alvarez, A. "Making It New." Review of *The Short Sharp Life of T. E. Hulme* and *Wilfred Owen*. *New York Review of Books* 15 May 2003: 28–30.
Auden, W. H. *Collected Poems.* New York: Modern Library, 2007.

Biber, Douglas. *Variation across Speech and Writing.* New York: Cambridge UP, 1988.

Chafe, Wallace L. *Discourse, Consciousness, and Time: The Flow and Displacement of Conscious Experience in Speaking and Writing.* Chicago: U of Chicago P, 1994.

Chafe, Wallace and Deborah Tannen. "The Relation between Written and Spoken Language." *Annual Review of Anthropology* 16 (1987): 383–407.

Chaytor, H. J. *From Script to Print: An Introduction to Medieval Vernacular Literature.* Cambridge, UK: W. Heffer, 1950.

Cushman, Ellen. *The Cherokee Syllabary: Writing the People's Perseverance.* Oklahoma: U of Oklahoma P, 2011.

Elbow, Peter. "The Believing Game or Methodological Believing. *Journal for The Assembly for Expanded Perspectives on Learning* 14 (Winter 2009): 1–11.

——. "Reflections on Academic Discourse: How it Relates to Freshmen and Colleagues." *College English* 53.2 (Feb. 1991): 135–155.

——. *Vernacular Eloquence: What Speech Can Bring to Writing.* Oxford: Oxford UP, 2012.

——. "Voice in Writing Again: Embracing Contraries." *College English* 70.2 (Nov. 2007): 168–188.

Halliday, M. A. K., *Complementarities in Language.* Beijing: Commercial Press, 2008.

Harris, Roy. *The Origin of Writing.* London: Duckworth, 1986.

Havelock, Eric A. *Preface to Plato.* Cambridge MA: Harvard UP, 1963.

Lepore, Jill. *A is For American: Letters and Other Characters in the Newly United States.* New York: Vintage, 2002.

McLuhan, Marshall. *Understanding Media: The Extension of Man.* 1st Edn. New York; McGraw Hill, reissued by MIT Press, 1994, with introduction by Lewis H. Lapham; reissued by Gingko Press, 2003

Murphy, James J., ed. *Quintilian on the Teaching of Speaking and Writing: Translations from Books One, Two, and Ten of the* Institutio Oratoria. Edwardville: Southern Illinois U P, 1987.

Nero, S., and Ahmad, D. *Vernaculars in the Classroom: Paradoxes, Pedagogy, Possibilities.* New York: Routledge, 2014.

Olson, David. "From Utterance to Text: The Bias of Language in Speech and Writing." *Harvard Educational Review* 47.3 (1977): 257–281.

Ong, Walter. *Orality and Literacy: The Technologizing of the Word.* New York: Methuen, 1982.

Pinker, Steven. *The Language Instinct: How the Mind Creates Language.* New York: HarperCollins, 2000.

Powers, Richard. *New York Times Book Review* 7 January 2007: http://www.nytimes.com/2007/01/07/books/review/Powers2.t.html?pagewanted=2&_r=1 (accessed 11/4/10).

Robinson, Andrew. *The Story of Writing: Alphabets, Hieroglyphs, and Pictograms.* London and NY: Thames and Hudson, 1995.

Tóibín, Colm. "The Shadow of Rose." Review of Tennessee Williams' Notebooks. *New York Review of Books* 20 Dec 2007: 38–44.

SECTION 1

HISTORICAL STORIES ABOUT THE DEVELOPMENT AND EFFECTS OF ALPHABETIC LITERACY

1.
ORIGINS AND FORMS OF WRITING
Denise Schmandt-Besserat and Michael Erard

Writing is a system of graphic marks that represent the units of a specific language. The units to be represented (whether individual sounds, syllables, parts of words, or some combination of all three) are a function of the structure of the language, the needs and traditions of the society that uses that system, and the capabilities of the human brain. *Writing* is a general term for a visual system distinct from art, and a mode of language use that is distinguished from, speaking, whereas *writing system* refers to a specific type of graphic marks that represent types of linguistic units. Other words for writing systems are *script* and *orthography*. Alphabets (such as the Roman alphabet), syllabaries (such as Cherokee or Ethiopic, which represent consonant + vowel syllables), abjads (such as Arabic, which represent only consonants), and logosyllabaries (such as Chinese, which represent words) are all types of writing systems.

Writing is a unique human achievement, and this chapter sketches some of the history of this achievement. It is distinct from art, as we discuss. We visit the three known origins of writing in Mesopotamia, China, and Mesoamerica to show how writing arose, in what forms, and how it spread. We also provide an overview of how writing systems have been studied in modern times, and we propose some ideas about what the future might hold for writing and writing systems.

Art and Writing

Humans created two major systems of visual symbols to express themselves and to communicate with others: art and writing. By visual symbols we mean markings standing for a meaning shared by a community. For example, in Western society, the picture of a dove evokes peace. It is a common assumption that art and writing are related and, in particular, that writing has its origin in pictures. However, both communication systems are fundamentally different, fully independent from each other, and play different roles in society:

Archaeological evidence shows that art preceded writing by some 25,000 years. The first evidence of it comes from France in the Paleolithic Aurignacian period about 30,000 BCE. The appearance of art does not coincide with any major physiological, technological, or economic human development. Therefore, it remains a mystery why image making appeared so relatively late in human cultural development. The first art

---

Schmandt-Besserat, Denise and Michael Erard. "Origins and Forms of Writing." *Handbook of Research on Writing: History, Society, School, Individual*, Text. ed Charles Bazerman. Mahwah, NJ: Erlbaum, 2007. 7–22.

creations consisted of lines, circular depressions called *cup marks,* incomplete sketches of animals, and a motif interpreted, as a female vulva, all pecked with a flint axe on stone boulders (Bahn & Vertut, 1988, 1997; Leroi-Gourhan, 1971). In the Gravettian period, about 23,000 BCE, small three-dimensional sculptures representing obese women become familiar. The same repertory of shapes made with the same technique were repeated in several rock shelters of southwestern France. They attest to the existence of an extended community of Paleolithic humans who communicated meaning via complex visual symbols that were stylized in various ways. A community, dispersed in time and space, communicating with visual symbols: All of these elements underlie the development of writing as well.

What did Paleolithic cup marks mean, and why were they associated with animal designs or vulvae? We will never know for certain. However, most scholars consider them to be representing the elements of a cosmology. The images stood for ideas of utmost significance for the society, such as the creation of the world, the meaning of death, and the principle of reproduction. According to this hypothesis, visual art dealt with the supernatural, the unknown, the feared, or the wanted. It was a powerful instrument of thought to conceive ideas and bring a community to forge a common understanding of the mysteries of life. By the late Upper Paleolithic and the following Mesolithic and Neolithic periods, art had become a worldwide phenomenon: No culture is known that does not foster art.

The Origins of Writing

The available evidence shows that writing arose autochthonously in three places of the world: in Mesopotamia about 3200 BCE, in China about 1250 BCE, and in Mesoamerica around 650 BCE, Devising a system of graphic symbols to represent the sounds of language is, in itself, a remarkable achievement. However, the spread of this system through a society and across a geographical area is also remarkable. After all, communicating with writing is impossible if the recipient of a written message does not know the meaning of the written symbols. Thus, when we refer to the *spread of writing,* we mean not only the dissemination of the concept of representing the sounds of language with graphic symbols or the migration of those symbols, but also the dissemination of the rules and standards of what the graphic signs represent. This was as important at the beginning of writing as it will be in the future. As recently as 2005, archaeology has played an active role in informing theories about the origins of writing, and archaeologists may someday discover evidence that China, Mesopotamia, and Mesoamerica influenced each other, or that other regions or cultures influenced them. Until such evidence is uncovered, it is reasonable to treat these regions separately and the writing systems that arose as unique.

Mesopotamia

The function of writing when it came about in 3200 BCE was exclusively economic. Whereas art dealt with the numinous, each sign of writing stood for a precise unit of a specific commodity—the things of mundane life. After 10,000 BCE, art became an integral part of every culture, whereas writing remained the asset of few civilizations. Moreover, art came without precedent, whereas the signs of writing derived their shape, meaning, format, and economic function from a 4,000-year-old counting system using clay counters called *tokens*. The long evolution from counting to writing can be summarized as follows (Schmandt-Besserat, 1996).

The Token System Antecedent of Writing

The token system coincided with the Neolithic Revolution, when animals and cereals were first domesticated. About 7500 BCE, probably in a Syrian village, farmers modeled counters in clay in various specific and striking shapes that were easy to recognize, remember, and duplicate. Each shape was assigned a meaning; A cone was a small measure of grain, a sphere stood for a large measure of grain, a cylinder for an animal of the herd, and an ovoid for a jar of oil. This invention was simple, but it was a great invention: It was the first visual code—the first system of artifacts created for the sole purpose of communicating information. Art communicated profound, but vague, ideas, but the tokens communicated concrete, discrete information on specific quantifies of merchandise such as grain and animals.

The token system was destined to a long life remaining in use for 4,000 years. Art's evolution paralleled technological advances such as the use of copper and bronze tools, whereas the tokens were driven by the needs of an economy of redistribution. When city-states came about, in the 4th millennium BCE, the tokens became a complex system with multiple shapes and multiple markings, incised or punched, to record the products of urban workshops such as wool, textiles, garments, mats, vessels, and tools, imported goods such as metal, or processed foods such as trussed ducks, honey, and bread. There were also new tokens to record goods with greater precision in order to satisfy the more stringent state administration, such as special tokens designating rams, ewes, and lambs (i.e., the sex and age of animals).

The token system shared with art one archaic feature. From the beginning of its use, around 7500 BCE, to the very end, around 3000 BCE, the tokens, like images, represented the number of units of goods in one-to-one correspondence. Six jars of oil were shown with 6 ovoids and 10 jars of oil with 10 ovoids. Keeping records with tokens was cumbersome and bulky.

Two-Dimensional Signs

About 3500 BCE, the temple economy of the Sumerian city of Uruk required keeping tokens in archives—perhaps to keep track of debts until they were settled. The temple administration invented envelopes consisting of small hollow clay balls in which tokens could be held together and be protected from tampering. The envelopes also offered a clay surface on which the temple officials as well as debtors could impress their seals to warrant the terms of the transaction represented by the tokens inside.

About 3500 BCE, the envelopes were perfected to make their content visible. The tokens were impressed on the surface showing how many of what shape were included inside. This invention was a major step toward writing because the three-dimensional tokens were reduced to two-dimensional markings.

Evidence from such cities such as Uruk in Mesopotamia, Susa in Elam, and Habuba Kabira in Syria shows tokens (dating from 3300–3200 BCE) imprinted on a solid clay ball—a tablet. Accordingly, the signs were no longer merely duplicating actual tokens held within. The tablets did altogether away with tokens, and by doing so, the signs became independent entities. The tablets were far more convenient than envelopes filled with tokens because they could display permanently one or even several accounts that could be viewed at a glance.

The Creation of Numerals

Signs traced with a stylus, rather than impressed with actual tokens, appeared at the Mesopotamien city of Uruk about 3100 BCE. These incised signs had the advantage of accurately illustrating the exact shape of the most intricate tokens and their particular markings. Incisions led to more than changed shapes, as they also marked the Introduction of numerals. The incised signs were never repeated in one-to-one correspondence. Numbers of jars of oil were no longer shown by the sign for jar of oil repeated as many times as the number of units of oil to record. The sign for jar of oil was preceded by numerals—signs for abstract numbers. Whereas the tokens fused together inextricably the concept "1" with that of a unit of merchandise, the incised signs abstracted the concept of *oneness* from that of the item counted.

The units of grain were used to express such abstract numbers as 1, 2 or 3 (and upwards). "1" was indicated by the impression of a cone token that formerly was a small measure of grain, and "10" by a sphere that represented a large measure of grain. It was a great economy of signs: 33 jars of oil were expressed by seven signs ($3 \times 10 + 3 \times 1 +$ "oil")—instead of 33. Most important, as a result of the abstraction of numbers, the signs for goods and those for numerals could evolve in separate ways. Writing and counting generated different sign systems.

The Sound of Speech Emulated

About 3000 BCE, the Sumerian city-state administration required recording the personal name of the individuals who gave or received the goods listed on the tablets. Phonograms—signs standing for sounds—were created. The new signs were simple, incised sketches with no concern for esthetics. They singled out things that were easy to draw that stood for the sound of the word they evoked. The drawing of a man's body stood for the sound "*lu*" and that of the mouth for "*Ka*," which were the sounds of the words for *man* and *mouth* in the Sumerian language. The syllables or words composing an individual's name were written like a rebus. For example, the modern name *Lucas* could have been written with the two signs mentioned earlier "lu - ka." The stage of pictography—writing with pictures—when the technique of writing came in its form closest to visual art, was in fact the time when writing became removed from the concrete world of logography to be formally connected with the sounds of speech by the extraordinary invention of phonograms.

The Parting From Accounting

In 2800 BCE, 400 years after the invention of clay tablets, writing still dealt exclusively with accounting. The texts listed merchandise received or dispensed by a temple administration, stipulated land donations, or compiled signs to be used by accountants for performing their tasks. But a scribe at the court of the kings of Ur, a southern Sumerian city, in about 2700 to 2600 BCE, innovated by using a chisel to inscribe gold, silver, and lapis lazuli objects to be deposited in tombs (Moorey, 1982; Woolley, 1934). The royal scribe of Ur did not list quantities of goods. His inscriptions had nothing to do with accounting. They consisted of a personal name such as *Meskalamdug* wrought on a gold bowl or a name and a title, "Puabi, Queen," carved on a lapis lazuli seal (Burrows, 1934).

For the first time, this scribe put writing to work for a function other than accounting. That new purpose was funerary. The Sumerian belief that the name of a deceased individual was to be spoken aloud at regular intervals in order for his or her ghost to exist in the underworld explains the funerary texts (Bayliss, 1973; Jonker, 1995; Niditch, 1996; Scurlock, 1988). Meskalamdug's name, couched in gold, suggests that casting the sounds of a name into writing was held equivalent to a perpetual utterance for the benefit of his ghost. After 5,000 years of accounting, the second function of writing was to guarantee the survival of the dead in the netherworld (Westenholz, 1993). At this point, for the first time, art and writing became complementary. The artifact enshrined the written word.

The Sentences of Speech Emulated

The concern for survival in the afterlife continued to bring art and writing together. About 2600 or 2500 BCE, a scribe inscribed small statues in the name of deceased individuals. He further added a prayer asking for a long afterlife to the god to whom the statue was dedicated (George, 1999). The inscription gave speech to the worshipper figure who addressed the gods in writing using sentences with subjects, verbs, and complements, bringing writing to model itself onto speech by adopting the syntax of spoken language. It was the powerful combination of sculpture and writing that was the true take-off of writing. About 2500 BCE, a Sumerian king was able to describe his victories in a lengthy text (Cooper, 1983). By 2000 BCE, writing was used for historical, religious, legal, scholarly, and literary texts, including poetry.

The Spread of Writing

Mesopotamia and its nearest neighbors Syria and Elam, in present-day Western Iran, are unique in presenting the evidence for the synchronic stages of tokens, envelopes, and tablets (Schmandt-Besserat, 1992). But the cognitive steps that led from logography to numerals and phonograms occurred only once in Mesopotamia.

The Mesopotamian writing system constitutes the prototype of the other Bronze Age writing systems of the Old World. When the Proto-Elamites created their own script, they borrowed simultaneously the concept of abstract numbers and phonetic signs from Mesopotamia (Hoyrup, 1994). Egypt, where the use of tokens in prehistory is not clearly attested, produced a full-blown writing system based on the rebus principle visibly imitating Mesopotamia. Carbon 14 dating disproves the claims for Egyptian primacy (Boehmer, Dreyer, & Kromer, 1993). About 2500 BCE, the Indus Valley Civilization devised a script that had no links with the Mesopotamian-like tokens recovered in pre-Harappan sites (Possehl, 1996). Crete probably adopted first the idea of tokens and then that of writing. This is suggested by the fact that Minoan clay counters in the shape of miniature vessels seem unrelated to the Linear A or B scripts used in the Aegean between 2200 and 1300 BCE (Poursat, 1994). The Mesopotamian tokens and writing loomed large over the process of civilization in the Old World.

The Cuneiform Script

The Mesopotamian script reached its classical period about 2200 to 2000 BCE when scribes used a reed stylus with a triangular end that produced cuneiform's distinctive wedge patterns. Though always remaining partly logographic (one sign = one concept), the script represented ever-more syllables, not individual sounds, making the script a syllabary (Walker, 1987). This first writing system played a vast role in the diffusion of writing: In the course of the third to first millennia BCE, it was adapted to languages of various families such as Akkadian and Eblaite (Semitic); Elamite (perhaps Dravidian); Hittite and Old Persian (Indo European); and Hurrian and Urartian (whose identification as Caucasian is disputed). The cuneiform script lost ground when Aramaic, written with a flowing hand on papyrus or parchment, became prevalent in the Near East. Cuneiform writing lingered in Mesopotamia until the Christian era.

The Alphabet

The alphabet was invented only once—which means that all the present alphabets, from Latin, Arabic, Greek, Cyrillic, Hebrew, Ethiopian, and Tamil to Navaho derive from the same first alphabet. The invention of the alphabet took place in the Near East, probably in present-day Lebanon, about 1700 BCE (Healey, 1990). Neither syllabic nor logographic, it owed nothing to the cuneiform; rather, it was a totally new system based on the identification of the distinctive sounds of a language and matching each with a specific sign. The first alphabet consisted of 22 letters, each standing for a phoneme—a single speech sound. The success of the alphabet was to streamline script. Compared to the some 600 cuneiform signs, the 22 letters were easy to learn allowing literacy to spread more widely. The letters of this first alphabet, however, only represented consonants.

The Phoenician cities that thrived on the coast of present-day Syria and Lebanon between 1000 and 300 BCE played an important role in the diffusion of the alphabet across the Mediterranean Sea, and in particular to Greece. (Markoe, 2000; Whitt, 1995).

Perhaps as early as 800 BCE, the Greeks adapted the Semitic alphabet to their Indo-European language by adding letters for vowels. This resulted in a 27-letter alphabet that made it easier to transcribe the spoken word and even easier to read, because all the sounds were indicated (Cook 1987). In turn, the Etruscans, who occupied the province of Tuscany in present-day Italy, starting in the eighth century BCE adopted the Greek alphabet by slightly modifying the shape of the letters (Bonfante, 1990). When Etruria was conquered by Rome in the first century BCE, the Etruscan alphabet became that of the Romans. The diffusion of the Latin alphabet followed the conquests of the Roman armies through Europe (Reynolds, 1991).

Chinese

Among these three origins of writing, Chinese is the only one that has an unbroken record of use in the last three millennia leading up to the modern time. The earliest evidence of Chinese characters dates to 1250 BCE. About 4,500 symbols have been identified on shards of turtle shell and cow bone, used in divination practices. Questions to an oracle were written on the shell or bone, which were then heated in the fire; the resulting cracks were read, and the answers given were also inscribed in the bone. About 1,500 of these 4,500 symbols have survived as modern Chinese characters. The oldest examples of oracle bone writing have been found in north central China in the Shang region. There is no evidence that the Shang were solely responsible for developing writing in China, but there is also no evidence of Chinese writing at any other place at an earlier time (Keightley, 1978, 1989).

From the beginning, Chinese was written vertically, the columns read right to left. (Modern conventions have also added horizontal, left-to-right reading.) Early Chinese writing had several variants. The "great seal" script, *ta chuan*, was used in 1200 to 800 BCE on bronze vessels and carved on character seals, and was also used in all other writing. Other seal scripts were the most diverse of formal writing. From 403 to 221 BCE, a number of independent states developed their own script styles, but from 221 to 206 BCE the Qin dynasty established a standard script called *hsiao chuan*, or "lesser seal script." This gave way to *li shu*, the "clerkly script," a straighter style that was easier to write, developed by the staff of the imperial democracy and used from 206 BCE to 220 CE. Around the second century CE, a third formal style, the standard script (or *kai shu*), was developed (Boltz, 1994).

Until the early 20th century, all dialects of Chinese were written in a literary dialect that dated to the late Old Chinese period, about 1100 BCE to 100 CE. This meant that literate Chinese wrote in a way they themselves did not speak. This form persisted, in part, because of the Chinese civil service's power in creating and maintaining the written standard for some 2,000 years. However, in the early 20th century, a reform movement in China adapted modern spoken Chinese as the basis for written Chinese. Now writing is done in Modern Standard Chinese, a dialect close to the Mandarin spoken in Beijing.

The most remarkable feature of Chinese writing is the size of its character set. Since around 100 CE, when the scholar Xu Shen created a dictionary of 9,353 characters, the number of characters has steadily increased to about 60,000. Most of these characters, however, are archaic words, variant characters, or proper names. For the modern Chinese writer and reader of Chinese, 1,000 characters account for 90% of all occurrences in texts, and 2,400 characters cover 99% of occurrences. In other words, only a slight fraction of the total number of characters is required to be fully literate in contemporary Chinese societies (Boltz, 1994).

In the West, a myth about Chinese writing has persisted. Because Chinese characters are written with elaborate series of pen strokes, and because Chinese calligraphy is done with brushes and ink, the characters have been considered small pictures that represent ideas. This is not the case, and numerous books have been devoted to dispelling this myth (DeFrancis, 1984). Most characters do represent speech sounds; 90% of the characters consist of a graphic element that indicates pronunciation, combined with another element that marks meaning.

Mesoamerica

In Mesoamerica—what is now southern Mexico and the countries of Central America—as many as 13 different writing systems had been developed by 900 CE by various civilizations (Lounsbury, 1989). The most visible of these is the Maya writing system, because it was written on stone on upright monuments know as *stelae,* and because major advances in Maya decipherment have been made in the last 20 years (Coe, 1999). Maya was written during the height of the civilization, from 250 to 900 CE through to the 16th century, when Christopher Columbus first encountered the Maya.

Maya characters are known as *glyphs,* about 800 of which are known to exist. Each glyph organizes several smaller elements known as graphemes and contains a main grapheme with one or more diacritics. The diacritics can appear to the left, right, top, or bottom of the main symbol. The glyphs represent morphemes (or basic units of words), syllables (consonant + vowel sequences), as well as semantic and phonological determinatives. Because there was no set standard for glyph construction, writers could present the same word in many different ways, often in the same texts, and writers took pleasure in creating these variants. Glyphs were always written in paired vertical stacks and read top to bottom, left to right, in a zig-zag fashion. The sequences of graphemes in a glyph are read, more or less, from the upper left corner to the lower right.

The Maya carved glyphs on stone stelae and painted them on ceramics and bark paper books called codices; archaeological and deciphering work is done with the stelae and other stone carvings as well as the codices. If writing in Mesopotamia is associated with economic functions, then in Mesoamerica writing is associated with calendrical calculations and the actions of kingly dynasties. Hundreds of codices existed and were used by the Maya; many were destroyed by the Europeans as pagan works; others hidden or lost by the Maya decomposed. (Since the 19th-century the extant codices have been copied and photographed; though they are known by the European cities where they reside—the Dresden Codex, the Madrid Codex, the Paris Codex, and the Grolier Codex—they are now distributed worldwide via the Web.)

Despite its prominence, Maya writing was not the oldest Mesoamerican writing, and archaeologists have attempted to establish its lineage more precisely. Some markings that may be precursors date as early as 11.00 BCE. The earliest writings that are recognizably antecedent to later scripts date to around 650 BCE in the states of Tabasco and Oaxaca, Mexico. In 2002, archaeologists M. Pohl, K. Pope, and C. von Nagy announced the discovery of a roller stamp and plaques with glyphs, which were found near the Olmec site of La Venta in Tabasco (Pohl, Pope, & Von Nagy, 2002; Stokstad, 2002). The discovery bolstered the theory that the Olmec had influenced other civilizations and cultures. From 400 BCE to 200 CE, three related writing systems were used in Mesoamerica. The Isthmian script (the descendent of the Olmec script and a logosyllabic script like the later Maya script) was used from the Mexican Gulf Coast through the Isthmus of Tehuantepec; the Oaxacan script was used in the Valley of Oaxaca; and the Maya script was used in an area that extended from the Yucatan peninsula to the foothills of the Guatemalan Highlands.

When Europeans arrived in Mexico, they outlawed the use of native writing systems. Indigenous Mesoamerican people have revived the use of glyphs in contemporary times as a symbol of their heritage.

Writing as Culture

The contemporary interest in the structure of writing systems is generally agreed to begin with I. J. Gelb, a philologist at the University of Chicago, whose 1952 book, *The Study of Writing*, was the first to categorize various writing systems in terms of their history and structure. Though many of his statements about writing's relationship to language have been corrected, his book sparked exploration into writing systems. Gelb even coined a name for this field; *grammatology*. (The word is perhaps better known among humanists as the title of a book by the French philosopher, Jacques Derrida—*Of Grammatology*.)

However, scholars' interest in the relationship between orality and literacy traditions began with Milman Parry in the 1920s (Jahandarie, 1999). Perry was a Harvard classicist who first showed that the texts of the ancient Greek poet Homer were primarily oral compositions. This closed a debate (ongoing at the time) about Homer's indentity and whether "Homer" was a single author or several. (Parry argued that Homer was a single, real person who assembled his unique epics from a number of essential themes and variations that had been passed down as part of an oral tradition.) Other early investigators, such as Eric Havelock (1976), sought to uncover how literacy shaped Greek society, and the impact of the alphabet on the organization of ideas, abstract, thought, and consciousness.

In the 1960s, Marshall McLuhan, a Canadian media critic, became a popular thinker on the effects of mass media and media technologies, such as television, which led him to consider how cultures that relied on aural/oral information differed from visual cultures (McLuhan 1962, 1964, Moos 1997, Gordon 2003). Many of McLuhan's colleagues and followers extended these ideas to thinking about the properties of cultures that did not have books or writing. Walter Ong argued that writing is a technology that restructures consciousness of individuals who use it and refocuses the energies of societies that utilize it (Ong 1982). Anthropologist Jack Goody, characterizing writing as a "technology of the intellect," tackled the oral-literate divide to show how writing influences religion, the economy law, and commerce (Goody 1977, 1987). David Olson argues that writing, not speech, determine our ability to reflect on ourselves (Olson and Torrance 1991, Olson 1994).

For most of the 20th century, linguists did not pay much attention to forms of written language, arguing that their task was to study language as it was spoken. In the 1970s, they found renewed interest in writing systems as evidence for abstract units of language and for insight into otherwise unobservable linguistic processes. The fact that many writing systems are alphabetic (because they represent individual sounds) suggests that individual sound segments called phonemes are fundamental to human language production. However, the fact that some writing systems encode syllables suggests that syllabic units are also fundamental. Anthropological linguists have been attentive to writing, beginning in the late 19th century, due to work describing languages indigenous to the Americas and recording narratives, oral poetry, and other verbal performance. Later they theorized how transcribing spoken utterances, conversations, and oral performances altered the interpretations of spoken discourse (Bauman & Sherzer, 1974).

Late in the 20th century, the academic attention to writing systems matured. This interest led to the publication of encyclopedic works on writing systems. These were novel because they collected language, writing, and cultural experts and combined these with state-of-the-art advances in computer printing that allowed all the characters in numerous writing systems to be printed. These works included *The Blackwell Encyclopedia of Writing Systems* (1999), edited by Florian Coulmas. Because of increased interest in teaching writing systems, several textbooks have also been published, such as *Writing Systems: An Introduction to Their Linguistic Analysis* (2002) by Florian Coulmas, and *Writing Systems: A Linguistic Approach* (2005) by Henry Rogers.

Decipherment

European scholars and explorers were deciphering ancient texts written in ancient, often no longer used, writing systems long before Milman Perry and I. J. Gelb's work. Three decipherments in particular captivated European imaginations, opening up aspects of unknown civilizations: the decipherment of Egyptian hieroglyphics, of cuneiform, and of Linear B.

In the early 19th century, a number of decipherment projects were launched, the most famous of which is the translation of the trilingual text (hieroglyphic, Coptic, and Greek) of the Rosetta stone by Jean Francois Champollion. The French scholar recognized that the hieroglyphic script was fundamentally phonetic. Using the obelisk of Philae, he noted that the names of Ptolemaios and Cleopatra had four letters in common—PT—and that these letters were shown in the expected order. Other names expanded the number of characters deciphered: Alexander, Philip, Atsinoe, Berenice, Caesar, and Claudius, Starting his work in 1808, Champollion by 1822 had drawn the connection between ancient Egyptian and Coptic, identified the difference between phonograms and logograms, compiled an impressive dictionary of ancient Egyptian, and established the first elements of a grammar (Chassagnard, 2001).

Cuneiform was first encountered by Europeans in the early 17th century CE, when travelers heard of a writing system made out of narrow, nail-shaped characters. (The word *cuneiform* comes from the Latin word *cuncus*, for "wedge.") Several scholars contributed to the decipherment of the cuneiform script. Among them, Henry Creswicke Rawlinson stands out as the heroic individual who between 1835 and 1844 made paper squeezes of parts of the trilingual (Old Persian, Akkadian, and Elamite) proclamation of Darius the Great inscribed on the rock of Behistun in Western Iran. This was daring because the inscriptions were carved on a steep cliff more than 300 feet above the ground, and could only be reached either from a flimsy scaffold or dangling down from on a rope. The column of 112 lines Rawlinson copied allowed him to recognize that the Akkadian cuneiform script was polyphonic; that is, each sign could stand for several sounds (Kramer, 1963). In 1851, his publication correctly identified Akkadian, the language spoken in Babylonia, as a Semitic language and established the first rudiments of its grammar (Walker, 1987).

One long-standing decipherment problem was the script called Linear B, which came from the Aegean island Knossos and from mainland Greece at the site of Pylos. It was finally deciphered in 1953 by Michael Ventris and John Chadwick (Chadwick, 1958). The script they discovered is the oldest surviving record of a Greek dialect called Mycenaean and was used between 1500 and 1200 BCE on Crete and southern Greece. A counterpart script, called Linear A, remains undeciphered.

The excitement for decipherment among Europeans was motivated by biblical scholarship and fueled by European colonial expansion into Asia and the Middle East. As the European powers moved through northern Africa, Persia, and Mesopotamia, they encountered ancient cities, archaeological sites, and other enduring monuments of civilizations that predated the ancient Greeks. Scholars' access to artifacts in European museums and libraries aided their work. Not all decipherment is finished, however. Presently, John S. Justeson is engaged in the study of the stele of La Mojjara, Mexico, making headway toward the understanding of the Epi-Olmec Hieroglyphic writing (Justeson & Kaufman, 1993). Some writing systems have never been successfully figured out because the language they represent are unknown. Among them are the Indus Valley Script, proto-Elamite, Proto-Elamite, Linear A, Meroïtic, and Rongo Rongo. Other artifacts, such as the Phaistos Disk, bear inscriptions that may or may not be writing. In the case of Rongo Rongo, a writing system on Easter Island, it is the only example of the writing system ever found.

The Spread of Writing

In 1986, the anthropologist of science Bruno Latour proposed a materialist explanation for the impact of writing on a society. In contrast to the distinctively mentalist or cognitivist arguments of Marshall McLuhan (1962, 1964), Walter Ong (1982), Jack Goody (1977, 1987a, 1987b), David Olson (1994), and others, Latour limits his arguments to how representational devices (drawings, charts, graphs, photos, and diagrams) allow scientists to make increasingly stronger arguments about the phenomena they study (Latour, 1986, 1990). Thus, representations succeed because they enable their users to do more. Without erasing the historical details, and without subsuming diverse places into the same developmental sequence, Latour's explanation extends to Maya astronomers, Chinese oracles, and Mesopotamian merchants. Writing systems may spread through the influence of religion, military and political conquest, or economic ties, but it persists for reasons that have to do with its utility for human work and its adaptability across spheres. One might use Latour to explain that many writing systems evolve toward the alphabetic, not because the alphabetic is inherently better but because it has social advantages over the representation of ideas, words, or syllables: It may be easier to learn, more easily adapted to other languages, and more efficiently ordered.

The Future of Writing

The history of writing has marked the interplay between linguistics, socioeconomics, and the forces of technological change, an interplay that will shape the future of writing. This future may not involve creating new symbols or diffusing new ways to write down languages. However, the evolution of technology, particularly the advent of the World Wide Web, more advanced data-processing technologies, and cheap, accessible personal computers have created technical challenges.

For instance, one challenge facing writers of Chinese was inputting the large number of characters with a standard keyboard. This problem, which has existed since the advent of publishing and of the typewriter, led to several systems for writing Chinese phonetically. One system, called *Pinyin,* is used in Mainland China; another system, called *bopomofo,* is used in Taiwan. Both (which were originally developed for students to learn characters more easily) have been employed in various inputting schemes using computers, for which no standard exists. Faster computer processors and cheaper computer memory has helped widen the impact of the inputting bottleneck on writing Chinese on computers.

Another challenge that faced computer users around the world was ensuring that different computing platforms, operating systems, and software programs could swap, share, and process text data, regardless of the writing system of the text. Computers do not store, send, or process letters or characters; rather, they process strings of numbers that are encoded by software and displayed on computer screens as the appropriate letters, numerals, punctuation marks, and other symbols. As an example, when computer A sends a string of numbers to computer B, both computers must share the same formula for turning those numerical strings into the appropriate visual symbols. The development of a universal standard for text encoding with computers would therefore be an important development for the future of writing (Erard, 2003).

The earliest computers could encode only limited character sets, such as Roman and Cyrillic. As personal computers spread globally and as the computer industry began looking for global markets, it became clear that many people in the world would purchase and use computers only if they could write their native scripts on them. In the late 1980s, computer scientists from IBM, Xerox-Parc, Apple, and other computer companies began working on a solution: a universal standard for text encoding that would be installed as part of the basic architecture of all hardware and software. This standard, now known as Unicode, contains encodings for 96,000 characters and 55 writing systems, from Chinese to Thai to Mongolian to Gothic. Approximately 70,000 of Unicode's encodings are for Chinese characters. However, about 100 writing systems, most of them used by small groups or of ancient or academic interest, remain to be encoded. These include Egyptian hieroglypic, cuneiform, Balinese, Javanese, and Tifinagh (or Berber). A group at the University of California-Berkeley called the Universal Scripts Initiative, is working on standardizing character sets for these minority writing systems in order to make them a part of the Unicode standard as soon as possible (Erard, 2003). This will ensure that Unicode is universal and allows as many people as possible to participate in the digital age.

The future of writing will also be determined by communications technologies. The rise of e-mail, chat rooms, and bulletin boards, as well as the widespread use of text messaging on cell phones, has created new symbols in Europe, North America, and Asia. In e-mail text, users invented "emoticons," graphic symbols that inventively combined punctuation marks to add emotional or intonational context to a writer's text (such as ":-)" to denote a positive or happy remark). Users of chat rooms and text messaging on cell phones have also developed abbreviations, phonetic spellings (as in English, using "lol" for "laugh out loud," "2" for "to," and "U" for "you"), and logograms that allow them to compress messages. In Japan and China, manufacturers of cell phones have created limited symbol sets built in to phones. In one system, the message "please call me" is displayed with an icon of a telephone, followed by *kure,* which is an abbreviated word for making a request. "Would you like to go out for a drink tonight" is displayed as a picture of a mug or cup, followed by a verb ending that is typically used for extending invitations (French, 2000). These types of unique symbols will continue to evolve, particularly with communication formats and devices that are strongly identified with youth cultures.

Another future development is that more of the world's languages will be written down. According to *Ethnologue* (Grimes and Grimes, 2005), a catalog of the world's languages, there are 6,912 languages spoken in the world as of 2004. Most of these are not written down because no writing systems have been developed or adapted for them yet. Because the writing system most often adapted for them is the Roman alphabet, the future favors the Roman alphabet. Not only is technology available in the Roman alphabet, most of the language workers, many of them missionaries, who are assigning writing systems to language use the Roman alphabet. Widely used in the world already, the Roman alphabet is written by more people in the world than any other.

References

Bahn, P., and Vertut, J. (1988). *Images of the Ice Age.* New York: Facts on File.
Bahn, P., and Vertut, J. (1997). *Journey through the Ice Age.* Berkeley: University of California Press.

Bayliss, M. (1973). The cult of the dead kin in Assyria and Babylonia. *Iraq, 35,* 115–125.
Bauman, R., and Sherzer, J. (Eds.). (1974). *Explorations in the ethnography of speaking.* London: Cambridge University Press.
Boehmer, R., Dreyer, G., & Kromer, B. (1993). Eine fruezeitliche 14C—Datierungen aus Abydos und Uruk *Mitteilungen des Deutschen Archaeologisches Instituts Abteilung Kairo, 49,* 63–68.
Boltz, W. G. (1994) *The origin and early development of the Chinese writing system.* New Haven, CT: American Oriental Society.
Bonfante, L. (1990) *Etruscan.* Berkeley: University of California Press.
Burrows, E. (1934). Inscribed material. In C. L. Woolley (Ed.), *Ur excavations; Vol. II, The royal cemetery* (Vol. 1, pp. 311–322). London: Oxford University Press.
Chadwick, J. (1958). *The decipherment of Linear B.* New York: Random House.
Chassagnard, G. (2001). *Les Freres Champollion, de Figeac aux Hieroglyphes,* Paris: Segnat Editions.
Coe, M. (1999). *Breaking the Maya code.* New York: Thames & Hudson.
Cook, B. E. (1987). *Greek inscriptions.* Berkeley: University of California Press.
Cooper, J. S. (1983). Reconstructing history from ancient inscriptions: The Lagash–Umma border conflict. *Sources From the Ancient Near East, 2*(1), 44–48.
Coulmas, F. (Ed.). (1999). *The Blackwell Encyclopedia of Writing Systems,* Oxford, England: Oxford University Press.
Coulmas, P. (2003). *Writing Systems: An Introduction to their Linguistic Analysis.* Cambridge, England: Cambridge University Press.
DeFrancis, J. (1984). *The Chinese language; Fact and fantasy.* Honolulu: University of Hawaii Press.
Derrida, J. (1976). *Of grammatology.* Baltimore: Johns Hopkins University Press.
Erard, M. (2003, September 25). "For the world's A B C's, he makes 1's and 0's." *The New York Times,* p. 000.
French, H. (2000, June 8). In e-mail wrinkle, cell phones are chatterboxes. *The New York Times,* p. 000.
Gelb, I. J. (1952). *A study of writing.* Chicago: University of Chicago Press.
George, A. (1999). *The epic of Gilgamesh.* London: Penguin.
Goody, J. (1977). *The domestication of the savage, mind.* Cambridge, England: Cambridge University Press.
Goody, J. (1987). *The interface between the written and the oral,* Cambridge, England: Cambridge University Press.
Goody, J. (1987). *The logic of writing and the organization of society.* Cambridge, England: Cambridge University Press.
Gordon, W. T. (Ed.). (2003). *Marshall McLuhan: Understanding media—the extensions of man.* Corte Madera, CA: Gingko.
Grimes, B., and Grimes, J. (Eds.). (2005). *Ethnologue.* Dallas, TX: Summer Institute of Linguistics.
Havelock, E. A. (1976). *Origins of Western literacy* (Monograph series 14). Toronto: Ontario Institute for Studies m Education.
Healey, J. (1990). *The early alphabet.* Berkeley: University of California Press.
Hoyrup, J. (1994). *Measure, number and weight.* Albany: State University of New York Press.
Jahandarie, K. (1999). *Spoken and written discourse: A multi-disciplinary perspective.* Stamford, CT: Ablex.
Jonker, G. (1995). *The topography of remembrance.* Leiden, Netherlands: E. J. Brill.
Justeson, J. S. & Kaufman, T. (1993). A decipherment of Epi-Olmec hieroglyphic writing. *Science, 259,* 1703–1711.

Keightley, D. N. (1978). *Sources of Shang history: The oracle-bone inscriptions of Bronze Age Chin.* Berkeley; University of California Press.

Keightley, D. N. (1989). The origins of writing in China: Scripts and cultural contexts. In W. Senner (Ed.), *The origins of writing* (pp. 171–202). Lincoln: University of Nebraska Press.

Kramer, S. (1963). *The Sumerians.* Chicago: University of Chicago Press.

Latour, B. (1986). "Visualization and Cognition: Thinking with Eyes and Hands," Knowledge and Society: Studies in the Sociology of Culture Past and Present, 6, 1–40.

Latour, B. (1990). Drawing things together. In M. Lynch & S. Woolgar (Eds.), *Representation in scientific practice* (pp. 19–68). Cambridge, MA: MIT Press.

Leroi-Gourhan, A. (1971). *Prehistoire de l'art accidental* Paris: Editions Lucien Mazenod.

Lounsbury, F. (1989). The ancient writing of middle America. In W. Senner (Ed.), *The origins of writing* (pp. 203–237). Lincoln: University of Nebraska Press.

Markoe, G. E. (2000). *Phoenicians.* Berkeley: University of California Press.

McLuhan, M. (1962). *The Gutenberg galaxy.* Toronto: A Mentor Book, University of Toronto.

McLuhan, M. (1964). *Understanding media.* New York: Mentor Book, New American Library.

Moorey, P. R. S. (1982). *Ur "of the Chaldees": A revised and updated version of Sir Leonard Wooley's "Excavations at Ur."* Ithaca, NY: Cornell University Press.

Moos, M. E. (Ed.), (1997). *Marshall McLuhan essays: Media research.* Amsterdam: Overseas Publishers Association.

Niditch, S. (1996). *Oral world and written word.* Louisville, KY: Westminster John Knox Press.

Olson, D. R. (1994). *The world on paper.* Cambridge, England: Cambridge University Press.

Olson, D. R., and Torrance, N. (1991). *Literacy and orality.* Cambridge, England: Cambridge University Press.

Ong, W. J. (1982). *Orality and literacy.* New York: Methuen.

Pohl, M., Pope, K., and Nagy, C. (2002). Olmec origins of Mesoamerican writing. *Science, 298*(5600), 1984–88.

Possehl, G. (1996). *Indus age: The writing system.* Philadelphia: University of Pennsylvania Press.

Poursat, J.-C. (1994). Les systemes primitifs de comptabilite en Crete minoenne In P. Ferioli, E. Fiandra, G. G. Fissore, & M. Frangipane (Eds.), *Archives before writing* (pp. 247–252). Rome: Ministero per i benì Cultirali e Ambientali Ufficìo Centrale per i benì Archivisti.

Reynolds, J. (1991). *Latin inscriptions.* Berkeley: University of California Press.

Rogers, H. (2005). *Writing systems: A linguistic approach.* Malden, MA: Blackwell.

Schmandt-Besserat, D. (1992). *Before writing.* Austin: University of Texas Press.

Schmandt-Besserat, D. (1996). *How writing came about.* Austin: University of Texas Press.

Scurlock, J. A. (1988). *Magical means of dealing with ghosts in ancient Mesopotamia.* Unpublished doctoral dissertation, University of Chicago.

Stokstad, E. (2002). Oldest New World writing suggests Olmec innovation. *Science, 298*(5600). Retrieved December 12, 2004, from Academic Search Premier.

Walker, C. B. F. (1987). *Cuneiform.* Berkeley: University of California Press.

Westenholz, J. G. (1993). Writing for posterity: Naram-Sin and Enmerkar. In A. F. Rainey (Ed.), *Kinattuta sha darati: Raphael Kutscher memorial volume* (p. 216). Tel Aviv: The Institute of Archeology of Tel Aviv University, 1993, 205–218.

Whitt, W. D. (1995). The story of the Semitic alphabet. In J. Sasson (Ed.), *Civilization of the ancient Near East* (Vol. 4, pp. 2379–2397). New York: Scribner's.

Woolley, C. L. (Ed.), (1934). *Ur excavations: Vol. II. The royal cemetery* (Vol. 1). London: Oxford University press.

2.
THE EMERGENCE OF A LITERATE RHETORIC IN GREECE
Richard Leo Enos

Introduction

In *A Study of Writing*, the preeminent philologist I. J. Gelb (1974) asserted that "the development of a full Greek alphabet . . . [Ellipsis in the original] is the last important step in the history of writing" (184). Gelb's claim is, of course, ripe for debate, but it also prompts the question, "What was the first great invention in literate rhetoric?" We know, as shown to us by George Kennedy (1963, 1999), Walter Ong (1982), and Eric Havelock (1963, 1982, 1986), that many of the heuristics of oral (primary) rhetoric were appropriated to literate (secondary) rhetoric when writing developed its own techne in classical Greece (Enos and Ackerman). Some components of oral rhetoric—such as "voice" and "tone"—persist even now in literate rhetoric. Today we are inclined to think of oral and written discourse as separate—and even autonomous—activities of expression. In fact, and as incredible as it may seem, the discovery that Greeks prior to Homer were not illiterate actually made front-page news in the Friday, April 9, 1954, issue of *The New York Times*! The front-page headline of reporter Sanka Knox's breaking news read, "Briton's Work Shows Early Greeks Had Ability to Write." In this story, Knox announced that young British "leisure-time" scholar Michael Ventris had deciphered a long-forgotten script and discovered that the writing on these "mud-colored clay [writing] tablets, sifted from the dust of a long-crumbled civilization in Greece and on Crete, is Greek from the pre-alphabetic days 500 years before Homer" (p. 1). Knox further asserted that "implications of Mr. Ventris' findings have rocked the archaeological world, and resultant tremors, scholars assume, will be felt in other areas of learning before long" (p. 1).

Knox's observation about the importance of these early Greek scripts proved to be prophetic. In the over half-century of research that has followed this "news," we have discovered that, in ancient Greece, oral and literate rhetoric were inextricably united, interactive and even recursive. That is, not only was writing often done in the service of oral discourse, but also such a phenomenon as reading silently was virtually non-existent (Stanford). Writing did eventually become an "art" unto itself, but this process

---

Enos, Richard Leo. "The Emergence of a Literate Rhetoric in Greece." *Rhetoric Society Quarterly* 36(3) (2006): 223–241.

was an evolutionary one, where features that we now associate exclusively with written composition often had oral antecedents. A re-examination of rhetorical heuristics that appear to be particular to writing will enable us not only to better understand the emergence of literate rhetoric in ancient Greece but also writing's eventual evolution from oral rhetoric.

The most obvious feature of writing that has oral antecedents is the alphabet itself. In the Greek alphabet, each of the twenty-four letters references a discrete, vocal feature of the language. After the alphabet provided the heuristic that made written composition facile for even children to learn and use, what was the first rhetorical "canon" that helped to structure meaning between writer and reader? This article argues that the first great invention in literate rhetoric was the paragraph. By "paragraphs" we mean large, macroscopic units whose division and arrangement reveal patterns of composing discourse and, indirectly, structuring thought for the purposes of communication. The paragraph, both for oral and written rhetoric, reveals not only some of the earliest efforts to structure meaning for others but also an epistemic shift from oral to written composition processes. That is, and much like the alphabet in this respect, the paragraph provides the transitional link between oral and literate rhetoric. Understanding nascent efforts to compose discourse systematically provides invaluable insight into the evolutionary process that created rhetoric, particularly if we recognize rhetoric as the systemization of heuristics that patterned discourse and nurtured creativity. To better understand the relationship—and therefore the transition—between oral and literate rhetoric, we will examine the most fundamental way of composing written discourse in Greece; paragraphing.

Taxis-Composition in the Pre-Literate Period

Paragraphs were indirectly a sign of oral classification and a precursor to the canon of arrangement. In the most general sense, it is difficult to think of any use of language that is not based on a system of arrangement. In respect to composition, the systematic patterning of paragraphs predates the discipline itself and persisted throughout Antiquity. The earliest use of this mode of arrangement in Greek discourse anticipates the emergence of rhetoric as a discipline and provides insights into how rhetoric evolved into an art or techne. Before the advent of writing, Greece was an oral culture. The techniques of oral composition are dramatically illustrated by three examples: Rhapsodes, Pre-Socratic Philosophers, and Sophists. The Rhapsodes composed and transmitted Homeric tales first by oral recitation and later with the aid of writing. In the nascent oral stage, Rhapodes, or aoidoi, used the cadence, rhythm and euphony (tonal quality) of Greek as an heuristic for arranging compositions. That is, the use of formulae was a way of both structuring and retaining epic tales. The patterns of arrangement used by Rhapsodes—although much more sophisticated—were aids to memorizing verse, similar to the way that a child might memorize a nursery tale by "chanting" out the story in a rhyming pattern. Another version of this phenomenon would be a contemporary singer who composes a repertoire of songs that can be performed based on the rhyming patterns in the prosody of the musical score. In this sense, the oral paragraph is a pattern of arrangement for recollection and creative composition.

Patterns of memory also facilitated the structuring of cognitive processes, which is evident in the fragmentary remains of the PreSocratic Philosophers and Sophists. Again, when orality dominated, concepts were formally patterned in the poetic cadence of prose rhythm. Yet, what were also transmitted in these oral formulae were pattern of thinking. For example, the antithetical structuring of discourse, by its nature, provides a correlative balancing that juxtaposes ideas through dissociation. Such a pattern of arrangement prompts individuals to understand by viewing concepts in discrete categories, often in the form of polar opposites. The Pre-Socratic and Sophistic notions of dissoi logoi and anti-logoi are illustrations of compositional patterns of paragraphing that not only have contrastive cadence but also induce understanding by juxtaposing ideas. Using dissoi logoi, for example, we could determine an individual's merits by establishing his or her position on a "good/evil" continuum. Using anti-logoi, to offer a related illustration, we could determine an individual's place under a particular concept—such as wealth—by saying, "He is by no means poor, but he is no Rockefeller either!" If we can also imagine how these heuristics of bi-polarity would be arranged in a correlative balance of antithetical notions, then we will have an illustration of the heuristic and epistemic potential for arrangement in composing thought and sharing meaning.

Compositional Features of Rhetoric: Linearity and Syntax

In writing, we also see that the structuring of a paragraph is based on the expectation that the writer and reader share some presumptions about how discourse should be structured. In this respect, any effort to communicate, oral or written, requires rhetor and audience to cooperate with each other by seeking patterns of discourse that create a harmony between what is anticipated and what is received by both the rhetor and the auditor or reader. While the term for "paragraph" (ἡ παραγραφή) does not appear in Homer (Iliad 6. 169; cf. 17.599), the notion of making "scratch marks" (γράφω) on a tablet does, and the earliest Greek scripts reveal diacritical marks to separate components in the writing process. These diacritical scratches are actually the earliest forms of the paragraph, making the paragraph one of the earliest forms of punctuation in the compositional process of Greek scripts. In this sense, "paragraphs" had their forerunners. Egyptian cartouches, for example, represent an encircling of a name to set it apart for royal or divine status (Casson).

Even in Greece, and long before the alphabet, the syllabic writing of the Bronze Age reveals a systemic "drawing around" of characters to chunk ideas and expression. The most vivid example of this concept of grouping ideas in a text is evident even in the composition of the hieroglyphic-type characters of the Bronze Age Phaestos Disk (Evans 22–28, 273–93; Doblhofer 267–70). Although its Cretan origin is still debated, the clay has movable pictographic "type" characters (Ventris and Chadwick 10; Gelb 1974, 157).

The other writings from Bronze Age Greece—clay tablets of syllabaries called Linear A and Linear B—show principles of systematic patterns through large stroke marks. In fact, the initial impression from one of their early discoverers, Sir Arthur Evans, was that these tablets were arranged in large orderly groups demarcated by a stroke mark, which he described as "paragraphs" because of the systematic gathering of symbols into groups (49).

It is reasonable to assume that early schemes to compose discourse were done for the sake of clarity and comprehension. The uniformity and compartmentalization of these characters reveal an ordering of ideas, in part, structured by the delineation of scratch marks. With the introduction of syllabary and linear scripts, particularly Linear B (c. 1450 BC), the use of paragraph markings became increasingly familiar and standardized. It is clear that concurrent with the use of a syllabary was a system of diacritical markings used as compositional units to set off sections of discourse. As Sterling Dow (1954) argues, Minoan writing was an instrumental function used to facilitate oral discourse (127–8). In short, the paragraph—as are all features of early Greek scripts—is an aid to memory and meaning in the transmission of oral discourse. As such, the early paragraph functions as an oral delimiter, a graphic instrument to facilitate verbal expression, rather than as an independent composing tool of written discourse.

Again, explicit archaeological evidence, predating Homer by several hundred years, reveals that this early form of the paragraph was already being standardized within an oral culture. Reporting on his pioneering work on Minoan excavations in 1909, Sir Arthur Evans describes a deposit of Linear B inscriptions on the North entrance passage of "exceptional size" showing "eight lines of inscription in characters of good style" (I: 48–9). Evans indicated that the sign-groups probably represented words ranging from two to five characters with "an upright line marking the termination of each" (49). Evans conjectures that "the total number of words seems to be twenty, divided into three paragraphs, the first ending on line 2, the second on line 6, and the third on line 8" (49). Evans includes a footnote in his archaeological report explaining that he considered these scratch markings to be "paragraphs" because of the blanks left by groups of succeeding lines (49, n.2). The delineated spacing made by scratch marks helps us understand why Evans would consider these markings to be "paragraphs" and reveals an early process of isolating topics through visual spacing. Evans' observations—made at the dawning of the 20th century—are consistent with Richard Young and Alton Becker's 1966 study on the lexical and grammatical cues of paragraph recognition.

Evans believed that these markings were significant and argued that "the whole physiognomy of this linear script" with its "espacement into distinct paragraphs," "attests a very considerable advance in the Art of Writing," even to the point of his claiming that its left-to-right regularity had a "European aspect" (I: 39, 40). For years, however, Evans' claims about paragraphs remained speculative observations, since decades passed before Michael Ventris deciphered Linear B and revealed that it was indeed a Greek linear syllabary. Ventris thus demonstrated that an archaic Greek script predated Homer by 500 years: beyond any doubt, the Mycenaean civilization was literate. In deciphering Linear B script, Ventris and Chadwick noted that these "paragraphs" appear as both longitudinal and horizontal cross-lines (111–12). Similar to Evans,

Ventris and Chadwick discovered that between paragraphs "the text is generally spaced by leaving one line vacant" (112). They also reported that, other than distinct punctuation by the commodity ideograms, changes in character size, and numbers which often occur at the end of a line, "there is no indication whatever of commas and full stops" (111). There is even one inscription from Pylos, which uses a formulaic expression to introduce a new paragraph, and another to suggest that occasionally two paragraphs are separated by cutting along one of the horizontal cross-lines (112). It is clear that these scripts characteristically use spacing or line strokes to separate units of discourse; literally, the "paragraphes" or scratching stroke around the writing is inherent in the earliest known compositional techniques of Hellenic discourse.

The erosion of the Greek syllabary script to a "Dark Age" dominated exclusively by oral literature (with attendant compositional and formulaic techniques), the introduction of the alphabet, and the subsequent literate revolution have been documented by such researchers as I. J. Gelb (1974), Eric Havelock (1982), Tony M. Lentz (1979, 1982), and Richard Leo Enos (1993). The consensus, after considerable debate, is that the Greek alphabet was adopted at some period between the tenth to the eighth century BC. Somewhat more contentious are the theories positing the development of scripts from retrograde, to boustrophedon, and eventually left-to-right direction. While variable directions of writing occur in early compositions, Greeks initially tended to follow the retrograde direction of Phoenician forerunners for their abecedarium but eventually emphasized their own compositional scheme called "boustrophedon," that is, reversing both the direction of the script and the characters themselves at the end of a line. The economy of this compositional scheme, both in effort and in the conservation of material, is obvious. In fact, writing left-to-right, right-to-left, or "snake-writing" (Schlangenschrift, in which the script curves to the shape of the writing material), seems to have been subject to the discretion of the writer. As A. G. Woodhead (1967) indicates, such scripts were actually a convenience to the reader, since one did not have to break at the end of a line but could follow the trail of words uninterrupted (25).

'Breaks" in ideas, manifested in physical markings called "interpuncts," did become important to Greek composers, as did the standardization of a more symmetrical, linear left-to-right script. As early writers evolved their script away from the boustrophedon system, the use and function of the paragraph again became more prevalent but, as will be discussed, more varied in its functions. In another style of composition during the pre-classical period, stoichedon, the letters are aligned both vertically and horizontally at equal spacing. This method requires that all characters face the same way and is clearly in conflict with the boustrophedon method. The adoption of the left-to-right direction of writing encouraged the stoichedon method to become the style during the classical period (Woodhead 30).

It is clear, however, that the Bronze Age linear scripts—and the linear scripts of a consistent direction—are a reasonable, if not necessary, development in the evolution of a compositional scheme. The study of the development of Greek scripts provides the basis for the following principle of composition: paragraphs become an important feature of composition when scripts become linear. It should be noted, however, that 'linearity" could be sacrificed to conform to the material written upon, such as vases and graffiti (Lang). Many of these examples of "graffiti," however, still have a distinctly linear quality. Theoretically, this principle could easily be extended to nonlinear scripts—or any writing system where delineation is desirable—but there is little doubt that the pre-Homeric linear scripts of Greece utilize various markings for the paragraph as an aspect of the syntax of the language. Although the concept of the paragraph expanded considerably as the development of Hellenic rhetoric continued, this principle in language syntax remained fixed.

The Compositional Features of Rhetoric: Paragraphs as Vocal Segregates

While writing with an alphabet became increasingly pervasive in the seventh and sixth centuries BC, it was often considered to be little more than an aid to memory, a macroscopic compositional technique to facilitate oral discourse. Similarly, reading silently was virtually unknown; hence, reading was a public rather than an intrapersonal activity (Stanford 1967). Further, the ability to isolate and thus "freeze" words synchronically was alien to Greeks; in fact, not only are characters strung together discursively without word breaks in early Greek scripts, but Greeks did not even think of words in isolation at all until the fifth century BC (Havelock 1982, 8). These conditions had a dominant impact on the concept of the paragraph. 'Paragraphing"—which should be seen as an activity in order to accurately reflect its dynamic nature in Greek composition—was an oral activity which used formulaic cues in the text to communicate to listeners-readers, many of whom were illiterate or may not have had easy access to the text. Thus, formulaic oral expressions take on the function of visual paragraph formats, and the concept of the "paragraph" takes on a plasticity to accommodate a variety of communication functions. The oral composing techniques of Hellenic rhapsodes were the basis for the formalization of the Iliad and Odyssey from an oral to a written text at some time near 560–500 BC, and the codification and standardization of these texts were based on principles of oral composition (Enos 1993).

Certainly in public texts, visual spacing and special markings serve to isolate critical ideas in the phonology of texts (Threatte 73–94). Extant inscriptions of victors lists at athletic and literary contests, honor rolls and other public texts calling for compartmentalization reveal the visual functions of the paragraph (Enos 1995). These visual spaces and strokes serve both syntagmatic and paradigmatic functions; they serve as punctuation marking of discrete lines and the form of a summary (Kenyon 27; Aristotle, Rhetoric 1409a). Such marks may indicate the end, not the beginning of a section and take the shape of a horizontal stroke (- - - -), a wedge (>), or ἡ διπλῆ, a terminating mark at the end of a text (7), or ἡ κορωνίς, or double point (:), or some other diacritical mark (Thompson). Several examples of a paragraphos appear in extant inscriptions. An excellent example of such paragraph-marking appears on an inscription stipulating book-lending regulations for The Library of Pantainos (Merritt).

The fact that this public inscription belongs to the age of Trajan (98–117 AD) testifies to the persistence of some of the punctuation marks of the paragraph beyond the Classical Period. In fact, the term for a specialized writing instrument (ἡ παραγραφίς) to make these markings was most likely derived from the term "ἡ παραγραφή" (Pollvcis Onomasticon 4. 18; 10.59). Frequently, as Thompson shows, if a final line were short in the preceding paragraph, a vacant space would be left and the new paragraph would begin with a slight scratch to mark the shift (68–70). Eventually the scratch and wedge marks were eliminated when the initial letter of the first full line was drawn back and projected into the margin (Thompson 68). In some cases, a letter began the first full line; in other instances, even in the middle of a word (Thompson 69). As standardized punctuation marks were being developed in Alexandrian schools, the termination of paragraphs was frequently accompanied by emphatic markings of dots and dashes (Thompson 70).

Paragraph markings, whether diacritical or vacant spaces, function as compositional determinants for separation; that is, such markings and spaces operate as "unarticulated phonograms" which cue conceptual and articulated estrangement. In this sense, paragraphs are the equivalent of vocal segregates by providing a visual taxis or categorical break that operates as a verbal/cognitive segregate. All such syntactic marks summarized above are indicators of a pause in the oral reading of the text; that is, the separation of physical space and the separation of acoustic, temporal space through a pause-break together cue the separation of ideas. These findings lead to the second principle of paragraph composition in Hellenic scripts: syntactic markings of Hellenic paragraphs are determinants of spatial, temporal and acoustic separation. Since speaking, reading, and writing were not seen as discrete phenomena, it is clear that paragraph cues would be global indicators of separation for all the senses that bear on communication. The markings of the paragraph were simultaneously cues for physical spacing, temporal pauses, and acoustic silence.

The Compositional Features of Rhetoric: Memory and Dissociation

The Classical Period provided both the greatest diversity and confluence in the concept of the paragraph. There is even evidence to indicate that the paragraph was a term of stage direction in the theatre, a cue to character change in drama and dialogues, and a term to distinguish the contrasting groups of a chorus or parabasis. Several prominent orators, such as Isocrates and Hyperides, illustrate the malleability of the meaning of the "paragraph" but consistently use forms of the term to distinguish exceptional or contrasting notions (Isocrates Antidosis 59; Hyperides, Against Demosthenes Frag, [c]; In Defense of Euxenippus 30). More than any other orator, however, Demosthenes reveals the intertwining oral and literary aspects of the paragraph throughout his forensic orations. In fact, the range of meanings for the paragraph is clearly apparent in forensic discourse. As a syntactic feature, the paragraph can mean a marked passage, marked time, a law written in parallel columns or a summary (Isocrates; Antidosis 59; Hyperides, Against Demosthenes Frag, [c]; Demosthenes, Against Aristocrates 63; Against Callipus 4; Aeschines, Against Ctesiphon 200, see also: Plato, Laws 785 A; Eustathius, Commentarii ad Homeri Iliadem 107.46; The Rhetoric of Aristotle, ed. with a commentary by Edward Meredith Cope and John Edwin Sandys, vol III [Cambridge: Cambridge Univ. Press, 1877 (reprinted Hildesheim: Georg Ohms Verlang, 1970)], p. 91 [note]).

Aristotle's perspective is especially revealing, for he uses the term "ἡ παραγραφή" in the Rhetoric to mean summary notations. As a legal term, however, the paragraph serves the functions of a special or counter plea, a point of admissibility, and an exception or emendation (Isocrates, Against Callimachus 1; Demosthenes, Against Lacritus 45, Against Phormio 17, Against Pantaenetus 33, Against Meidias 84, Against Boeotus 1.9; Hyperides, In Defense of Euxenippus 30, see also: Pollvcis Onomasticon 8. 57, 58). In certain instances, the term "ἡ παραγραφή" is the technical name for a type of forensic oration that constitutes a special plea (e.g., Demosthenes, Against Zenothemis, Against Nausimachus, Against Lacritus; Isocrates, Against Callimachus). In fact, D. A. Russell indicates that the paragraph, or "demurrer," functioned as a legal objection and was a standard feature of Greek declamation (Russell 38, 45, 60, 61, 101, 121, 139; Isager and Hansen 123–32). One inscription now in the British Museum even uses the term "paragraph" to indicate a point of stipulation in a contractual agreement (Inscriptiones Graecae: Inscriptiones Atticae, Euclidis Anno Posteriores, 2 [2], 1176.20). Aristotle, as indicative of its oral/written nature, uses the paragraph in the Rhetoric to indicate a summary functioning as a closing statement (1409a). In this revealing passage Aristotle refers to the paragraph as a mark of punctuation in a text to provide a visual cue to aid the memory of the rhetor in the cadence of the periodic structure of oral delivery. Aristotle's discussion of the paragraph as a compositional aid to facilitate listeners—coupled with its function in litigation—illustrates that the paragraph not only indicates distinctions but also concepts that are seen as contrasting in ways that are compatible with the notions of dissoi logoi and anti logoi that were discussed earlier. The use of the paragraph as a means of dissociation provides the third principle of paragraph composition in Hellenic rhetoric: the paragraph serves as an aid to memory in the structuring of written and oral composition when contrasting notions need to be articulated for purposes of argument and/or style.

The Compositional Features of Rhetoric: Invention and Structure

The various functions and derivative terms for the paragraph in oral and written composition extend our notion of its nature considerably, pointing to the likelihood that formulaic expressions, and even deviations in pitch, would necessitate written cues. In essence, physical markings function as written cues for phonological features of oral delivery: the written paragraph markings are mimetic codes for oral paragraphing. This analysis reveals that the written compositional techniques of paragraphing aid in the arrangement of oral discourse and serve an inventional function that provides generic distinctions for comparing and contrasting concepts. The paragraph can serve as an heuristic to facilitate the invention and structuring of ideas since it aids not only in arrangement but also the contrasting of concepts. Similarly, the paragraph, particularly in terms of style and forensic argument mentioned above, functions to help construe ideas in contrasting ways and clearly echoes back to the notion of dissoi logoi, or the invention of concepts by structuring antithetical notions (Vernant 122–3; Kerferd 5, 31–2). As discussed earlier, one of the earliest methods of structuring thought in Hellenic discourse is to establish ideas in opposition so that parameters for meaning can be established (Perry 410–18). Prominent PreSocratics such as Empedocles, and distinguished Sophists such as Gorgias, established epistemologies based on the principle of dissociation (Enos 1993). The conceptual framework for structuring antithetical concepts, the predisposition to set off ideas in correlative fashion, is apparent in the dissociation of notions and the euphony of language. Such a quality, characteristic of the oral style of Hellenic rhetoric, is echoed in the inscribed paragraph as an aid both for the separation and contrasting of ideas. The heuristic potential of the paragraph in Hellenic rhetoric is captured in the fourth principle of composition: during the Classical Period, the paragraph functioned as a means of inventing and structuring contrasting notions and thus served an heuristic function as well as an aid to memory.

The heuristic potential of the paragraph in Hellenic rhetoric complements the observations made by Richard Young and Patricia Sullivan in an essay on contemporary composition: "Why Write? A Reconsideration" (Young and Sullivan 1984). In their essay, Young and Sullivan argue that structuring principles in composition facilitate not only short-term memory but also invention (223–25). Young and Sullivan's discussion deals with contemporary issues in composition. However, the parallel of this phenomenon with the paragraph and classical discourse is clear: the structuring of the paragraph provides an heuristic not only to organize thought but also an environment to create discourse. Such an observation, while in a different historical and linguistic context, is nonetheless consistent with the findings of this study of the emergence of a literate rhetoric in Greece.

Conclusion

The principles discussed here illustrate both the diversity and unity of the paragraph as an oral/literary phenomenon. Yet the formalization of the paragraph as an aspect of composition is inevitable once we realize its early nature and evolution. As individuals learned to read and write silently, as literacy began to spread, and as orality and literacy began to separate, the concept of the paragraph increasingly became a mark of written style. Even ancient references after the Classical Period began to reveal that the oral dynamics were being removed from the concept of the paragraph as it evolved to little more than a compositional technique. George Kennedy discusses the transformation of rhetoric from a primary oral function to a secondary literary function under the concept of "letteraturizzazione" (Kennedy 1999). The shift in rhetoric, which Kennedy discusses generally, can be applied specifically to the paragraph. Clearly, the paragraph emerged in Greek rhetoric as perhaps the earliest compositional technique for the punctuation of symbols to isolate and orchestrate ideas.

The observations advanced in this essay reveal an inextricable binding of oral and written expression. Throughout the Classical Period, a diversity of forms and expressions in oral and written notions of the paragraph is evident. This diversity ranges from physical spacing through scratch marks, to visual cues, to oral and written composition, all of which served as both aids to memory and to heuristic processes. In the sense of Kennedy's discussion of letteraturizzazione, the separation of orality from literacy also transformed the meaning of a "paragraph." The separation of oral and written discourse stripped the oral aspects from the concept of the paragraph, relegating it solely to a formatting function of style. The results of this research indicate that the concept of the paragraph in Greek rhetoric has several dimensions and evolutionary stages, including oral, graphic, temporal, acoustic, legal, syntactic, and heuristic.

The observations advanced in this essay illustrate the benefits of assimilating methods of composition research for a more sensitive understanding of rhetoric's history. Discussing the relationship between language and writing, I. J. Gelb argued (1975) that "very little work has been done in the field of relations of writing to language. Philologists have been concerned mainly with the historical evolution of writing and have paid little attention to the interrelations between writing and language (64)." Gelb goes on to argue that linguists, on the other hand, are more concerned with spoken languages than with writing. "When interested in written languages," Gelb claims, "they have often limited their study to living written languages, especially those written in pre-alphabetic systems (64)." Gelb argues, and this review illustrates, that an historical approach to composition encourages an understanding of situated discourse practices rather than an autonomous, independent system of inquiry. That is, viewing the paragraph diachronically pointedly reveals the dynamic relationship between orality and literacy in Greek rhetoric.

Studies on the contemporary use of the paragraph reveal that our historical predispositions are imprecise; specifically, the paragraph is not merely a formulaic convention but rather a conceptual notion in the inventive process of composition. While contemporary research has pointed to the complexity of the paragraph, historians of rhetoric have done comparatively little to explain its development and endurance. As is true with many aspects of rhetoric, the unit of discourse known as the paragraph its nature and origin—evolved out of ancient discourse. This inquiry into the paragraph, and its derivative terms in Greek rhetoric through the Classical Period, complements current composition research about the paragraph's nature and development and thus contributes to our understanding from another important perspective. The central observation of this study is that the paragraph grew out of oral discourse and exhibited a diversity of functions in Ancient Greece that are only partially realized through the paragraph's present-day function in writing. Reconstructing the paragraph's multiple dimensions in Ancient Greece requires an examination of its historical development, which reveals that the complexity of the paragraph now apparent in modern research parallels and complements the complexity of the paragraph in Antiquity. Gelb's assertion about the alphabet being the last great invention in writing will need to be modified as we continue to re-examine features of writing that have oral antecedents.

References

Aeschines. *Against Ctesiphon.*
Aristotle. *The Rhetoric of Aristotle.* Ed. with commentary, Edward Meredith Cope and John Edwin Sandys, vol. 3. Cambridge: Cambridge University Press, 1877. Hildesheim: Georg Ohm Verlang, 1970.

Casson, Lionel. *Ancient Egypt.* New York: Time-Life Books, 1971. 150–51.

Demosthenes. *Against Aristocrates.*

———. *Against Boeotus.*

———. *Against Callipus.*

———. *Against Lacritus.*

———. *Against Meidias.*

———. *Against Nausimachus.*

———. *Against Pantaenetus.*

———. *Against Phormio.*

———. *Against Zenothemis.*

Doblhofer, Ernst. *Voices in Stone: The Decipherment of Ancient Scripts and Writings.* Trans. Mervyn Savill. New York: Collier Books, 1975.

Dow, Sterling. "Minoan Writing." *American Journal of Archaeology* 58 (April 1954): 78–129.

Enos, Richard Leo. *Greek Rhetoric Before Aristotle.* Prospect Heights, IL: Waveland Press, 1993.

———. *Roman Rhetoric: Revolution and the Greek Influence.* Prospect Heights, IL: Waveland Press, 1995.

Enos, Richard Leo and Elizabeth Odoroff. "The Orality of the 'Paragraph' in Greek Rhetoric." *Pre/Text* 6 (Spring/Summer 1985): 51–65.

Enos, Richard Leo and John Ackerman. "Walter J. Ong and the Archaeology of Orality and Literacy: A Theoretical Model for Historical Rhetoric." *Media, Consciousness and Culture: Explorations of Walter Ong's Thought.* Eds. Bruce Gronbeck, Thomas J. Farrell, and Paul A. Soukup. Newbury Park, CA: Sage Publications, 1991. 108–120.

Eustathius. *Commentarii ad Homeri Iliadem.*

Evans, Arthur J. "The Palace Archives of Mycenaean Cnossus." *The Athenaeum* 3786 (May 19, 1900): 634.

———. *Scripta Minoa: The Written Documents of Minoan Crete with Special Reference to the Archives of Knossos.* vol. 1. Oxford: Clarendon Press, 1909.

Gelb, I. J. "Records, Writing, and Decipherment." *Language & Texts: The Nature of Linguistic Evidence.* Ed. Herbert H. Paper. Ann Arbor, MI: Center for the Coordination of Ancient and Modern Study, 1975.

———. *A Study of Writing.* Revised edn. Chicago, IL: University of Chicago Press, 1974.

Havelock, Eric A. *The Literate Revolution in Greece and Its Cultural Consequences.* Princeton, NJ: Princeton University Press, 1982.

———. *The Muse Learns to Write: Reflections on Orality and Literacy from Antiquity to the Present.* New Haven and London: Yale University Press, 1986.

———. *Preface to Plato.* Cambridge, MA and London: The Belknap Press of Harvard University Press, 1963, 1982.

Homer. *Iliad.*

Hyperides. *Against Demosthenes, Frag. [c].*

———. *In Defense of Euxenippus.*

Inscriptions Graecae: Inscriptiones Atticae, Euclidis Anno Posteriores. Ed. Iohannes Kirchner. Chicago, IL: Ares Publishers, Inc., 1974; Berlin: 1913–1940.

Isager, Signe, and Mogens Herman Hansen. *Aspects of Athenian Society in the Fourth Century BC: A historical introduction to and commentary on the paragraphs/speeches and the speech Against Dionysodorus in the Corpus Demosthenicum XXXII–XXXVIII and LVI.* Trans. Judith Hsiang Rosenmeier. Odense, Denmark: Odense University Press, 1975.

Isocrates. *Against Callimachus.*

———. *Antidosis.*
Kennedy, George A. *The Art of Persuasion in Greece.* Princeton, NJ: Princeton University Press, 1963.
———. *Classical Rhetoric and its Christian and Secular Tradition from Ancient to Modern Times.* 2nd edn. Chapel Hill, NC: University of North Carolina Press, 1999.
Kenyon, Frederic G. *The Palaeography of Greek Papyri.* Oxford: Clarendon Press, 1899.
Kerferd, G. B. *The Sophistic Movement.* Cambridge: Cambridge University Press, 1981.
Knox, Sanka. "Briton's Work Shows Early Greeks Had Ability to Write." *New York Times* 9 (Friday, April, 1954): 1, C18.
Lang, Mabel. *Graffiti in the Athenian Agora.* Princeton, NJ: American School of Classical Studies, 1974.
Lentz, Tony M. "The Oral Tradition of Interpretation: Reading in Hellenic Greece as Described by Ancient Authors." Ph.D. dissertation, The University of Michigan, 1979.
———. "Writing as Sophistry: From Preservation to Persuasion." *Quarterly Journal of Speech* 68 (February 1982): 60–68.
Merritt, Benjamin D. (ed.). *Inscriptions from the Athenian Agora.* Princeton, NJ: American School of Classical Studies at Athens, 1966, no. 32. (I 2729, Hesperia 5 [1936]: 41–3; suppl. 8, 268–72).
Ong, Walter J. *Orality and Literacy: The Technologizing of the Word.* London and New York: Methuen, 1982; London and New York: Routledge, 1993.
Perry, Ben Edwin. "The Early Greek Capacity for Viewing Things Separately." *Transactions of the American Philological Association* 68 (1937): 410–418.
Plato. *Laws.*
Pollvcis Onomasticon.
Russell, D. A. *Greek Declamation.* Cambridge: Cambridge University Press, 1983.
Stanford, W. B. *The Sound of Greek: Studies in the Greek Theory and Practice of Euphony.* Berkeley, CA: California Press, 1967.
Thompson, Edward Maune. *A Handbook of Greek and Latin Palaeography.* Chicago, IL: Ares, 1975.
Threatte, Leslie. *The Grammar of Attic Inscriptions.* Berlin: Walter De Gruyter, 1980.
Ventris, Michael and John Chadwick. *Documents in Mycenaean Greek.* 2nd edn. Cambridge: Cambridge University Press, 1973.
Vernant, Jean Pierre. *The Origins of Greek Thought.* English edn. Ithaca, NY: Cornell University Press, 1982.
Woodhead, A. G. *The Study of Greek Inscriptions.* Cambridge: Cambridge University Press, 1967.
Young, Richard E., and Alton L. Becker. "The Role of Lexical and Grammatical Cues in Paragraph Recognition." *Studies in Language and Language Behavior.* Progress Report II, Contract: OE5–14–036. Ann Arbor, MI: The University of Michigan Center for Research on Language and Language Behavior, 1966.
Young, Richard E., and Patricia Sullivan. "Why Write? A Reconsideration." *Essays on Classical Rhetoric and Modern Discourse.* Eds. Robert J. Connors, Lisa S. Ede, and Andrea A. Lunsford. Carbondale and Edwardsville, IL: Southern Illinois University Press, 1984. 215–225.

3.
THE CONSEQUENCES OF LITERACY
Jack Goody and Ian Watt

The accepted tripartite divisions of the formal study both of mankind's past and present are to a considerable extent based on man's development first of language and later of writing. Looked at in the perspective of time, man's biological evolution shades into prehistory when he becomes a language-using animal; add writing, and history proper begins. Looked at in a temporal perspective, man as animal is studied primarily by the zoologist, man as talking animal primarily by the anthropologist, and man as talking and writing animal primarily by the sociologist.

That the differentiation between these categories should be founded on different modes of communication is clearly appropriate; it was language that enabled man to achieve a form of social organisation whose range and complexity was different in kind from that of animals: whereas the social organisation of animals was mainly instinctive and genetically transmitted, that of man was largely learned and transmitted verbally through the cultural heritage. The basis for the last two distinctions, those based on the development of writing, is equally clear: to the extent that a significant quantity of written records are available the pre-historian yields to the historian; and to the extent that alphabetical writing and popular literacy imply new modes of social organisation and transmission, the anthropologist tends to yield to the sociologist.

But why? And how? There is no agreement about this question, nor even about what the actual boundary lines between non-literate and literate cultures are. At what point in the formalisation of pictographs or other graphic signs can we talk of "letters", of literacy? And what proportion of the society has to write and read before the culture as a whole can be described as literate?

These are some of the many reasons why the extent to which there is any distinction between the areas and methods peculiar to anthropology and sociology must be regarded as problematic; and the difficulty affects not only the boundaries of the two disciplines but also the nature of the intrinsic differences in their subject matter.[1] The recent trend has been for anthropologists to spread their net more widely and engage in the study of industrial societies side by side with their sociological colleagues. We can no longer accept the view that anthropologists have as their objective the study of primitive man, who is characterised by a "primitive mind", while sociologists, on the other hand, concern themselves with civilised man, whose activities are guided by "rational thought" and tested by "logico-empirical procedures". The reaction against such ethnocentric views, however, has now gone to the point of denying that the distinction between non-literate and literate society has any significant validity. This position seems contrary to our personal observation; and so it has seemed worthwhile to enquire whether there may not be, even from the most empirical and relativist standpoint, genuine illumination to be derived from a further consideration of some of the historical and analytic problems connected with the traditional dichotomy between non-literate and literate societies.

The Cultural Tradition in Non-Literate Societies

For reasons which will become clear it seems best to begin with a generalised description of the ways in which the cultural heritage is transmitted in non-literate societies, and then to see how these ways are changed by the widespread adoption of an easy and effective means of written communication.

When one generation hands on its cultural heritage to the next, three fairly separate items are involved. First, the society passes on its material plant, including the natural resources available to its members. Secondly, it transmits standardised ways of acting. These customary ways of behaving are only partly communicated by verbal means; ways of cooking food, of growing crops, of handling children may be transmitted by direct imitation. But the most significant elements of any human culture are undoubtedly channelled through words, and reside in the particular range of meanings and attitudes which members of any society attach to their verbal symbols. These elements include not only what we habitually think of as customary behavior but also such items as ideas of space and time, generalised goals and aspirations, in short the *weltanschauung* of every social group. In Durkheim's words, these categories of the understanding are "priceless instruments of thought which the human groups have laboriously forged through the centuries and where they have accumulated the best of their intellectual capital".[2] The relative continuity of these categories of understanding from one generation to another is primarily ensured by language, which is the most direct and comprehensive expression of the social experience of the group.

The transmission of the verbal elements of culture by oral means can be visualised as a long chain of interlocking conversations between members of the group. Thus all beliefs and values, all forms of knowledge, are communicated between individuals in face-to-face contact; and, as distinct from the material content of the cultural tradition, whether it be cave paintings or hand-axes, they are stored only in human memory.

The intrinsic nature of oral communication has a considerable effect upon both the content and the transmission of the cultural repertoire. In the first place it makes for a directness of relationship between symbol and referent. There can be no reference to "dictionary definitions", nor can words accumulate the successive layers of historically validated meanings which they acquire in a literate culture. Instead the meaning of each word is ratified in a succession of concrete situations, accompanied by vocal inflexions and physical gestures, all of which combine to particularize both its specific denotation and its accepted connotative usages. This process of direct semantic ratification, of course, operates cumulatively; and as a result the totality of symbol-referent relationships is more immediately experienced by the individual in an exclusively oral culture, and is thus more deeply socialised.

One way of illustrating this is to consider how the range of vocabulary in a non-literate society reflects this mode of semantic ratification. It has often been observed how the elaboration of the vocabulary of such a society reflects the particular interests of the people concerned. The inhabitants of the Pacific island of Lesu have not one, but a dozen or so, words for pigs,[3] according to sex, color, and where they come from—a prolixity which mirrors the importance of pigs in a domestic economy that otherwise includes few sources of protein. The corollary of this prolixity is that where common emphases and interests, whether material or otherwise, are not specifically involved, there is little verbal development. Malinowski reported that in the Trobriands the outer world was only named insofar as it yielded useful things, useful, that is, in the very broadest sense;[4] and there is much other testimony to support the view that there is an intimate functional adaptation of language in non-literate societies, which obtains not only for the relatively simple and concrete symbol-referents involved above, but also for the more generalized "categories of understanding" and for the cultural tradition as a whole.

In an essay he wrote in collaboration with Mauss, "De quelques formes primitives de classification",[5] Durkheim traces the interconnections between the ideas of space and the territorial distribution of the Australian aborigines, the Zuni of the Pueblo area and the Sioux of the Great Plains. This intermeshing of what he called the collective representations with the social morphology of a particular society is clearly another aspect of the same directness of relationship between symbol and referent. Just as the more concrete part of a vocabulary reflects the dominant interests of the society, so the more abstract categories are often closely linked to the accepted terminology for pragmatic pursuits. Among the LoDagaa of Northern Ghana, days are reckoned according to the incidence of neighboring markets; the very word for day and market is the same, and the "weekly" cycle is a six-day revolution of the most important markets in the vicinity, a cycle which also defines the spatial range of everyday activities.[6]

The way in which these various institutions in an oral culture are kept in relatively close accommodation one to another surely bears directly on the question of the central difference between literate and non-literate societies. As we have remarked, the whole content of the social tradition, apart from the material inheritances, is held in memory. The social aspects of remembering have been emphasised by sociologists and psychologists, in particular Maurice Halbwachs.[7] What the individual remembers tends to be what is of critical importance in his experience of the main social relationships. In each generation, therefore, the individual memory will mediate the cultural heritage in such a way that its new constituents will adjust to the old by the process of interpretation that Bartlett calls "rationalizing" or the "effort after meaning"; and whatever parts of it have ceased to be of contemporary relevance are likely to be eliminated by the process of forgetting.

The social function of memory—and of forgetting—can thus be seen as the final stage of what may be called the homeostatic organisation of the cultural tradition in non-literate society. The language is developed in intimate association with the experience of the community, and it is learned by the individual in face-to-face contact with the other members. What continues to be social relevance is stored in the memory while the rest is usually forgotten: and language—primarily vocabulary—is the effective medium of this crucial process of social digestion and elimination which may be regarded as analogous to the homeostatic organisation of the human body by means of which it attempts to maintain its present condition of life.

In drawing attention to the importance of these assimilating mechanisms in non-literate societies, we are denying neither the occurrence of social change, nor yet the "survivals" which it leaves in its wake. Nor do we overlook the existence of mnemonic devices in oral cultures which offer some resistance to the interpretative process. Formalised patterns of speech, recital under ritual conditions, the use of drums and other musical instruments, the employment of professional remembrancers—all such factors may shield at least part of the content of memory from the transmuting influence of the immediate pressures of the present. The Homeric epics, for instance, seem to have been written down during the first century of Greek literature between 750 and 650 BC, but "they look to a departed era, and their substance is unmistakably old".[8]

With these qualifications, however, it seems correct to characterize the transmission of the cultural tradition in oral societies as homeostatic in view of the way in which its emphasis differs from that in literate societies. The description offered has, of course, been extremely abstract; but a few illustrative examples in one important area—that of how the tribal past is digested into the communal orientation of the present—may serve to make it clearer.

Like the Bedouin Arabs and the Hebrews of the Old Testament, the Tiv people of Nigeria give long genealogies of their forebears which in this case stretch some twelve generations in depth back to an eponymous founding ancestor.[9] Neither these genealogies, nor the Biblical lists of the descendants of Adam, were remembered purely as feats of memory. They served as mnemonics for systems of social relations. When on his deathbed Jacob delivered prophecies about the future of his twelve sons, he spoke of them as the twelve tribes or nations of Israel. It would seem from the account in Genesis that the genealogical tables here refer to contemporary groups rather than to dead individuals;[10] the tables presumably serve to regulate social relations among the twelve tribes of Israel in a manner similar to that which has been well analysed in Evans-Pritchard's work on the Nuer of the Southern Sudan and in Fortes' account of the Tallensi of Northern Ghana.[11]

Early British administrators among the Tiv of Nigeria were aware of the great importance attached to these genealogies, which were continually discussed in court cases where the rights and duties of one man towards another were in dispute. Consequently they took the trouble to write down the long lists of names and preserve them for posterity, so that future administrators might refer to them in giving judgement. Forty years later, when the Bohannans carried out anthropological field work in the area, their successors were still using the same genealogies.[12] However, these written pedigrees now gave rise to many disagreements; the Tiv maintained that they were incorrect, while the officials regarded them as statements of fact, as records of what had actually happened, and could not agree that the unlettered indigenes could be better informed about the past than their own literate predecessors. What neither party realised was that in any society of this kind changes take place which require a constant readjustment in the genealogies if they are to continue to carry out their function as mnemonics of social relationships.

These changes are of several kinds: those arising from the turnover in personnel, from the process of "birth and copulation and death"; those connected with the rearrangement of the constituent units of the society, with the migration of one group and the fission of another; and lastly those resulting from the effects of changes in the social system itself, whether generated from within or initiated from without. Each of these three processes (which we may refer to for convenience as the processes of generational, organisational and structural change) could lead to alterations of the kind to which the administration objected.

It is obvious that the process of generation leads in itself to a constant lengthening of the genealogy; on the other hand, the population to which it is linked may in fact be growing at quite a different rate, perhaps simply replacing itself. So despite its increasing length the genealogy may have to refer to just as many people at the present time as it did fifty, a hundred, or perhaps two hundred years ago. Consequently the added depth of lineages caused by new births needs to be accompanied by a process of genealogical shrinkage; the occurrence of this telescoping process, a common example of the general social phenomenon which J. A. Barnes has felicitously termed "structural amnesia", has been attested in many societies, including all those mentioned above.[13]

Organisational changes lead to similar adjustments. The state of Gonja in Northern Ghana is divided into a number of divisional chiefdoms, certain of which are recognised as providing in turn the ruler of the whole nation. When asked to explain their system the Gonja recount how the founder of the state, Ndewura Jakpa, came down from the Niger Bend in search of gold, conquered the indigenous inhabitants of the area and enthroned himself as chief of the state and his sons as rulers of its territorial divisions. At his death the divisional chiefs succeeded to the paramountcy in turn. When the details of this story were first recorded at the turn of the present century, at the time the British were extending their control over the area, Jakpa was said to have begotten seven sons, this corresponding to the number of divisions whose heads were eligible for the supreme office by virtue of their descent from the founder of the particular chiefdom. But at the same time as the British had arrived, two of the seven divisions disappeared, one being deliberately incorporated in a neighboring division because its rulers had supported a Mandingo invader, Samori, and another because of some boundary changes introduced by the British administration. Sixty years later, when the myths of state were again recorded, Jakpa was credited with only five sons and no mention was made of the founders of the two divisions which had since disappeared from the political map.[14]

These two instances from the Tiv and the Gonja emphasise that genealogies often serve the same function that Malinowski claimed for myth; they act as 'charters' of present social institutions rather than as faithful historical records of times past.[15] They can do this more consistently because they operate within an oral rather than a written tradition and thus tend to be automatically adjusted to existing social relations as they are passed by word of mouth from one member of the society to another. The social element in remembering results in the genealogies being transmuted in the course of being transmitted; and a similar process takes place with regard to other cultural elements as well, to myths, for example, and to sacred lore in general. Deities and other supernatural agencies which have served their purpose can be quietly dropped from the contemporary pantheon; and as the society changes, myths too are forgotten, attributed to other personages, or transformed in their meaning.

One of the most important results of this homeostatic tendency is that the individual has little perception of the past except in terms of the present; whereas the annals of a literate society cannot but enforce a more objective recognition of the distinction between what was and what is. Franz Boas wrote that for the Eskimo the world has always been as it is now:[16] it seems probable, at least, that the form in which nonliterate societies conceive the world of the past is itself influenced by the process of transmission described. The Tiv have their genealogies, others their sacred tales about the origin of the world and the way in which man acquired his culture. But all their conceptualisations of the past cannot help being governed by the concerns of the present, merely because there is no body of chronologically ordered statements to which reference can be made. The Tiv do not recognise any contradiction between what they say now and what they said fifty years ago, since no enduring records exist for them to set beside their present views. Myth and history merge into one: the elements in the cultural heritage which cease to have a contemporary relevance tend to be soon forgotten or transformed; and as the individuals of each generation acquire their vocabulary, their genealogies, and their myths, they are unaware that various words, proper-names and stories have dropped out, or that others have changed their meanings or been replaced.

Kinds of Writing and Their Social Effects

The pastness of the past, then, depends upon a historical sensibility which can hardly begin to operate without permanent written records; and writing introduces similar changes in the transmission of other items of the cultural repertoire. But the extent of these changes varies with the nature and social distribution of the writing system; varies, that is, according to the system's intrinsic efficacy as a means of communication, and according to the social constraints placed upon it, that is, the degree to which use of the system is diffused through the society.

Early in prehistory, man began to express himself in graphic form; and his cave paintings, rock engravings and wood carvings are morphologically, and presumably sequentially, the forerunners of writing. By some process of simplification and stylisation they appear to have led to the various kinds of pictographs found in simple societies.[17] While pictographs themselves are almost universal, their development into a self-sufficient system capable of extended discourse occurs only among the Plains Indians.[18]

Pictographs have obvious disadvantages as means of communication. For one thing a vast number of signs is needed to represent all the important objects in the culture. For another, since the signs are concrete, the simplest sentence requires an extremely elaborate series of signs: many stylised representations of wigwams, footprints, totemic animals and so on are required just to convey the information that a particular man left there a few days ago. Finally, however elaborately the sytem is developed, only a limited number of things can be said.

The end of the fourth millennium saw the early stages of the development of more complex forms of writing, which seem to be an essential factor in the rise of the urban cultures of the Orient. The majority of signs in these systems were simply pictures of the outside world, standardised representations of the object signified by a particular word; to these were added other devices for creating word signs or logograms, which permitted the expression of wider ranges of meaning. Thus in Egyptian hieroglyphics, the picture of a beetle was a code sign not only for that insect but also for a discontinuous and more abstract referent "became".[19]

The basic invention used to supplement the logograms was the phonetic principle, which for the first time permitted the written expression of all the words of a language. For example, by the device of phonetic transfer the Sumerians could use the sign for *ti*, an arrow, to stand for *ti*, life, a concept not easy to express in pictographic form. In particular, the need to record personal names and foreign words encouraged the development of phonetic elements in writing.

But while these true writing systems all used phonetic devices for the construction of logograms (and have consequently been spoken of as word-syllabic systems of writing), they failed to carry through the application of the phonetic principle exclusively and systematically.[20] The achievement of a system completely based upon the representation of phonemes (the basic units of meaningful sound) was left to the Near Eastern syllabaries, which developed between 1500–1000 BC, and finally to the introduction of the alphabet proper in Greece. Meanwhile these incompletely phonetic systems were too clumsy and complicated to foster widespread literacy, if only because the number of signs was very large; at least six hundred would have to be learned even for the simplified cuneiform developed in Assyria, and about the same for Egyptian hieroglyphs.[21] All these ancient civilisations, the Sumerian, Egyptian, Hittite and Chinese, were literate in one sense and their great advances in administration and technology were undoubtedly connected with the invention of a writing system; but when we think of the limitations of their systems of communication as compared with ours, the term "protoliterate", or even "oligoliterate", might be more descriptive in suggesting the restriction of literacy to a relatively small proportion of the total population.[22]

Any system of writing which makes the sign stand directly for the object must be extremely complex. It can extend its vocabulary by generalisation or association of ideas, that is, by making the sign stand either for a more general class of objects, or for other referents connected with the original picture by an association of meanings which may be related to one another either in a continuous or in a discontinuous manner. Either process of semantic extension is to some extent arbitrary or esoteric; and as a result the interpretation of these signs is neither easy nor explicit. One might perhaps guess that the Chinese sign for a man carries the general meaning of maleness; it would be more difficult to see that a conventionalised picture of a man and a broom is the sign for a woman; it's a pleasing fancy, no doubt, but not one which communicates very readily until it has been learned as a new character, as a separate sign for a separate word, as a logogram. In Chinese writing a minimum of 3000 such characters have to be learned before one can be reasonably literate;[23] and with a total repertoire of some 50,000 characters to be mastered, it normally takes about twenty years to reach full literate proficiency. China, therefore, stands as an extreme example of how, when a virtually non-phonetic system of writing becomes sufficiently developed to express a large number of meanings explicitly, only a small and specially trained professional group in the total society can master it, and partake of the literate culture.

Although systems of word signs are certainly easier to learn, many difficulties remain, even when these signs are supplemented by phonemic devices of a syllabic sort. Other features of the social system are no doubt responsible for the way that the writing systems developed as they did: but it is a striking fact that—for whatever ultimate causes—in Egypt and Mesopotamia, as in China, a literate elite of religious, administrative and commercial experts emerged and maintained itself as a centralised governing bureaucracy on rather similar lines. Their various social and intellectual achievements were, of course, enormous; but as regards the participation of the society as a whole in the written culture, a wide gap existed between the esoteric literate culture and the exoteric oral one, a gap which the literate were interested in maintaining. Among the Sumerians and Akkadians writing was the pursuit of scribes and preserved as a "mystery", a "secret treasure". Royalty were themselves illiterate; Ashurbanipal (668–626 BC) records that he was the first Babylonian king to master the "clerkly skill".[24] "Put writing in your heart that you may protect yourself from hard labour of any kind", writes an Egyptian of the New Kingdom: "The scribe is released from manual tasks; it is he who commands".[25] Significantly, the classical age of Babylonian culture, beginning under Hammurabi in the late eighteenth century BC, appears to have coincided with a period when the reading and writing of Akkadian cuneiform was not confined to a small group, nor to one nation; it was then that nearly all the extant literature was written down, and that the active state of commerce and administration produced a vast quantity of public and private correspondence, of which much has survived.

These imperfectly phonetic methods of writing survived with little change for many centuries;[26] so too did the cultures of which they were part.[27] The existence of an elite group, which followed from the difficulty of the writing system, and whose continued influence depended on the maintenance of the present social order, must have been a powerfully conservative force, especially when it consisted of ritual specialists;[28] and so, it may be surmised, was the nature of the writing system itself. For pictographic and logographic systems are alike in their tendency to reify the objects of the natural and social order; by so doing they register, record, make permanent the existing social and ideological picture. Such, for example, was the tendency of the most highly developed and longest-lived ancient writing system, that of Egypt, whose society has been described with picturesque exaggeration as "a nation of fellahin ruled with a rod of iron by a Society of Antiquaries".

This conservative or antiquarian bias can perhaps be best appreciated by contrasting it with fully phonetic writing; for phonetic writing, by imitating human discourse, is in fact symbolising, not the objects of the social and natural order, but the very process of human interaction in speech: the verb is as easy to express as the noun; and the written vocabulary can be easily and unambiguously expanded. Phonetic systems are therefore adapted to expressing every nuance of individual thought, to recording personal reactions as well as items of major social importance. Non-phonetic writing, on the other hand, tends rather to record and reify only those items in the cultural repertoire which the literate specialists have selected for written expression; and it tends to express the collective attitude towards them.

The notion of representing a sound by a graphic symbol is itself so stupefying a leap of the imagination that what is remarkable is not so much that it happened relatively late in human history, but rather that it ever happened at all. For a long time, however, these phonetic inventions had a limited effect because they were only partially exploited: not only were logograms and pictograms retained, but a variety of phonograms were used to express the same sound. The full explicitness and economy of a phonetic writing system "as easy as A B C" was therefore likely to arise only in less advanced societies on the fringes of Egypt or Mesopotamia, societies which were starting their writing system more or less from scratch, and which took over the idea of phonetic signs from adjoining countries, and used them exclusively to fit their own language.[29] These phonetic signs could, of course, be used to stand for any unit of speech, and thus developed either into syllabaries or into alphabets. In a few cases, such as Japanese, the particular nature of the language made it possible to construct a relatively simple and efficient syllabary; but as regards the great majority of languages the alphabet, with its signs for individual consonants and vowels, proved a much more economical and convenient instrument for representing sounds. For the syllabaries, while making writing easier, were still far from simple;[30] they were often combined with logograms and pictographs.[31] And whether by necessity or tradition or both, pre-alphabetic writing was still mainly restricted to elite groups. The Mycenean script disappeared completely after the 12th century BC, a fact which was possible because of the very restricted uses of literacy and the close connection between writing and palace administration.[32] It is doubtful whether any such loss could have occurred in Greece after the introduction of a complete alphabetic script, probably in the eighth century BC.

The alphabet is almost certainly the supreme example of cultural diffusion:[33] all existing or recorded alphabets derive from Semitic syllabaries developed during the second millennium. Eventually there arose the enormous simplification of the Semitic writing system, with its mere twenty-two letters; and then only one further step remained: the Greek script, which is, of course, much closer than the Semitic to the Roman alphabet, took certain of the Semitic signs for consonants which the Greek language didn't need, and used them for vowels, which the Semitic syllabary did not represent.[34] The directness of our inheritance from these two sources is suggested by the fact that our word "alphabet" is the latinized form of the first two letters of the Greek alphabet, "alpha", derived from the Semitic "alphh", and "beta", from the Semitic "beth".

The reason for the success of the alphabet, which David Diringer calls a "democratic" script as opposed to the "theocratic" scripts of Egypt, is itself based on the fact that, uniquely among writing systems, its graphic signs are representations of the most extreme and most universal example of cultural selection—the basic phonemic system. The number of sounds which the human breath stream can produce is vast; but nearly all languages are based on the formal recognition by the society of only forty or so of these sounds. The success of the alphabet (as well as some of its incidental difficulties) comes from the fact that its system of graphic representation takes advantage of this socially-conventionalized pattern of sound in all language systems; by symbolizing in letters these selected phonemic units the alphabet makes it possible to write easily and read unambiguously about anything which the society can talk about.

The historical picture of the cultural impact of the new alphabetic writing is not altogether clear. As regards the Semitic system, which was widely adopted elsewhere, the evidence suggests that—in part perhaps because of the intrinsic difficulties of the system, but mainly because of the established cultural features of the societies which adopted it—the social diffusion of writing was slow. There was, for one thing, a strong tendency for writing to be used as a help to memory rather than as an autonomous and independent mode of communication; and under such conditions its influence tended towards the consolidation of the existing cultural tradition. This certainly appears to be true of India and Palestine.[35] Gandz notes, for example, that Hebrew culture continued to be transmitted orally long after the Old Testament had begun to be written down. As he puts it, the introduction of writing:

> did not at once change the habits of the people and displace the old method of oral tradition. We must always distinguish between the *first introduction* of writing and its *general diffusion.* It often takes several centuries, and sometimes even a millennium or more, until this invention becomes the common property of the people at large. In the beginning, the written book is not intended for practical use at all. It is a divine instrument, placed in the temple "by the side of the ark of the covenant that it may be there for a witness" (Deuteronomy, xxxi, 26), and remains there as a holy relic. For the people at large, oral instruction still remained the only way of learning, and the memory—the only means of preservation. Writing was practiced, if at all, only as an additional support for the memory {...}

It was not, in fact, until some six centuries after the original Hebrew adoption of the Semitic writing system that, at the time of Ezra (ca. 444 BC), an official "generally recognized text" of the Torah was published, and the body of the religious tradition ceased to be "practically . . . a sealed book" and became accessible to anyone who chose to study it.[36]

Even so, of course, as the frequent diatribes against the scribes in the Gospels remind us,[37] there remained a considerable gap between the literati and the laymen; the professionals who plied their trade in the market-place belonged to "families of scribes", perhaps organized as guilds, within which the mystery was handed down from father to son.[38]

Anything like popular literacy, or the use of writing as an autonomous mode of communication by the majority of the members of society, is not found in the earliest societies which used the Semitic writing system; it was, rather, in the sixth and fifth centuries BC in the city states of Greece and Ionia that there first arose a society which as a whole could justly be characterized as literate. Many of the reasons why literacy became widespread in Greece, but not in other societies which had Semitic, or indeed any other, simple and explicit writing systems, necessarily lie outside the scope of this essay; yet considerable importance must surely be attributed to the intrinsic advantages of the Greek adaptation of the Semitic alphabet, an adaptation which made it the first comprehensively and exclusively phonetic system for transcribing human speech.[39] The system was easy, explicit and unambiguous—more so than the Semitic where the lack of vowels is responsible for many of the cruxes in the Bible: for instance, since the consonant in the Hebrew words is the same, Elijah may have been fed by "Ravens" or "Arabs."[39a] Its great advantage over the syllabaries lay in the reduction of the number of signs and in the ability to specify consonant and vowel clusters. The system was easy to learn: Plato sets aside three years for the process in the Laws,[40] about the time taken in our schools today; and the much greater speed with which alphabetic writing can be learned is shown, not only by such reports as those of the International Institute of Intellectual Cooperation in 1934,[41] but also by the increasing adoption of the Roman script, and even more widely of alphabetic systems of writing, throughout the world.

The extensive diffusion of the alphabet in Greece was also materially assisted by various social, economic and technological factors. In the first place the 8th century saw a great burst of economic activity following the revival of the eastern trade which had declined after the Mycenean collapse in the 12th century.[42] Secondly, while the Greek society of the period had, of course, its various social strata, the political system was not strongly centralized; especially in the Ionic settlements there appears to have been a good deal of flexibility and in them we discern the beginnings of the Greek city state. Thirdly, the increased contact with the East brought material prosperity and technological advance. The wider use of iron, the advent of the true Iron Age, was perhaps one of the results.[43] More closely connected with literacy was the fact that trade with Egypt led to the importation of papyrus; and this made writing itself easier and less expensive, both for the individual writer and for the reader who wanted to buy books: papyrus was obviously much cheaper than parchment made from skins, more permanent than wax tablets, easier to handle than the stone or clay of Mesopotamia and Mycenae.

The chronology and extent of the diffusion of literacy in Greece remains a matter of debate. With the Mycenean collapse in the 12th century, writing disappeared; the earliest Greek inscriptions in the modified Semitic alphabet occur in the last two decades of the 8th century.[44] Recent authorities suggest the new script was adopted and transformed about the middle of the 8th century in Northern Syria.[45] The extensive use of writing probably came only slowly in the 7th century, but when it eventually came it seems to have been used in a very wide range of activities, intellectual as well as economic, and by a wide range of people.[46]

It must be remembered, of course, that Greek writing throughout the classical period was still relatively difficult to decipher, as words were not regularly separated;[47]

that the copying of manuscripts was a long and laborious process; and that silent reading as we know it was very rare until the advent of printing—in the ancient world books were used mainly for reading aloud, often by a slave. Nevertheless, from the sixth century onwards literacy seems to be increasingly presumed in the public life of Greece and Ionia. In Athens, for example, the first laws for the general public to read were set up by Solon in 593–4 BC; the institution of ostracism early in the fifth century assumes a literate citizen body—6,000 citizens had to write the name of the person on their potsherds before he could be banished;[48] there is abundant evidence in the fifth century of a system of schools. teaching reading and writing[49] and of a book-reading public— satirized already by Aristophanes in *The Frogs*;[50] while the final farm of the Greek alphabet, which was established fairly late in the fifth century, was finally adopted for use in the official records of Athens by decree of the Archon Eucleides in 403 BC.

Alphabetic Culture and Greek Thought

The rise of Greek civilization, then, is the prime historical example of the transition to a really literate society. In all subsequent cases where a widespread introduction of an alphabetic script occurred, as in Rome, for example, other cultural features were inevitably imported from the loan country along with the writing system; Greece thus offers not only the first example of this change, but also the essential one for any attempt to isolate the cultural consequences of alphabetic literacy.

The fragmentary and ambiguous nature of our direct evidence about this historical transformation in Greek civilization means that any generalizations must be extremely tentative and hypothetical; but the fact that the essential basis both of the writing systems and of many characteristic cultural institutions of the Western tradition as a whole are derived from Greece, and that they both arose there simultaneously, would seem to justify the present attempt to outline the possible relationships between the writing system and those cultural innovations of early Greece which are common to all alphabetically-literate societies.

The early development of the distinctive features of Western thought is usually traced back to the radical innovations of the pre-Socratic philosophers of the sixth century BC. The essence of their intellectual revolution is seen as a change from mythical to logico-empirical modes of thought. Such, broadly speaking, is Werner Jaeger's view; and Ernst Cassirer writes that "the history of philosophy as a scientific discipline may be regarded as a single continuous struggle to effect a separation and liberation from myth".[51]

To this general picture there are two kinds of theoretical objection. First, that the crucial intellectual innovations—in Cassirer as in Werner Jaeger—are in the last analysis attributed to the special mental endowments of the Greek people; and insofar as such terms as "the Greek Mind" or "genius" are not simply descriptive, they are logically dependent upon extremely questionable theories of man's mature and culture. Secondly, such a version of the transformation from "unphilosophical" to "philosophical" thought assumes an absolute—and untenable—dichotomy between the "mythical" thought of primitives and the "logico-empirical" thought of civilized man.

The dichotomy, of course, is itself very similar to Lévy-Bruhl's earlier theory of the "prelogical" mentality of primitive peoples, which has been widely criticised. Malinowski and many others have demonstrated the empirical elements in non-literate cultures,[52] and Evans-Pritchard has carefully analyzed the "logical" nature of the belief systems of the Azande of the Sudan;[53] while on the other hand the illogical and mythical nature of much Western thought and behavior is evident to anyone contemplating either our past or our present.

Nevertheless, although we must reject any dichotomy based upon the assumption of radical differences between the mental attributes of literate and non-literate peoples, and accept the view that previous formulations of the distinction were based on faulty premises and inadequate evidence, there may still exist general differences between literate and non-literate societies somewhat along the lines suggested by Lévy-Bruhl. One reason for their existence, for instance, may be what has been described above: the fact that writing establishes a different kind of relationship between the word and its referent, a relationship that is more general and more abstract, and less closely connected with the particularities of person, place and time, than obtains in oral communication. There is certainly a good deal to substantiate this distinction in what we know of early Greek thought. To take, for instance, the categories of Cassirer and Werner Jaeger, it is surely significant that it was only in the days of the first widespread alphabetic culture that the idea of "logic"—of an immutable and impersonal mode of discourse—appears to have arisen; and it was also only then that the sense of the human past as an objective reality was formally developed, a process in which the distinction between "myth" and "history" took on decisive importance.

Myth and History

Non-literate peoples, of course, often make a distinction between the lighter folk-tale, the graver myth, and the quasi-historical legend.[54] But not so insistently, and for an obvious reason. As long as the legendary and doctrinal aspects of the cultural tradition are mediated orally, they are kept in relative harmony with each other and with the present needs of society in two ways; through the unconscious operations of memory, and through the adjustment of the reciter's terms and attitudes to those of the audience before him. There is evidence, for example, that such adaptations and omissions occurred in the oral transmission of the Greek cultural tradition. But once the poems of Homer and Hesiod, which contained much of the earlier history, religion and cosmology of the Greeks, had been written down, succeeding generations were faced with old distinctions in sharply aggravated form: how far was the information about their Gods and heroes literally true? how could its patent inconsistencies be explained? and how could the beliefs and attitudes implied be brought into lines with those of the present?

The disappearance of so many early Greek writings, and the difficulties of dating and composition in many that survive, make anything like a clear reconstruction impossible. Greek had of course been written, in a very limited way, during Mycenean times. At about 1200 writing disappeared and the alphabet was not developed until some four hundred years later. Most scholars agree that in the middle or late eighth century the Greeks adapted the purely consonantal system of Phoenicia, possibly at the trading port of al Mina (Poseidon?). Much of the early writing consisted of "explanatory inscriptions on existing objects—dedications on offerings, personal names on property, epitaphs on tombs, names of figures in drawings".[55] The Homeric poems were written down between 750 and 650 BC, and the seventh century saw first the recording of lyric verse and then (at the end) the emergence of the great Ionian school of scientist philosophers.[56] Thus within a century or two of the writing down of the Homeric poems, many groups of writers and teachers appeared, first in Ionia and later in Greece, who took as their point of departure the belief that much of what Homer had apparently said was inconsistent and unsatisfactory in many respects. The logographers, who set themselves to record the genealogies, chronologies and cosmologies which had been handed down orally from the past, soon found that the task led them to use their critical and rational powers to create a new individual synthesis. In non-literate society, of course, there are usually some individuals whose interests lead them to collect, analyse and interpret the cultural tradition in a personal way; and the written records suggest that this process went considerably further among the literate elites of Egypt, Babylon and China, for example. But perhaps because in Greece reading and writing were less restricted to any particular priestly or administrative groups, there seems to have been a more thorough-going individual challenge to the orthodox cultural tradition in sixth-century Greece than occurred elsewhere. Hecataeus, for example, proclaimed at about the turn of the century, "What I write is the account I believe to be true. For the stories the Greeks tell are many and in my opinion ridiculous",[57] and offered his own rationalizations of the data on family traditions and lineages which he had collected. Already the mythological mode of using the past, the mode which, in Sorel's words, makes it "a means of acting on the present",[58] has begun to disappear.

That this trend of thought had much larger implications can be seen from the fact that the beginnings of religious and natural philosophy are connected with similar critical departures from the inherited traditions of the past; as W.B. Yeats wrote, with another tradition in mind, "Science is the critique of myths, there would be no Darwin had there been no *Book* of Genesis".[59] Among the early pre-Socratics there is much evidence of the close connection between new ideas and the criticism of the old. Thus Xenophanes of Colophon (*fl. ca.* 540 BC) rejected the "fables of men of old", and replaced the anthropomorphic gods of Homer and Hesiod who did "everything that is disgraceful and blameworthy among men" with a supreme god, "not at all like mortals in body and mind";[60] while Heraclitus of Ephesus (*fl. ca.* 500 BC), the first great philosopher of the problems of knowledge, whose system is based on the unity of opposites expressed in the *Logos* or structural plan of things, also ridiculed the anthropomorphism and idolatry of the Olympian religion.[61]

The critical and sceptical process continued, and according to Cornford, "a great part of the supreme god's biography had to be frankly rejected as false, or reinterpreted as allegory, or contemplated with reserve as mysterious myth too dark for human understanding."[62] On the one hand the poets continued to use the traditional legends for their poems and plays; on the other the prose writers attempted to wrestle with the problems with which the changes in the cultural tradition had faced them. Even the poets, however, had a different attitude to their material. Pindar, for example, used *mythos* in the sense of traditional stories, with the implication that they were not literally true; but claimed that his own poems had nothing in common with the fables of the past.[63] As for the prose writers, and indeed some of the poets, they had set out to replace myth with something else more consistent, with their sense of the *logos*, of the common and all-encompassing truth which reconciles apparent contradictions.

From the point of view of the transmission of the cultural tradition, the categories of understanding connected with the dimensions of time and space have a particular importance. As regards an objective description of space, Anaximander (b. 610 BC) and Hecataeus (*fl. ca.* 510–490), making use of Babylonian and Egyptian techniques, drew the first maps of the world.[64] Then their crude beginnings were subject to a long process of criticism and correction—by Herodotus[65] and others; and from this emerged the more scientific cartography of Aristotle, Eratosthenes and their successors.[66]

The development of history appears to have followed a rather similar course, although the actual details of the process are subject to much controversy. The traditional view gave priority to local histories which were followed by the more universal accounts of Herodotus and Thucydides. Dionysius of Halicarnasus writes of the predecessors of these historians who "instead of co-ordinating their accounts with each other ... treated of individual peoples and cities separately ... They all had the one same object, to bring to the general knowledge of the public the written records that they found preserved in temples or in secular buildings in the form in which they found them, neither adding nor taking away anything; among these records were to be found legends hallowed by the passage of time ... "[67]

Jacoby however has insisted "the whole idea is wrong that Greek historiography began with local history."[68] As far as Athens is concerned, history begins with the foreigner Herodotus who, not long after the middle of the fifth century, incorporated parts of the story of the town in his work because he wanted to explain the role it played in the great conflict between East and West, between Europe and Asia. The aim of Herodotus' *History* was to discover what the Greeks and Persians "fought each other for";[69] and his method was *historia*—personal inquiry or research into the most probable versions of events as they were to be found in various sources. His work rested on oral tradition and consequently his writings retained many mythological elements. So too did the work of the logographer, Hellanicus of Lesbos, who at the end of the fifth century wrote the first history of Attica from 683 to the end of the Peloponnesian war in 404. Hellanicus also tried to reconstruct the genealogies of the Homeric heroes, both backwards to the Gods and forwards to the Greece of his own time; and this inevitably involved chronology, the objective measurement of time. All he could do, however, was to rationalize and systematize largely legendary materials.[70] The development of history as a documented and analytic account of the past and present of the society in permanent written form took an important step forward with Thucydides, who made a decisive distinction between myth and history, a distinction to which little attention is paid in non-literate society.[71] Thucydides wanted to give a wholly reliable account of the wars between Athens and Sparta; and this meant that unverified assumptions about the past had to be excluded. So Thucydides rejected, for example, the chronology that Hellanicus had worked out for the prehistory of Athens, and confined himself very largely to his own notes of the events and speeches he related, or to the information he sought out from eye-witnesses and other reliable sources.[72]

And so, not long after the widespread diffusion of writing throughout the Greek world, and the recording of the previously oral cultural tradition, there arose an attitude to the past very different from that common in non-literate societies. Instead of the unobtrusive adaptation of past tradition to present needs, a great many individuals found in the written records, where much of their traditional cultural repertoire had been given permanent form, so many inconsistencies in the beliefs and categories of understanding handed down to them that they were impelled to a much more conscious, comparative, and critical attitude to the accepted world picture, and, notably to the notions of God, the universe and the past. Many individual solutions to these problems were themselves written down, and these versions formed the basis for further investigations.[73]

In non-literate society, it was suggested, the cultural tradition functions as a series of interlocking face-to-face conversations in which the very conditions of transmission operate to favor consistency between past and present, and to make criticism—the articulation of inconsistency—less likely to occur; and if it does, the inconsistency makes a less permanent impact, and is more easily adjusted or forgotten. While scepticism may be present in such societies, it takes a personal, non-cumulative form; it does not lead to a deliberate rejection and reinterpretation of social dogma so much as to a semi-automatic readjustment of belief.[74]

In literate society, these interlocking conversations go on; but they are no longer man's only dialogue; and insofar as writing provides an alternative source for the transmission of cultural orientations it favors awareness of inconsistency. One aspect of this is a sense of change and of cultural lag; another is the notion that the cultural inheritance as a whole is composed of two very different kinds of material; fiction, error and superstition on the one hand; and on the other, elements of truth which can provide the basis for some more reliable and coherent explanation of the gods, the human past and the physical world.

Plato and the Effects of Literacy

One area of this process can be described as the replacement of myth by history; but of course *historia* in the Greek sense, meaning "inquiry", can be viewed much more broadly as an attempt to determine reality in every area of human concern; and in many of these areas it was the Greeks who provided us with the bases of our present categories of understanding.

The actual role of writing in the development of this conceptual framework is more largely a matter of inference than in the particular case of history proper; but when we turn from the processes of collective development and transmission in their chronological perspective to the particular process of transmission from one individual to another, we can find something a little more definite than inference to go on; for in the writings of the Greek who shows most consciousness of the difference between oral and literate thoughtways, Plato, the greater completeness and intensity of oral transmission is discussed and emphasized.

Plato was born about 427 BC, long after the widespread diffusion of the alphabet in the Greek world. Many of the characteristic institutions of literate culture had already appeared: there were schools for children from the age of six and upwards;[75] and professional scholars and philosophers, such as the Sophists, had replaced the traditional expounders of the lore of the past, such as the *Eupatridai,* noble families in whom had earlier been vested the right to interpret the laws. Both the schools and the Sophists are discussed in an early Platonic dialogue, the *Protagoras,* where Socrates is shown to be suspicious of the new professional teachers and authors who have turned wisdom into a market-place commodity, a commodity which is dangerous unless the buyer already has "understanding of what is good and evil".[76] But it is in the *Phaedrus* and the *Seventh Letter* that we find the most explicit criticism of writing as a means of conveying thoughts and values.

In the *Phaedrus,* Socrates takes up the "nature of good and bad speaking and writing" and tells how the Egyptian king Thamus rebuked the God Theuth for claiming that his invention of writing would provide "a recipe for memory and wisdom": ". . . If men learn this," Thamus concludes, "it will implant forgetfulness in their souls: they will cease to exercise memory because they rely on that which is written, calling things to remembrance no longer from within themselves, but by means of external marks; what you have discovered is a recipe not for memory, but for reminder. And it is no true wisdom that you offer your disciples, but only its semblance; for by telling them of many things without teaching them you will make them seem to know much, while for the most part they know nothing; and as men filled, not with wisdom, but the conceit of wisdom, they will be a burden to their fellows."[77]

The emphasis on memory,[78] the repository of the cultural tradition in oral society, is significant; and it is appropriate that Socrates should deliver his attack on writing in the form of a fable or myth, in a distinctively oral and non-logical mode of discourse. The ensuing discussion, and several other discussions, of which the most important occurs in the *Seventh Letter,* make clear that the objections to writing are twofold: it is inherently shallow in its effects; and the essential principles of truth can only be arrived at dialectically.

Writing is shallow in its effects because reading books may give a specious sense of knowledge, which in reality can only be attained by oral question and answer; and such knowledge in any case only goes deep when it "is written in the soul of the learner."[79] The reasons which Plato, or his spokesman Socrates, gives for holding dialectic to be the true method of pursuing essential knowledge are very close to the picture given above of the transmission of the cultural tradition in oral society. For the dialectic method is, after all, an essential social process, in which the initiates pass on their knowledge directly to the young; a process, indeed, in which only a long personal relationship can transcend the inherent incapacity of mere words to convey ultimate truths—the forms or ideas which alone can give unity and coherence to human knowledge. As Plato puts it in the *Seventh Letter,* such knowledge can be passed on only when "after personal assistance in these studies from a guide, after living for some time with that guide, suddenly a flash of understanding, as it were, is kindled by a spark that leaps across, and once it has come into being within the soul it proceeds to nourish itself."[80]

What is at issue here is not only the intimate understanding which comes from long personal contact, but also the inherent advantages which living speech is given over the written word by virtue of its more immediate connection with the act of communication itself. The first advantage is that possible confusions or misunderstandings can always be cleared up by question and answer; whereas "written words," as Socrates tells Phaedrus, "seem to talk to you as though they were intelligent, but if you ask them anything about what they say, from a desire to be instructed, they go on telling you just the same thing for ever." The second intrinsic advantage is that the speaker can vary his "type of speech" so that it is "appropriate to each nature . . . addressing a variegated soul in a variegated style . . . and a simple soul in a simple style." And so, in the *Phaedrus,* Socrates concludes that "anyone who leaves behind him a written manual, and likewise anyone who takes it over from him, on the supposition that such writing will provide something reliable and permanent, must be exceedingly simple-minded."[81]

To some extent Plato's arguments against writing are specific reflections of the incapacity of words alone to convey the Ideas, and of the initiate's usual reluctance to share his esoteric lore except on his own terms;[82] while in the perspective of the later history of epistemology, Plato's position must be seen as an indication of his prescient awareness of the danger of using abstract words about whose referents no common agreement or identity of understanding has been established. Plato's reservations about writing must also be seen in relation to the preference which Greek culture shares with Roman for the more living quality of the spoken as opposed to the written word[83]—the general argument at this particular point in the *Phaedrus* is concerned with the advantages of extempore as compared with written speeches.

Nevertheless the *Phaedrus* and the *Seventh Letter* seem to provide good evidence that Plato considered the transmission of the cultural tradition was more effective and permanent under oral conditions, at least as regards the individual's initiation into the world of essential values. The endless ferment of new ideas at the end of the fifth century in Athens, and the growing scepticism about religion and ethics, bore eloquent witness to how writing down the accumulated lore of the past had fostered a critical attitude; but whatever the dismay of Plato at some features of the process, he himself could not escape it. Plato, of course, was largely critical in his thought. The majority of his dialogues are arguments against the views of other philosophers; and even his most practical and constructive writings, such as *The Republic* and *The Laws,* are in large part continuations of the debates which had begun with the pre-Socratic criticisms and rationalizations of the anthropomorphism of the body of traditional myths; myths which were sanctified by the preeminent authority of Homer, from whom, as Plato wrote in *The Republic* "all men have learned from the beginning".[84]

It would be wrong, therefore, to represent Plato as a whole-hearted protagonist of the oral tradition. Neither he nor Socrates were intransigent enemies of literate culture;

Socrates did not write books himself, but Xenophon tells us that he would "turn over and peruse in company with his friends ... the treasures of the wise men of old, which they have left written in books";[85] while the scale, the complexity of organization, and the high literary finish of *The Republic,* led Wilamowitz-Moellendorff to hail Plato as the first true author.[86] One must assume, therefore, a much more complex attitude to the new problems of the literate culture; the increase both in the number of books and readers, and consequently in the public awareness of historical change which books fostered, had made the problems inescapable by the end of the fifth century in Athens; and Plato was torn between his interest and understanding of the prosaic, analytic and critical procedures of the new literate thoughtways on the one hand, and his occasional nostalgias for the "unwritten customs and laws of our ancestors,"[87] along with the poetic myths in which they were enshrined.

Logic and the Categories of Understanding

The importance of Plato in the later history of philosophy, of course, lies primarily in that aspect of his work which looks forward, and which did much to define the methods of Western thought; the present argument therefore requires a brief consideration of how far these are intrinsically connected with writing. Obviously the great majority of Greek ideas have their roots in their specific historical and social circumstances, for many of which one can find earlier sources and analogues in the great civilizations of the Near East and elsewhere. Yet it does not seem to be merely a matter of ethnocentric prejudice to say that in two areas at least the Greeks developed intellectual techniques that were historically unique, and that possessed intrinsic empirical advantages which led to their widespread adoption by most subsequent literate cultures: the first area is epistemological, where the Greeks developed a new kind of logical method; and the second area is that of taxonomy, where the Greeks established our accepted categories in the fields of knowledge—theology, physics, biology and so forth.

In the former, Plato is essentially an heir of the long Greek enterprise of trying to sort out truth, *episteme,* from current opinion, *doxa*. This epistemological awareness seems to coincide with the widespread adoption of writing, probably because the written word suggests an ideal of definable truths which have an inherent autonomy and permanence quite different from the phenomena of the temporal flux and of contradictory verbal usages. In oral cultures, words—and especially words like "God," "Justice," "Soul," "Good"—may hardly be conceived of as separate entities, divorced both from the rest of the sentence and its social context. But once given the physical reality of writing, they take on a life of their own; and much Greek thought was concerned with attempting to explain their meanings satisfactorily, and to relate these meanings to some ultimate principle of rational order in the universe, to the *logos*.

It was, of course, Plato and Aristotle who conceived that there might be a special intellectual procedure for this process; who imagined the possibility of a system of rules for thinking itself, rules which were quite distinct from the particular problem being thought about and which offered a more reliable access to truth than current opinion. In the *Phaedrus,* for example, Socrates is made to speak of the proper method for arriving at the truth in general; and this method consists in disregarding the body of popular assumptions, and instead, analysing each idea by an initial definition of terms, followed by the development of a unified argument with "a middle and extremities so composed as to suit each other and the whole work." This is to be achieved by "divisions and collections," by analysis of a problem into its constituent elements, and by subsequent rational synthesis.[88]

This logical procedure seems essentially literate. On general grounds, because, as Oswald Spengler put it, "writing ... implies a complete change in the relations of man's waking-consciousness, in that it *liberates it from the tyranny of the present* ... the activity of writing and reading is infinitely more abstract than that of speaking and hearing."[89] On more practical grounds too, because it is difficult to believe that such a large and complex series of arguments as are presented in *The Republic*, for instance, or in Aristotle's *Analytics*, could possibly be created, or delivered, much less completely understood, in oral form.

There is also some fairly convincing evidence to suggest a more directly causal connection between writing and logic. The Greek word for an "element" was the same word as for a "letter of the alphabet"; and in *The Statesman* Plato compares the first basic principles of his philosophy with the child's first contact with the alphabet,[90] on the grounds that each principle or letter is the key to an infinitely greater number of words or ideas than the particular ones through which it is learned. Plato develops this idea in the *Theaetetus* when Socrates compares the process of reasoning to the combination of irreducible elements or letters of the alphabet into syllables which, unlike their constituent letters, have meaning: "the elements or letters are only objects of perception, and cannot be defined or known; but the syllables or combinations of them are known and ... apprehended".[90a] From this it is not far to the way the letters of the alphabet are used to symbolise the manipulation of general terms in Aristotelian logic; the set sequence of the premises, arguments and conclusions of a syllogism have been represented by letters of the alphabet ever since Aristotle so used them in the *Analytics*. It is further significant that Aristotle felt that he had made his greatest philosophical contribution in the field of logic; for, as he says in *De Sophisticis Elenchis*, "on the subject of reasoning we had nothing else of an earlier date to speak of at all."[91]

The same process of dissection into abstract categories, when applied not to a particular argument but to the ordering of all the elements of experience into separate areas of intellectual activity, leads to the Greek division of knowledge into autonomous cognitive disciplines which has since become universal in Western culture and which is of cardinal importance in differentiating literate and non-literate cultures, Plato made one important step in this direction, for he developed both the word and the notion of theology to designate a separate field of knowledge.[92] This kind of strict separation of divine attributes from the natural world, and from human life, is virtually unknown among non-literate peoples.[93] Neglect of this fact has led to much misunderstanding of the non-empirical and magico-religious aspects of their culture: but the neglect is itself a tribute to the depth of the literate tradition's acceptance of the categories of understanding which it has inherited from Greece.

Plato, however, was too much the disciple of Socrates to take the compartmentalization of knowledge very far. This was left to his pupil, Aristotle, and to his school;[94] by the time of the death of Aristotle in 322 BC most of the categories in the field of philosophy, natural science, language and literature, had been delineated, and the systematic collection and classification of data in all of them had begun.

With Aristotle the key methods and distinctions in the world of knowledge were fully, and for the most part permanently, established; and so, of course, were its institutions. It was Aristotle, according to Strabo,[95] who was the first man to collect books, and who taught the kings of Egypt to set up libraries; and although there had actually been earlier private collectors of books, Aristotle's library is the first of which much is known; it is from his collections that our word "museum" derives; and if "academy" commemorates the school of Plato, *lycée* carries us back to Aristotle's *Lyceum*.

Literate Culture: Some General Considerations

It is hardly possible, in this brief survey, to determine what importance must be attributed to the alphabet as the cause or as the necessary condition of the seminal intellectual innovations that occurred in the Greek world during the centuries that followed the diffusion of writing; nor, indeed, does the nature of the evidence give much ground for believing that the problem can ever be fully resolved. The present argument must, therefore, confine itself to suggesting that some crucial features of Western culture came into being in Greece soon after the existence, for the first time, of a rich urban society in which a substantial portion of the population was able to read and write; and that, consequently, the overwhelming debt of the whole of contemporary civilization to classical Greece must be regarded as in some measure the result, not so much of the Greek genius, as of the intrinsic differences between non-literate (or proto-literate) and literate societies; the latter being mainly represented by those societies using the Greek alphabet and its derivatives. If this is so, it may help us to take our contrast between the transmission of the cultural heritage in non-literate and alphabetically-literate societies a little further.

To begin with, the case of alphabetic reading and writing was probably an important consideration in the development of political democracy in Greece: in the fifth century a majority of the free citizens could apparently read the laws, and take an active part in elections and legislation. Democracy as we know it, then, is from the beginning associated with widespread literacy; and so to a large extent is the notion of the world of knowledge as transcending political units: in the Hellenic world diverse people and countries were given a common administrative system and a unifying cultural heritage through the written word. Greece is therefore considerably closer to being a model for the world-wide intellectual tradition of the contemporary literate world than those earlier civilizations of the Orient which each had its own localised traditions of knowledge: as Oswald Spengler put it, *"Writing is the grand symbol of the Far"*.[96]

Yet although the idea of intellectual, and to some extent political, universalism is historically and substantively linked with literate culture, we too easily forget that this brings with it other features which have quite different implications, and which go some way to explain why the long-cherished and theoretically feasible dream of an "educated democracy" and a truly egalitarian society has never been realized in practice. One of the basic premises of liberal reform over the last century and a half has been that of James Mill, as it is described in the *Autobiography* of his son, John Stuart Mill:

> So complete was my father's reliance on the influence of reason over the minds of mankind, whenever it is allowed to reach them, that he felt as if all would be gained if the whole population were taught to read, if all sorts of opinions were allowed to be addressed to them by word and in writing, and if, by means of the suffrage they could nominate a legislature to give effect to the opinions they adopted.[97]

All these things have been accomplished since the days of the Mills, but nevertheless "all" has not been "gained"; and some of the causes of this may be found in the intrinsic effects of literacy on the transmission of the cultural heritage, effects which can be seen most clearly by contrasting them with their analogues in non-literate society.

The writing down of some of the main elements in the cultural tradition in Greece, we say, brought about an awareness of two things: of the past as different from the present; and of the inherent inconsistencies in the picture of life as it was inherited by the individual from the cultural tradition in its recorded form. These two effects of widespread alphabetic writing, it may be surmised, have continued and multiplied themselves ever since, and at an increasing pace since the development of printing. "The printers," Jefferson remarked, "can never leave us in a state of perfect rest and union of opinion,"[98] and as book follows book and newspaper newspaper, the notion of rational agreement and democratic coherence among men has receded further and further away, while Plato's attacks on the venal purveyors of knowledge in the market place have gained increased relevance.

But the inconsistency of the totality of written expression is perhaps less striking than its enormous bulk and its vast historical depth. Both of these have always seemed insuperable obstacles to those seeking to reconstruct society on a more unified and disciplined model: we find the objection in the book-burners of all periods; and it appears in many more respectable thinkers. In Jonathan Swift, for example, whose perfectly rational Houyhnhnms "have no letters", and whose knowledge, "consequently ... is all traditional".[99] These oral traditions were of a scale, Swift tells us, that enabled "the historical part" to be "easily preserved without burthening their memories." Not so with the literate tradition, for, lacking the resources of unconscious adaptation and omission which exist in the oral transmission, the cultural repertoire can only grow; there are more words than anybody knows the meaning of—some 142,000 vocabulary entries in a college dictionary like the *Webster's New World*. This unlimited proliferation also characterises the written tradition in general: the mere size of the literate repertoire means that the proportion of the whole which any one individual knows must be infinitesimal in comparison with what obtains in oral culture. Literate society, merely by having no system of elimination, no "structural amnesia", prevents the individual from participating fully in the total cultural tradition to anything like the extent possible in non-literate society.

One way of looking at this lack of any literate equivalent to the homeostatic organization of the cultural tradition in non-literate society is to see literate society as inevitably committed to an ever-increasing series of culture lags. The content of the cultural tradition grows continually, and in so far as it affects any particular individual he becomes a palimpsest composed of layers of beliefs and attitudes belonging to different stages in historical time. So too, eventually, does society at large, since there is a tendency for each social group to be particularly influenced by systems of ideas belonging to different periods in the nation's development; both to the individual, and to the groups constituting society, the past may mean very different things.

From the standpoint of the individual intellectual, of the literate specialist, the vista of endless choices and discoveries offered by so extensive a past can be a source of great stimulation and interest; but when we consider the social effects of such an orientation, it becomes apparent that the situation fosters the alienation that has characterized so many writers and philosophers of the West since the last century. It was surely, for example, this lack of social amnesia in alphabetic cultures which led Nietzsche to describe "we moderns" as "wandering encyclopaedias", unable to live and act in the present and obsessed by a "'historical sense', that injures and finally destroys the living thing, be it a man or a people or a system of culture."[100] Even if we dismiss Nietzsche's views as extreme, it is still evident that the literate individual has in practice so large a field of personal selection from the total cultural repertoire that the odds are strongly against his experiencing the cultural tradition as any sort of patterned whole.

From the point of view of society at large, the enormous complexity and variety of the cultural repertoire obviously creates problems of an unprecedented order of magnitude. It means, for example, that since Western literate societies are characterized by these always increasing layers of cultural tradition, they are incessantly exposed to a more complex version of the kind of culture-conflict that has been held to produce *anomie* in oral societies when they come into contact with European civilization, changes which, for example, have been illustrated with a wealth of absorbing detail by Robert Redfield in his studies of Central America.[101]

Another important consequence of alphabetic culture relates to social stratification. In the proto-literate cultures with their relatively difficult nonalphabetic systems of writing, there existed a strong barrier between the writers and the non-writers; but although the "democratic" scripts made it possible to break down this particular barrier, they led eventually to a vast proliferation of more or less tangible distinctions based on what people had read. Achievement in handling the tools of reading and writing is obviously one of the most important axes of social differentiation in modern societies; and this differentiation extends on to more minute differences between professional specializations so that even members of the same socio-economic groups of literate specialists may hold little intellectual ground in common.

Nor, of course, are these variations in the degree of participation in the literate tradition, together with their effects on social structure, the only causes of tension. For, even within a literate culture, the oral tradition—the transmission of values and attitudes in face-to-face contact—nevertheless remains the primary mode of cultural orientation, and, to varying degrees, it is out of step with the various literate traditions. In some respects, perhaps, this is fortunate. The tendency of the modern mass-communications industries, for example, to promote ideals of conspicuous consumption which cannot be realized by more than a limited proportion of society, might well have much more radical consequences but for the fact that each individual exposed to such pressures is also a member of one or more primary groups whose oral converse is probably much more realistic and conservative in its ideological tendency; the mass media are not the only, and they are probably not even the main, social influences on the contemporary cultural tradition as a whole.

Primary group values are probably even further removed from those of the "high" literate culture, except in the case of the literate specialists. This introduces another kind of culture conflict, and one which is of cardinal significance for Western civilization. If, for example, we return to the reasons for the relative failure of universal compulsory education to bring about the intellectual, social and political results that James Mill expected, we may well lay a major part of the blame on the gap between the public literate tradition of the school, and the very different and indeed often directly contradictory private oral traditions of the pupil's family and peer group. The high degree of differentiation in exposure to the literate tradition sets up a basic division which cannot exist in non-literate society: the division between the various shades of literacy and illiteracy. This conflict, of course, is most dramatically focussed in the school, the key institution of society. As Margaret Mead has pointed out:

> Primitive education was a process by which continuity was maintained between parents and children ... Modern education includes a heavy emphasis upon the function of education to create discontinuities—to turn the child ... of the illiterate into the literate.[102]

A similar and probably even more acute stress develops in many cases between the school and the peer group; and quite apart from the difficulties arising from the substantive differences between the two orientations, there seem to be factors in the very nature of literate methods which make them ill-suited to bridge the gap between the street-corner society and the blackboard jungle.

First, because although the alphabet, printing, and universal free education have combined to make the literate culture freely available to all on a scale never previously approached, the literate mode of communication is such that it does not impose itself as forcefully or as uniformly as is the case with the oral transmission of the cultural tradition. In non-literate society every social situation cannot but bring the individual into contact with the group's patterns of thought, feeling and action: the choice is between the cultural tradition—or solitude. In a literate society, however, and quite apart from the difficulties arising from the scale and complexity of the "high" literate tradition, the mere fact that reading and writing are normally solitary activities means that insofar as the dominant cultural tradition is a literate one, it is very easy to avoid; as Bertha Phillpotts wrote in her study of Icelandic literature:

> Printing so obviously makes knowledge accessible to all that we are inclined to forget that it also makes knowledge very easy to avoid... A shepherd in an Icelandic homestead, on the other hand, could not avoid spending his evenings in listening to the kind of literature which interested the farmer. The result was a degree of really national culture such as no nation of today has been able to achieve.[103]

The literate culture, then, is much more easily avoided than the oral one; and even when it is not avoided its actual effects may be relatively shallow. Not only because, as Plato argued, the effects of reading are intrinsically less deep and permanent than those of oral converse; but also because the abstractness of the syllogism and of the Aristotelian categorizations of knowledge do not correspond very directly with common experience. The abstractness of the syllogism, for example, of its very nature disregards the individual's social experience and immediate personal context; and the compartmentalization of knowledge similarly restricts the kind of connections which the individual can establish and ratify with the natural and social world. The essential way of thinking of the specialist in literate culture is fundamentally at odds with that of daily life and common experience; and the conflict is embodied in the long tradition of jokes about absent-minded professors.

It is, of course, true that contemporary education does not present problems exactly in the forms of Aristotelian logic and taxonomy; but all our literate modes of thought have been profoundly influenced by them. In this, perhaps, we can see a major difference, not only with the transmission of the cultural heritage of oral societies, but with those of proto-literate ones. Thus Marcel Granet relates the nature of the Chinese writing system to the "concreteness" of Chinese thought, and his picture of its primary concentration on social action and traditional norms suggests that the cultural effect of the writing system was in the direction of intensifying the sort of homeostatic conservation found in non-literate cultures; it was indeed conceptualised in the Confucian *tao-'tung*, or "orthodox transmission of the way." In this connection it may be noted that the Chinese attitude to formal logic, and to the categorization of knowledge in general, is an articulate expression of what happens in an oral culture.[104] Mencius, for example, speaks for the non-literate approach in general when he comments: "Why I dislike holding to one point is that it injures the tao. It takes up one point and disregards a hundred others."[105]

The social tension between the oral and literate orientations in Western society is, of course, complemented by an intellectual one. In recent times the Enlightenment's attack on myth as irrational superstition has often been replaced by a regressive yearning for some modern equivalent of the unifying function of myth: "have not," W. B. Yeats asked, "all races had their first unity from a mythology that marries them to rock and hill?"[106]

In his nostalgia for the world of myths Plato has had a long line of successors. The Rousseauist cult of the Noble Savage, for instance, paid unwitting tribute to the strength of the homogeneity of oral culture, to the yearning admiration of the educated for the peasant's simple but cohesive view of life, the timelessness of his living in the present, the unanalytic spontaneity that comes with an attitude to the world that is one of absorbed and uncritical participation, a participation in which the contradictions between history and legend, for example, or between experience and imagination, are not felt as problems. Such, for example, is the literary tradition of the European peasant from Cervantes' Sancho Panza to Tolstoy's Platon Karataev. Both are illiterate; both are rich in proverbial lore; both are untroubled by intellectual consistency; and both represent many of the values which, it was suggested above, are characteristic of oral culture. In these two works, *Don Quixote* and *War and Peace*, which might well be considered two of the supreme achievements of modern Western literature, an explicit contrast is made between the oral and literate elements of the cultural tradition. Don Quixote himself goes mad by reading books; while, opposed to the peasant Karataev, stands the figure of Pierre, an urban cosmopolitan, and a great reader. Tolstoy writes of Karataev that—in this like Mencius or like Malinowski's Trobrianders—he:

> did not, and could not, understand the meaning of words apart from their context. Every word and every action of his was the manifestation of an activity unknown to him, which was his life. But his life, as he regarded it, had no meaning as a separate thing. It had a meaning only as part of a whole of which he was always conscious.[107]

Tolstoy, of course, idealizes; but conversely, even in his idealization he suggests one major emphasis of literate culture and one which we immediately associate with the Greeks—the stress upon the individual; Karataev does not regard "his life ... as a separate thing". There are, of course, marked differences in the life-histories of individual members of non-literate societies: the story of Crashing Thunder differs from that of other Winnebago,[108] that of Baba of Karo from other Hausa women;[109] and these differences are often given public recognition by ascribing to individuals a personal tutelary or guardian spirit. But on the whole there is less individualization of personal experience in oral cultures, which tend, in Durkheim's phrase, to be characterized by "mechanical solidarity"[110] —by the ties between like persons, rather than by a more complicated set of complementary relationships between individuals in a variety of roles. Like Durkheim, many sociologists would relate this greater individualization of personal experience in literate societies to the effects of a more extensive division of labor. There is no single explanation; but the techniques of reading and writing are undoubtedly of very great importance. There is, first of all, the formal distinction which alphabetic culture has emphasised between the divine, the natural, and the human orders; secondly, there is the social differentiation to which the institutions of literate culture give rise; third, there is the effect of professional intellectual specialization on an unprecedented scale; lastly, there is the immense variety of choice offered by the whole corpus of recorded literature; and from these four factors there ensues, in any individual case, the highly complex totality deriving from the selection of these literate orientations and from the series of primary groups in which the individual has also been involved.

As for personal awareness of this individualization, other factors doubtless contributed, but writing itself (especially in its simpler, more cursive forms) was of great importance. For writing, by objectifying words, and by making them and their meaning available for much more prolonged and intensive scrutiny than is possible orally, encourages private thought; the diary or the confession enables the individual to objectify his own experience, and gives him some check upon the transmutations of memory under the influences of subsequent events. And then, if the diary is later published, a wider audience can have concrete experience of the differences that exist in the histories of their fellow men from a record of a life which has been partially insulated from the assimilative process of oral transmission.

The diary is, of course, an extreme case; but Plato's dialogues themselves are evidence of the general tendency of writing to increase the awareness of individual differences in behavior, and in the personality which lies behind them;[111] while the novel, which participates in the autobiographical and confessional direction of such writers as St. Augustus, Pepys and Rousseau, and purports to portray the inner as well as the outer life of individuals in the real world, has replaced the collective representations of myth and epic.

From the point of view of the general contrast between oral and alphabetically literate culture, then, there is a certain identity between the spirit of the Platonic dialogues and of the novel[112]: both kinds of writing express what is a characteristic intellectual effort of literate culture, and present the process whereby the individual makes his own more or less conscious, more or less personal selection, rejection and accommodation, among the conflicting ideas and attitudes in his culture. This general kinship between Plato and the characteristic art form of literate culture, the novel, suggests a further contrast between oral and literate societies: in contrast to the homeostatic transmission of the cultural tradition among non-literate peoples, literate society leaves more to its members; less homogeneous in its cultural tradition, it gives more free play to the individual, and particularly to the intellectual, the literate specialist himself; it does so by sacrificing a single, ready-made orientation to life. And, insofar as an individual participates in the literate, as distinct from the oral, culture, such coherence as a person achieves is very largely the result of his personal selection, adjustment and elimination of items from a highly differentiated cultural repertoire; he is, of course, influenced by all the various social pressures, but they are so numerous that the pattern finally comes out as an individual one.

Much could be added by way of development and qualification on this point, as on much else that has been said above. The contrast could be extended, for example, by bringing it up to date and considering later developments in communication, from the invention of printing and of the power press, to that of radio, cinema and television. All these latter, it may be surmised, derive much of their effectiveness as agencies of social orientation from the fact that their media do not have the abstract and solitary quality of reading and writing, but on the contrary share something of the nature and impact of the direct personal interaction which obtains in oral cultures. It may even be that these new modes of communicating sight and sound without any limit of time or place will lead to a new kind of culture: less inward and individualistic than literate culture, probably, and sharing some of the relative homogeneity, though not the mutuality, of oral society.

To speculate further on such lines would be to go far beyond the purposes of this essay; and it only remains to consider briefly the consequences of the general course of the argument for the problem as it was posed at the outset in terms of the distinction between the disciplines primarily (though not exclusively) concerned in the analysis of non-literate and literate societies, that is, anthropology and sociology.

One aspect of the contrast drawn between non-literate and alphabetic culture would seem to help explain one of the main modern trends in the development of anthropology: for part of the progress which anthropology has made beyond the ethnocentrism of the 19th century surely derives from a growing awareness of the implications of one of the matters discussed above: an awareness, that is, of the extent to which, in the culture of oral societies, non-Aristotelian models[113] are implicit in the language, the reasoning, and the kinds of connection established between the various spheres of knowledge. The problem has been approached in many ways; particularly illuminating, perhaps, in Dorothy D. Lee's contrast between the 'lineal' codifications of reality in Western culture, and the 'non-lineal' codifications of the Trobriand Islanders; and there, incidentally, although Aristotle is not mentioned, his characteristically analytic, teleological and relational thinking is recognizable in the governing attitudes that Dorothy Lee presents as the typical literate mode of thought in contrast to that of the Trobrianders.[114] Benjamin Lee Whorf makes a similar point in his contrast of Hopi with SAE (standard average European). He sees the "mechanistic way of thinking" of Europeans as closely related to the syntax of the languages they speak, "rigidified and intensified by Aristotle and the latter's medieval and modern followers",[115] The segmentation of nature is functionally related to grammar; Newtonian space, time and matter, for example, are directly derived from SAE culture and language.[116] He goes on to argue that "our objectified view of time is ... favorable to historicity and to everything connected with the keeping of records, while the Hopi view is unfavorable thereto." And to this fact he links the presence of:

1. Records, diaries, bookkeeping, accounting, mathematics stimulated by accounting.
2. Interest in exact sequences, dating, calendars, chronology, clocks, time wages, time graphs, time as used in physics.
3. Annals, histories, the historical attitude, interest *in* the past, archaeology, attitudes of introjection towards past periods, e.g. classicism, romanticism.[117]

Many of these features are precisely those which we have mentioned as characteristic of societies with easy and widespread systems of writing. But while Whorf and other anthropological linguists have noted these differences between European institutions and categories on the one hand and those of societies like the Trobriands and the Hopi on the other, they have tended to relate these variations to the languages themselves, giving little weight to the influence of the mode of communication as such, to the intrinsic social consequences of literacy.[118]

On the other hand, what has been said about literacy and the consequent developments of Greek thought leading to the logical methods and to the categories of Aristotle may seem to attribute to one individual, and to the civilization to which he belonged, a kind of absolute claim to intellectual validity to which neither the philosopher, the anthropologist, nor the historian of ancient civilization, is likely to assent. The currency of such diffuse assumptions in general long ago moved John Locke to an unwonted burst of wintry humour: "God has not been so sparing to men to make them barely two-legged creatures, and left it to Aristotle to make them rational",[119] Nevertheless Locke's own treatment of the "forms of argumentation" and of "the division of the sciences" is itself recognisably within the tradition that derives from Aristotle and his time; and so, in some important ways, is the literate culture, not only of the West, but of the civilized world today. There is obviously some more or less absolute efficacy in the organization of human knowledge which appears in the thoughtways of the first substantially literate culture, although its definition (which could hardly be more difficult) is well beyond the scope of this paper. Max Weber saw as the essential differentiating factor of Western civilization the "formal rationality" of its institutions; and this, in turn, he regarded as a more fully developed and more exclusively practise, version of the ordinary human tendency to act reasonably—to behave with "substantive rationality". For Weber "formal rationality" was merely an institutionalised form of this general tendency working through "rationally established norms, by enactment, decrees, and regulations"[120] rather than through personal, religious, traditional or charismatic allegiances. Weber's differentiation in some respects parallels the differentiation made above between oral and alphabetic culture and in various places he anticipates part of the argument advanced in this paper.[121]

The present study then, is an attempt to approach a very general problem from one particular point of view. In that perspective it suggests one reason for what has been widely remarked upon in the comparison between anthropology and sociology: the relative incompleteness of sociological analyses as compared with those of anthropology, and the tendency for anthropologists studying European societies to limit their observations to village communities or family groups. For, quite apart from differences of scale and complexity of social structure, there are two other dimensions of analysis which can in practice be largely disregarded by the anthropologist but not by the student of literate societies.

First the reifying of the past in written record means that sociology must inevitably be the more deeply concerned with history. The kinds of practical and theoretical issues involved here are numerous, for the great importance of the historical dimension, and its very different kind of impact on various social groups, obviously poses acute methodological problems. At the most general level, the analytic model of the sociologist must take into account the fact that from one point of view his data include materials accumulated from earlier cultures and periods, and that the existence of these records greatly increases the possible alternative ways of thinking and behaving for the members of the society he is studying, as well as influencing their action in other ways. This added complexity means that certain aspects of the past continue to be relevant (or at least potentially so) for the contemporary scene; and it also means that when functional theoretical models are used, the interconnections can hardly be as direct or immediate as those the anthropologist might expect in non-literate societies.

Secondly, the sociologist must in any case recognize that since in alphabetic society much of the homeostatic function of the oral tradition works at the inward and individual rather than at the overt and public level, sociological descriptions, which inevitably deal primarily with collective life, are considerably less complete than those of anthropology, and consequently provide a less certain guide to understanding the behavior of the particular individuals of whom the society is composed.

Summary

Recent anthropology has rightly rejected the categorical distinctions between the thinking of "primitive" and "civilized" peoples, between "mythopoeic" and "logico-empirical" modes of thought. But the reaction has been pushed too far: diffuse relativism and sentimental egalitarianism combine to turn a blind eye on some of the most basic problems of human history. Where the intellectual differences in the cultural traditions of complex and simple societies are given adequate recognition, the explanations offered are unsatisfactory. In the case of Western civilization, for example, the origins are sought in the nature of the Greek genius, in the grammatical structure of the Indo-European languages, or, somewhat more plausibly, in the technological advances of the Bronze Age and the associated developments in the division of labor.

In our view, however, insufficient attention has been paid to the fact that the urban revolution of the Ancient Near East produced one invention, the invention of writing, which changed the whole structure of the cultural tradition. Potentially, human intercourse was now no longer restricted to the impermanency of oral converse. But since the first methods of writing employed were difficult to master, their effects were relatively limited, and it was only when the simplicity and flexibility of later alphabetic writing made widespread literacy possible that for the first time there began to take concrete shape in the Greek world of the 7th century BC a society that was essentially literate and that soon established many of the institutions that became characteristic of all later literate societies.

The development of an easy system of writing (easy both in terms of the materials employed and the signs used) was more than a mere pre-condition of the Greek achievement; it influenced its whole nature and development in fundamental ways. In oral societies the cultural tradition is transmitted almost entirely by face-to-face communication; and changes in its content are accompanied by the homeostatic process of forgetting or transforming those parts of the tradition that cease to be either necessary or relevant. Literate societies, on the other hand, cannot discard, absorb, or transmute the past in the same way. Instead, their members are faced with permanently recorded versions of the past and its beliefs; and because the past is thus set apart from the present, historical enquiry becomes possible. This in turn encourages scepticism; and scepticism, not only about the legendary past, but about received ideas about the universe as a whole. From here the next step is to see how to build up and to test alternative explanations: and out of this there arose the kind of logical, specialized, and cumulative intellectual tradition of sixth-century Ionia. The kinds of analysis involved in the syllogism, and in the other forms of logical procedure, are clearly dependent upon writing, indeed upon a form of writing sufficiently simple and cursive to make possible widespread and habitual recourse both to the recording of verbal statements and then to the dissecting of them. It is probable that it is only the analytic process that writing itself entails, the written formalization of sounds and syntax, which make possible the habitual separating out into formally distinct units of the various cultural elements whose indivisible wholeness is the essential basis of the "mystical participation" which Lévy-Bruhl regards as characteristic of the thinking of non-literate peoples.

One of the problems which neither Lévy-Bruhl nor any other advocate of a radical dichotomy between "primitive" and "civilized" thought has been able to resolve is. the persistence of "non-logical thinking" in modern literate societies. But, of course, we must reckon with the fact that in our civilization, writing is clearly an addition, not an alternative, to oral transmission. Even in our *buch und lesen* culture, childrearing and a multitude of other forms of activity both within and outside the family depend upon speech: and the relationship between the written and the oral traditions must be regarded as a major problem in Western cultures.

A consideration of the consequences of literacy in these terms, then, throws some light not only upon the nature of the Greek achievement but also upon the intellectual differences between simple and complex societies. There are, of course, many other consequences we have not discussed—for instance, the role of writing in the running of centralized states and other bureaucratic organizations; our aim has only been to discuss in very general terms some of the more significant historical and functional consequences of literacy.[122]

Notes

1 Some writers distinguish the field of Social Anthropology from that of Sociology on the basis of its subject matter (i.e. the study of non-literate or non-European peoples), others on the basis of its techniques (e.g. that of participant observation). For a discussion of these points, see Siegfried F. Nadel, *The Foundations of Social Anthropology* (London, 1951), p. 2.
2 Émile Durkheim, *The Elementary Forms of the Religious Life*, trans, Joseph W. Swain (London, 1915), p. 19.
3 Hortense Powdermaker, *Life in Lesu* (New York, 1933), p. 292. See also *Language, Thought, and Culture*, ed. Paul Henle (Ann Arbor, 1958), pp. 5–18.
4 Bronislaw Malinowski, "The Problem of Meaning in Primitive Languages", in C. K. Ogden and I. A. Richards, *The Meaning of Meaning* (London, 1936), pp. 296–336, esp. p. 331. But see also the critical comments by Claude Lévi-Strauss, La *Pensée Sauvage* (Paris, 1962), pp. 6, 15–16.
5 *L'Année sociologique,* 7 (1902–3), pp. 1–72. See also S. Czarnowski, "Le morcellement de l'étendue et sa limitation dans la religion et la magie", *Actes du congrès international d'histoire des religions* (Paris, 1925), 1, pp. 339–359.
6 Jack Goody, unpublished field notes, 1950–52. See also E. E. Evans-Pritchard, *The Nuer* (Oxford, 1940), chapter 3, "Time and Space", and David Tait, *The Konkomba of Northern Ghana* (London, 1961), pp. 17 ff. For a general treatment of the subject, see A. Irving Hallowell,

"Temporal Orientations in Western Civilisation and in a Preliterate Society", *American Anthropologist*, 39 (1937), pp. 647–670.
7 *Les Cadres sociaux de la mémoire* (Paris, 1925); "Mémoire et société", *L'Année sociologique*, 3e série, 1 (1940–8), pp. 11–177; *La Mémoire collective*, Paris, 1950. See also Frederic C. Bartlett on the tendency of oral discourse to become an expression of ideas and attitudes of the group rather than the individual speaker, in *Remembering* (Cambridge, 1932), pp. 265–7, and *Psychology and Primitive Culture* (Cambridge, 1923), pp. 42–3, 62–3, 256.
8 M. I. Finley, *The World of Odysseus* (New York, 1954), p. 26.
9 Laura Bohannan, "A Genealogical Charter", *Africa*, 22 (1952), pp. 301–15; Emrys Peters, "The Proliferation of Segments in the Lineage of the Bedouin of Cyrenaica", *Journal of the Royal Anthropological Institute*, 90 (1960), pp. 29–53. See also Godfrey and Monica Wilson, *The Analysis of Social Change* (Cambridge, 1945), p. 27.
10 Ch. 49; further evidence supporting this assumption is found in the etymology of the Hebrew term *Toledot*, which originally denoted "genealogies", and assumed also the meaning of "stories and accounts" about the origin of a nation. "In this sense the term was also applied to the account of the creation of heaven and earth" [Solomon Gandz, "Oral Tradition in the Bible" in *Jewish Studies in Memory of George A. Kohut*, ed. Salo W. Baron and Alexander Marx (New York, 1935), p. 269].
11 *The Nuer* (Oxford, 1940); "The Nuer of the Southern Sudan" in *African Political Systems*, ed. Meyer Fortes and Edward Evan Evans-Pritchard (London, 1940); Meyer Fortes, *The Dynamics of Clanship among the Tallensi* (London, 1945).
12 "A Genealogical Charter", p. 314.
13 John A. Barnes, "The Collection of Genealogies", *Rhodes-Livingstone Journal. Human Problems in British Central Africa*, 5 (1947), pp. 48–56, esp. p. 52; Meyer Fortes, "The Significance of Descent in Tale Social Structure", *Africa*, 14 (1944), p. 370; Evans-Pritchard, *The Nuer*, pp. 199–200; Peters, "The Proliferation of Segments", p. 32. See also I. G. Cunnison, *The Luapula Peoples of Northern Rhodesia* (Manchester, 1959), pp. 108–14.
14 Jack Goody, unpublished field notes, 1956–7; the heads of the divisions who could not succeed to the paramountcy also claimed descent from sons of the founding ancestor, Jakpa, but this was not an intrinsic part of the myth as usually told, and in any case their number remained constant during the period in question.
15 *Myth in Primitive Psychology* (London, 1926), pp. 23, 43.
16 Franz Boas, "The Folklore of the Eskimo", *Journal of American Folklore*, 64 (1904), p. 2. Lévi-Strauss treats the absence of historical knowledge as one of the distinctive features of *la pensée sauvage* in contrast to *la pensée domestiquée* (*La Pensée sauvage*, p. 349).
17 Ignace J. Gelb, *A Study of Writing* (Chicago, 1952), pp. 24ff.
18 C. F. and F. M. Voegelin, "Typological Classification of Systems with Included, Excluded and Self-sufficient Alphabets", *Anthropological Linguistics*, 3 (1961), pp. 84, 91.
19 Voegelin, "Typological Classification", pp. 75–76.
20 C. F. and F. M. Voegelin classify all these systems (Chinese, Egyptian, Hittite, Mayan and Sumerian-Akkadian) as "alphabet included logographic systems": because they make use of phonetic devices, they include, under the heading "self-sufficient alphabets", systems which have signs for consonant-vowel sequences (i.e. syllabaries), for independent consonants (IC), e.g. Phoenician, or for independent consonants plus independent vowels (IC + IV), e.g. Greek. In this paper we employ "alphabet" in the narrower, more usual, sense of a phonemic system with independent signs for consonants and vowels (IC + IV).
21 Gelb, *Study of Writing*, p. 115; David Diringer, *The Alphabet: A Key to the History of Mankind* (New York, 1948), pp. 48, 196.
22 "Protoliterate" is often employed in a rather different sense, as when S. N. Kramer ["New Light on the Early History of the Ancient Near East", *American Journal of Archaeology*, 52 (1948), p. 161] uses the term to designate the Sumerian phase in Lower Mesopotamia when writing was first invented. There seems to be no generally accepted usage for societies where there is a fully developed but socially restricted phonetic writing system. Sterling Dow ["Minoan Writing", *American Journal of Archaeology*, 58 (1954), pp. 77–129] characterises two stages of Minoan

society: one of "stunted literacy", where little use was made of writing at all (Linear A); and one of "special literacy" where writing was used regularly but only for limited purposes (Linear B). Stuart Piggott refers to both these conditions under the name of "conditional literacy" [*Approach to Archaeology* (London, 1959), p. 104].

23 Alfred C. Moorhouse, *The Triumph of the Alphabet* (New York, 1953), pp. 90, 163.
24 G. R. Driver, *Semitic Writing* (London, 1954, rev. ed.), pp. 62, 72.
25 *cit*. V. Gordon Childe, *Man Makes Himself* (London, 1941), pp. 187–8; see also *What Happened in History* (London, 1942), pp. 105, 118.
26 "Egyptian hieroglyphic writing remained fundamentally unchanged for a period of three thousand years", according to David Diringer [*Writing* (London, 1962), p. 48]. He attributes the fact that it never lost its cumbrousness and elaboration to "its unique sacredness" (p. 50).
27 Many authorities have commented upon the lack of development in Egypt after the initial achievements of the Old Kingdom: for a discussion (and a contrary view), see John A. Wilson in *Before Philosophy*, ed. H. Frankfort and others (London, 1949), pp. 115–16 [pub. in U.S.A. as *The Intellectual Adventure of Ancient Man* (Chicago, 1946)].
28 "The world view of the Egyptians and Babylonians was conditioned by the teaching of sacred books; it thus constituted an orthodoxy, the maintenance of which was in the charge of colleges of priests" [Benjamin Farrington, *Science in Antiquity* (London, 1936), p. 37]. See also Gordon Childe, *What Happened in History*, p. 121.
29 Gelb, *Study of Writing*, p. 196, maintains that all the main types of syllabary developed in just this way. Driver rejects the possibility that the Phoenician alphabet was invented on Egyptian soil, as it would have been "stifled at birth" by the "deadweight of Egyptian tradition, already of hoary antiquity and in the hands of a powerful priesthood" (*Semitic Writing*, p. 187).
30 "Immensely complicated", Driver calls the pre-alphabetic forms of writing Semitic (*Semitic Writing*, p. 67).
31 For Hittite, see O. R. Gurney, *The Hittites* (London, 1952), pp. 120–21. For Mycenean, see John Chadwick, *The Decipherment of Linear B* (Cambridge, 1958).
32 Chadwick, *The Decipherment of Linear B*, p. 130; see also "A Prehistoric Bureaucracy", *Diogenes*, 26 (1959), pp. 7–18.
33 As is exhaustively documented in David Diringer, *The Alphabet, A Key to the History* of *Mankind* (New York, 1948).
34 *The Alphabet*, pp. 214–218. On the "accidental" nature of this change see C. F. and F. M. Voegelin, "Typological Classification", pp. 63–4.
35 According to Ralph E. Turner, *The Great Cultural Traditions* (New York, 1941), I, pp. 346, 391, the Hebrews took over the Semitic system in the eleventh century BC, and the Indians a good deal later, probably in the eighth century BC.
36 Gandz, "Oral Tradition in the Bible", pp. 253–4.
37 *e.g.* Luke, 20; Matthew, 23; in the 7th century BC, even kings and prophets employed scribes, Jer. xxxvi, 4, 18.
38 Driver, *Semitic Writing*, pp. 87–90, where he instances the case of one scribe who having no son "taught his wisdom to his sister's son".
39 "If the alphabet is defined as a system of signs expressing single sounds of speech, then the first alphabet which can justifiably be so called is the Greek alphabet". Gelb, *Study of Writing*, p. 166.
39a I. Kings 17, iv-vi; see A *Dictionary of the Bible* . . . ed. James Hastings (New York, 1898–1904), *s.v.* "Elijah".
40 810 a. From the ages 10 to 13.
41 *L'Adoption universelle des caractères latins* (Paris, 1934); for more recent developments and documentation, see William S. Gray, *The Teaching of Reading and Writing: An International Survey*, Unesco Monographs on Fundamental Education X (Paris, 1956), especially pp. 31–60.
42 Chester G. Starr, *The Origins of Greek Civilization* (New York, 1961), pp. 189–190, 349 ff.
43 Starr, *The Origins of Greek Civilization*, pp. 87–88, 357.
44 Starr, *The Origins of Greek Civilization*, p. 169.

45 L. H. Jeffery, *The Local Scripts of Archaic Greece* (Oxford, 1961), p. 21; R. M. Cook and A. G. Woodhead, "The Diffusion of the Greek Alphabet", *American Journal of Archaeology*, 63 (1959), pp. 175–78. For North Syria, see Sir Leonard Woolley, *A Forgotten Kingdom* (London, 1953).
46 Chester Starr speaks of its use by "a relatively large aristocratic class" (p. 171) and Miss Jeffery notes that "writing was never regarded as an esoteric craft in early Greece. Ordinary people could and did learn to write, for many of the earliest inscriptions which we possess are casual graffiti" (p. 63).
47 Frederic G. Kenyton, *Books and Readers in Ancient Greece and Rome* (2nd ed., Oxford, 1951), p. 67.
48 Jérôme Carcopino, *L'Ostracisme athénien* (Paris, 1935), pp. 72–110.
49 *Protagoras*, 325 d.
50 1. 1114; in 414 BC. See also Plato, *Apology,* 26 d, and the general survey of Kenyon, *Books and Readers in Ancient Greece and Rome*.
51 *The Philosophy of Symbolic Forms* (New Haven, 1955), II, p. xiii; and *An Essay on Man* (New York, 1953), especially pp. 106–130, 281–3. For Werner Jaeger, see especially *The Theology of The Early Greek Philosophers* (Oxford, 1947).
52 "Magic, Science and Religion" in *Science, Religion and Reality,* ed. Joseph Needham (New York, 1925), reprinted *Magic, Science and Religion* (New York, 1954), p. 27. For an appreciation of Lévy-Bruhl's positive achievement, see Evans-Pritchard, "Lévy-Bruhl's Theory of Primitive Mentality", *Bulletin of the Faculty of Arts, University of Egypt,* 2 (1934), pp. 1–36. In his later work, Lévy-Bruhl modified the rigidity of his earlier dichotomy.
53 *Witchcraft, Oracles and Magic Among the Azande* (Oxford, 1937). See also Max Gluckman's essay, "Social Beliefs and Individual Thinking in Primitive Society", *Memoirs and Proceedings of the Manchester Literary and Philosophical Society,* 91 (1949–50), pp. 73–98. From a rather different standpoint, Lévi-Strauss has analysed "the logic of totemic classifications" (*La Pensée sauvage*, p. 48 ff.) and speaks of two distinct modes of scientific thought; the first (or "primitive") variety consists in "the science of the concrete", the practical knowledge of the handy man (*bricoleur*), which is the technical counterpart of mythical thought (p. 26).
54 e.g. the Trobriands (Malinowski, *Myth in Primitive Psychology*, pp. 33ff).
55 Jeffery, *The Local Scripts of Archaic Greece*, p. 46.
56 "It was in Ionia that the first completely rationalistic attempts to describe the nature of the world took place" [G. S. Kirk and J. E. Raven, *The Presocratic Philosophers* (Cambridge, 1957), p. 73]. The work of the Milesian philosophers, Thales, Anaximander and Anaximenes, is described by the authors as "clearly a development of the genetic or genealogical approach to nature exemplified by the Hesiodic *Theogony*" (p. 73).
57 F. Jacoby, *Die Fragmente der Griechischen Historiker*, Vol. I, *Genealogie und Mythographie* (Berlin, 1923), fr. 1.a.
58 *Reflections on Violence*, trans. T. E. Hulme (New York, 1941), p. 136; *cit.* Robert Redfield, *The Primitive World and its Transformations* (Ithaca, New York, 1953), p. 125.
59 *cit.* Joseph Hone, *W. B. Yeats* (London, 1942), p. 405 (our italics).
60 Hermann Diels, *Die Fragmente der Vorsokratiker* (Berlin, 1951), fr. 11, 23; see also John Burnet, *Early Greek Philosophy* (2nd ed. London, 1908), pp. 131, 140–141, and Werner Jaeger, *The Theology of the Early Greek Philosophers* (Oxford, 1947), pp. 42–7; Kirk and Raven, *The Presocratic Philosophers*, pp. 163 ff.
61 Diels, *Fragmente der Vorsokratiker,* fr. 40, 42, 56, 57, 106; see also Francis M. Cornford, *Principium Sapientiae: The Origins of Greek Philosophical Thought* (Cambridge, 1952), pp. 112 ff.; Kirk and Raven, *The Presocratic Philosophers*, pp. 182 ff.
62 Francis M. Cornford, *Greek Religious Thought from Homer to the Age of Alexander* (London, 1923), xv-xvi. See also Burnet, *Early Greek Philosophy*, p. 1.
63 1st Olympian Ode.
64 See Eric H. Warmington, *Greek Geography* (London, 1934), pp. xiv, xxxviii.
65 *History*, 4, 36–40.
66 Warmington, *Greek Geography*, pp. xvii-xviii, xli ff.
67 *Cit.* Lionel Pearson, *Early Ionian Historians* (Oxford, 1939), p. 3.

68 Felix Jacoby, *Atthis* (Oxford, 1949), p. 354.
69 *History*, I, l. See also Moses I. Finley (ed.), *The Greek Historians* (New York, 1959), pp. 4 ff.
70 See Pearson, *Early Ionian Historians*, pp. 152–233, especially pp. 193, 232–33.
71 See, for instance, Bronislaw Malinowski, *Argonauts of the Western Pacific* (London, 1922), pp. 290–333.
72 Thucydides, *History*, I, 20–22, 97. For a picture of note-taking *(hypomnemata)* among Athenians, see *Theaetetus*, 142 c-143 c.
73 Felix Jacoby notes that "fixation in writing, once achieved, primarily had a preserving effect upon the oral tradition, because it put an end to the involuntary shiftings of the *mnemai* (remembrances), and drew limits to the arbitrary creation of new *logoi* (stories)" (*Atthis*, 1949, p. 217). He points out that this created difficulties for the early literate recorders of the past which the previous oral *mnemones* or professional "remembrancers" did not have to face: whatever his own personal view of the matter, "no true Atthidographer could remove Kekrops from his position as the first Attic king ... Nobody could take away from Solon the legislation which founded *in nuce* the first Attic constitution of historical times." Such things could no longer be silently forgotten, as in an oral tradition.

The general conclusion of Jacoby's polemic against Wilamowitz's hypothesis of a "pre-literary chronicle" is that "historical consciousness ... is not older than historical literature" (p. 201).
74 As writers on the indigenous political systems of Africa have insisted, changes generally take the form of rebellion rather than revolution; subjects reject the King, but not the kingship. See Evans-Pritchard, *The Divine Kingship of the Shilluk of the Nilotic Sudan* (The Frazer lecture, Cambridge, 1948), pp. 35ff; Max Gluckman, *Rituals of Rebellion in South-East Africa* (The Frazer lecture, 1952), Manchester, 1954.
75 See Henri-Irénée Marrou, *Histoire de l'éducation dans l'antiquité* (Paris, 1948), pp. 76–7, 84–6, 94, 139–142, 150–2.
76 *Protagoras*, 313 e.
77 259 e; 274–275. From Reginald Hackforth's translation in his *Plato's Phaedrus* (Cambridge, 1952).
78 A great deal of relevant information, and a wealth of further references, are given in the valuable article by James A. Notopoulos, "Mnemosyne in Oral Literature," *Transactions of the American Philological Association*, 69 (1938), pp. 465–93.
79 *Phaedrus*, 276 a.
80 341 c-d. [trans. R.S. Bluck, *Plato's Life and Thought* (London, 1949)].
81 *Phaedrus*, 275 d; 277 c; 275 c.
82 For a modern example, see Alexandra David-Neel and Lama Yongden, *The Secret Oral Teachings in Tibetan Buddhist Sects* (Calcutta, 1959).
83 See especially William Chase Greene, "The Spoken and the Written Word", *Harvard Studies in Classical Philology*, 60 (1951), pp. 23–59.
84 606 e [Jaeger, *Theology of the Early Greek Philosophers*, pp. 42, 211. See also Cornford, *Principium Sapientiae*, pp. 154–5.
85 *Memorabilia*, i, 6, 16. See also *Phaedo*, 98–99; *Phaedrus*, 230 d-e.
86 *Platon* (Berlin, 1919), 1, 389.
87 See especially Plato's *Laws* 793 a-c. Plato is shown to represent both the old veneration and the new distrust of Homer in H. V. Apfel's "Homeric Criticism in the Fourth Century BC", *Transactions of the American Philological Association*, 69 (1938), p. 247.
88 264 c; 265 d-266 b; 277 b-c.
89 *The Decline of the West*, trans. C. F. Atkinson (New York, 1934), II, p. 149.
90 *Statesman*, 278: See also *Cratylus*, 424 b-428 c.
90a *Theaetetus*, 201–202. The analogy is continued to the end of the dialogue.
91 184 b. There were, of course, many precursors, not only Plato and his laws of the dialectic but the Sophists and grammarians with their semantic interests (see John Edwin Sandys, *A History of Classical Scholarship* (Cambridge, 1921), 1, pp. 27, 88 ff).
92 Jaeger, *Theology of the Early Greek Philosophers*, pp. 4–5.

93 This question is discussed in greater detail by Jack Goody in "Religion and Ritual: the Definitional Problem", *British Journal of Sociology*, 12 (1961), pp. 142–164.
94 See, for example, Alfred E. Taylor, Aristotle (London, 1943), pp. 24–39.
95 *Geography*, 608–9, cit. Sandys, *History of Classical Scholarship*, I, p. 86. See also *ibid.*, pp. 76–114 and James Westfall Thompson, *Ancient Libraries* (Berkeley, 1940), pp. 18–21.
96 *Decline of the West*, II, 150.
97 *Autobiography of John Stuart Mill*, ed. John J. Coss (New York, 1924), p. 74.
98 Cit. Harold A. Innis, "Minerva's Owl", *The Bias of Communication* (Toronto, 1951), p. 24. Harold Innis was much occupied with the larger effects of modes of communication, as appears also in his *Empire and Communications* (Oxford, 1950). This direction of investigation has been taken up by the University of Toronto review *Explorations;* and the present authors are also indebted to the as yet unpublished work of Professor E. A. Havelock on the alphabetic revolution in Greece. Among the many previous writers who have been concerned with the Greek aspect of the problem, Nietzsche [*Beyond Good and Evil* (Edinburgh, 1909), p. 247], and Jose Ortega y Gasset ["The Difficulty of Reading", *Diogenes*, 28 (1959), pp. 1–17] may be mentioned. Among those who have treated the differences between oral and literate modes of communication in general, David Reisman ["The Oral and Written Traditions", E*xplorations*, 6 (1956), pp. 22–28, and *The Oral Tradition, the Written Word and the Screen Image* (Yellow Springs, Ohio, 1956)] and Robert Park ["Reflections on Communication and Culture", *American J. of Sociology*, 44 (1938), pp. 187–205] are especially relevant here.
99 *Gulliver's Travels*, Part IV, ch. 9, ed. Arthur E. Case (New York, 1938), p. 296.
100 "The Use and Abuse of History", *Thoughts out of Season*, trans. Adrian Collins (Edinburgh, 1909), pp. 33, 9.
101 *Chan Kom, a Maya Village* (Washington, D.C., 1934); *The Folk Culture of Yucatan* (Chicago, 1941); *A Village that Chose Progress: Chan Kom Revised* (Chicago, 1950); and for a more general treatment, *The Primitive World and its Transformations* (Ithaca, New York, 1953), pp. 73, 108. See also Peter Worsley, *The Trumpet Shall Sound* (London, 1957). For the concept of *anomie*, see Émile Durkheim, *Le Suicide* (Paris, 1897), Book 11, Ch. V.
102 "Our Educational Emphases in Primitive Perspective", *American Journal of Sociology*, 48 (1943), p. 637.
103 *Edda and Saga* (London, 1931), pp. 162–3.
104 Marcel Granet, La *Pensée chinoise* (Paris, 1934), especially pp. vii-xi, 8–55; see also Hu Shih, *The Development of the Logical Method in Ancient China* (Shanghai, 1922).
105 Cit. I. A. Richards, *Mencius on the Mind* (London, 1932), p. 35.
106 *Autobiographies* (London, 1955), p. 194.
107 Leo Tolstoy, *War and Peace*, trans. Louise and Aylmer Maude (New York, 1942), pp. 1078–9.
108 Paul Radin, *Crashing Thunder; the Autobiography of an American Indian* (New York, 1926), and *Primitive Man as Philosopher* (New York, 1927).
109 Mary F. Smith, *Baba of Karo, a Woman of the Muslim Hausa* (London, 1954).
110 Émile Durkheim, *The Division of Labor in Society*, trans. G. Simpson (New York, 1933), p. 130.
111 In the *Theaetetus*, for example, emphasis is placed on the inner dialogue of the soul in which it perceives ethical ideas "by comparing within herself things past and present with the future" (186 b).
112 Jaeger, *Paideia* (Oxford, 1944), II, 18, speaks of the dialogues and the memoirs by many members of the circle of Socrates as "new literary forms invented by the Socratic circle . . . to re-create the incomparable personality of the master."
113 Just as it has been argued that a proper understanding of Homer depends upon a "non-Aristotelian literary criticism" which is appropriate to oral literature: James A. Notopoulos, "Parataxis in Homer: a New Approach to Homeric Literary Criticism", *Transactions of the American Philological Association*, 80 (1949), pp. 1, 6.
114 "Codifications of Reality: Lineal and Nonlineal", in *Freedom and Culture* (Englewood Cliffs, New Jersey, 1959), pp. 105–120; see also her "Conceptual Implications of an Indian Language", *Philosophy of Science*, 5 (1938), pp. 89–102.

115 "Languages and Logic", *Technological Review*, 43 (1941), reprinted in *Language, Thought, and Reality, Selected Writings of Benjamin Lee Whorf* (New York, 1956), p. 238.
116 "The Relation of Habitual Thought and Behavior to Language", *Language, Culture, and Personality, Essays in Memory of Edward Sapir*, ed. by Leslie Spier (Menasha, Wis., 1941), reprinted in *Language, Thought, and Reality*, p. 153.
117 *op. cit.* p. 153.
118 For example in his paper "A linguistic consideration of thinking in primitive communities" (*Language, Thought and Reality*, pp. 65–86), Whorf discusses Lévy-Bruhl's account of the thinking of primitive man as characterized by *participation mystique*, and suggests that the differences are related to the structure of language. No mention is made of the role of writing and he seems to see language itself as the independent variable, although in his later paper on "Habitual thought", he does make a passing reference to writing, as well as to the *interdependence* of language and culture (p. 153). Lévi-Strauss, who is much concerned with the linguistic aspects of the problem, makes no mention of the role of literacy in his analysis of the differences between *la pensée sauvage* and *la pensée domestiquée*, but again the actual process of domestication is peripheral to his study (1962).
119 *Essay Concerning Human Understanding*, Book IV, ch. 17, 84.
120 *From Max Weber, Essays in Sociology*, trans. H. H. Gerth and C. Wright Mills (New York, 1946), pp. 298–9. See also *The Theory of Social and Economic Organisation*, trans. A. M. Henderson and Talcott Parsons (New York, 1947), pp. 184–6.
121 Especially in the "Author's Introduction" to *The Protestant Ethic*, trans. Talcott Parsons (London, 1930), pp. 13–31, where Weber gives a rapid but comprehensive survey of the problem of "what combination of circumstances" made some aspects of Western civilization "lie in a line of development having *universal* significance and value". See also his lecture "Science as a Vocation" (*From Max Weber,* especially pp. 138–143).
122 The authors are much indebted to John Beattie, Glyn Daniel, Lloyd Fallers, Moses Finley, Joseph Fontenrose, Harry Hoijer, the late Alfred Kroeber, Simon Pembroke and Nur Yalman for reading and commenting upon earlier versions of this paper. They are also grateful to the Center for Advanced Studies in the Behavioral Sciences, California, for the opportunity of working together on the manuscript in Spring, 1960.

4.
WRITING IS A TECHNOLOGY THAT RESTRUCTURES THOUGHT[1]
Walter J. Ong, SJ

I

Literacy is imperious. It tends to arrogate to itself supreme power by taking itself as normative for human expression and thought. This is particularly true in high-technology cultures, which are built on literacy of necessity and which encourage the impression that literacy is an always to be expected and even natural state of affairs. The term "illiterate" itself suggests that persons belonging to the class it designates are deviants, defined by something they lack, namely literacy. Moreover, in high-technology cultures—which, more and more, are setting the style for cultures across the world—since literacy is regarded as so unquestionably normative and normal, the deviancy of illiterates tends to be thought of as lack of a simple mechanical skill. Illiterates should learn writing as they learned to tie their shoe-laces or to drive a car. Such views of writing as simply a mechanical skill obligatory for all human beings distort our understanding of what is human if only because they block understanding of what natural human mental processes are before writing takes possession of consciousness. These views also by the same token block understanding of what writing itself really is. For without a deep understanding of the normal oral or oral-aural consciousness and noetic economy of humankind before writing came along, it is impossible to grasp what writing accomplished.

...

Functionally literate persons, those who regularly assimilate discourse such as this, are not simply thinking and speaking human beings but chirographically thinking and speaking human beings (latterly conditioned also by print and by electronics). The fact that we do not commonly feel the influence of writing on our thoughts shows that we have interiorized the technology of writing so deeply that without tremendous effort we cannot separate it from ourselves or even recognize its presence and influence. If functionally literate persons are asked to think of the word "nevertheless", they will all have present in imagination the letters of the word—vaguely perhaps, but unavoidably—in handwriting or typescript or print. If they are asked to think of the word "nevertheless" for two minutes, 120 seconds, without ever allowing any letters at all to enter their imaginations, they cannot comply. A person from a completely oral

---

Ong, Walter. "Writing is a Technology that Restructures Thought." *The Written Word: Literacy in Transition*. Ed. Gerd Baumann. NY: Oxford UP, 1986. 23–50.

background of course has no such problem. He or she will think only of the real word, a sequence of sounds, "ne-ver-the-less". For the real word "nevertheless", the sounded word, cannot ever be present all at once, as written words deceptively seem to be. Sound exists only when it is going out of existence. By the time I get to the "the-less", the "never" is gone. To the extent that it makes all of a word appear present at once, writing falsifies. Recalling sounded words is like recalling a bar of music, a melody, a sequence in time. A word is an event, a happening, not a thing, as letters make it appear to be. So is thought: "This is paper" is an occurrence, an event in time. We grasp truth articulately only in events. Articulated truth has no permanence. Full truth is deeper than articulation. We find it hard to recognize this obvious truth, so deeply has the fixity of the written word taken possession of our consciousness.

The oral world as such distresses literates because sound is evanescent. Typically, literates want words and thoughts pinned down—though it is impossible to "pin down" an event. The mind trained in an oral culture does not feel the literate's distress: it can operate with exquisite skill in the world of sounds, events, evanescences. How does it manage? Basically, in its noetic operations it uses formulaic structures and procedures that stick in the mind to complement and counteract the evanescent: proverbs and other fixed sayings, epithets, that is, standard, expected qualifiers (the *sturdy* oak, the *brave* warrior, *wise* Nestor, *clever* Odysseus), numerical sets (the three Graces, the seven deadly sins, the five senses, and so on), balance, rhythms of all sorts ("Blessed are the poor in spirit, for theirs is the kingdom of heaven")—anything to make it easy to call back what Homer recognized were "winged words". Primary oral culture also keeps its thinking close to the human life world, personalizing things and issues, and storing knowledge in stories. Categories are unstable mnemonically. Stories you can remember. In its typical mindset, the oral sensibility is out to hold things together, to make and retain agglomerates, not to analyse (which means to take things apart)—although, since all thought is to some degree analytic, it does analyse to a degree. Pressed by the need to manage an always fugitive noetic universe, the oral world is basically conservative. Exploratory thinking is not unknown, but it is relatively rare, a luxury orality can little afford, for energies must be husbanded to keep on constant call the evanescent knowledge that the ages have so laboriously accumulated. Everybody, or almost everybody, must repeat and repeat and repeat the truths that have come down from the ancestors. Otherwise these truths will escape, and culture will be back on square one, where it started before the ancestors got the truths from their ancestors.

...

II

Writing was an intrusion, though an invaluable intrusion, into the early human lifeworld, much as computers are today. It has lately become fashionable in some linguistic circles to refer to Plato's condemnation of writing in the *Phaedrus* and the Seventh Letter. What is seldom if ever noticed, however, is that Plato's objections against writing are essentially the very same objections commonly urged today against computers by those who object to them (Ong 1982: 79–81). Writing, Plato has Socrates say in the *Phaedrus*, is inhuman, pretending to establish outside the mind what in reality can only be in the mind. Writing is simply a thing, something to be manipulated, something inhuman, artificial, a manufactured product. We recognize here the same complaint that is made against computers: they are artificial contrivances, foreign to human life.

Secondly, Plato's Socrates complains, a written text is basically unresponsive. If you ask a person to explain his or her statement, you can get at least an attempt at explanation: if you ask a text, you get nothing except the same, often stupid words which called for your question in the first place. In the modern critique of the computer, the same objection is put, "Garbage in, garbage out". So deeply are we into literacy that we fail commonly to recognize that this objection applies every bit as much to books as to computers. If a book states an untruth, ten thousand printed refutations will do nothing to the printed text: the untruth is there for ever. This is why books have been burnt. Texts are essentially contumacious.

Thirdly, Plato's Socrates urges, writing destroys memory. Those who use writing will become forgetful, relying on an external source for what they lack in internal resources. Writing weakens the mind. Today, some parents and others fear that pocket calculators provide an external resource for what ought to be the internal resource of memorized multiplication tables. Presumably, constant repetition of multiplication tables might produce more and more Albert Einsteins. Calculators weaken the mind, relieve it of the setting-up exercises that keep it strong and make it grow. (Significantly, the fact that the computer manages multiplication and other computation so much more effectively than human beings do, shows how little the multiplication tables have to do with real thinking.)

Fourthly, in keeping with the agonistic mentality of oral cultures, their tendency to view everything in terms of interpersonal struggle, Plato's Socrates also holds it against writing that the written word cannot defend itself as the natural spoken word can: real speech and thought always exist essentially in the context of struggle. Writing is passive, out of it, in an unreal, unnatural world. So, it seems, are computers: if you punch the keys they will not fight back on their own, but only in the way they have been programmed to do.

...

The new technology of writing, it is now clear, was operating in Plato's lifeworld in ways far too convoluted for even Plato to understand. The technology of writing was not merely useful to Plato for broadcasting his critique of writing, but it also had been responsible for bringing the critique into existence. Although there was no way for Plato to be explicitly aware of the fact, his philosophically analytic thought, including his analysis of the effects of writing, was possible only because of the effects that writing was having on mental processes. We know that totally oral peoples, intelligent and wise though they often are, are incapable of the protracted, intensive linear analysis that we have from Plato's Socrates. Even when he talks, Plato's Socrates is using thought forms brought into being by writing. In fact, as Eric Havelock has beautifully shown in his *Preface to Plato* (1963), Plato's entire epistemology was unwittingly a programmed rejection of the archaic preliterate world of thought and discourse. This world was oral, mobile, warm, personally interactive (you needed live people to produce spoken words). It was the world represented by the poets, whom Plato would not allow in his Republic, because, although Plato could not formulate it this way, their thought processes and modes of expression were disruptive of the cool, analytic processes generated by writing.

. . .

III

In downgrading writing, Plato was thinking of writing as an external, alien technology, as many people today think of the computer. Because we have by today so deeply interiorized writing, made it so much a part of ourselves, as Plato's age had not yet made it fully a part of itself, we find it difficult to consider writing to be a technology as we commonly assume printing and the computer to be. Yet writing (and especially alphabetic writing) is a technology, calling for the use of tools and other equipment, styli or brushes or pens, carefully prepared surfaces such as paper, animal skins, strips of wood, as well as inks or paints, and much more. Writing technologies have differed in different parts of the world. In their own indigenous technologies of writing, East Asia—China, Korea, and Japan—typically used not pens but brushes, not liquid ink in ink-horns or inkwells, but ink blocks, on which the wet brush was rubbed as in making water-colour paintings, in this sense "painting" rather than "writing" (etymologically, "scratching") their texts.

. . .

Although we take writing so much for granted as to forget that it is a technology, writing is in a way the most drastic of the three technologies of the word. It initiated what printing and electronics only continued, the physical reduction of dynamic sound to quiescent space, the separation of the word from the living present, where alone real, spoken words exist.

IV

Once reduced to space, words are frozen and in a sense dead. Yet there is a paradox in the fact that the deadness of the written or printed text, its removal from the living human lifeworld, its rigid visual fixity, assures its endurance and its potential for being resurrected into limitless living contexts by a limitless number of living readers. The dead, thing-like text has potentials far outdistancing those of the simply spoken word. The complementary paradox, however, is that the written text, for all its permanence, means nothing, is not even a text, except in relationship to the spoken word. For a text to be intelligible, to deliver its message, it must be reconverted into sound, directly or indirectly, either really in the external world or in the auditory imagination. All verbal expression, whether put into writing, print, or the computer, is ineluctably bound to sound forever.

Nevertheless, by contrast with natural, oral speech, writing is completely artificial. There is no way to write "naturally". Oral speech is fully natural to human beings in the sense that every human being in every culture who is not physiologically or psychologically impaired learns to talk. Moreover, while talk implements conscious life, its use wells up naturally into consciousness out of unconscious or subconscious depths, though of course with the conscious as well as unconscious co-operation of society. Despite the fact that they govern articulation and thought processes themselves, grammar rules or structures normally originate, live, and function far below the level at which articulation functions. You can know how to use the grammatical rules or structures and even how to set up new rules or structures that function clearly and effectively without being able to state what they are. Of all the hundreds of thousands of grammar rules or structures that have been at work in all the tens of thousands of languages and dialects of humankind, only the tiniest fraction have ever been articulated at all.

Writing or script differs as such from speech in that it is not inevitably learned by all psychologically or physiologically unimpaired persons, even those living in highly literate cultures. Moreover, the use of writing or script does not inevitably well up out of the unconscious without the aid of stated rules. The process of putting spoken language into writing is governed by consciously contrived, articulated procedures: for example, a certain pictogram will be consciously determined to stand for a certain specified word or concept, or *a* will be consciously ruled to represent a certain phoneme, *b* another, and so on. (This is not at all to deny that the writer-reader situation created by writing is deeply involved with unconscious processes which are at work in composing written texts once one has learned the explicit, consciously controlled rules for transposing sound into a visual code.)

To say writing is artificial is not to condemn it but to praise it. Like other artificial creations and indeed more than any other, writing is utterly invaluable and indeed essential for the realization of fuller, interior, human potentials. Technologies are not mere exterior aids but also interior transformations of consciousness, and never more than when they affect the word. Such transformations of consciousness can be uplifting, at the same time that they are in a sense alienating. By distancing thought, alienating it from its original habitat in sounded words, writing raises consciousness. Alienation from a natural milieu can be good for us and indeed is in many ways essential for fuller human life. To live and to understand fully, we need not only proximity but also distance. This writing provides for, thereby accelerating the evolution of consciousness as nothing else before it does.

Technologies are artificial, but—paradox again—artificiality is natural to human beings. Technology, properly interiorized, does not degrade human life but on the contrary enhances it. The modern orchestra, for example, is a result of high technology. A clarinet is an instrument, which is to say a tool. A piano is an intricate, hand-powered machine. An organ is a huge machine, with sources of power—pumps, bellows, electric generators, motors—in motion before the organ is touched by its operator.

. . .

The fact is that by using the mechanical contrivance a clarinettist or pianist or an organist can express something poignantly human that cannot be expressed without the mechanical contrivance. To achieve such expression effectively, of course, the musician has to have interiorized the technology, made the tool or machine a second nature, a psychological part of himself or herself. Art imitates nature. Art follows nature, and joins itself to nature. Art is second nature. But it is not nature. *Natura* in Latin, like *physis* in Greek, means birth. We are not born with art but add it to ourselves. Mastering a musical tool, making it one's own, calls for years of mechanical "practice", learning how we can make the tool do mechanically all that it can do. Little boys and girls know how boring it can be. Yet such shaping of the tool to one's self, learning a technological skill, is hardly dehumanizing. The use of a technology can enrich the human psyche, enlarge human spirit, set it free, intensify its interior life.

I instance the modern orchestra here to make the point that writing is an even more deeply interiorized technology than the performance of instrumental music is. To understand what writing is, which means to understand it in relation to its past, to orality, one must honestly face the fact that it is a technology.

...

VII

One of the most generalizable effects of writing is separation. Separation is also one of the most telling effects of writing and hence can serve here to give some final form to this discussion. Writing is diaeretic. It divides and distances, and it divides and distances all sorts of things in all sorts of ways. Distancing or "distanciation" is one of the effects of writing commonly discussed by those coming from the Husserlian and Heideggerian traditions, such as Paul Ricoeur (1981), but their discussions are highly specialized and abstractly schematic, paying little if any attention to the actual history of writing, its growth out of orality, or to the socio-psychological complexities this history presents us with—that is, to the sort of things earlier detailed here. Their phenomenology is fundamentally synchronic, not diachronic. And without a diachronic phenomenology, our present situation does not show its true contours for we do not become aware of how matters stood before writing, and to that extent, as earlier stated, are relatively unaware of what writing truly is.

Many of the phenomena here associated with separation or division or distancing could also be discussed under various other headings, some of them less abstract headings than separation or division, but few other headings would be so handily inclusive. My observations here on separation or distancing will be condensed and, if only for that reason, should serve, I hope, to open discussion and to suggest further study. Here, then, are some of the ways in which writing separates or divides. Writing ties together so many things in so many interrelations that some of the itemizations here inevitably overlap.

1. Writing separates the known from the knower. It promotes "objectivity". Any writing system does this, but the alphabet does so most of all, since it most thoroughly dissolves all sounds into spatial equivalents. Havelock (1976) has shown how the ancient Greeks' invention of the first fully vocalic alphabet, the most radical of all writing systems, gave them their intellectual ascendancy by providing access to the

thorough intellectual "objectivity" that led to modern science, and modern forms of thought generally, although the science of the ancient Greeks remained far more rhetorically structured and far more embedded in the human lifeworld than our science is today.

. . .

Enhanced separation of the known from the knower is probably the most fundamental value of writing, from its beginnings to the present. Between knower and known writing interposes a visible and tangible object, the text. The objectivity of the text helps impose objectivity on what the text refers to (see Olson). Eventually writing will create a state of mind in which knowledge itself can be thought of as an object, distinct from the knower. This state of mind, however, is most fully realized only when print intensifies the object-like character of the text.

However, whatever its intimate effects on knowledge, the physical text is not itself knowledge, for knowledge, verbalized or other, can exist only in a knowing subject. In place of knowledge once possessed and formulated verbally by a living person, texts substitute coded marks outside any knower which a knowing subject possessed of the code can use to generate knowledge in himself or herself. Knowledge itself is not object-like: it cannot be transferred from one person to another physically even in oral communication, face-to-face, or *a fortiori* in writing. I can only perform actions—produce words—which enable you to generate the knowledge in yourself. The concept of "medium" or "media" applied to human communication uses an analogy which is useful but nevertheless so gross, and so inconspicuously gross, that it regularly falsifies what human communication is. I myself try to avoid the term now, though I have used it in earlier books and articles. "Medium" applies properly to manual or machine transferral of pattern, not to human communication. Since knowledge cannot be physically transferred verbally from one human person to another but must always be created by the hearer or reader within his or her own consciousness, interpretation is always in play when one listens or when one reads.

2. Whereas oral cultures tend to merge interpretation of data with the data themselves, writing separates interpretation from data. Asked to repeat exactly what they have just said, persons from a primary oral culture will often given an interpretation of what they originally said, insisting and clearly believing that the interpretation is exactly what they said in the first place (Olson, citing Ruth Finnegan). They have difficulty in grasping what literates mean by word-for-word repetition. The text provides a new scenario. The text is a visual given, a datum, separate from any utterer or hearer or reader. What one says (or writes) about the text is something else, distinct from the text-object and what it as such represents. This is not to deny that any understanding of a text always involves interpretation: for what the object-like text represents is not an object, but words. It is simply to state that the status of interpretation becomes different with writing.

3. Writing distances the word from sound, reducing oral-aural evanescence to the seeming quiescence of visual space. But this distancing is not total or permanent, for every reading of a text consists of restoring it, directly or indirectly, to sound, vocally or in the imagination.

4. Whereas in oral communication the source (speaker) and the recipient (hearer) are necessarily present to one another, writing distances the source of the communication (the writer) from the recipient (the reader), both in time and in space. It is as easy to read a book by a person long dead or by a person thousands of miles away as it is to read one by a friend sitting at your elbow. Oral communication provides no comparable condition until the invention of sound recordings, which, however, depend on writing for their existence and, despite their aura of immediacy, distance speaker and hearer even more than writing does, interposing between the two mechanisms far more complicated than those of writing and print, and abolishing all direct relationship to lived time.

5. Writing distances the word from the plenum of existence. In their original, spoken condition, words are always part of a context that is predominantly non-verbal, a modification of a field of personal relationships and object-relationships. The immediate context of spoken words is never simply other words. The immediate context of textualized words is simply other words.

6. By distancing the word from the plenum of existence, from a holistic context made up mostly of non-verbal elements, writing enforces verbal precision of a sort unavailable in oral cultures. Context always controls the meaning of a word. In oral utterance, the context always includes much more than words, so that less of the total, precise meaning conveyed by words need rest in the words themselves. Thus in a primary oral culture, where all verbalization is oral, utterances are always given their greater precision by nonverbal elements, which form the infrastructure of the oral utterance, giving it its fuller, situational meaning. Not so much depends on the words themselves. In a text, the entire immediate context of every word is only other words, and words alone must help other words convey whatever meaning is called for. Hence texts force words to bear more weight, to develop more and more precisely "defined"—that is "bordered" or contrastive meanings. Eventually, words used in texts come to be defined in dictionaries, which present the meaning of words in terms of other words. Oral cultures present the meaning of words by using them (Goody 1968). Oral people are generally altogether uninterested in defining words by other words (Ong 1982: 53–4, citing Luria 1976). What the word "tree" means is determined by putting the word in non-verbal context, as in pointing to a tree, not by saying in words what "tree" means.

7. Writing separates past from present. Primary oral cultures tend to use the past to explain the present, dropping from memory what does not serve this purpose in one way or another, thus homogenizing the past with the present, or approximating past to present. To use Jack Goody's term, their relationship with the past is homeostatic. By freezing verbalization, writing creates a distanced past which is full of puzzles because it can refer to states of affairs no longer effectively imaginable or can use words no longer immediately meaningful to any living persons.

8. Writing separates "administration"—civil, religious, commercial, and other—from other types of social activities. "Administration" is unknown in oral cultures, where leaders interact non-abstractly with the rest of society in tight-knit, often rhetorically controlled, configurations. "Administration" can have two senses: (1) a distinct

group able to oversee and manage, in a more or less abstractly structured fashion, complex social wholes or activities or (2) the work such a group actually does. In both senses administration comes into being with the development of written documentation and scribal expertise. At first, in more marginally textualized society, administrators relied on scribes for exploitation of the possibilities of textuality but, with wider and deeper textualization, eventually found it advantageous to be able to read and write themselves (Stock 1983; Cressy, Laqueur, and Stevens in Resnick 1983).

9. Writing makes it possible to separate logic (thought structure of discourse) from rhetoric (socially effective discourse). The invention of logic, it seems, is tied not to any kind of writing system but to the completely vocalic phonetic alphabet and the intensive analytic activity which such an alphabet demands of its inventors and subsequently encourages in all sorts of noetic fields. All formal logic in the world, down to that used for computers, stems from the ancient Greeks (the later development of some formal logic in India, which may have been an independent development, came only after Greek logic had effectively taken over and of course after India had use of the alphabet).

10. Writing separates academic learning (*mathēsis* and *mathēma*) from wisdom (*sophia*), making possible the conveyance of highly organized abstract thought structures independently of their actual use or of their integration into the human lifeworld. Wisdom regards not abstractions but holistic situations and operations in the density of the real human lifeworld. Learning by apprenticeship, with which academic learning contrasts, had kept even specialized knowledge integrated into this lifeworld and had helped to keep wisdom as the noetic as well as the practical ideal. When cultures first assimilate writing, however, they tend to put wise sayings into texts. New technologies of the word always reinforce earlier conditions of utterances but at the same time transform them. But wise sayings in texts are denatured: they do not function the way they function in oral cultures. Oral cultures do not recite lists of decontextualized wise sayings, such as are found in biblical wisdom literature, but, in fact, quite commonly and even typically use such sayings separately as parrying devices in real-life agonistic oral exchange. Once wise sayings are written down, oral culture is weakening, though its demise may take many hundreds of years. Today Ibo entrepreneurs in Onitsha in Nigeria are printing and selling collections of proverbs to marginally oral people who are unaware of the fuller implications of literacy, much as Erasmus was doing for residually oral Europeans almost five hundred years ago.

11. Writing can divide society by giving rise to a special kind of diglossia, splitting verbal communication between a "high" language completely controlled by writing even though also widely spoken (Learned Latin in the European Middle Ages) and a "low" language or "low" languages controlled by speech to the exclusion of writing. Besides Learned Latin, the other high languages created and sustained by writing to produce similar diglossia have been Sanskrit, Classical Arabic, Rabbinical Hebrew (all alphabetically written) and Classical Chinese (written, but not in the alphabet). In all these cases the high language has been not only a written language but also a sex-linked language, no longer a mother tongue, used only by males (with exceptions so

few as to be negligible). As social structures changed with the advance of technologies and women worked their way out of the massive responsibilities of pre-technological household management (which often included highly skilled crafts and even major manufacturing activities) and into academic education, the diglossia was reduced and gradually eliminated. As women entered academia, some did learn the high languages, but only when these were on the wane and no longer used as languages of instruction or of normal academic discourse. Of the tens of thousands of books written in Learned Latin through the eighteenth century and beyond, virtually none are by women. Instead, women helped put the low, vernacular languages in competition with the high language. Eventually one or another dialect of various low languages was taken over by writing and replaced the original high language. This has happened to all the high languages just mentioned—which are in fact the major high languages of the world—with the partial exception of Classical Arabic in the still linguistically fluid Arabic-speaking world.

12. Writing differentiates grapholects, those "low"-language dialects which are taken over by writing and erected into national languages, from other dialects, making the grapholect a dialect of a completely different order of magnitude and effectiveness from the dialects that remain oral. The grapholect which we know as standard English has an active or recuperable vocabulary of perhaps a million and a half words, as compared with the relatively few thousand words available in dialects without written resources (see, for example, Laughlin 1975 on Tzotzil). For this exponential development, the lexicon of a grapholect requires print as well as writing, for dictionaries are print products. (Imagine producing multiple copies of *Webster's Third International Dictionary* or of the *Oxford English Dictionary* by hand.)

13. Writing divides or distances more evidently and effectively as its form becomes more abstract, which is to say more removed from the sound world into the space world of sight. "Abstract" in fact means removed, distanced, from *abstrahere*, to draw out or to draw away from. The alphabet in its various forms is the most abstract writing form. We have already noted that Tzeng and Wang (1983) have reported—though more work remains to be done here—how writing and reading Chinese characters involve the right cerebral hemisphere of the brain more than do writing and reading the alphabet, which involve the left hemisphere more. The right hemisphere normally implements totalizing, intuitive, less abstractive or less analytic processes; the left hemisphere is more analytic—and more involved in the alphabet. As has been seen, formal logic, modern science, and ultimately the computer have their historical roots in the fully vocalic alphabet, the most analytic of the writing systems, dissolving all sound as such into spatial equivalents, in principle, if never completely in fact. (The alphabet, it should be recalled, was invented only once: all alphabets in the world—Greek, Roman, Glagolitic, Cyrillic, Arabic, Sanskrit, Korean, etc.—derive in one way or another, directly or indirectly, from the ancient Semitic alphabet, which, however, in contrast to Greek, did not and still does not have letters for vowels.)

14. Perhaps the most momentous of all its diaeretic effects in the deep history of thought is the effect of writing when it separates being from time. This separation has been detailed in a recent major monograph by Eric Havelock (1983), "The Linguistic

Task of the Presocratics, Part One: Ionian Science in Search of an Abstract Vocabulary". We know that all philosophy depends on writing because all elaborate, linear, so-called "logical" explanation depends on writing. Oral persons can be wise, as wise as anyone, and they can of course give some explanation for things. But the elaborate, intricate, seemingly endless but exact cause-effect sequences required by what we call philosophy and by extended scientific thinking are unknown among oral peoples, including the early Greeks before their development of the first vocalic alphabet. Havelock's newly seminal work, however, goes beyond showing that elaborate explanatory thinking depends upon writing and the revisionary, back-tracking operations made possible by such a time-obviating mechanism. His new monograph shows more precisely that the development of the content, the subject-matter of metaphysics itself, with its concentration on being as being, depended internally upon the elaboration of writing. Havelock's work is based upon extraordinarily careful analysis of pre-Socratic texts and upon cautious reconstruction of antecedents of the texts. Here I can only attempt to suggest in a quite sweeping, but I believe accurate way what Havelock's point comes to as related to the line of thought I have been pursuing.

Oral speech and thought narrativizes experience and the environment, whereas philosophy, which comes into being slowly after writing, is radically anti-narrative. Plato did not want story-telling poets in his republic. The philosophical enterprise required the coinage of a large number of abstract nouns. Havelock (1983: 20) cites some which around the end of the fifth century BC had become common tender for dealing with the cosmic environment: matter (*hulē*), dimension (*megethos*), space (*chōra*), body (*sōma*), void (*kenon*), motion (*kinēsis* or *phora*), change (*alloiōsis*, *metabolē*), rest (*stasis*). Besides such nouns, "the conceptual task also required the elimination of verbs of doing and acting and happening . . . in favor of a syntax which states permanent relationships between conceptual terms systematically" (p. 14). In this new noetic economy, Heraclitus suggests (p. 25) that "is" (*esti*) should replace the use of all other verbs and even of the past and future of the verb "to be" (*einai*). Parmenides brings this reorganization of thought to completion: the imagistic, narrativistic Homeric references to the world are replaced "by the thought world of conceptual science" (pp.28–9). In brief, the Homeric verb *kinein*, which refers not so much to our concept of "motion" as to the earlier concept of "commotion" (the disturbance inherent in any kind of real action, not a disembodied abstraction such as *kinēsis*), yields to *einai*, "to be", which is not commotion at all (p. 38). Becoming becomes being. The mobile oral world has been supplanted by the quiescent text, and Plato's immutable ideas have been provided with their action-free, seemingly timeless chirographic launching pad.

One is struck by similarities between the ancient Greek situation reported by Havelock and that which Luria found among illiterates as compared to literates among the folk he studied in the southwestern Soviet Union (reported in Ong 1982: 49–57). Asked, "What is a tree? Define a tree," the illiterate peasant replies, "Why should I? Everyone knows what a tree is." To learn what a thing *is* one does not use definitions. To grasp an object's essence, one does not talk about the object, but, as has earlier been noted here, one *points* to the object physically or metaphorically. One deals with existing beings as such indexically, not verbally. Words in an oral culture are used typically not to set up static definitions but to discourse actively on the way a thing acts or behaves or operates in the human lifeworld. Words in oral cultures paradigmatically go with action and with things that act. As writing is interiorized, verbalization migrates from a predominantly action frame to a predominantly "being" frame: the verb *to be* becomes more urgent than it had ever been in an oral culture. The quest is on to find Aristotle's *to ti ēn einai;* that is, "what it is to be" or "what being is".

. . .

VIII

Print and electronics continue with new intensification and radical transformations the diaeretic programme initially set in motion by writing. They separate knower from known more spectacularly than writing does. Between the knower and the known print interposes elaborate mechanical contrivances and operations of a different order of complexity than writing. The computer achieves the ultimate (thus far) in separation of the knower and the known (the subject of discourse): between the two it interposes limitlessly complex structures of mechanically articulated "bits" of information, each consisting of the ultimate in divisive patterning, the dichotomy or binary division, which translates into "yes–no" or "is–isn't". Putting the simplest statement of, say, a dozen words on to a page in a word processor involves operations inside the machine, totally remote from the human lifeworld, which are thousands, perhaps millions, of times more complex than writing or even letterpress printing, though unimaginably less complex than the activities of the human cerebrum.

. . .

In the case of the computer we are clearly dealing with physical separation of knower and known. But in the case of writing as well, it is the physical separation, the interposition of the text, created by a technology, that makes possible the psychological separation between the self and the object of its knowledge. Moreover, as is evident in computer programming, new tracks for thought are imposed by the new technologies. And the software of the computer vigorously interposes even another consciousness or other consciousnesses—the programmer or programmers—between the knower and the known.

. . .

XI

As the digital computer can be to a degree, so writing is self-corrective to a degree. It has in itself the cure for the chirographic squint commonly afflicting cultures that have deeply interiorized writing. Because it so radically separates knower from known, writing can distance us from writing itself. Writing has enabled us to identify the orality that was antecedent to it and to see how radically it differs from that orality. Writing has the power to liberate us more and more from the chirographic bias and confusion it creates, though complete liberation remains impossible. For all states of the word—oral, chirographic, typographic, electronic—impose their own confusions, which cannot be radically eliminated but only controlled by reflection.

In the noetic world, separation ultimately brings reconstituted unity. This is true of naming at the oral stage. Calling an object a "tree", as has been seen, puts the object "out there", as different from the knower. In place of empathetic identification, the name sets up a relatively clear subject–object relationship. But this very relationship makes for a new kind of intimacy. Now, in certain ways, the knower can deal with the tree better on its own terms, rather than on terms unreflectively imposed by the knower. He or she can better appreciate what the tree is on its own as distinct from the knower—although of course distinctness from the knower is never totally realized. With the use of names, the inarticulate identification of the infant with the surrounding world is replaced by verbally implemented distancing. The new distancing submerges the original empathetic identification in a flood of new awarenesses but does not entirely do away with it. And indeed, as distancing increases beyond those ranges made available by oral naming through the vaster distances opened by writing and print—and now electronics—the original empathetic identification becomes more and more recuperable at the level of conscious reflectivity. That is to say, with writing and its sequels, empathetic identification can be attended to as we are attending to it now, and as oral folk could not attend to it. Of course, the original innocence of the pristine empathetic identification can never be repossessed directly. Civilization entails such discomforts, for that is what they are. (Freud's title should be translated "Civilization and its Discomforts" (*Unbehagen*), not "Discontents".) Human knowledge demands both proximity and distance, and these two are related to one another dialectically. Proximity perceptions feed distancing analyses, and vice versa, creating a more manageable intimacy.

As a time-obviating, context-free mechanism, writing separates the known from the knower more definitely than the original orally grounded manœuvre of naming does, but it also unites the knower and the known more consciously and more articulately. Writing is a consciousness-raising and humanizing technology. So is print, even more, and, in its own way, so is the computer. But that is another story, which has yet to be told or written or printed or processed in the course of this series.

Note

1. This is an edited version of the original long essay by Ong. I have borrowed the editing done by Ellen Cushman, Eugene R. Kintgen, Barry M. Kroll, and Mike Rose in their volume, *Literacy: A Critical Sourcebook*, 19–31. I am grateful for their work.

References

Goody, J. and I. Watt 1968: "The Consequences of Literacy", in J. Goody (ed.), *Literacy in Traditional Societies*, 27–84. Cambridge: Cambridge University Press.

Graff, H. J. (ed.) 1981: *Literacy and Social Development in the West: A Reader*, Cambridge Studies in Oral and Literate Culture, 3. Cambridge and New York: Cambridge University Press.

Havelock, E. A. 1963: *Preface to Plato.* Cambridge, Mass.: Belknap Press of Harvard University Press.

——. 1976: *Origins of Western Literacy.* Toronto: Ontario Institute for the Study of Education.

——. 1983: "The Linguistic Task of the Presocratics, Part One: Ionian Science in Search of an Abstract Vocabulary", in K. Robb (ed.), *Language and Thought in Early Greek Philosophy*, 7–82. La Salle, Ill.: Hegeler Institute, Monist Library of Philosophy.

Hoskin, K. W. (n.d.): "The History of Education and the History of Writing". Review article, manuscript from the author.

Laughlin, R. W. 1975: *The Great Tzotzil Dictionary of San Lorenzo Zinacatan.* Washington, DC: Smithsonian Institution Press.

Luria, A. R. 1976: *Cognitive Development: Its Cultural and Social Foundations*, trans. M. Lopez-Morillas and L. Solataroff; ed. M. Cole. Cambridge, Mass.: Harvard University Press.

Olson, D. R. (n.d.): *The World on Paper.* Book in preparation, draft-manuscript from the author.

Ong, W. J. 1982: *Orality and Literacy.* London: Methuen.

Resnick, D. (ed.) 1983: *Literacy in Historical Perspective.* Washington, DC: Library of Congress.

Stock. B. 1983: *The Implications of Literacy: Written Language and Models of Interpretation in the Eleventh and Twelfth Centuries.* Princeton, NJ: Princeton University Press.

Tzeng, O. J. L. and W. S.-Y. Wang 1983: "The First Two R's", in *American Scientist*, 71: 452–6.

5.
NARRATIVES OF LITERACY: CONNECTING COMPOSITION TO CULTURE
Beth Daniell

In 1986 Lester Faigley analyzed three competing theories of the writing process: the expressive, the cognitive, and the social. Although calling for a synthesis, Faigley was clearly endorsing the social view. He identified four strands of research which contributed to the social perspective he was advocating: post-structuralist theories of language, sociology of science, ethnographies of literacy and language, and Marxism. Two of these four—ethnography and Marxism—contributed texts about literacy that were instrumental in helping composition studies make what has been called the social turn (Trimbur, "Taking"; Bizzell, *Academic* 202). Indeed the move in composition studies away from the individualistic and cognitive perspectives of the seventies and early eighties toward the social theories and political consciousness that prevail today was encouraged, pushed along, impelled by competing narratives of literacy. These days, literacy—the term and concept—connects composition, with its emphasis on students and classrooms, to the social, political, economic, historical, and cultural.

In thinking about the relations of literacy and composition, I have found helpful Jean-Francois Lyotard's notions of the grand narratives of modernism and the little narratives of postmodernism. Lyotard argues in *The Postmodern Condition* that in the modern age knowledge is justified, or legitimated, through narrative. The legitimacy of an idea, a work, or a proposal depends, in other words, on its contribution to one of two grand narratives. As Lyotard puts it, "The mode of legitimation... which reintroduces narrative as the validity of knowledge, can thus take two routes, depending on whether it represents the subject of the narrative as cognitive or practical, as a hero of knowledge or a hero of liberty" (31). Subjected to the skepticism of the postmodern age, these "totalizing" metanarratives, according to Lyotard, have been deconstructed and replaced by a proliferation of little narratives. It is my contention that various narratives of literacy have influenced and continue to shape the images we in composition studies have of who we are, what we do, and how we do it. Using Lyotard as a terministic screen to examine these narratives brings to light a number

---

Daniell, Beth. "Narratives of Literacy." *College Composition and Communication*. 50.3 (February 1999): 393–410.

of issues: the conflicted politics of composition studies over the last two or three decades, the relationship of theory and ideology, the ethical questions of research, the problematics of separating the spiritual from academic study.

Background: Two Literacy Arguments

In the 1980s there were two different controversies over literacy. One concerned E. D. Hirsch's notion of cultural literacy. This argument, which reached its climax in the late eighties, arose out of Hirsch's claim that a body of common cultural "facts" would solve the problems of American education, which he saw as failing both minority students and the body politic. Critics charged Hirsch and liked-minded folk, such as William Bennett and Allan Bloom, with conservatism, elitism, insensitivity to regional, social, racial, and ethnic differences, naiveté in uncritically accepting standardized test scores, and nostalgia for a golden age that never was. Hirsch's book *Cultural Literacy*, the articles and comments in MLA's *Profession 88*, Patricia Bizzell's "Arguing About Literacy," and Mike Rose's *Lives on the Boundary* document this controversy.

The other literacy debate focused on the literacy-orality theory espoused by Eric Havelock and Walter Ong among others, a view of literacy also known as the great leap or great divide theory and the autonomous model. This view of literacy I have come to see as a version of the grand narrative Lyotard calls the narrative of "speculation," that is, the one that is "more philosophical," the one that has to do with cognition (31). This narrative legitimates knowledge by explaining our universal "primordial origins," according to Mark Mullen (548), and thus offering a path to progress: If we understand the origins of, say, literacy, then we will know how literacy changes the thinking of human beings and will understand how individuals progress and how cultures advance.

Predating Hirsch's literacy work, literacy-orality theory has roots, proponents, and critics in a number of fields: anthropology, sociolinguistics, education, history, as well as classics—Havelock's disciplinary home—and English studies—Ong had been president of MLA. While I give attention in this essay to the great divide or great leap narrative and the work that deconstructed it, I do not want to give the impression that the two literacy arguments were unrelated. The connection between the two controversies is explained in Bizzell's "Arguing about Literacy" article: even though, as Bizzell puts its, "the concept of 'cultural literacy' has emerged as a corrective to 'Great Divide' literacy theories" (144), both views, she argues, protect the status quo while at the same time claiming to show how the intellectual capabilities of students can be augmented.

Literacy and Orality

In great leap or great divide narratives, literacy is not merely encoding and decoding sound in and from inscribed symbols or even, to use Ann Berthoff's definition, "the realized capacity to construct and construe in graphic form representations of our recognitions" (142). In great leap accounts, literacy becomes a theoretical construct in binary opposition with orality; on each side of the dichotomy or single continuum are contrasting modes of speech, composition, behavior, and thought (see Ong, *Orality* 37–57). In their strong versions, literacy-orality theories assert that simply reading and writing with a Greek-derived alphabet—that is, an alphabet with both consonants and vowels—actually causes fundamental advances—great developmental leaps—in human cognition. These cognitive leaps then bring about alterations not only in the consciousness of individuals but also in cultures. In this view, literacy is an individual mental act which only later brings about certain social and cultural conditions. Literacy thus marks the great divide between advanced, complex cultures and traditional ones. In *Literacy in Theory and Practice*, Brian Street refers to this perspective as the autonomous model because it depicts literacy as standing alone, acomextual, a thing that exists independent of culture.

The Great Leap Narrative

The earliest proponents of the great leap grand narrative were both keen rhetoricians and master storytellers. The best rendition of the story is Havelock's 1963 *Preface to Plato*. In preliterate Greece, the story goes, the knowledge and values necessary for the survival of the culture were transmitted through poetry. The content was tradition, the language formulaic. Weaving together familiar stories and formulas, the poet constructed the poem itself in a public oral performance wherein both bard and audience entered into an almost trance-like, or "mimetic," state. At about the time of Plato, literacy had become sufficiently internalized that the mental energy previously needed for the memorization of the poetic formulas was released. This newly released mental energy allowed for the questioning and analyzing of the stories, thus breaking the mimetic spell. This narrative explains, then, the origin of Plato's dialectic as well as his reasons for banishing the poets from his Republic. In strong versions of the great leap narrative, literacy is seen as the origin of independent, analytical thought, and in weaker versions as a causal factor.

In "The Consequences of Literacy," also from 1963, Jack Goody and Ian Watt take up the tale, asserting that Aristotle and the next generation of Greek thinkers used these literate modes of thought to develop systematized abstract thinking, such as the syllogism, the categories, and the taxonomies in various fields. Later, according to Ong in several articles and books, the technology of print made literacy accessible to a greater number of people, thus releasing more mental energy for abstract thinking in many new fields. Western culture underwent a recapitulation and an extension of the great leap. The climax occurred, David Olson says in "From Utterance to Text," when British thinkers like John Locke began to use the essay to explore abstract problems and to create new theoretical knowledge; in this so-called essayist literacy, meaning is found in the text, not in the relationship of writer to audience, or in the context. Offering a single theory which accounts for everything, this version of Lyotard's narrative of speculation, as Patrick Fuery and Nick Mansfield might explain it, "sees the human race as ascending towards the greatest possible understanding of itself, the purest possible self-consciousness of its inner value and potential" (137–38).

Farrell's Proposal

The Havelock-Ong depiction of orality and literacy has been used profitably by such historians of rhetoric as Richard Enos, Jan Swearingen, and Kathleen Welch, but in composition it proved more controversial. In the seventies and early eighties the great leap narrative of literacy was taken up, sometimes with enthusiasm, because research in composition was dominated by inner-directed, cognitive theories of writing. These views, as Bizzell points out in "Cognition, Convention, and Certainty," posited the cause of poor writing by students in the faulty minds of the students themselves rather than in inequitable social conditions. The depiction of orality was thought by some, including Ong himself ("Literacy"), to be useful in describing the thought patterns and the language, particularly the written language, of first-year students, basic writers, and minority students in American colleges and universities.

The most controversial, though by no means the only, pedagogical proposal based on the Havelock-Ong narrative of literacy was Thomas J. Farrell's 1983 *CCC* article "IQ and Standard English." Here Farrell argues that writing teachers should require African American students to learn "the full deployment" of the verb to be, which Farrell sees as a literate, not oral linguistic form. Citing Ong's assertions that oral languages reflect an agonistic, participatory mind-set (see Ong, *Orality* 43–46), Farrell asserts that oral languages have only action verbs; only literate languages develop the copulative verb necessary for stating propositions (475). Regarding inner-city African American culture as "a residual form of what Walter J. Ong calls a primary oral culture" (473), Farrell argues that if African American students learned the standard forms of to be, they could then think propositionally, thereby raising their scores on standardized IQ tests.

The immediate reaction among many in the composition community was outrage. In 1984 *CCC* printed four responses (Greenberg, Hartwell, Himley, and Stratton). Karen Greenberg pulled no punches, linking Farrell's notions with other "racist" theories of language deprivation (460); R. E. Stratton called the article "offensive" (469); Patrick Hartwell said he was "soundly ticked off" (461). Greenberg and Hartwell criticized Farrell's understanding of be-deletion in African American dialects (see also Walters [185] on copula absence in other languages). Swearingen organized a panel for the 1986 CCCC including both Farrell and his critics and then edited those papers for a special issue of *Pre/Text*. In a 1988 article Rose charged several cognitive theories including the literacy-orality binary with reductionism, arguing that the theories he examined take attention away from "the immediate social and linguistic conditions in which the student composes" ("Narrowing" 295). Concern over Farrell's proposal is the subtext of many of the papers included in the MLA *Right to Literacy* collection. Throughout all this criticism ran the conviction that Farrell's plan and the thinking it was based on would prove both educationally and psychologically damaging for students.

The Ethnographic Narratives

Much of the criticism leveled at Farrell and at Ong and Havelock during this time drew on anthropological and sociolinguistic research into language and literacy, among which were a number of ethnographic studies that cast doubt on the Havelock-Ong narrative by telling different stories of literacy. These competing narratives showed that literacy does not work the same way in all cultures or that the specific cognitive properties or linguistic structures claimed as consequences of literacy do in fact exist in oral cultures. Some of this research, briefly summarized in my paper in the *Pre/Text* special issue, can be found in collections edited by William Frawley and by Deborah Tannen. Key work across the range of literacy studies, from theorists of the great divide to its critics, comprises an anthology by Eugene Kintgen, Barry Kroll, and Mike Rose.

One study often cited in arguments against great leap theories is Shirley Brice Heath's decade-long ethnography of literacy and language in the Piedmont Carolinas. In "Protean Shapes," Heath shows that spoken language in an African-American community, which according to Ong's model could be classified as "residually oral," can have far more complex syntax than literate language with the same message, speaker, and audience. Heath's stories of literacy in three different communities argue that it is more useful to regard orality and literacy not as a single continuum, but rather as two continua, two traditions, that meet, intersect, and cross in specific human situations (112). Heath's Carolina study remains the single most comprehensive project on literacy carried out in United States, and her book *Ways with Words*, despite later criticism, is a standard item on Ph.D. reading lists in rhetoric and composition.

Cross-cultural work, such as Keith Basso's analysis of an Apache word game and Niyi Akinnaso's explanation of Yoruba cowry shell divination ritual, refutes other specific great leap claims. Perhaps the most important cross-cultural study was the research of Sylvia Scribner and Michael Cole among the Vai people of northern Africa. From comparisons of three distinctly different groups of literates sharing the same culture, Scribner and Cole conclude that mental abilities typically associated with literacy are better understood not as consequences of literacy, but rather as qualities imparted by Western schooling. Scribner and Cole's *The Psychology of Literacy*, like Heath's work, has become standard reading in composition studies.

Shaking the Foundations

Besides using evidence from ethnographic studies of literacy to question the validity of the binary oppositions of the great leap, some scholars have sought other ways to undermine its foundations. For example, in *Literacy in Theory and Practice* Street points to flaws in both research and logic in Goody's argument to assert that literacy is never autonomous, never separate, never innocent or neutral, but always embedded in and embodying the practices, beliefs, and values of a culture, always therefore ideological. In *Social Literacies* Street criticizes Ong's work on methodological, empirical, and theoretical grounds. Despite his recognition of the role imagination plays in the human sciences, Street issues warnings about the dangers of Ong's "if I were a horse" method to researchers tempted to make pronouncements about the minds of people not available for questioning (155). John Halverson closely examines the primary classical texts to conclude that Havelock's reading of Homer, the basis of great divide depictions of primary oral cultures, is inaccurate: "Havelock's portrait of Homer as the didactic, encyclopedic custodian of tradition lacks verification from the Homeric poems" (156) Taking another tack, sociolinguist Keith Walters urges readers to look at the political work of the great leap narrative; its claim that alphabetic literacy causes its users to think more logically than people in cultures without alphabetic literacy or without a writing system is, Walters says, "an idea that many Westerners find appealing, no doubt because it 'explains' what they perceive to be the superiority of Western culture" (175).

The Literacy for Liberation Narrative

In addition to these moves, those who sought to refute the totalizing and conservative Havelock–Ong account of literacy turned as well to Marxist critiques of education. Chief among these was the theoretical writing of Brazilian educator Paulo Freire, especially his *Pedagogy of the Oppressed*. Using his own experience in teaching adult literacy, Freire argues persuasively that literacy can be a tool for liberating people from political and economic oppression. Other Marxist analyses, underscored by historical studies (see Graff; Resnick and Resnick), demonstrated the gate-keeping role literacy has played under industrialized capitalism (see Douglas). Marxist theory reinforced the message of ethnographic work like Heath's "What No Bedtime Story Means": that schooling in the United States as well as in the Third World is a class-based enterprise, serving the status quo and making few allowances for students whose home experiences with language and literacy deviated from middle-class "ways with words." Elspeth Stuckey's *The Violence of Literacy* stripped many people of their last vestiges of naive and romantic belief in literacy as an open door to the middle class. In the society around us we could see that restricting access to literacy is an effective way to deprive particular groups of power.

Such studies and observations persuaded many in composition that what counts as literacy in a given time and place is determined by social, economic, and political factors rather than by some prior definition. The Marxist perspective on literacy thus served as a valuable corrective to the blind devotion of American scholarship to the individual and its traditional myopia toward power as factor in human institutions. To see reading and writing as social practice mediated and regulated by institutions instead of as a free-standing, individual mental operation supplied composition with a different lens to use in looking at our students, their texts, and our own work. The idea that writing and writing instruction were deeply connected with power became, with Berlin's histories, a mainstream idea.

Despite all these benefits, Marxist work on literacy also looks like a version of the other grand narrative Lyotard identifies in *The Postmodern Condition*, the one he associates with the practical, with liberty, the one he calls "more political" (31). Fuery and Mansfield describe this grand narrative as "assess[ing] things according to how much they contribute to the eventual production of a society that is equal, just, and free" (137). In the Freire version of the emancipation narrative, a middle- or upper-class academic goes with his or her privileged graduate students, all of them ready to "'die', in order to be reborn through and with the oppressed" (Freire 127), into the villages or barrios where they find that "the people" want to learn to read and write. The academics study the people and their environment to collect the culturally significant "generative words" that are used not only to teach reading and writing but also to impart political awareness. Since Portuguese is a language whose words are comprised mainly of consonant-vowel combinations (with few consonant clusters), these generative words can be separated into syllables which also have separate meanings. As the adult students participate in the "culture circle," examining the slides the teachers present and responding to problems the teachers pose, they easily discover the cultural and political meaning of the generative words. Because the words resonate with meaning (as opposed to, say, "see Dick run"), adult students quickly learn the alphabet and the phonemic values of the letters. At the same time—seemingly automatically or inevitably—they develop what Freire calls *conscientização*, usually translated as critical consciousness and defined by Freire as "learning to perceive social, political, and economic contradictions, and to take action against the oppressive elements of reality" (19, note 1). Within three weeks, an adult is reading. This method has been used successfully in a number of Third World countries—so well in fact that Brazil's 1964 military junta exiled Freire for sixteen years.

Because those drawn to teaching are almost always motivated by a desire to help others, the Freire literacy narrative strikes a chord with people in composition, a discipline centered on pedagogy. This story was and is especially appealing to those of us who began teaching English in the sixties and seventies because to this cohort its leftist critique rings true and because, when we first read it, it seemed to offer a model for our idealistic goal of changing the structures of an unjust society. It is a particularly compelling vision for those whose careers began in open admissions programs or other War on Poverty projects, not an unusual background among people in composition studies. Freire quickly became an icon, like Mina Shaughnessy.

The problem with grand narratives is the unfortunate human tendency to overgeneralize from them: The Freire narrative has been used to support a discourse that sometimes seems to assume that all our students are oppressed. Of course some are. Some college students live daily with poverty and fear, and some, maybe even most in particular settings, suffer from racism and other prejudices. Community colleges and technical colleges are, certainly, on the frontlines of social and economic injustice, and far too many public schools are behind the lines. It would take either an incredible optimist or a complete ignoramus to deny the inequities in American society and in American education. But by the world's standards, most of the students who enroll in the classes we teach—especially in private colleges and large state universities—are not oppressed. They are not Freire's Third World adult illiterates, and our job is not now, if it ever was, to recruit for a leftist revolution. Rather, our task is to help students learn to read and write critically so that they can carry out the tasks of their lives with some control in an increasingly complex culture in which levels of literacy "accumulate" quickly (Brandt, "Accumulating"); this includes giving them the machinery by which to critique the world around them. But to speak of our students as either victims of oppression or the children of oppressors is too easy a characterization of the complicated social, political, and economic situation of the United States at century's end. It is a killer dichotomy unproductive in teaching actual American students, who come in varieties of ethnicity, race, religion, region, sexual preference, and socioeconomic background no binary can account for.

The point is that we must all be careful of literacy narratives that make us feel good, not just those narratives that explain away social injustice by calling some people oral and others literate, but also those that cast some of us in the role of "hero[es] of liberty" (Lyotard 31). Freire has shown that a "banking" pedagogy can support oppressive structures elsewhere in society and that literacy and literacy learning can be liberatory in some situations. But we have learned from experience that neither Freire's methods nor his critique will automatically bring critical consciousness to North America.

The Other Freire Narrative

Perhaps we have misunderstood the Freire narrative. We thought he was saying that teaching a language's literacy code by means of certain generative words would create critical consciousness and thus invite social critique, which would in turn allow us to reshape society. The most clearly written and relentlessly honest account I know of the search for social change through education is the introductory essay in Bizzell's *Academic Discourse and Critical Consciousness*. In this intellectual autobiography, Bizzell tells of her struggle to use education to create a more just and democratic society. She tells how she had thought that

> learning academic discourse [could] change the thinking of basic writers in much the same way that literacy, according to Paulo Freire, changes Brazilian peasants. Freire believes that human beings can "detach themselves from the world"; that when they 'enter into" social reality from this detached perspective, the "true interrelations" they will "discover" will embody injustices which the people will then be able to diagnose and correct. At this point they will have embarked on the process Freire calls "critical consciousness."
>
> (19)

What Bizzell comes to understand and what she shares with us in this powerful essay is that critical consciousness is not the result of a method, whether Freire's pedagogy of the oppressed or academic discourse, the term she uses for the essayist literacy described by Olson as the end point of the great leap narrative. Critical consciousness, which includes action toward social justice, does not reside in the intellectual distancing that a method allows; it comes instead from another source, as I learned at CCCC in 1988 from Ann Berthoff.

As Professor Berthoff (in her own inimitable way) asked a question in discussion after a panel, she remarked that Freire's pedagogy results as much from his Catholicism as from his Marxism. At once Freire made sense to me in a new (and, at the same time, very old) way. Freire's *Pedagogy of the Oppressed* is marked not just by

Marxist terminology but by the language of Christianity as well: rebirth, conversion, communion. Freire seems as interested in the spiritual salvation of the elites as he is in the political and economic salvation of the oppressed. What is missing in most North American accounts of Freire's method is the intense *I-thou* relation he calls for between teacher and student. Freire is never afraid, for example, to use the word love in his educational philosophy, to argue that education is an act of love, and therefore of courage.

In looking back over her struggle with Freire's philosophy, Bizzell says that she has come to see that "within Brazilian Roman Catholic society, Freire is readily recognized as a kind of 'liberation-theology' Catholic, pursuing left-wing political goals out of an ultimate concern for the souls of his students" (21). Few American academics are familiar with both traditions. Cornel West is an exception, as he demonstrates when he writes in *Keeping Faith: Philosophy and Race in America* that "the Marxist tradition is indispensable, yet inadequate" and "the moral vision and ethical norms I accept are derived from the prophetic Christian tradition" (133).

What Freire offers North America is not a method of teaching literacy we can carry from the Third World to the First, but an attitude of profound love for the human beings we teach. Being treated as if one is worthy, as if one's life is important, as if what one has to say is significant and deserving attention, as if one is—yes—a fellow child of God, allows some people, even the most silenced, to "come to voice," to use bell hooks' term, and, in so doing, to see the world and themselves differently. Freire taps into that striving, in his students, in his teachers, and in his readers, for something beyond ourselves, offering a spiritual perspective on the teaching of literacy: Not a grand narrative where we get to be heroes of an economic revolution but a grander narrative that calls us to be laborers in the vineyard, a narrative that is problematic indeed in a culture that values the separation of public and spiritual life.

The Little Narratives

Beyond Ong's narrative of cognition or Freire's narrative of liberation, we find a number of recent studies that may, if we continue with Lyotard's terms, be referred to as the little narratives of literacy (31, 60). These are more or less postmodern studies of reading and writing. Employing a variety of research methods, coming from several academic traditions, and, not unexpectedly, ranging in quality, the little narratives help us "gaze in wonderment at the diversity of discursive [and literate] species, just as we do at the diversity of plant or animal species" (Lyotard 26).

Just as Michael Holzman has pointed out the "post-Freirean" local focus of several adult literacy programs, so too the little narratives almost all examine literacy in particular local settings. While the little narratives of literacy offer valuable insights about various specific literate practices and while they may theorize on the these practices, they seldom make theoretical statements that claim to be valid for literate persons in general or literate cultures in general. These studies assume, rather, that literacy is multiple, contextual, and ideological. In addition, those taking a cultural studies approach distrust narratives in which one group becomes powerful because of the adoption of a presumably neutral technology. Using ethnographic methods, offering "thick descriptions," and exhibiting familiarity with Marxist and feminist critiques of language and culture, these analyses sometimes show the complexity of the relationship of orality and literacy, or spoken and written language, in actual practice. Taken as a whole, the little narratives argue as well that the relationship between literacy and oppression or freedom is rarely as simple as we have thought.

Interestingly, many of the little narratives—but not all—are written by women, and many of their subjects—but not all—are women. One of the earliest was Janice Radway's *Reading the Romance*, an examination of middle-class women's reading of romance novels. Allowing her subjects to speak for themselves, Radway captures the contradiction between the ideological content of the romance books and the ideological function of the women taking the time to read away from their roles as caregivers. Linda Brodkey's "On the Subject of Class and Gender in 'The Literacy Letters,'" Jennifer Horsman's *Something in My Mind Besides the Everyday*, and Anne Gere's "Kitchen Tables and Rented Rooms: The Extracurriculum of Composition" open windows into the literacy—and lives—of poor and working class women, often revealing the gap between these women and the middle-class teachers and social workers who try to help them.

Deborah Brandt's recent interviews with a number of adults of varying ages and backgrounds tease out the ambiguities and poignancies of acquiring and using literacy in America in the 20th century ("Accumulating"). Though Brandt shows how literacy has allowed for social mobility or contributed to the construction of identity, her work also takes into account the losses that have been, and are still, part of the price of literacy. Similarly, Kim Donehower's research focuses on often contradictory experiences of literacy acquisition in a mountain community in western North Carolina. Gere's *Intimate Practices*, a work of meticulous scholarship, shows how the reading and writing in women's clubs of the late 19th and early 20th centuries helped create community and identity for these women, while at the same time connecting them to the wider political and cultural issues of their times and providing them a means for speaking for the interests of their ethnic, racial, and religious groups.

Another group of studies, perhaps speaking to the spiritual issue raised by Freire, examines the relations of literacy and religion or spirituality: for example, Beverly Moss's study of literacy in three African American churches in Chicago; Andrea Fishman's work on reading and writing in an Amish community; Cushla Kapitzke's analysis of the literate practices of a Seventh-Day Adventist congregation in Australia; my own examination of literacy among women in Al-Anon ("Composing"). While these researches support the assertion of historical studies like those by the Resnicks and Goody (Introduction) that religion and literacy are inextricably intertwined in many societies, they point as well at the variety this relationship can take.

As the little narratives proliferate, the grand narratives seem to lose their power. The little narratives offer other images of what it means to be or to become literate in this culture and its various subcultures. They show people reading and writing for specific purposes: for entertainment, for personal growth, for identity formation, for community, for privacy, as well as for problem solving, for receiving and transmitting information, for economic advancement, or for political empowerment of oneself or of one's group. Varying in their overt politicization, the little narratives show that the modernist promise of literacy—economic security, upward mobility, political freedom, intellectual achievement, middle-class values, personal fulfillment—is inequitably fulfilled. But they also show that some people use literacy to make their lives more meaningful, no matter what their economic and political circumstances are.

Cultural Connections

Despite contemporary disillusion with the grand narratives of modernism, both the Havelock-Ong and the Freire narratives have contributed valuable perspectives to composition studies. Even those who take issue with the great leap narrative, as I do, realize that the Havelock-Ong narrative helped us look at the relations between literacy and culture, a relationship ignored when talk about literacy is in terms of words per minute or grade level. Further, when used with awareness of their limitations, the concepts of orality and literacy, which made the great leap narrative attractive in the first place, can function as a valuable heuristic, as we see in two recent essays. While both Annabelle Sreberny-Mohammadi's "Media Integration in the Third World: An Ongian Look at Iran" and Jimmie Killingsworth's "Product and Process, Literacy and Orality" use language from the Havelock-Ong theory, neither does so in ways that separate people into groups based on mental abilities. In Sreberny-Mohammadi's and Killingsworth's hands, literacy-orality theory becomes part of the toolbox of concepts for analyzing speech and writing, rather than a means of labeling individuals and groups or explaining everything.

From the arguments in the 1980s about the great leap theory, a number of benefits have ensued. First, it became clear that context means more than the room the student is in when she composes a school assignment. Second, anthropological studies demonstrated that literacy is both multiple and multicultural, that it varies not only from culture to culture but within cultures as well. We learned that literacy isn't one thing, and we have learned that it is more accurate to speak of literacies than of literacy. Third, foregrounding ethnographic research, the great divide debate offered composition studies another model for research besides the ed psych pre-test, post-test, or think-aloud case study approaches.

The Marxist critiques of education by Freire and others also emphasized the relations between literacy and culture by teasing out specific connections between reading and writing or their lack, on the one hand, and social, political, and economic forces, on the other. These studies demonstrate that literacy, including instruction in writing, is woven into a society's structures of power. But perhaps most important, with his literacy narrative Freire has left composition studies two crucial articles of faith concerning pedagogy: First, there is a difference between imparting knowledge (the banking concept) and sharing it (authentic dialogue). And, second, we teach out of relationship.

The little narratives of literacy connect composition to culture, further, by moving research in composition away from a narrow focus on writing only in the classroom to writing as part of everyday life, into what Gere has called the extracurriculum of composition. It is worth noting, as well, that several of the researchers who write the little narratives of literacy claim composition and rhetoric as their area of specialization (some are products of graduate programs in comp and rhetoric) and CCCC and *CCC* as major venues through which they share their work. This body of research responds to the questions a post-process composition studies should be concerned with: Why and how do people in our culture read and write when they are not compelled to by the state? What are the functions and forms of these various literacies? What do these practices mean to the participants? to composition studies? to the wider culture? How do those meanings vary from this group to that? The partial answers provided by the little narratives offer a richer perspective than we once had on the writing our students may do outside our classrooms or the writing they may be called to do. The little narratives underscore the fact that we are teaching actual not abstract students to write, not just for the next professor but for life in the culture.

In addition, because the little narratives take for granted the diversity of literacy, they often focus on the confluence of literacy with race, class, and gender. Like other postmodern work in composition as well as other disciplines, the little narratives are marked by a tension between Foucauldian determinism and human agency, showing the power of institutions to control people by controlling their literacy and the power of individuals and groups to use literacy to act either in concert with or in opposition to this power. As the little narratives make clear, literacy can oppress or resist or liberate, and the best of these studies present the simultaneity of these ideological contradictions. Taken together, these researches, as Fuery and Mansfield say of postmodernism, "remain ... implacably opposed to fixed and universal principles of meaning and value" but at the same time "promote diversity and improvement on a local, or molecular, scale" (136). In other words, the little narratives present many truths about literacy, not one Truth about it, and while they may show how to correct one injustice, they do not argue that this correction can eliminate all injustice or even a similar injustice elsewhere.

Implications

Looking at the narratives of literacy makes several issues obvious. The first is the conflicted politics of composition. One grand narrative expresses a conservative view of literacy, based on elitist notions of reading and writing and protecting the status quo. The other is leftist, ranging from mildly reformative to radically revolutionary. Skeptical of grand claims, the postmodern little narratives question both positions. Another issue that the competing narratives of literacy bring to the fore is the relations of theory and ideology. That is, the totalizing metanarratives make it clear that theories are not neutral statements merely describing phenomena, but actually promote (self -) interested world views. The studies that were used against the great leap narrative began to give us, in addition, an awareness of our own ethnocentric, class-based assumptions about literacy. The little narratives continue this process, as I realized when a graduate student reporting on Denny Taylor and Catherine Dorsey-Gaines' *Growing Up Literate: Learning from Inner-City Families* remarked, "I had no idea I could learn anything about literacy from these people."

Hence the concern of many postmodern researchers with the ethics of their research and writing, a third issue that emerges from a survey of the narratives of literacy. Examples of the self-conscious research and writing practices of such scholars can be found in Peter Mortensen and Gesa Kirsch's *Ethics and Representation in Qualitative Studies of Literacy*. Writers of little narratives typically foreground their own positionality, stating explicitly their own assumptions and biases. In addition, they often allow the voices of their subjects to be heard, more or less effectively, along with their own. The challenge is to let subjects be subjects and not turn them into objects, a charge leveled at cultural critics whose commentaries sometimes come across as condescending and disrespectful. This challenge is particularly relevant when the participants in our studies are people whose values do not coincide with those of academic researchers. An example, and indeed another issue that the literacy narratives reveal, is the problematics of analyzing and reporting on the literate and discursive practices of religious and spiritual groups.

At end of his 1986 article Faigley called for the social view of writing to pay attention to the new technologies of communication and to develop historical awareness; lessons from the literacy narratives contribute to these areas. Journals like *Computers and Composition* and books like Tharon Howard's *A Rhetoric of Electronic Communities* now examine the relations between spoken and written language which are emerging in the hybrid forms of electronic literacy. This exploration is enriched by an awareness of the literacy research, as Cynthia Selfe and Susan Hilligoss have demonstrated in their collection *Literacy and Computers*. Both the great leap criticism and the newer little narratives can serve as a corrective to the enthusiasm which sometimes causes people to argue that the supposedly neutral computer technologies will make us smarter or make us free. In addition, recent historical studies like Gere's *Intimate Practices* and Janet Cornelius' "*When I Can Read My Title Clear*"—which examine rich traditions of literacy among clubwomen at the turn of the century and African Americans during slavery—remind us to be cautious with statements about the historical relations of literacy (and orality), on the one hand, and race, class, or gender, on the other. Such works inform us that the dominant tradition is not the only one, that counter-traditions run along side, that history is usually more complex than it is presented.

In 1996, a decade after Faigley's call for a social perspective, Brandt institutionalized the connection of composition, literacy, and culture by saying, in the *Encyclopedia of Composition and Rhetoric*, that literacy is a term that now "illuminates the ways that individual acts of writing are connected to larger cultural, historical, and social and political systems" ("Literacy" 392). The little narratives of literacy can help us examine these connections, for they show, as John Trimbur has put it, "how individuals and groups engage in self-formation not as an autonomous activity but as a practice of everyday life" ("Composition" 130–31).

Works Cited

Akinnaso, Niyi. "The Literate Writes and the Nonliterate Chants: Written Language and Ritual Communication in Sociolinguistic Perspective." *Linguistics and Literacy*. Ed. William Frawley. New York: Plenum, 1982. 7–36.

Basso, Keith. Rev. of *The Domestication of the Savage Mind*, by Jack Goody. *Language in Society* 9 (1980): 72–80.

Berlin, James. *Writing Instruction in Nineteenth-Century American Colleges*. Carbondale: Southern Illinois UP, 1984.

——. *Rhetoric and Reality: Writing Instruction in American Colleges, 1900–1985*. Carbondale: Southern Illinois UP, 1987.

Berthoff, Ann E. "I. A. Richards and the Concept of Literacy." *The Sense of Learning*. Portsmouth: Boynton, 1990. 136–149.

Bizzell, Patricia. *Academic Discourse and Critical Consciousness*. Pittsburgh: U of Pittsburgh P, 1992.

——. "Arguing about Literacy." *College English* 50 (1988): 141–53.

——. "Cognition, Convention, and Certainty: What We Need to Know about Writing." *Pre/Text* 3 (1982): 213–43.

Brandt, Deborah. "Accumulating Literacy: Writing and Learning to Write in the Twentieth Century." *College English* 57 (1995): 649–668.

——. "Literacy." *Encyclopedia of Rhetoric and Composition*. Ed. Theresa Enos. New York: Garland, 1996. 392–394.

Brodkey, Linda. "'On the Subject of Class and Gender in 'The Literacy Letters.'" College English 51 (1989): 125–41.

Cornelius, Janet Duitsman. *"When I Can Read My Title Clear": Literacy, Slavery, and Religion in the Antebellum South*. Columbia: U of South Carolina P, 1991.

Daniell, Beth. "Against the Great Leap Theory of Literacy." *Pre/Text* 7 (1986): 181–93.

——. "Composing (as) Power." *CCC* 45 (1994): 238–46.

Donehower, Kim. "The Power of Literacy: How Ordinary People Understand Literacy as a Means for Social Change." CCCC, Phoenix, March 1997.

Douglas, Wallace. "Rhetoric for the Meritocracy." *English in America: A Radical View of the Profession*. Richard Ohmann. New York: Oxford UP, 1976. 97–132.

Faigley, Lester. "Competing Theories of Process: A Critique and a Proposal." *College English* 48 (1986): 527–41.

Farrell, Thomas J. "IQ and Standard English." *CCC* 34 (1983): 470–84.

Fishman, Andrea. *Amish Literacy: What and How It Means*. Portsmouth: Heinemann, 1988.

Frawley, William, ed. *Linguistics and Literacy*. New York: Plenum, 1982.

Freire, Paulo. *Pedagogy of the Oppressed*. Trans, Myra Bergman Ramos. New York: Seabury, 1970.

Fuery, Patrick and Nick Mansfield. *Cultural Studies and the New Humanities: Concepts and Controversies*. Melbourne: Oxford UP, 1997.

Gere, Anne Ruggles. *Intimate Practices: Literacy and Cultural Work in U.S. Women's Clubs, 1880–1920*. Urbana: U of Illinois P, 1997.

——. "Kitchen Tables and Rented Rooms: The Extracurriculum of Composition." *CCC* 45 (1994): 75–91.

Goody, Jack and Ian Watt. "The Consequences of Literacy," *Comparative Studies in Society and History* 5 (1963): 304–45.

——. Introduction. *Literacy in Traditional Societies*. Ed. Jack Goody. Cambridge: Cambridge UP, 1968. 1–26.

Graff, Harvey J. *The Legacies of Literacy: Continuities and Contradictions in Western Culture and Society*. Bloomington: Indiana UP, 1987.

Greenberg, Karen, Patrick Hartwell, Margaret Himley, and R. E. Stratton. "Responses to Thomas J. Farrell, 'IQ and Standard English' (with a reply by Thomas J. Farrell)." *CCC* 35 (1984): 455–78.

Halverson, John. "Havelock on Greek Orality and Literacy." *Journal of the History of Ideas* 53 (1992): 148–63.

Havelock, Eric. *Preface to Plato*. Cambridge: Harvard UP, 1963.

Heath, Shirley Brice. "Protean Shapes in Literacy Events: Ever-Shifting Oral and Literate Traditions." *Spoken and Written Language: Exploring Orality and Literacy*. Ed. Deborah Tannen. Norwood: Ablex, 1982. 91–117.

——. *Ways With Words*. New York: Cambridge UP, 1983.

——. "What No Bedtime Story Means: Narrative Skills at Home and School." *Language in Society* 11 (1982): 49–76.

Hirseh, E. D., Jr. *Cultural Literacy: What Every American Needs to Know*. Boston: Houghton, 1987.

Holzman, Michael. "A Post-Freirean Model for Adult Literacy Education." *College English* 50 (1988): 177–89.

hooks, bell. *Talking Back: Thinking Feminist, Thinking Black*. Boston: South End P, 1989.

Horsman, Jennifer. *Something in My Mind Besides the Everyday: Women and Literacy*. Toronto: Women's P, 1990.

Howard, Tharon. *A Rhetoric of Electronic Communities*. Greenwich: Ablex, 1998.

Kapitzke, Cushla. *Literacy and Religion: The Textual Politics and Practice of Seventh-Day Adventism*. Philadelphia: Benjamins, 1995.

Kintgen, Eugene R., Barry Kroll, and Mike Rose, eds. *Perspectives on Literacy*. Carbondale: Southern Illinois UP, 1988.

Killingsworth, Jimmie. "Product and Process, Literacy and Orality: An Essay on Composition and Culture." *CCC* 44 (1993): 26–39.

Lunsford, Andrea A., Helene Moglen, and James Slevin, eds. *The Right to Literacy*. New York: MLA, 1990.

Lyotard, Jean-Francois. *The Postmodern Condition: A Report on Knowledge*. Trans. Geoff Bennington and Brian Massumi. Minneapolis: U of Minnesota P, 1984.

Mortensen, Peter and Gesa E. Kirsch. *Ethics and Representation in Qualitative Studies of Literacy*. Urbana: NCTE, 1996.

Moss, Beverly J., "Creating a Community: Literacy in African-American Churches." *Literacy Across Communities*. Ed. Beverly J. Moss. Creskill: Hampton P, 1994, 147–78.

Mullen, Mark. "Postmodernism." *Encyclopedia of Rhetoric and Composition*. Ed. Theresa Enos. New York: Garland, 1996. 547–48.

Olson, David R. "From Utterance to Text: The Bias of Language in Speech and Writing." *Harvard Educational Review* 47 (1977): 257–81.

Ong, Walter J., Jr., S. J. "Literacy and Orality." *ADE Bulletin* 58 (1978): 1–7.

——. *Orality and Literacy: The Technologizing of the Word*. London: Methuen, 1982.

Radway, Janice A. *Reading the Romance: Women, Patriarchy, and Popular Literature*. Chapel Hill: U of North Carolina P, 1984.

Resnick, Daniel P., and Lauren B. Resnick. "The Nature of Literacy: An Historical Exploration." *Harvard Educational Review* 47 (1977): 370–85.

Rose, Mike. "Narrowing the Mind and Page: Remedial Writers and Cognitive Reductionism." *CCC* 39 (1988): 267–302.

———. *Lives on the Boundary*. New York: Free P. 1989.

Scribner, Sylvia, and Michael Cole. *The Psychology of Literacy*. Cambridge: Harvard UP, 1981.

Selfe, Cynthia L., and Susan Hilligoss. *Literacy and Computers: The Complications of Teaching and Learning with Technology*. New York: MLA, 1994.

Sreberny-Mohammadi, Annabelle. "Media Integration in the Third World: An Ongian Perspective." *Media, Consciousness, and Culture*. Eds. Bruce E. Gronbeck, Thomas J. Farrell, and Paul A. Soukup. Newbury Park: Sage, 1991. 133–46.

Street, Brian V. *Literacy in Theory and Practice*. New York: Cambridge UP, 1984.

———. *Social Literacies: Critical Approaches to Literacy in Development, Ethnography and Education*. New York: Longman, 1995.

Stuckey, J. Elspeth. *The Violence of Literacy*. Portsmouth: Boynton, 1991.

Swearingen, C., Jan, ed. *The Literacy/Orality Wars*, Special Issue. *Pre/Text 7* (1986). 115–218

Tannen, Deborah, ed. *Spoken and Written Language: Exploring Orality and Literary*, Norwood: Abler, 1982.

Taylor, Denny and Catherine Dorsey-Gaines. *Growing Up Literate: Learning from Inner City Families*. Portsmouth: Heinemann, 1988.

Trimbur, John. "Composition Studies: Postmodern or Popular." *Into the Field; Sites of Composition Studies*. Ed. Anne Ruggles Gere. New York: MLA, 1993. 115–32.

———. "Taking the Social Turn: Teaching Writing Post-Process." *CCC* 45 (1994): 108–18.

Walters, Keith. "Language, Logic, and Literacy." *The Right to Literacy*. Eds. Andrea A. Lunsford, Helene Moglen, and James Slevin. New York: MLA, 1990. 173–88.

West, Cornel. *Keeping Faith: Philosophy and Race in America*. New York: Routledge, 1993.

6.
LITERACY AND THE WRITING VOICE: THE INTERSECTION OF CULTURE AND TECHNOLOGY IN DICTATION
Lee Honeycutt

In the late 13th century, an interesting shift took place in the visual representation of authors within European iconography. For 4 centuries prior to this, those composing the written word were most often shown dictating their works instead of writing them, with church fathers either dictating to their own secretaries or transcribing the divine voice of God themselves. But in the late 13th century, noted church fathers such as St. Paul and St. John began appearing as writing down their own words instead of dictating. By the early 14th century, both church and secular authors were shown almost exclusively reading and writing silently (Saenger, 1982, pp. 388–389).

This change in visual representation, of course, reflects the culmination of a centuries-long shift from oral literacy to silent composing processes, the latter of which persist to this day. But as Welch (1999), Ong (1982), and others have noted, we appear to be living within a historical period in which the primacy of silent reading and writing is being contested by a "secondary orality" supported by various technologies. Among these is voice-recognition dictation software, which allows authors to speak into a headset and see their words appear instantly on the computer screen, with varying degrees of accuracy. Although currently used mostly by disabled authors or those with dire speed requirements, voice recognition has the potential to be a useful technology for bridging the spoken and written word. If so, it will take its place among a number of other emerging communication technologies designed to support the multiple literacies of the postmodern era. Looking at the long history of dictation—from its roots in classical rhetoric to today's voice-recognition software—can help us understand how shifts in current Western literacy practices are often formulated by compromises between technological intent and social and cultural constraints. That is the purpose of this article: to document historical changes in the practice of dictation that might in turn help us understand the technological and cultural mediation of voice recognition in the digital age.

To begin, I examine the history of dictation practices in late antiquity and the Middle Ages to show not only how silent writing is a fairly recent phenomenon in Western civilization but also how even slight changes in the material conditions of reading and writing altered the relationship of author to text and may do so once again should voice recognition become widely adopted in the future. In examining the history of dictation, I employ Vygotsky's (1981) historical-genetic method to demonstrate the various ways in which dictation practices have changed with technological innovation across the full spectrum of Western history. Although Vygotsky used this method to explore the origins of certain human psychological functions and their relation to signs, Haas (1999) has demonstrated its usefulness in examining the multidimensional nature of literacy practices as they intersect with mediating technologies over time: "A Vygotskian approach to the study of technology ... suggests (a) that multiple technologies for literacy exist, (b) that their history-of-use is complex and overlapping, and (c) that technology's uses are tied intrinsically to other human activities" (p. 213).

Second, I concentrate on the technological support of dictation practices—from the introduction of the typewriter in the late 19th century to the present day use of voice-recognition technology—to demonstrate how technological implementations are often affected by reigning cultural practices in ways that sometimes diverge from intended design. The study of how human actions are mediated by tools has been a hallmark of Soviet activity theory from its inception, but Cole (1996) has done much to highlight the "duality of mediation," or how tool use is constrained by past and current cultural forces:

Cultural mediation implies a mode of developmental change in which the activities of prior generations are cumulated in the present as the specifically human part of the environment. This form of development, in turn, implies the special importance of the social world in human development, since only other human beings can create the special conditions needed for development to occur, (p. 145)

As a generation that has known mostly silent writing, we might be tempted at first to dismiss computerized dictation as a technological gimmick that disrupts our embedded silent literacy practices. And we might be right. But as my cultural-historical analysis will show, dictation has often served as a useful bridge between the spoken and written word, depending on certain cultural and technological factors present in society.

In closing, I speculate on how professional communicators might use voice recognition—amid a diverse palette of other emerging communication technologies—to once again bridge these two modes of literacy. Its success, I argue, will depend largely on how well it is integrated with socially constructed rhetorical practices that are mediated by both coexisting technologies and certain social and economic factors regulating these technologies. In time, professional communicators may find voice recognition a useful literacy tool not only for harnessing the power of secondary orality but also for supporting some forms of collective authorship.

History of Dictation

Long before its use in modern business offices, dictation served as a distinct tool of literacy within the ancient world.

Dictation in Late Antiquity

As most students of rhetoric know, the ancient Greeks, along with other early societies throughout the Mediterranean, had long used sophisticated memory devices and oral delivery to transmit cultural narratives across generations. When writing was introduced, dictation served as a bridge by which people transferred information from one mode of storage to another, from their cultural memory to papyrus scrolls, much like information is being transferred today from paper to digital form. For example, some scholars have argued that the Odyssey of Homer was originally an oral composition retained in collective memory for some time before eventually being dictated into written form.[1]

But long after writing evolved in the early Mediterranean basin, orality and dictation remained important parts of the literacy landscape. For example, dictation was used as a method of book production by Roman publishers, who employed multiple scribes to jot down the dictation of a single reader, thus producing "the largest number of copies ... in the shortest time" (Skeat, 1956, p. 189). Dictation was also favored by Rome's educated class for writing letters and other short documents. According to Plutarch (1999), Julius Caesar dictated from horseback during the Gallic War, often using more than one secretary at once, and throughout his rule, he used dictation to maintain an extensive network of correspondence with friends and allies all over the city and empire (p. 316). In addition, we know from Cicero's (1978) numerous extant letters that he sometimes dictated to his slave Tiro, who in turn penned his own treatise, Notae Tironianae, about a shorthand method he developed and used.[2] But dictation was not Cicero's preferred method of composition, as we know from a letter to his brother Quintus (Cicero, 1978, p. 285).

According to Murphy (1974), responding to a letter in one's own handwriting was considered a sign of politeness in learned Roman society, due probably to the uniqueness of a personally handwritten response compared to the more widely used practice of dictation (p. 198). But despite such rules of etiquette, dictation remained a frequent social, business, and government literacy practice within the late empire—though not without its critics. Quintilian (1903), for one, cautioned against dictation, fearing it not only eradicated the editorial function of slower manual writing but also disrupted the silent reflection necessary for good writing:

> From my disapprobation of carelessness in writing, it is clearly enough seen what I think of the fine fancy of dictation; for in the use of the pen, the hand of the writer, however rapid, as it cannot keep pace with the celerity of his thoughts, allows them some respite; but he to whom we dictate urges us on, and we feel ashamed at times to hesitate, or stop, or alter, as if we were afraid to have a witness of our weakness. Hence it happens, that not only inelegant and casual expressions, but sometimes unsuitable ones, escape us, while our sole anxiety is to make our discourse connected; expressions which partake neither of the accuracy of the writer nor of the animation of the speaker; while, if the person who takes down what is dictated, prove, from slowness in writing, or from inaccuracy in reading, a hindrance, as it were, to us, the course of our thought is obstructed, and all the fire that had been conceived in our mind is dispelled by delay, or, sometimes, by anger at the offender

> ... In short, to mention once for all the strongest argument against dictation, privacy is rendered impossible by it; and that a spot free from witnesses, and the deepest possible silence, are the most desirable for persons engaged in writing, no one can doubt.
>
> (X, iii, 19–20, 22)

Such cautions aside, dictation was popular among the Romans for perhaps another reason: Their reading methods remained closely tied to a predominant orality. As a rule, Roman books and letters contained no punctuation, case distinction, or word separation, reflecting the fact that letters and syllables—not individual words—were the primary units of meaning. Reciting aloud to others or softly to themselves, Roman readers scanned the text syllable by syllable to extract meaning[3] According to Saenger (1982), Romans viewed writing as "essentially a transcription which, like modern musical notation, became an intelligible message only when it was performed orally to others or to oneself" (pp. 370–371). Thus, although the written word was an important mode of information storage and message transmission, it remained almost exclusively a means by which to recreate discursive products born into a predominantly oral world.

Dictation in the Middle Ages

As Roman prominence faded, however, the uses of dictation began to change. After the fall of the Roman Empire, dictation took on another function within a fragmented society in which literacy was often the exception rather than the rule. Instead of educated and literate Caesars, remains of the empire were sometimes ruled by illiterate barbarian kings who needed assistance in communicating their messages over vast distances if they hoped to keep their minions in line. Following the conquest of Italy by Theodoric the Ostrogoth in A.D. 489, for example, Cassidorius served as quaestor to the illiterate king and was ultimately responsible for much of the royal communication:

> A Julius Caesar or a Cicero was perfectly capable of both composition and transcription, because each man was a well-educated person ... But for a ruler like Theodoric or Charlemagne, the personal handwriting skill did not exist. No doubt the practice of verbatim dictation could still have been employed, but the comparatively low educational level of the dictating person would surely have militated against any high degree of excellence in the resulting compositions.
>
> (Murphy, 1974, p. 198)

Dictation, in such situations, was not a strict transcription of spoken words but instead an ad hoc elaboration of vocalized royal gist.

In a variety of manifestations, the act of dictation remained a popular mode of composing throughout the early Middle Ages yet was distinctly different from Roman practices. For one, there was no form of shorthand such as that used by Cicero's secretary. Instead, 12th-century authors dictated their mental prose to scribes who often jotted down edited summaries of the words they heard. Afterward, secretaries had to reconstruct the authors' intentions, resulting in an early form of collaborative writing (Saenger, 1982, pp. 381–382). Indeed, composition in the Middle Ages was a form of distributed cognition that often involved the participation of multiple minds from invention to finished product. As Carruthers (1990) pointed out, medieval composing entailed a number of distinct stages, beginning with invention, a meditative, recollective process in which composers searched their own mental inventory. The results of this search were called the res, a fleshed-out gist or rough draft of the composition that still needed editing and reworking. Following invention was compositio, in which the products of invention were used to craft a more fully formed draft called the dictamen.[4] Compositio often involved the use of waxed tablets or other correctable media, but if the author was mature and experienced, the process could be entirely mental. After the dictamen was completed, a scribe would copy it on a more permanent surface for submission to the public for commentary (Carruthers, 1990, pp. 194–195).

Although different in form from its Roman counterpart, dictation during the Middle Ages was still closely linked with a predominant orality resembling that of the Romans. The written word was slowly achieving a venerated position within the medieval world, but dictation remained the favored method of composition. This method, as Clanchy (1979) noted, sustained a gap between the material production of written works and the concept of being literate:

> A person might be able to write, yet not be considered literate ... Literacy involved being learned in Latin, whereas writing was the process of making a fair copy on parchment, which was the art of the scribe. Some authors ... did their own writing, but they are the exceptions and they distinguished that activity from composition.
>
> (p. 218)

One of the most important genres of composition during the Middle Ages was the dictated letter, which served as the foundation for the ars dictaminis, a pedagogical movement that kept rhetorical theory alive during what has traditionally been viewed as a dark period in the history of rhetoric (see Camargo, 1988, for an alternative historiography). Occurring between the early 11th and late 13th centuries, the ars dictaminis was a popular form of applied rhetoric that involved teaching the art of letter writing based on principles of Ciceronian rhetoric. Although the movement later devolved into formulaic methods that quashed all true forms of invention, it initially drew inspiration from two ancient rhetorical treatises—Cicero's De Inventione and the pseudo-Ciceronian Rhetorica ad Herennium (Patt, 1978, p. 152). Both of these standards of the ancient rhetorical canon emphasized, among other things, the extensive use of elaborate memory systems for aiding the rhetor in delivery of a speech.

Discussion of medieval dictation practices often brings up the paradox that many institutions in which dictation supposedly took place were monasteries with strict rules about maintaining silence. How could monks toiling under such rules use oral composition practices to carry out their work? As Saenger (1982) explained, most monastic orders for many centuries saw no conflict between practicing oral composition and adhering to the vow of silence:

> According to their rule, twelfth-century Cluniac monks were judged to have violated their vows of silence only when a word they spoke was not written in the text. Through oral readings and rote memorization Benedictine monks retained the biblical and patristic passages they would later use during the hours reserved for silent meditation. Oral composition was similarly not usually construed as a violation of the vow of silence. Thus, treatises on the ars dictaminis, which explained the rhythmic rules of the cursus, were composed by Cistercian monks, who lived under a rule of silence more strict than that of the Benedictines.
>
> (p. 383)

By the 14th century, however, composition practices had largely fallen silent due to a number of factors that began to take place as early as the 7th century. First of all, as Latin texts spread across Europe to the outer boundaries of the empire, they moved further and further into isolated territories of vernacular language, far removed from their original oral base. There in the hinterlands, the scriptum continua of written Roman letters proved more difficult to decipher for monastic scribes with a poor command of Latin. To compensate, authors began placing spaces between words so they could be read aloud properly.

Although it was at first received hesitantly on the Continent, this separation of text into discrete words represented a "major advance toward silent reading" (Saenger, 1982, p. 377), and during the next 3 centuries, word separation and silent reading—as well as silent writing—came to be accepted literacy practices throughout Europe. Due to a stubborn residual orality, however, the shift to silent reading and writing practices occurred so slowly over many generations that it was almost imperceptible to those living during the time (Clanchy, 1979, p. 219). For example, the composition of Latin scholastic texts shifted from dictation to silent writing relatively quickly, but texts written in Romance vernaculars, which were more closely tied to a living language, continued to be dictated for a much longer period because of their listening audience and a lack of orthographic uniformity (Saenger, 1997, p. 266). As Ong (1982) put it, "Latin had undergone a sound-sight split" (p. 113).

Although this shift in the modes of written production was reflected in changes to iconographic representations of scribes and authors during these centuries, such representations failed to capture the immense psychological changes that occurred in how authors viewed their texts:

> As a result of the new ease in writing, the author achieved a new sense of intimacy and privacy in his work. In solitude he was personally able to manipulate drafts on separate quires and sheets. He could see his manuscript as a whole, develop internal relationships, and eliminate redundancies common to the dictated literature of the twelfth century. He could also, at his leisure, easily add supplements and revisions to his text at any point before forwarding it to a scriptorium for publication.
>
> (Saenger, 1982, p. 390)

Perhaps the greatest change came from the author's holistic view of the emerging text. For centuries, dictating authors had been plagued with not being able to easily visualize what they had already dictated. As a result, they were torn between recalling what they had already dictated and what they wished to say in the future. But with the advent of silent reading and writing practices, at least one part of this cognitive memory load was obviated, allowing authors to concentrate more purely on production of what they wanted to say.

This shift in how authors viewed their texts was also at least partly responsible for a profound longitudinal change in cultural perceptions of authorship. According to Petrucci (1995), during the late Middle Ages, distinctions between dictation by "memory and voice alone, without hand or eye" and the continuatio scribendi, or continuous writing, of silent composition showed how gradual increases in autograph writing were "situated in the context of a complex and vast transformation of the intellectual professions themselves" (pp. 148–149). For example, Bonaventura da Bagnoregio observed at the time four distinct types of writers: the scriptor, who wrote the work of others, adding or changing nothing; the compilator, who wrote the work of others, making additions that are not his own; the commentator, who wrote the work of others and his own work, but only as secondary material; and the auctor, who wrote his own work and that of others, but mostly his own. Bonaventura placed this last category, which represented the "new intellectual of scholastic/university culture," at the very top of a hierarchical progression based entirely on the practice of writing, linking the scribe and the author without any break in continuity as it embraced and defined the entire panorama of possible intellectual activities within the institutional and physical framework of the operations of writing. (Petrucci, 1995, p. 149)

Yet Woodmansee (1994) observed that "while Bonaventura's auctor seems to be making a substantial (original) contribution of his own, he does so as part of an enterprise conceived collaboratively" (p. 17). In essence, the idea of individual authorship had taken root in the late Middle Ages but existed in a world of written literacy that was still predominantly oral and collaborative in nature.

As I discuss next, this germinal notion of individualized authorship took several centuries to become firmly entrenched in European culture, where it was supported not only by technological changes in the means of production and distribution but by cultural and philosophical changes that still reverberate today in professional attitudes toward writing and authorship.

The Demise of Memoria

Just as the ancients had relied on commonplaces to guide their delivery of speeches, so too did dictating authors in late antiquity and the Middle Ages use highly evolved memory systems to sustain dictation of lengthy works and to avoid the excess of copia, or redundancies, that marked much writing during this period. According to Carruthers (1990), one of the foremost authors of the Middle Ages to use mnemonic techniques during dictation was Thomas Aquinas, who regularly dictated his longer works to secretaries, sometimes using more than one scribe at a time. In his early works, Aquinas often jotted down a rough draft in a shorthand style illegible to anyone but himself, then dictated these rough notes to his secretaries. In later works, such as the Summa Theologica, however, he skipped the jotted draft altogether and dictated directly to his secretaries "as if a great torrent of truth were pouring into him from God," as one witness put it (Carruthers, 1990, p. 6). But for many authors who did not have an advanced sense of memory to guide their planning and production of text, dictation was often merely a string of off-the-cuff remarks orally transmitted to a scribe.

With the advent of silent writing, however, the distance between author and written product collapsed, allowing authors to edit out—as they composed—certain pleonasms endemic to speech and oral-based thought:

> Eliminating redundancy on a significant scale demands a time-obviating technology, writing, which imposes some kind of strain on the psyche in preventing expression from falling into its more natural patterns. The psyche can manage the strain in part because handwriting is physically such a slow process—typically about one-tenth of the speed of oral speech ... With writing, the mind is forced into a slowed-down pattern that affords it the opportunity to interfere with and reorganize its more normal, redundant processes.
> (Ong, 1982, p. 40)

Ong (1982) discussed at length the way writing restructures consciousness, and though some might label him a technological determinist for such thinking, his comparison of orality's redundancies and writing's reflective reorganization of thought focuses solely on affordances brought about by changes in the material conditions of composition. The opportunities for reflection and revision afforded by silent writing undoubtedly contributed to the decline of dictation as the primary form of composing, but other changes appear to have contributed as well, such as improvements in writing tools and the greater availability of cheaper paper.

Whatever the reasons, by the late 14th century, silent composing had largely displaced dictation, which was relegated to the emerging professional class of bureaucratic notaries. As dictation waned, the ars dictaminis also began to fade and was subsumed into a broader range of formal rhetorical pedagogy that included training in speechmaking and lectures, commentaries on the Ciceronian rhetorics, and a special 2-year course on the art of being a notary (Camargo, 1995, p. 90).

Precipitated in some part by the fading popularity of dictation and the advent of silent writing, the steady decline in the memory arts began during this period, though memoria would not be eclipsed by methods of rational empiricism for several centuries. In the 16th century, Peter Ramus would move memoria as well as invention and arrangement under the province of dialectic, leaving only style and delivery to rhetoric proper. As Welch (1999) has argued, the result was that "'style' and a narrow idea of delivery then received more emphasis and ... a more imbalanced style or language decoration gathered great power that continues today" (p. 150). The void within rhetoric caused by Ramus's division of the canons was filled during the next 2 centuries by a number of logicians and new rhetoricians whose works—including Joseph Priestley's Course of Lectures on Oratory and Criticism in 1762 and George Campbell's

Philosophy of Rhetoric in 1776—touted introspective forms of method and invention based on rational and empirical accounts of the mind (Crowley, 1990). The result, as Crowley (1990) noted, was that memory and invention moved away from their traditional moorings in collective opinion, as espoused by the ancients, to reside solely within the mind of the individual author.

Although some might argue that advances in textual storage technologies contributed in large part to the demise of memoria, Crowley (1993) believed it fell victim to three ideas that emerged within modernism, namely, the sovereignty of individual authors, language as a medium reflecting thought, and preference for the rational method as a means of invention (p. 41). Ultimately, however, memoria fell into decline from a mixture of both cultural and technological factors. Memoria, as Crowley has shown, was a socially based heuristic system reduced to an individual cognitive activity in part by certain intellectual trends within modernism. Yet recent work in activity theory has analyzed memory as not only an individual cognitive process but also a social process grounded in collective action (Scribner & Beach, 1993).

The individualizing trends of modernism may have done much to erase the traditionally collective nature of memoria, but we cannot overlook other events associated with the rise of individualism during this period. Foucault (1979) has done much to show how various trends within modernism affected what he called the "author function"—the institutional way in which certain discourses exist, circulate, and function within society over time. For Foucault, one of the primary traits of the author function is that it affects the operation of discourse differently across time and cultures, with the Middle Ages and early modernism having vastly different perceptual notions of authorship. Barthes (1977) has argued that this modern notion of individualized authorship grew out of several trends in European history at the dawn of the modern era, namely "English empiricism, French rationalism and the personal faith of the Reformation" (pp. 142–143).

Concurrent with these philosophical changes in modernism were economic and technological changes that also contributed to the concept of the individual author. It is no mere historical coincidence, for example, that the eventual demise of memoria roughly coincided with the greatest expansion of literacy technology up to that time—the printing press. As Baron (2000) has argued, the expanded distribution of written works via print eventually led to legal and economic changes in the definition of authorship, first as a legal mechanism and then as an economic one: "Authors gain[ed] increasing recognition in legal proceedings involving the disposition of their work, from being held criminally responsible to being recognized as at least original owners" (p. 65).

The centuries following the introduction of the printing press saw an explosion in the textualization of information that earlier had been transmitted through oral tradition. As Tebeaux (1997) has noted, this textualization contributed not only to the rise of individualism but also to early forms of technical writing:

> By the second decade of the seventeenth century, the expanding ontent of technical books suggested that with appropriate and sufficient knowledge, the individual could do anything—raise silkworms, bring a child into the world, repair highways, recognize and

treat disease. Knowledge acquired through schools and personal reading made the individual's horizons limitless. White oral transmission of information was limited by the individual's memory, textualized knowledge—properly written and displayed—could be read, re-read, and then used for reference. In the true spirit of Aquinas, the individual had become, by way of the text, the measure of things. By command of text man had become, as it were, master of his own destiny.

(p. 13)

Instead of vilifying Ramus for dividing the rhetorical canon, Tebeaux (1997) credited him with inspiring new forms of printed text based on visual principles for organizing and classifying arguments and information. These principles eventually led to widespread changes in typography and page design that emphasized clarity and readability. What had once been warehoused in the halls of memoria was now committed by individual authors to the printed page—in both textual and graphic form—for easy reference by individuals, who more and more read silently to themselves in isolation. During several centuries, a series of technological, economic, and intellectual forces had converged to bring the chattering literacy of late antiquity and the Middle Ages to a close. Dictation had been eclipsed by silent writing.

Technologies of the Word

The previous history of dictation has shown how even slight changes in the material conditions of writing production had a social impact on the process of composition as a literacy practice. As recent work in activity theory has demonstrated, the mediation of tools or artifacts has been overlooked in social analyses for many years, especially when it applies to production of language (Cole & Engestrom, 1993). In this section, I demonstrate how increasingly complex literacy tools developed during the next several centuries helped renew interest in dictation as an important bridge between burgeoning written literacy and the emerging concept of secondary orality. But I also show how the introduction of these technologies was often culturally mediated through existing literacy practices with roots formed in previous centuries.

Dictation and Silent Literacy

In addition to making composition more of a singular literacy practice that allowed authors to focus on removing redundancies and other oral artifacts from their emerging texts, silent reading and writing became during the Protestant Reformation extremely useful tools for formulating and communicating dissenting religious views in private. Although the printing press did much to help spread Protestant religious and political views throughout Europe, Saenger (1982) noted that silent reading and writing practices were also instrumental in spreading reformist ideas among Europe's elite, who could consume and transmit these ideas in private without immediate fear of reprisal from Rome. In addition, as silent writing helped reduce the real and psychological distance between author and page, it eliminated dependency on the labor of others. During the Middle Ages, the composing process had been a two-tiered system of literacy in which one person composed and the other transcribed. In many regards, the longer dictation persisted as a primary mode of composition, the longer written literacy remained the province only of the ruling elite, the only ones capable of affording a scribe. Once silent writing caught on, dictation was relegated to limited and specialized uses because it perpetuated this two-class system of elite author and lower-class amanuensis. Because silent composing was as cheap as the paper and pen used to write, it was much more democratic than dictation, which required a servant or hired hand, at least until supporting technologies were introduced in the 20th century.

Following its decline in the Middle Ages, dictation was used mainly by authors who either disdained the physical act of writing or were disabled from writing in a silent manner. Blind like the poet Homer many centuries before, John Milton, for example, dictated Paradise Lost to his daughters. But given the gradual spread of written literacy throughout Europe during the Renaissance, Milton's dictation practices were decidedly different from those of scribes in late antiquity and the Middle Ages. As Goody (1987) explained, Milton's dictation cannot compare to that of the Romans:

> Obviously Milton used verse forms and styles that were developed through writing; the theme itself is the creation of high literate culture, the product of a developing tradition. "Oral composition" in such a context is quite a different process from composition in a purely oral culture,
>
> (p. 92)

The difference between modern dictation and those of the ancients, then, is one mainly of context. In late antiquity and the early Middle Ages, the written word in many respects was intended to mimic the oral word that was favored by those cultures. Latin texts contained no punctuation or word divisions, making their production and reading closely tied to the predominant orality. Modern dictation practices, however, work in the opposite direction. Modern dictators use secondary orality to mimic the artifacts of an entrenched written literacy. Not only that, Milton was writing within a cultural milieu in which the notion of the individual author had firmly taken root.

Like centuries of scribes before them, Milton's daughters used only a pen to take dictation, but in the late 19th century, the invention of the typewriter helped create renewed interest in dictation for many authors. Foremost among these was Henry James, who in 1896 developed a chronic pain in his right wrist caused by long years at his writing desk. As a result, he tried dictating to a shorthand stenographer, but after growing impatient waiting for shorthand to be transcribed into text, he soon began dictating straight to a typist. This new method of composition initially raised concerns by critics about the effects on his prose style, to which James answered, "I can be trusted ... not to be simplified by any shortcut or falsified by any facility"

(Edel, 1969, p. 176). But as one of his biographers noted, stylistic differences were bound to emerge:

> Henry James writing, and Henry James dictating, were different persons. His sentences were to become, in time, elaborate—one might indeed say baroque—filled with qualifications and parentheses; he seemed often in a letter to begin a sentence without knowing what its end would be, and he allowed it to meander river-like into surprising turns and loops ... Certain indirections and qualifications had always existed. But the spoken voice was to be heard henceforth in James's prose, not only in the rhythm and ultimate perfection of his verbal music, but in his use of colloquialisms and in a more extravagant play of fancy, a greater indulgence in elaborate and figured metaphors, and in great proliferating similes.
> (Edel, 1969, pp. 176–177)

As the pain in his wrist subsided, James eventually returned to writing certain private letters by hand in the evenings. And he continued to use handwriting for composing both plays and short stories, realizing that a concise style was necessary for such compact genres. But for the remainder of his life, James composed all prose and much of his public correspondence by dictating to a typist.

The Divisions of Literacy Labor

Yet the typewriter did more than help renew interest in dictation among a few literary authors with severe cases of wrist strain. As Yates (1989) has noted, the typewriter was instrumental in the rise of a systems approach to business management that focused on efficiency and cost reduction at all levels of production. Prior to the typewriter, dictation played only a limited role in the business world, but in the 1880s, businesses began adopting the new invention on a much wider scale, and from then on, typing and stenography emerged among office workers as complementary skills for the rapid production of documents. According to Yates, the merging of these skills led to the complete separation of document composition from final production and served the efficiency goals of systems management quite well:

> By taking physical production out of the hands of those who composed the messages, stenographers and typists reduced the amount of time the highly paid executive spent on correspondence. The typewriter itself decreased the amount of less expensive clerical time taken to transcribe correspondence from dictation or from a handwritten draft. Moreover, by replacing illegible scrawls with neat, print-like text, the typewriter reduced both the time needed to read the document initially and the time needed to locate a given document in the files later. Finally, the large workforce of trained typists and secretaries helped standardize the formats and conventions for the new genres of internal written communication.
> (p. 44)

The adoption of dictation machines in the early 20th century created an even more distinct disconnect between the dictated word and its physical manifestation. The early Ediphone and Dictaphone machines of the late 19th century had housed the recorder and player in a single unit; however, in the early 20th century, equipment manufacturers began producing two separate machines, one used by executives for recording dictation and a second used by the transcriptionist (Morton, 2001). Dictation had always created a gap between composition and written production, but this new line of dictation machines separated the two even further, transforming the spoken words of corporate executives into material artifacts that could be replayed asynchronously by workers in the typing pool. Author and scribe no longer had to be present in the same room, which as you will recall, was one of Quintilian's (1903) reasons for eschewing dictation: "We feel ashamed at times to hesitate, or stop, or alter, as if we were afraid to have a witness of our weakness" (X, iii, 19). Transcriptionists were still needed to type recorded words onto paper, but dictating authors were now able to compose in private. With this division of labor came a somewhat greater textual responsibility on the part of the originating author. Scribes and dictators had formed a system of distributed cognition during late antiquity and the Middle Ages, but with the distancing quality of this new dictation technology, transcribers served less as collaborators in the writing process and more as conduits to the final textual product. Transcribers undoubtedly performed some grammar and spell-checking functions of the general skills secretary, but the dictating author was now more responsible for managing the form and content of the emerging text.

For a number of reasons, though, Dictaphones were never as universally adopted as typewriters. First, unlike the typewriter, the Dictaphone was designed and marketed for use solely by executives as a way to achieve even greater efficiency because secretaries could spend more time typing instead of taking shorthand. Second, as Lupton (1993) noted, some executives were resistant to the methods of systems management:

Executives often have resisted relinquishing their personal assistants, who are a sign of status as well as a source of consistent, customized help. Likewise, executive secretaries pride themselves on the specialized knowledge and range of skills involved in working with one "boss." (p. 53)

Third, the closely supervised nature of the transcription pool and the repetitive boredom of typing letters made the pools unpopular environments, and those who were later promoted to private secretary positions resisted using the Dictaphone because it was a symbol of lower-class employment. Generally, transcriptionists also disliked using the Dictaphone because the recordings were hard to understand and the headsets were uncomfortable (Morton, 2001).

The technological transformation of office work also helped create a sexual division of office labor that has persisted to this day. Prior to the Civil War, clerks who performed office work had been overwhelmingly male. But during the war, women came forward to fill emergency labor shortages in some offices, and between the advent of the typewriter and the beginning of the Great Depression, the number of women filling clerical positions continued to rise, encouraged to some extent by the advent of the typewriter and Dictaphone. In 1880, 40% of the stenographers and typists were women; by 1900, more than 75% were women, and by 1930, almost 95% were women (Davies, 1982, pp. 79–80). Although Lupton (1993) and Yates (1989) believed the typewriter's increasing popularization helped boost the number of women working in business offices, Lubar (1993) felt the typewriter played only a minor role in the sexual division of office work during this period:

> The growing number of educated women looking for work in the late 1800s was a more important factor, as were managerial decisions to establish a division of labor in clerical work. Women who acquired the specialized skill needed to run the machine fit neatly into the new subdivided structure of work. Because it was a new machine, with no tradition of either a male or a female operator, the typewriter allowed women to come into the office without appearing to take over men's work. By 1920 office work was being done largely by women. Women office workers were, for the most part, young, unmarried, and living with their families. Most were from lower-middle-class backgrounds. They were under strict supervision at work, and were usually expected to quit when they got married,
>
> (p. 36)

Even though office work was often monotonous, the female office worker was portrayed in popular literature and film during the first part of the 20th century as an exciting urban adventurer; the "flapper" of the 1920s, for example, was most often a typist (Lupton, 1993, p. 45). Some postcards from this period even portrayed female clerical workers as seductive "vamps" engaged in affairs with their employers (Fine, 1990, pp. 108–109). Following the Great Depression, advertisements often portrayed the typewriter as being operated solely by women and as mediating between the active decision making of male bosses and the passive service of female secretaries, who were seen as mere extensions of the machine's functionality. According to Lupton (1993), only the introduction of personal computers in the 1980s began to dissociate the keyboard from "women's work" and the female body; as a result, "young men now are encouraged to learn touch-typing in high school, enabling them to operate computer keyboards not only as managers and technicians but as secretaries and 'temps'" (p. 48).

Looking closely at trends in this technological history of dictation, we can see that many of the beliefs driving the systems approach to management during the late 19th and early 20th centuries had their roots in some of the same modernist concepts that Crowley (1993) felt were responsible for the demise of memoria: faith in rationalism, the sovereignty of individual authors, and adherence to the scientific method. In their efforts to wring maximum efficiency out of every single worker, proponents of systems management introduced technological supports for dictation that disrupted the traditionally collaborative relationship between dictator and scribe. Many executives and secretaries resisted such technological initiatives because of entrenched cultural attitudes toward both their work activities and their social position as workers. Male executives were not inclined to give up their personal secretaries, who were both status symbols and close collaborators. Secretaries resisted the change because as a transcriptionist, they were relegated to lower-class status within the firm and restricted to boring, repetitive work, often for multiple bosses; as a personal secretary, on the other hand, they were assigned to only one executive and usually worked on multiple tasks throughout the day. Although technologically enhanced dictation was practiced in many larger firms with separate typing pools, dictation machines were never used by a critical mass of companies because their very use went against the prevailing cultural practices of office work, some of which were inherited from literacy practices extending back several centuries. Despite modernism's emphasis on individual authorship, dictation in professional communication apparently was still largely a social act.

Dictation and the Future of Professional Communication

Despite advances in audiotape technology that made dictation easier to record and play back than it was with the wax cylinders and wires of earlier dictation machines, the use of dictation equipment in professional settings never reached the levels hoped for by early designers. At the peak of the Dictaphone's popularity in the early 1920s, only about 20,000 machines were sold each year compared to more than 500,000 typewriters sold annually (Morton, 2001). During the 1950s, the Dictaphone Company's audiotape systems became synonymous with dictation equipment and were used during the next three decades by a number of large corporations supporting typing pools. In response, Tebeaux (1983) suggested adding dictation training to the technical writing curriculum to better prepare students for the technological environment that awaited them in the workforce. She argued that learning to use dictation to compose would help students not only to produce first drafts more efficiently but also to produce writing that was more speech-like and, in the long run, to become more fluent writers. But Tebeaux could not have predicted that many of the centralized word-processing centers at that time would be gone in just a few short years. As personal computers reached the corporate desktop in the late 1980s, dictation and typing pools began to fall by the wayside. Individuals who had used dictation to compose began switching over to word processors because they were easy to use for composing, revising, and storing electronic documents. For example, Howard Gardner (personal communication, June 6, 2002), author of the theory of multiple intelligences, had dictated most of his academic work for years prior to this time, but when word processors came into vogue, he stopped dictating altogether. After the 1980s, dictation and transcription systems seem to have prospered only in limited areas of professional communication in which speed of composition is important, such as in legal and medical communication.

In the mid-1980s, voice-recognition technology began to emerge in the commercial market, and Spooner (1988) soon noted how this technology, by using the spoken word to quickly produce a visual representation of the emerging text, combined the primary benefits of dictation machines and word processors. Although dictating authors had relied for centuries on memory to guide the production of text, they were able to access their text only through scribal read out. With voice-recognition technology came perhaps the greatest material change in the production of dictated documents—the ability to draw instantaneously on previously produced text. At least one study (Reece & Gumming, 1996) has suggested this technology may actually lessen the need for preproduction planning when dictating,

The early voice-recognition systems that emerged in the mid-1980s were clumsy, inaccurate, and awkward because they were based on discrete speech recognition models in which authors had to pause between every word for the system to parse their speech. By 1994, researchers had developed continuous speech recognition models that allowed dictators to speak at a normal conversational pace, with slightly higher recognition accuracy rates. But in a study of such systems, Karat, Halverson, Horn, and Karat (1999) found that novices often got caught in a repeating cascade of errors because they tried to correct recognition inaccuracies using speech commands whereas experienced users tended to rely on keyboarding to make such corrections. The novices quickly realized that errors were often related to the quality of their speech, yet they seemed unable to sense these speech-related errors as easily as the errors they made during touchtyping. As a result, the novices either constantly monitored the screen for errors or relied more heavily on proofreading to find them.

If recognition inaccuracies can be held to a tolerable level in the future—either through technical advances or user training—then voice-recognition technology may have important impacts on professional communication, depending on a number of factors. As Bolter and Grusin (1999) have argued, new digital technologies are more than just technical artifacts; they "constitute networks or hybrids that can be expressed in physical, social, aesthetic, and economic terms. Introducing a new media technology does not mean simply inventing new hardware and software, but rather fashioning (or refashioning) such a network" (p. 19). Although technical improvements will likely be made, we should expect, given our knowledge about the history of dictation, that the future role of voice recognition in the writing process will be mediated by coexisting communication technologies and by such cultural factors as attitudes toward individual authorship and the prevalence of oral modes of literacy.

The Mediation of Competing and Companion Technologies

The keyboard, of course, is as old as the typewriter itself, but the typewriter did not become a ubiquitous writing instrument overnight. In fact, the invention was largely ignored when first introduced in the late 19th century. E. Remington & Sons, a gun, sewing machine, and farm implement manufacturer, introduced the first commercially viable typewriter in the United States in 1874. But the company had difficulty selling the invention because of poor marketing and because few people could type faster than they could write in cursive hand (Baron, 2000, p. 201). Faced with poor sales, Remington eventually sold the invention to one of its sales agents, William Wyckoff, who began an aggressive marketing campaign and opened typing schools throughout the country to train clerks in how to use it. By the late 1880s, touch-typing techniques using all 10 fingers had been developed, and speed-typing contests were held on a regular basis, with winners soon breaking the 100-word-per-minute mark. Without Wyckoff's orchestrated marketing and training, the typewriter might have languished even longer before people saw its utility as a literacy tool. Even when it became popular, most people used it as a scribal tool for transcription and duplication, not as a direct tool of authoring, as we use computers in the digital age.

Today, keyboarding is such a popular literacy skill that we can hardly imagine voice recognition displacing it anytime soon. Even simple attempts to replace the inefficient QWERTY keyboard arrangement—developed by inventor Christopher Sholes to prevent typebars from jamming on his early typewriters—with the more efficient Dovarak arrangement have met with stiff resistance. As the experienced users in the study by Karat et al. (1999) demonstrated, voice recognition and keyboarding at this stage of development seem to work best as complementary technologies, allowing a writer to quickly produce a rough draft via speech and then correct errors and revise the document using the keyboard. But as Baron (2000) has pointed out, the "overriding production issue through the ages has been speed" (p. 198). And perhaps accuracy too. If word recognition accuracy increases to the point at which users can consistently produce clean drafts faster than they can with keyboarding, then voice recognition has a chance of becoming a widely adopted literacy tool in the corporate workplace. If it does not, voice recognition, for the foreseeable future, will be adopted mostly by disabled people. A person who types 120 words per minute is unlikely to consider voice recognition—especially with its initially poor accuracy rates—as an alternative to keyboarding.

You can, however, achieve fairly high recognition accuracy rates—but only if you make a concerted effort to improve your pronunciation and diction and speak in continuous phrases so that the computer can parse your speech correctly. Yet few people today seem accustomed to composing text in fluent, continuous sentences, whether orally or with a keyboard. For many, word processing has promoted a style of writing in which people test out phrases on the screen and then immediately revise them before moving forward with composing. In a recent study of 34 students using voice-recognition technology (Honeycutt, 2004), I found students had an average accuracy rate of 94% when reading a prepared text to check the accuracy of their voice models; however, their accuracy rates began to plummet when they began composing actual essays. In poststudy interviews, most students cited recognition errors as their greatest obstacle in using the program, and many reported that voice recognition interfered with their normal style of writing in which they type out a few rough phrases or sentences and then revise before moving on to the next section. What this study clearly demonstrates is that achieving acceptable recognition accuracy entails much practice, almost to the exclusion of using the keyboard. Few people with embedded keyboarding skills will take the time for such practice unless they are convinced that it will increase the speed with which they are able to compose. But because of the initially low accuracy rates of voice recognition, the time saved using it to compose may be offset by the extra time spent proofreading and revising for recognition errors. Proofreading, of course, is necessary in keyboarding as well, but because of homonyms, voice-recognition technology might always require extremely close proofreading.

Keyboarding, however, is not the only input technology with which voice recognition will have to compete. In addition to speed and accuracy, people adopt such technologies because of convenience. Many technology companies, for example, are manufacturing input devices that draw on the tradition of handwriting. Personal digital assistants (PDAs) and the newer tablet PCs have a digital stylus to help users input data. Although convenient in some social situations in which keyboarding might be awkward, these input devices are considerably slower than keyboarding and in some situations can be just as inaccurate as voice recognition. Most support optional keyboards as a result.

We also cannot overlook the convergent possibilities of the cell phone. Already, digital audio recorders, such as the Olympus DS-3000®, can be used to replay prerecorded dictation sessions through a desktop voice-recognition program such as Dragon's NaturallySpeaking® or IBM's ViaVoice®. Although digital recorders do not provide external representation of text, such recording technology may one day appear in future versions of the cell phone with small screens for immediate textual representation. Currently, cell phone users can perform extremely accurate dictation, albeit with a human touch, using a program such as Dial Dictate®, which allows people to phone their dictation into a centralized recording server. The digital audio files are then sent to office personnel for transcription.

Although I hesitate to make any concrete predictions about future technology use for fear of being wrong, I can easily envision a future in which all three types of input technology—keyboarding, voice, and stylus-coexist for the professional communicator who will learn to switch back and forth between them based on tacit rules of speed, accuracy, and convenience. Learning to move from one to another with fluency and grace may take time, but digital composition tools of the future will almost certainly allow us to transform voice to text when we need it. Whether we use such tools with regularity, however, may be influenced by factors other than technology.

Attitudes Toward Authorship

In their critique of Romantic notions of authorship, Barthes (1977) and Foucault (1979) focused most of their attention on perceptions of individual authors within the field of literary criticism and not on authors within more mundane fields such as journalism, the sciences, and professional communication. Within such fields, collaborative authoring has flourished for quite some time, as Lunsford and Ede (1990) documented in their examination of collaborative writing practices. In exposing the myth of singular authorship, Lunsford and Ede showed how the "constructed nature of authorship—and challenges to the traditional concept—appear in many contemporary sources in the sciences and humanities, in corporations and in libraries" (pp. 101–102).

Still, professional communication does occur within a culture that generally prizes individual authorship, particularly as it is legally manifested in the concept of intellectual property. Although modern copyright law has evolved to support individual authorship, it has paid little attention to collective authoring in its many forms. As Jaszi (1994) has noted, "At base ... the law is not so much systematically hostile to works that do not fit the individualistic model of Romantic 'authorship' as it is uncomprehending of them" (p. 38). Yet many legal scholars and literacy theorists are beginning to speculate about how this emphasis on individual authorship is being changed by the advent of modern communication technologies. Although this impact is often portrayed in the media as a battle between the recording industry and those who download digital audio files off the Internet, it ultimately has much broader significance in protections for individual authors and future recognition of collective forms of authorship. Woodmansee (1994), for one, believed that communication technologies are hastening the death of the individual author myth in Western culture:

> As the collaborative nature of contemporary research and problem-solving fosters multiple authorship in more and more spheres, electronic technology is hastening the demise of the illusion that writing is solitary and originary. Even in the still relatively primitive applications that are widely available ... the computer is dissolving the boundaries essential to the survival of our modern fiction of the author as the sole creator of unique, original works... In a variety of ways, electronic communi-cation seems to be assaulting the distinction between mine and thine that the modern authorship construct was designed to enforce.
> (pp, 25–26)

Woodmansee (1994) referred primarily to interactive bulletin boards and annotated electronic texts, seeing them as analogous to the Renaissance commonplace book, in which the compiler "composed, transcribed, commented on, and reworked the writings of others—all in apparent indifference to the identity of their originators and without regard to ownership" (p. 27). In this regard, electronic technology might easily be seen as helping to revive the collective sense of memoria on which dictation so relied during the Middle Ages. Whether the collective nature of these technologies is any match for the powerful economic forces supporting copyright law and its monetary protection of individual authors remains to be seen.

But even if our composing memories become less individual and more collective, either through technical or social means, certain features of voice-recognition technology might prevent its use from being the collaborative effort that dictation was in past eras. In the technology's current state, accurate recognition rates depend on quiet environments without background noise; contrast that with a collaborating author's ability to type, as primary scribe, onto a projected computer screen during a noisy group invention session. Replicating such a scenario with voice recognition would be difficult. Just as the Dictaphone turned collaborating scribes into mere transcriptionists during the early 20th century, voice recognition in its present state would tend to squelch the contributions of copresent collaborators and render primary responsibility for composing to the dictating author. In addition, at present the program's recognition of the dictating voice stream is tied to an individual voice model that is constructed when first using the program. Thus, those who have not created such a model during initialization are excluded from dictating; in contrast, keyboarding is open to anyone who has learned to type. Such limitations present serious impediments to the often acoustically messy work of copresent collaborative authoring.

Voice recognition could more easily be used, however, in distributed forms of collaboration in which contributors might dictate sections of a document or report at their private workstations and then e-mail the resulting text to persons responsible for primary revision and editing. Or individuals might even dictate their section of a report to a portable digital audio recorder and then e-mail the audio file to the primary editor, who could run it through a voice-recognition program containing a model of the contributor's voice, Such centralized systems are already being used in medical transcription and may eventually be used in professional communication as well.

Such is the paradoxical nature of voice-recognition technology in its present state. The ability of this technology to decipher the human voice stream is so tenuous that it requires a physical isolation that is unnecessary for silent writers using a pen or keyboard. Future manifestations of the technology may lessen some of this need for acoustical isolation, but at present, voice-recognition technology seems to trap writers in the very Romantic garrets from which so many are eager to free them.

The Effects of Secondary Orality

As Ong (1982) and others have argued, our society appears to be entering a historical period in which the primacy of silent reading and writing is being contested by a secondary orality supported by various technologies. Few would contest the fact that television, radio, and the telephone have done much during the past century to displace the printed word as the focal point of Western literacy. Even written forms of professional communication seem to be more and more speech-like, especially as they are written in permeable electronic formats. As Baron (2000) has shown, most styles of English writing—with the exception of 18th-century formal prose—have taken a decidedly conversational tone, especially as literacy has increased:

In the nineteenth century, mass schooling reinforced the growth of popular literacy that had begun to emerge in the eighteenth century, and the more oral, accessible style of middle-class novels and short stories became the norm. These trends have continued ever since, (p. 77)

Past literacy researchers tended to view speech and writing as dichotomous forms of communication, but many linguists today (Biber, 1988; Chafe, 1985; Tannen, 1982) instead see them as polar ends of a continuum of various genres exhibiting elements of both modes. Dictation seems best situated along such a continuum at a point closer to writing than to speech, which has little in common with dictation in terms of context and purpose. With the exception of public speaking, speech is primarily interactive orality in the presence of others whereas dictation, in its most frequent form, is autonomous writing produced via the spoken word. Some aspects of written voice may be influenced by the act of speech dictation, but for the most part, dictation is a distinct form of writing and not a form of speech, at least for mature writers. Dictation today emulates a strong legacy of written literacy.

We cannot ignore, however, the fact that modern dictation takes place within a society that is quickly being dominated by oral forms of communication. The phenomenal rise of the cell phone as a tool of professional communication is testament to a technologized orality that seems to know no spatial or temporal bounds. But as Ong (1982) noted, secondary orality is decidedly different from the orality of the ancients because it is supported in so many ways by an underlying textual literacy. Although many may prize the convenience and speed of the cell phone, professional communicators still treasure the opportunities for reflection, thoroughness, and syntactical economy that writing affords. That may be why e-mail remains the most popular communication tool within many organizations; at Microsoft, for example, day-to-day communication between workers takes place predominately via e-mail, with very little occurring via telephone (Brown & Duguid, 2000). E-mail may have many speech-like qualities due to our secondary orality, as Baron (2000) noted, but it also provides us with opportunities for reflection and revision traditionally afforded by silent writing.

Voice recognition appears poised to take advantage of both types of literacy. Potentially, it can draw on the oral literacy skills so dominant in our society to fashion forms of textual literacy still treasured for their organization and economy of expression. Its future adoption may depend on how much organizations value the interplay between speech and text and on workplace variables such as convenience, accuracy, and speed. For example, two professions in which dictation is often used today—law and medicine—seem to value dictation for its convenience in noting ideas, writing correspondence, and documenting client data on the fly during hurried parts of the workday. Both professions currently hire extensive administrative staff to transcribe this dictation from audio to text, but voice recognition is beginning to make inroads into both professions as a way of reducing labor costs. The leading voice-recognition program, Dragon's NaturallySpeaking®, offers versions of the software with recognition vocabularies specialized for each profession. Such programs have been adopted by a number of physicians during the past few years, and some hospitals have initiated voice-recognition programs into their larger work systems. Massachusetts General Hospital in Boston, for example, adopted a voice-recognition system in 1998 and was able to achieve annual savings of U.S. $530,000 and decrease report throughput times by 50% (Antiles, Couris, Schweitzer, Rosenthal, & Da Silva, 2000).

But two separate studies comparing voice-recognition software and human transcription services came to different conclusions. In their comparison of two emergency room physicians who each used one of the two systems, Zick and Olsen (2001) found that voice-recognition charts were produced faster and with almost the same accuracy as those produced with transcription. Al-Aynati and Chorneyko (2003), on the other hand, found a greater disparity in accuracy rates in their study of the two types of systems used in a hospital pathology department. Transcription services had significantly higher accuracy rates than did voice recognition, and the time needed to revise transcribed reports was about half that of the voice-recognition reports. Despite these differences, however, they concluded that voice recognition would be commonly used in pathology departments in the future. At present, the medical profession seems on the cusp of adopting voice-recognition systems wholesale even though accuracy is a continuing concern. In this particular context, voice recognition could have fatal consequences if dictated reports are not carefully proofread for recognition errors. Labor and confidentiality issues complicate the picture, and Weber (2003) has described two competing visions of how dictation might be used in the medical profession's future. One involves a high-tech scenario in which all but a few older physicians use a host of mobile devices and input methods—including touch screen and both speech and handwriting recognition—to develop electronic health records from empirically refined templates and other codified input fields. In the other, low-tech, scenario, many physicians resist these new technology systems because they impede their traditional work flows and interactions with patients and use templates that limit the physician's freedom of expression. The future is often difficult to predict, but Weber believed that by 2006, the medical transcription industry will resemble a combination of these competing visions.

Even if recognition errors were completely eradicated, voice recognition's widespread adoption might rely more on whether an organization values conversations and other forms of oral literacy and is willing to support voice-recognition technology as a result. In organizations such as Microsoft, where most professional transactions take place via the embedded textual technology of keyboarding, voice recognition seems to have less chance of prospering than it does in, say, the medical profession. In addition, the nature of orality itself may hamper the adoption of voice recognition. As Shneiderman (2000) has argued, voice recognition has failed to be adopted widely beyond the disabled community because vocalization itself disrupts problem solving in general as both cognitive skills are handled by the same part of the brain. His argument, however, rests on theories about parts of the brain being dedicated to single mental functions and does not take into account the possibility of multiple forms of literacy in which some people, for example, might be more gifted speakers than others. Shneiderman's argument may hold true for many steeped in the fairly recent Western tradition of silent reading and writing, but those with developed oral literacy skills may find voice recognition an attractive alternative.

The embedded nature of silent writing itself may also be key to the technology's future adoption. If a new generation of young students is offered a choice of using either voice recognition or keyboarding or both, what will their decisions be, and what effect will they have on our concept of written literacy? Such a question might bring forth visions of future classrooms full of chattering verbal writers explicating their invention strategies with a combined decibel level rivaling that of the nearest airport. But as I mentioned earlier, the technical requirements of voice recognition may ensure its private use because background noise can interfere with the accuracy of word recognition. Unlike dictation prior to the 20th century, we might expect voice recognition to be a private literacy technology. We once thought that of the telephone, but as proven by the existence of aurally mesmerized cell phone users roaming the public commons, nothing is certain in our exploding digital world. It does not take much imagination to envision future students sitting on park benches or walking down the sidewalk while dictating e-mail or research papers into a portable digital audio recorder for the computer to transcribe later. As I mentioned, such devices already exist. If public dictation becomes common, how will we distinguish these writers from the disturbed who are simply mumbling or talking to themselves? Our society has no taboo against locking yourself in a room for hours and writing silently on paper or screen. But we definitely consider it odd if you lock the door and start talking to yourself. Lewis (1999), a novelist who uses voice recognition regularly, said that he closes his study windows for this very reason:

> Weather permitting, I usually write with the windows open, but since I've started dictating, I've closed them because the idea of a passerby listening in is as horrifying as the idea of a reader looking over my shoulders, I wonder, too, sometimes if any of my neighbors can hear me engaged in the apparently insane process of talking to myself for hours on end.
> (p. 86)

If voice recognition eventually becomes a popular mode of writing production, we may find ourselves debating what are acceptable limits for public oral composition, much as we discuss the etiquette of holding cell phone conversations in public areas. With voice recognition, invention may become too much of a social act—though that never seemed much of a problem for the ancients.

Notes

1 This thesis was first proposed during the 1930s by Milman Parry, whose thinking influenced a generation of scholars thereafter (Thomas, 1992, p. 12). For further explorations of this theme, see Kirk (1976) and Goody (1987). For a recent reassessment of such claims, see Janko (1998).
2 According to Pitman (1891), Cicero was actually the inventor of this shorthand method, which was later expanded on by Seneca and Cyprian, the bishop of Carthage. The treatise is extant but according to Pitman remained dormant in European libraries between the 5th and 15th centuries.
3 Arguments by Saenger (1997) and others that the Greeks and Romans were largely unfamiliar with silent reading practices have been disputed in recent scholarship. Gavrilov (1997), for example, traced the lineage of this argument through several sources and argued it stems from a selective reading of the Confessions of St. Augustine, who remarked wondrously about seeing St. Ambrose reading silently to himself. Burnyeat (1997), in turn, cited a passage from Ptolemy in which the philosopher discussed the role that silent reading plays in study and contemplation. In an older article, Knox (1968) discussed the limited use of silent reading in ancient Greece.
4 Murphy (1974) noted that; "the precise etymology of the medieval Latin word dictamen has not yet been traced, but it seems fair to conclude that it is derived from the classical Latin verb dicto, dktare because of the connection between 'dictation' and letters which were dictated. Again, the term itself reveals a concern for the oral-written relationship" (p. 195)

References

Al-Aynati, M. M., & Chorneyko, K. A. (2003). Comparison of voice-automated transcription and human transcription in generating pathology reports. Archives of Pathology and Laboratory Medicine, 127, 721–725.
Antiles, S., Couris, J., Schweitzer, A., Rosenthal, D., & Da Silva, R. Q. (2000). Project planning, training, measurement and sustainment: The successful implementation of voice recognition. Radiology Management, 22, 18–31.
Baron, N. S. (2000). *Alphabet to email: How written English evolved and where it's heading.* London: Routledge Kegan Paul.
Barthes, R. (1977). The death of the author. In S. Heath (Ed.), *Image, music, text* (pp. 142–148). New York: Hill and Wang.
Biber, D. (1988). *Variation across speech and writing.* New York: Cambridge University Press.

Bolter, J. D., & Grusin, R. (1999). *Remediation: Understanding new media.* Cambridge, MA: MIT Press.

Brown, J. S., & Duguid, P. (2000). *The social life of information.* Boston: Harvard Business School Press.

Burnyeat, M. F. (1997). Postscript on silent reading. Classical Quarterly, 47, 74–76.

Camargo. M. (1988). Toward a comprehensive art of written discourse: Geoffrey of Vinsauf and the ars dictaminis. Rhetorica, 6, 167–194.

Camargo. M. (1995). Between grammar and rhetoric: Composition teaching at Oxford and Bologna in the late Middle Ages. In W. B. Horner (Ed.), *Rhetoric and pedagogy: Its history and practice* (pp. 83–94). Mahwah, NJ: Lawrence Erlbaum.

Carruthers, M. J. (1990). *The book of memory: A study of memory in medieval culture.* Cambridge, UK: Cambridge University Press.

Chafe, W. L. (1985). Linguistic differences produced by differences between speaking and writing. In D. R. Olson, N. Torrance, & A. Hildyard (Eds.), Literacy, language, and learning (pp. 105–123). London: Cambridge University Press.

Cicero. (1978). *Cicero's letters to his friends* (Vol. 2, D. R. S. Bailey, Trans.). New York: Penguin.

Clanchy, M. T. (1979). From memory to written record: England 1066–1307. London: Arnold.

Cole, M. (1996). *Cultural psychology: A once and future discipline.* Cambridge, MA: Belknap.

Cole, M., & Engestrom, Y. (1993). A cultural-historical approach to distributed cognition. In G. Salomon (Ed.), *Distributed cognitions: Psychological and educational considerations* (pp. 1–46). New York: Cambridge University Press.

Crowley, S. (1990). *The methodical memory: Invention in current-traditional rhetoric.* Carbondale: Southern Illinois University Press.

Crowley, S. (1993). Modern rhetoric and memory. In J. F. Reynolds (Ed.), *Rhetorical memory and delivery: Classical concepts for contemporary composition and communication* (pp. 31–44). Hillsdale, NJ: Lawrence Erlbaum.

Davies, M. W. (1982). *Woman's place is at the typewriter: Office work and office workers 1870–1930.* Philadelphia: Temple University Press.

Edel, L. (1969), *The life of Henry James: The master (1901–1916).* New York: Avon.

Fine, L. M. (1990). *The souls of the skyscraper: Female clerical workers in Chicago, 1870–1930.* Philadelphia: Temple University Press.

Foucault, M. (1979). What is an author? In J. V. Harari (Ed.), *Textual strategies: Perspectives in post-structuralist criticism* (pp. 141–160). Ithaca, NY: Cornell University Press.

Gavrilov, A. K. (1997). *Techniques of reading in classical antiquity.* Classical Quarterly, 47, 56–73.

Goody, J. (1987). *The interface between the written and the oral.* New York: Cambridge University Press.

Haas, C. (1999). *On the relationship between old and new technologies. Computers and Composition,* 16, 209–228.

Honeycutt, L. (2004). *The role of planning in writing with voice recognition software.* Unpublished manuscript.

Janko, R. (1998). *The Homeric poems as dictated texts.* Classical Quarterly, 48, 1–13,

Jaszi, P. (1994). On the author effect: Contemporary copyright and collective creativity. In M. Woodmansee & P. Jaszi (Eds.), *The construction of authorship: Textual appropriation in law and literature* (pp. 29–56). Durham, NC: Duke University Press.

Karat, C., Halverson, C, Horn, D., & Karat, J. (1999). Patterns of error and correction in large vocabulary continuous speech recognition systems. In *Proceedings of the SIGCHI*

Conference on Human Factors in Computing Systems (pp. 568–575). Pittsburgh: ACM Press.

Kirk, G. S. (1976). *Homer and the oral tradition.* Cambridge, UK: Cambridge University Press.

Knox, B. M. W. (1968). *Silent reading in antiquity.* Greek, Roman, and Byzantine Studies, 9, 421–435.

Lewis, J. (1999, April/May). How to kill your keyboard. *Civilization*, 6, 84–87.

Lubar, S. (1993). *Infoculture: The Smithsonian book of information age inventions.* Boston: Houghton Mifflin,

Lunsford, A., & Ede, L, (1990). *Singular texts/plural authors: Perspectives on collaborative writing.* Carbondale: Southern Illinois University Press.

Lupton, E. (1993). *Mechanical brides; Women and machines from home to office.* New York: Princeton Architectural Press.

Morton, D. L., Jr. (2001). Men, women, and sound: The history of the office dictation machine. Retrieved May 27, 2003, from http://www.recording-history.org/HTML/men_womenl.htm

Murphy, J. J. (1974). *Rhetoric in the Middle Ages: A history of rhetorical theory from Saint Augustine to the Renaissance.* Berkeley: University of California Press.

Ong, W. J. (1982). *Orality and literacy: The technologizing of the word.* New York: Routledge Kegan Paul.

Patt, W. D. (1978). The early ars dictaminis as response to a changing society. *Viator*, 9, 133–155.

Petrucci, A. (1995). *Writers and readers in medieval Italy.* New Haven, CT: Yale University Press.

Pitman, I. (1891). *A history of shorthand* (3rd ed.), London: Pitman & Sons.

Plutarch, (1999). *Roman lives: A selection of eight Roman lives* (R. Waterfield, Trans.). Oxford, UK: Oxford University press.

Quintilian, (1903). *Institutes of oratory: Or, education of an orator* (Vol. 2, J. S. Watson, Trans.). London: Bell and Sons.

Reece, J. E., & Cumming, G. (1996). Evaluating speech-based composition methods: Planning, dictation, and the listening word processor. In C. M. Levy & S. E. Ransdell (Eds.), *The science of writing: Theories, methods, individual differences, and applications* (pp. 361–380). Mahwah, NJ: Lawrence Erlbaum.

Rehr, D. (n.d.). It's the machine dictators love. Yesterday's office. Retrieved March 2, 2003, from http://www.yesterdaysoffice.com/index.cfm?fuseaction=ShowArticle&articleid=3

Saenger, P. (1982). Silent reading: Its impact on late medieval script and society. *Viator*, 13, 367–414.

Saenger, P. (1997). *Space between words: The origins of silent reading.* Stanford, CA: Stanford University Press.

Scribner, S., & Beach, K. (1993). An activity theory approach to memory. *Applied Cognitive Psychology*, 7, 185–190.

Shneiderman, B. (2000). The limits of speech recognition. *Communications of the ACM*, 43(9), 63–65.

Skeat, T. C. (1956). The use of dictation in ancient book production. *Proceedings of the British Academy*, 42, 179–208.

Spooner, M. (1988). Dictating to the machine: Voice activated computer technology. *English Education*, 20, 109–115.

Tannen, D. (1982). The oral/literate continuum in discourse. In D. Tannen (Ed.), *Spoken and written language: Exploring orality and literacy* (pp. 1–16). Norwood, NJ: Ablex.

Tebeaux, E. (1983). Keeping technical writing relevant (or, how to become a dictator). *College English*, 45, 174–183.

Tebeaux, E. (1997). *The emergence of a tradition: Technical writing in the English Renaissance*, 1475–1640. Amityville, NY: Baywood.

Thomas, R. (1992). *Literacy and orality in ancient Greece*. New York: Cambridge University Press.

Vygotsky, L. S. (1981). The genesis of higher mental functions. In J. V. Wertsen (Ed.), *The concept of activity in Soviet psychology* (pp. 144–188). Armonk, NY: Sharpe.

Weber, J. (2003). Tomorrow's transcription tools: What new technology means for healthcare. *Journal of the American Health Information Management Association*, 74, 39–43.

Welch, K. E. (1999). *Electric rhetoric: Classical rhetoric, oralism, and a new literacy*. Cambridge, MA: MIT Press.

Woodmansee, M. (1994). On the author effect: Recovering collectivity. In M. Woodmansee & P. Jaszi (Eds.), *The construction of authorship: Textual appropriation in law and literature* (pp. 15–28). Durham, NC: Duke University Press.

Yates, J. (1989). *Control through communication: The rise of system in American management*. Baltimore: Johns Hopkins University press.

Zick, R. G., & Olsen, J. (2001). Voice recognition software versus a traditional transcription service for physician charting in the emergency department. *American Journal of Emergency Medicine*, 19, 295–298.

SECTION 2

ANALYSES OF HOW SPEECH AND WRITING RELATE TO EACH OTHER

7.
WRITING AND SPEAKING
Douglas Biber and Camilla Vásquez

> Thought has always worked by opposition,
> Speech/Writing
> High/Low . . .
> Does this mean something?
> Cixous (1975, p. 90)

The past several decades have seen many shifts in perspective in the study of writing and speaking. In the early 20th century, a number of structural linguists (e.g., Sapir, Bloomfield) stressed the primacy of speech over writing, positing that writing was essentially an artifact of spoken language Later scholars, working from a broader social perspective (e.g., Goody, 1968; Goody & Watt, 1968), documented the historical development and diffusion of different types of writing systems in various Western and non-Western cultures, and explored the social and cultural implications of the introduction of the technology of literacy, by analyzing some of the earliest functions of written texts. Other researchers in this tradition, most notably Olson and Ong, have argued that the introduction of literacy has had consequences for cognition, society, and language use. The work of Olson and Ong has come to be associated with an autonomous view of writing and with characterizations of writing as "detached, and self-contained" (Ong, 1982, p. 132) and "able to stand in as an unambiguous and autonomous representation of meaning" (Olson, 1977, p. 258).

At the same time, several early researchers suggested that the linguistic characteristics of speech and writing are fundamentally different. For example, DeVito (1967), Olson (1977), and Kay (1977) argued that the language of writing is more explicit, decontextualized, and therefore autonomous than speech, with referents being explicitly identified, and background assumptions and logical relations being overtly encoded in the text itself. Other researchers have claimed that writing is more structurally complex than speech, with longer sentences (or t-units) and a greater use of subordination (e.g., Chafe, 1982; O'Donnell, 1974).

Despite the many studies carried out in the 1970s and early 1980s, there was little agreement on the salient linguistic characteristics of the two modes. Several studies examined linguistic features such as sentence length, number of subordinate clauses, and the frequency of passive constructions in speech and writing (e.g., Chafe,

---

Biber, Douglas., & Vásquez, Camilla. "Writing and Speaking." *Handbook of Research on Writing: History, Society, School, Individual, Text*. Ed. Charles Bazerman. Mahwah, NJ: Erlbaum, 2007. 535–548.

1982; Kay, 1977; Kroll, 1977; O'Donnell, 1974). These studies generally concluded that written language is structurally elaborated, complex, formal, and abstract, whereas spoken language is concrete, context-dependent, and structurally simple. Some studies, however, found almost no linguistic differences between speech and writing (Blankenship, 1962), whereas others (Halliday, 1979; Poole & Field, 1976) actually claimed that speech is more elaborated than writing (see the survey of research in Biber, 1988, chap. 3).

The 1980s saw a reaction to these earlier perspectives on literacy as opposed to orality (i.e., as autonomous, cognitive, and linguistic). During this decade, several studies appeared that called into question overgeneralization made about speech and writing (e.g., Frawley, 1982; Tannen, 1982), and yet other more culturally or socially oriented studies focused less on the differences between oral and literate production and more on their diverse functions in particular social contexts (e.g., Heath, 1982; Street, 1984). And as the technical view of literacy as a mode of linguistic production independent of social context gradually came under increasing scrutiny, the work of Scribner and Cole (1981) also demonstrated that many of the cognitive effects that had been ascribed to literacy were instead the results of particular educational practices. A great deal of recent research on literacy—particularly anthropological and ethnographic approaches—has broadened the scope of inquiry, by viewing both oral and literate production as embedded in complex social practices. These anthropological, ethnographic, or ideological (Street, 1984) approaches to literacy have been useful in identifying the relationship between language and macrostructures (culture, power, etc.) and have therefore provided numerous insights into connections between literacy practices and schooling (e.g., Heath, 1982; Scribner & Cole, 1981; etc.); however, such studies have not been expressly concerned with specific linguistic differences between speaking and writing.

Over this same period, researchers in linguistics began to recognize the importance of linguistic differences within each mode and the inadequacy of simple dichotomous comparisons of spoken and written language. For example, Akinnaso (1982), Tannen (1982, 1985), and Beaman (1984) all argue that linguistic studies should be based on comparisons of the same task in speech and writing to isolate the effect of mode. That is, many earlier studies were based on a comparison of a single spoken variety to a single written variety but these were often not matched for factors such as purpose and the amount of preplanning (e.g., a comparison of face-to-face conversation to a preplanned written essay). In contrast, the approach advocated by Tannen, Beaman, and others required that subjects perform the same task in speech and writing, usually producing spontaneous narratives. By controlling the task, researchers hoped to isolate the effect of the spoken versus written mode on linguistic form.

This line of research leads naturally to more general issues of register variation, where *register* is used as a cover term to refer to a language variety that is defined by situational characteristics and communicative purposes (examples of different registers include conversation, lectures, novels, biology research articles, etc.). Rather than focusing on the simple dichotomy of speech versus writing, the study of register variation entails a much broader scope of investigation; for example: To what extent do spoken registers differ from one another linguistically? That is, what are the patterns of linguistic variation among varieties with*in* the spoken mode? Similarly what kinds of linguistic differences exist among written registers? Studying the full range of registers within each mode (i.e., spoken and written) allows for a much more comprehensive framework to address the question of whether there are overall differences between speech and writing.

Research questions such as these motivated the development of multidimensional analysis (e.g., Biber 1986, 1988, 1995). Studies in this research tradition have used large corpora of naturally occurring texts to represent the range of spoken and written registers in a language. These registers are compared with respect to dimensions of variation, comprising constellations of linguistic features that typically co-occur in texts (see the section Multidimensional Analyses of Spoken and Written Register Variation). Each dimension is distinctive in three respects:

1. It is defined by a distinctive set of co-occurring linguistic features.
2. It is associated with distinctive communicative functions.
3. There are distinctive patterns of register variation associated with each dimension.

Several general patterns and conclusions about spoken and written language have emerged from multidimensional studies:

1. Some dimensions are strongly associated with spoken and written differences; other dimensions have little or no relation to speech and writing.
2. There are few, if any, absolute linguistic differences between spoken and written registers.
3. However, there are strong and systematic linguistic differences between stereotypical speech and stereotypical writing, that is, between conversation and written informational prose.
4. The spoken and written modes differ in their linguistic potential: They are not equally adept at accommodating a wide range of linguistic variation. In particular, there is an extremely wide range of linguistic variation among written registers, because writers can choose to employ linguistic features associated with stereotypical speech. In contrast, there is a more restricted range of linguistic variation among spoken registers, in part because the real-time production circumstances of the spoken mode make it difficult to employ many of the linguistic features associated with stereotypical informational writing.

In the next section, we survey the characteristic linguistic features of stereotypical speech and writing, showing how these two extremes of the spoken and written modes are dramatically different in their patterns of language use. Then, in the following section, we briefly survey the results of multidimensional studies to support the claim that the two modes differ in their linguistic potential, describing the overall linguistic relationship between speech and writing.

Stereotypical Speech and Writing: Conversation Versus Informational Prose

As noted previously, there are many different registers found within the spoken and written modes. However, it is possible to identify particular registers that are especially typical of each mode. Conversation and informational expository prose fit this description, and these two registers can thus be regarded as stereotypically spoken and written registers (see also Tannen, 1982; Biber, 1995, who use the terms *oral* and *literate* for this distinction).

The characterization of conversation as stereotypical speaking is not controversial: All languages and cultures have conversational interactions, and it can be considered the unmarked means of spoken communication universally. The communicative focus in conversation is typically on (inter)personal rather than informational concerns, and meaning can be clarified and jointly negotiated by participants. For these reasons, conversational interactions require fast, efficient communication, but they have relatively little need for a precise, dense packaging of information. These communicative priorities match the real-time production circumstances of the spoken mode. In other words, the real-time production of speech enables fast, easy communication, and facilitates direct interaction among participants, but it is less well-suited for highly informational or precise communication. (In contrast, the written mode would be slow and cumbersome for communication in face-to-face interactional situations.)

The characterization of informational expository prose as stereotypical writing is more controversial. Exposition differs from conversation in that it is not universal. Many speakers and cultures have literate competencies and traditions but lack expository registers. As a result, some researchers have claimed that expository registers are not representative of the written mode. For example, authors such as Street (1984, 1993) argue that academic exposition has been regarded as stereotypical writing simply because it is the most highly valued register of the intellectual elite in Western societies. According to this view, expository informational prose is not noteworthy for the way that it exploits the linguistic and communicative resources of the written mode; rather, the special status of expository prose is attributed to the fact that Western scholars have typically used this form of discourse for their own written communications. In contrast, we would argue that informational exposition is special in both its communicative/situational characteristics and its linguistic characteristics—because it maximally exploits the resources of the written mode. In particular, exposition maximally exploits the opportunities for carefully planned and revised expression made possible by the written mode, and thus it shows extreme characterizations of informational density, elaboration, and precision.

The communicative resources provided by the written mode are not necessarily obvious, to individual speakers or to developing cultures. As Goody (1977, 1986) and Stubbs (1980) point out, writers learn to exploit the resources of the written mode only gradually over time, in contrast to speakers' abilities to use the spoken mode, which appears to be native to all cultures. For example, Stubbs (1980) notes that it took nearly 100 years after the invention of printed books before page numbers were regularly added for the benefit of readers, and modern devices such as a table of contents and indexes appeared even later. Similarly, beginning readers do not immediately realize that written materials can be processed in different ways from speech. For example, written materials can be read at different speeds, depending on the difficulty of the material and the purposes of the reader. In addition, individuals can selectively process written materials in a nonlinear fashion, reading only those parts that are particularly interesting or relevant. It also takes time for writers to learn to exploit the production opportunities for planning and revision, in order to produce carefully integrated, informational prose.

We certainly would not claim that written exposition is in any sense better than other written registers, or that it is necessarily desirable for all cultures and speakers to develop proficiency in expository registers. However, we regard informational exposition as stereotypical writing in that it has the opposite situational and communicative characteristics from conversation: both exposition and conversation make maximal use of the communicative resources provided by their respective modes. As a result, a linguistic comparison/contrast of conversation and expository prose provides a description of the styles of expression associated with the exploitation of those communicative resources.

Linguistic Comparison/Contrast of Conversation and Academic Prose

One analytical approach that has been especially productive for studying register variation is corpus-based analysis, with its emphasis on the representativeness of the database, and its associated computational tools, which are used to investigate distributional patterns across registers and across discourse contexts in large text collections (for introductions to this analytical approach, see Biber, Conrad, & Reppen, 1998; Hunston, 2002; Kennedy, 1998; McEnery & Wilson, 1996; Meyer 2002). The recent *Longman Grammar of Spoken and Written English* (*LGSWE;* Biber, Johansson, Leech, Conrad, & Finnegan, 1999) applies corpus-based analyses to show how any grammatical feature can be described for both its structural characteristics and its patterns of use across spoken and written registers. The analyses in the *LGSWE* are based on texts from four registers: conversation, fiction, newspaper language, and academic prose. Although these are general registers, they differ in important ways from one another (e.g., with respect to mode, interactiveness, production circumstances, purpose, and target audience). The analyses were carried out on the Longman Spoken and Written English (LSWE) Corpus, which contains approximately 20 million words of text overall, with approximately 4 to 5 million words from each of these four registers.

Because the *LGSWE* systematically includes grammatical descriptions of conversation and academic prose, this reference work provides one of the most comprehensive surveys of the linguistic differences between stereotypical speech and writing. These two registers have been found to consist of dramatically different patterns of use for nearly every linguistic feature. Table 7.1 lists some of the features that are especially characteristic of conversation, whereas Table 7.2 lists features that are especially characteristic of academic prose. The Appendix [not printed here] provides examples and definitions for each of these features.

Many of the grammatical features typical of conversation, listed in Table 7.1, reflect a heavy reliance on verbs, adverbs, and pronouns rather than on complex noun phrases. These features result in the dense use of short, simple clauses. However, it also turns out that several dependent-clause features are much more common in conversation than in other registers. For example, complement clauses controlled by verbs, especially *that*-clauses and *WH*-clauses, are found frequently in conversation. (The complementizer *that* is frequently omitted in these structures.) Such grammatical features are often used to express speaker stance (personal attitudes or evaluations) in conversation: The controlling verb expresses the stance, whereas the complement clause contains the new information. The following excerpt from a conversation illustrates these features. Notice especially the dense use of verbs, pronouns, and *that* complement clauses. We have underlined the start of all *that*-clauses and WH-clauses, and inserted the symbol <> to mark places where the complementizer *that* has been omitted.

B: Well not the organizer surely, oh I <u>know</u> I would have <u>thought</u> you'd have to, [unclear] shoot it.
A: I'm <u>sure that</u> the social services require psychiatric or—
B: Mm, I would've thought so.
A: Obviously medical <unclear> <u>what</u> you're doing. Mhm, but they're to be qualified people involved. But I would have <u>expected that</u> the whole thing would have to be operated by, somebody who was qualified.
B: I don't know, because like, you know like the doctors <unclear>
A: <unclear> I <u>think</u> it sort of <u>depends how</u> big that you want to get involved in.

Taken together, these conversational features reflect two of the most important situational characteristics of typical speech: restriction to real-time production (resulting in a reliance on clausal structures rather than complex noun phrases), and a focus on personal involvement (resulting in the dense use of linguistic features to express stance).

In contrast, Table 7.2 lists major grammatical features that are especially common in academic prose. Three linguistic features are especially prevalent in this type of writing: nouns, adjectives, and prepositional phrases. In addition, there are many related specific features that are especially characteristic of academic prose (e.g., nominalizations, noun phrases with multiple modifiers). In contrast, verbs are much less common in academic prose than in conversation (although there are specific verb categories that are common in academic prose, such as the copula *be,* existence verbs, derived verbs, and passive-voice verbs.) The dense use of complex noun phrase structures reflect the informational/ideational focus of academic prose, together with the opportunity for careful crafting and revision of the text enabled by the written mode. The following short excerpt from a university textbook illustrates many of these features. We have underlined all nouns and marked prepositions in **bold**.

<u>Wildlife photography</u> represents the nonconsumptive <u>use</u> **of** <u>wildlife</u>, which is the <u>use</u>, **without** <u>removal</u> or <u>alteration</u>, **of** natural <u>resources</u>. **For** much **of** this <u>century</u>,

the <u>management</u> **of** <u>wildlife</u> **for** the <u>hunter</u> has been emphasized **by** <u>wildlife managers</u>. **In** recent <u>years</u>, however, <u>management</u> **for** nonconsumptive <u>uses</u> **such as** <u>wildlife</u> <u>photography</u> and <u>bird-watching</u> has received more <u>attention.</u>

It is noteworthy that not all dependent-clause types are more common in informational written prose than in conversation. Rather, specific clause types have their own distributions, reflecting their primary communicative functions and apparently their production difficulty. For example, finite relative clauses are much more common in expository writing than in conversation; these clauses serve informational functions, being used for nominal specification and elaboration. In contrast, many complement clause types are considerably more common in conversation than in academic prose; these clauses are used primarily to express stance; thus they are a preferred structure in conversation, despite their apparent structural complexity. Many of these structures are formed through the use of lexical bundles; semifrozen recurrent multiword expressions such as *I don't know why* _____ (see *LGSWE*, chap. 13; Biber, Conrad, & Cortes, 2004). As a result, the dense use of these complement clause constructions does not pose a difficult production task in conversation.

Table 7.1 Grammatical Features That Are Especially Common in Conversation But Relatively Rare in Academic Prose (based on a survey of the Longman Grammar of Spoken and Written English, with page citations)

Feature	Specific pattern of use
Verbs and verb phrases:	
Lexical verbs: overall pp. 65, 359	Almost one third of all content words in conversation are lexical verbs
Mental verbs pp. 366, 368	E.g., *know, think, see, want, mean*
Phrasal verbs pp. 409, 424	E.g., *come on, get up, get off, find out, go on*
Present tense p. 456 ff.	Approximately 70% of all verb phrases in conversation are present tense
Progressive aspect p. 462 ff.	three times more common in conversation than in academic prose
Modal verbs p. 486 ff.	About twice as common in conversation than in the written registers; especially *can, will, would*
Semimodal verbs p. 486 ff.	Common only in conversation; especially *have to, (had) better, (have) got to, used to*
Adverbs:	
Simple adverbs p. 540–2, 560–3	Twice as common in conversation; e.g., *here, there, now, then, just, really*
Adjectival forms used as adverbs pp. 542–3	common only in conversation; e.g., *It's running <u>real good</u>*
Amplifiers pp. 564–6	Twice as common in conversation, especially *very, so, really/real, too*
Stance adverbs pp. 859, 867–71	Over twice as common in conversation, especially *really, actually, like, maybe*

(continued)

(Table 7.1 continued)

Feature	Specific pattern of use
Pronouns:	
Personal pronouns pp. 92, 235, 237, 333, 334	four times more common in conversation, especially *I, you, it*
Demonstrative pronoun *that* pp. 349–50	Extremely common only in conversation
Simple clause features:	
Questions pp. 211 ff.	Common only in conversation
Imperatives pp. 221–220	Common only in conversation
Stranded prepositions in WH-questions pp. 106–107	Common only in conversation
Coordination tags pp. 116–7	Common only in conversation, e.g., *or something* (but note the use of *etc.* in writing)
Dependent clause features:	
Verb + *that* complement clause pp. 668–70, 674–5	Five times more common in conversation, especially think, *know, guess* + *that*-clause
Complementizer *that* omission (vs. retention) pp. 680–683	The preferred use in conversation (over 80% of all that-clauses omit the complementizer)
Verb + WH complement clauses pp. 688–9	Much more common in conversation, especially *know* + WH-clause
Conditional adverbial clauses p. 821 ff.	Twice as common in conversation

Note: Based on a survey of the Longman Grammar of Spoken and Written English, with page citations.

Multidimensional Analyses of Spoken and Written Register Variation

Multidimensional (MD) analysis was developed as a corpus-based methodological approach to: (a) identify the salient linguistic co-occurrence patterns in a language, in empirical/quantitative terms, and (b) compare spoken and written registers in the linguistic space defined by those co-occurrence patterns. The approach was first used in Biber (1985, 1986) and then developed more fully in Biber (1988, 1995). As noted in earlier, MD analysis is based on the assumption that all registers have distinctive linguistic patterns of use (associated with their defining situational characteristics). Thus, MD studies of speech and writing set out to describe the linguistic similarities and differences among a range of spoken registers, and similarly among a range of written registers—and to then compare speech and writing within the context of a comprehensive analysis of register variation.

In the present chapter, we have space for only a brief summary of the major patterns of variation resulting from MD studies. Readers are referred to Biber (1988, 1995) or Conrad and Biber (2001; chaps. 1 and 2) for the details of these studies.

MD analysis uses factor analysis to reduce a large number of linguistic variables to a few basic parameters of linguistic variation. In MD analyses, the distribution of individual linguistic features is analyzed in a corpus of texts. Factor analysis is then used to identify the systematic co-occurrence patterns among those linguistic features—the dimensions—and then texts and registers are compared along each

Table 7.2 Grammatical Features That Are Especially Common in Academic Prose But Relatively Rare in Conversation (based on a survey of the Longman Grammar of Spoken and Written English)

Feature	Pattern of use
Nouns and noun phrases:	
Nouns: overall p. 65	Approximately 60% of all content words in academic prose are nouns
Nouns vs. pronouns pp. 235–236	Nouns are much more common than pronouns in academic prose, especially in object positions
Plural nouns pp. 291–229	Four times more common in informational writing than in conversation
Nominalizations pp. 322–3	Over 10 times more common in academic prose, especially nouns formed with *–tion* and *–ity*
Definite article *the* pp. 267–9	Three times more common in academic prose than in conversation
Noun phrases with modifiers p. 578	60% of all noun phrases in academic prose have a modifier
	In contrast, Approximately. 90% of the noun phrases in conversation are a single pronoun with no modifier
Nouns as premodifiers p. 589–596	Approximately. 10 times more common in academic prose (and newspapers)
Noun phrases with Postmodifiers p. 606–608	Approximately. Six times more common in academic prose (and newspapers)
Noun phrases with multiple postmodifiers p. 640–644	Approximately. 10 times more common in academic prose
Appositive noun phrases as post-modifiers in noun phrases p. 606, 638–40	Approximately. Five times more common in academic prose (and newspapers)
Adjectives and adjective phrases:	
Adjectives: overall p. 65, 506	Adjectives are four times more common in academic prose than in conversation
Attributive adjectives p. 506, 589	Approximately Seven times more common in academic prose
Derived adjectives pp. 531–533	Approximately 10 times more common in academic prose, especially adjectives formed with *–al*
Verbs and verb phrases:	
Copula *be* Copular verb *become* pp. 359–360, 437–439	Twice as common in academic prose
Existence verbs (e.g., *include, involve, indicate*) pp. 366, 369, 419	Twice as common in academic prose
Verbs with inanimate subjects pp. 378–380	Common only in academic prose
Derived verbs pp. 400–403	Approximately Three times more common in academic prose, especially verbs formed with *re-* and *–ize*

(continued)

(Table 7.2 continued)

Feature	Pattern of use
Passive voice pp. 476–480, 937–40	Approximately 10 times more common in academic prose, especially the "short" passive (with no *by*-phrase)
Dependent Clause features:	
Relative clauses with the relative pronoun *which* pp. 609–612	Approximately 10 times more common in academic prose
Participle clauses as postmodifiers in noun phrases p. 606, 630–632	Approximately 10 times more common in academic prose (and newspapers)
That-clauses as noun complement clauses pp. 647–651	Over 10 times more common in academic prose, especially with the head nouns *fact, possibility, doubt, belief, assumption*
To-clauses as noun complement clauses pp. 647–51	over 10 times more common in academic prose (and newspapers), especially with the head nouns *attempt, ability, capacity, effort, right*.
Abstract' noun + *of* + *ing*-clause (e.g., *methods of assessing error*) pp. 653–655	over 10 times more common in academic prose, especially with the head nouns *way, method, possibility, effect, problem, process, risk*
Extraposed clauses pp. 672–5, 722–4	over 10 times more common in academic prose, especially *that*-clauses controlled by the adjectives *clear, (un)likely,* and *(im)possible*; and *to*-clauses controlled by the adjectives *(im)possible, difficult, hard, important, necessary*
Other features:	
Prepositions p. 92	Over twice as common in academic prose
Of-phrases pp. 301–302	over 10 times more common in academic prose
Prepositional phrases as postmodifiers in noun phrases p. 606–608, 634–638	Over Five times more common in academic prose (and newspapers)
Dual Gender reference: pp. 316–317	Common only in academic prose e.g., *he or she, his or her, he/she*

Note: Based on survey of the Longman Grammar of Spoken and Written English, with page citations.

dimension. Each dimension comprises a group of linguistic features that usually co-occur in texts (e.g., nouns, attributive adjectives, prepositional phrases); these co-occurrence patterns are identified statistically using factor analysis. The co-occurrence patterns are then interpreted to assess their underlying situational, social, and cognitive functions. Many dimensions have positive and negative sets of co-occurring features. Rather than reflecting importance, the positive and negative signs identify two groupings of features that occur in a complementary pattern as part of the same factor. That is, when the features with positive loadings occur together frequently in a text, the features with negative loadings are markedly less frequent in that text, and vice versa.

For example, Dimension 1 in the 1988 MD analysis has both positive and negative features. The negative features include nouns, long words, prepositional phrases, type/token ratio, and attributive adjectives. These features reflect an informational focus, a careful integration of information in a text, and precise lexical choice. Text Sample 1 (technical academic prose) illustrates these co-occurring linguistic characteristics in an academic article:

> Apart from these general group-related aspects, there are also individual aspects that need to be considered. Empirical data show that similar processes can be guided quite differently by users with different views on the purpose of the communication.

This text sample is typical of written expository prose in its dense integration of information: frequent nouns and long words, with most nouns being modified by attributive adjectives or prepositional phrases (e.g., <u>general group related aspects</u>, <u>individual aspects</u>, <u>empirical data</u>, <u>similar processes</u>, <u>users with different views on the purpose of the communication</u>).

The set of positive features on Dimension 1 is more complex, although all of these features have been associated with interpersonal interaction, a focus on personal stance, and real-time production circumstances. For example, first- and second-person pronouns, *WH*-questions, emphatics, amplifiers, and sentence relatives can all be interpreted as reflecting interpersonal interaction and the involved expression of personal stance (feelings and attitudes). Other positive features are associated with the constraints of real-time production, resulting in a reduced surface form, a generalized or uncertain presentation of information, and a generally fragmented production of text; these include *that* deletions, contractions, proverb DO, the pronominal forms, and final (stranded) prepositions. Text Sample 2 (office hours—School of Business) illustrates the use of positive Dimension 1 features in a formal conversation (university office hours) from the T2K-SWAL Corpus:

> Instructor: Now here's what you should do if you want me to go over your graduation papers—you gotta do it this semester because if you wait until the summer or the fall—
> Student: Uh huh.
> Instructor: Then you'll have to go through somebody else and it'll just take longer.
> Student: Yeah, so I can do that then and what do I—do you just file?
> Instructor: You can go down to Rosemary's office and get the papers, two sets of papers one for the college of business and one for the university.
> Student: And I can do it now.
> Instructor: Mhm, you can do it this semester and if she says no, you tell her why.
> Student: OK.

Overall Dimension 1 marks interactional, stance-focused, and generalized content (the positive features) versus high informational density and precise word choice (the negative features). Two separate communicative parameters seem to be represented here: the primary purpose of the writer/speaker (involved vs. informational), and the production circumstances (those restricted by real time constraints vs. those enabling careful editing possibilities). Reflecting both of these parameters, the interpretive label

Involved Versus Informational Production was proposed for the dimension underlying this factor.

The 1988 MD analysis showed that English registers vary along five major dimensions associated with different functional considerations, including: interactiveness, involvement and personal stance, production circumstances, informational density, informational elaboration, narrative purposes, situated reference, persuasiveness or argumentation, and impersonal presentation of information. Two of these dimensions have no systematic relationship to speech and writing (Dimension 2: Narrative Discourse; and Dimension 4: Argumentation). However, the other three dimensions identify sharp distinctions between oral and literate registers, where the term *oral* is used to refer to stereotypical speech (i.e., conversation), and the term *literate* is used to refer to stereotypical writing (i.e., academic prose or other kinds of formal, informational prose). On Dimension 1: Involved Versus Informational Production, conversation is at one extreme, marked as extremely involved and restricted by real-time production circumstances; academic prose is at the other extreme, marked as extremely informational and carefully crafted and edited (see previous discussion). On Dimension 3: Elaborated Versus Situated Reference, conversation is at one extreme, marked as extremely situated in reference (frequent time and place adverbials); academic prose is at the other extreme, marked as extremely elaborated in reference (frequent relative-clause constructions). On Dimension 5, academic prose is at one other extreme, marked by impersonal styles of presentation (frequent passive constructions), whereas conversation is at the other extreme.

The 1988 MD analysis indicates that the spoken and written modes can be exploited in extreme ways, resulting in register characterizations not found in the other mode. There are fundamental differences in the production circumstances of speech and writing, and these differences provide the potential for styles of expression in writing that are not normally feasible in speech. In addition, spoken registers rarely adopt the extreme informational communicative focus of written expository registers. (Even classroom teaching is much more interactive and involved in purpose than typical written expository registers; see Biber, Conrad, Reppen, Byrd, & Helt, 2002). Thus, written academic prose and official documents are highly informational (Dimension 1), elaborated in reference (Dimension 3), and impersonal (Dimension 5) —extreme linguistic characterizations not found in any spoken register.

However, despite the existence of these oral/literate dimensions, no dimension identifies an absolute distinction between speech and writing. On Dimension 1, written registers can be involved (e.g., personal letters), whereas spoken registers can be moderately informational (e.g., prepared speeches). And on Dimensions 3 and 5, written registers such as fiction and personal letters are similar to conversation in being situated and not impersonal.

These same basic patterns have been found in the MD analyses of Somali and Korean: In both of these languages, there are several oral/literate dimensions that distinguish between conversation at one extreme and written informational prose at the other extreme. At the same time, there are few dimensions that define an absolute contrast between speech and writing. Rather, most dimensions show some overlap among spoken and written registers. The Lexical Elaboration dimension in the Somali analysis—consisting of once-occurring words, type-token ratio, nominalizations, and so on—comes the closest to defining an absolute spoken–written contrast: No spoken Somali register makes dense use of these features, whereas all written registers (except textbooks) rely extensively on these features.

Consideration of all MD analyses to date reveals an additional pattern that is less easily noticed: The range of linguistic variation among written registers is typically much greater than the range of variation among spoken registers. Written production gives the author maximum freedom to manipulate the linguistic characteristics of a text in response to numerous situational influences, including communicative purpose, interactiveness, personal involvement and sometimes the desire to adopt a colloquial (even conversational) style. In contrast, spoken language is constrained by the need to produce language in real time. As a result, regardless of the speaker's focus on informational communicative purposes, spoken registers tend to be relatively oral with respect to all linguistic dimensions. For example, even classroom teaching is relatively oral in its MD profile (see Biber et al., 2002). In contrast, written registers show a much wider range of linguistic characteristics, because an author has ample time to exploit either oral or literate features depending on the primary communicative purposes. Thus, written registers like personal letters and e-mail messages tend to be oral in their MD profiles.

Conclusion

In this chapter, we have provided a brief and selective survey of previous research concerned with the linguistic differences between speech and writing. In illustrating some of the major linguistic differences found between stereotypical registers of the spoken and written modes of production, namely conversation and informational prose, we have argued that the modes differ considerably in. their linguistic potential. The systematic differences associated with conversation and expository prose (as illustrated by numerous findings from the *LGSWE*) can be attributed to the defining situational characteristics as well as production circumstances of the two registers. Furthermore, although MD analyses have shown that there are few, if any, absolute linguistic differences between the spoken and written modes, there are strong and systematic linguistic differences between the registers of conversation and written informational prose—not only in English, but in. other languages as well. In addition, MD analyses have revealed a more subtle difference between speech and writing: Spoken registers employ a restricted range of linguistic styles, whereas writers can shape their texts in whatever fashion that they want. These differences, we have argued, are clearly linked to the differing situational and production opportunities and constraints of the two modes. Thus, we conclude that any discussion of the linguistic differences between speech and writing must take into account the complex patterns of register variation within the two modes, while also recognizing the inherent restrictions on language production in the spoken mode relative to the written mode.

References

Akinnaso, F. (1982). On the differences between spoken and written language. *Language and Speech, 25*, 97–125.

Beaman, K. (1984). Coordination and subordination revisited: Syntactic complexity in spoken and written narrative discourse. In D. Tannen (Ed.), *Spoken and written language; Exploring orality and literacy* (pp. 45–80). Norwood, NJ; Ablex.

Besnier, N. (1988). The linguistic relationships of spoken and written Nukulaelae registers. *Language, 64*, 707–736.

Biber, D. (1988). *Variation across speech and writing.* Cambridge, England: Cambridge University Press.

Biber, D. (1995). *Dimensions of register variation: A cross-linguistic comparison.* Cambridge, England: Cambridge University Press.

Biber, D., & Clark, V. (2000). Historical shifts in modification patterns with complex noun phrase structures: How long can you go without a verb? In T. Fanego, M.J. López-Couso, & J. Pérez-Guerra (Eds.), *English historical syntax and morphology* (pp. 43–66). Amsterdam: Benjamins.

Biber, D., & Conard, S. (2001). Register variation: A corpus approach. In D. Schiffrin, D. Tannen, & H. Hamilton (Eds.), *The handbook of discourse analysis* (pp. 175–196). Oxford, England: Blackwell.

Biber, D., Conrad, S., & Cortes, V. (2004). *If you look at . . .*: Lexical bundles in university teaching and textbooks. *Applied Linguistics, 25*, 371–405.

Biber, D., Conard, S., & Reppen, R. (1998). *Corpus linguistics: Exploring language structure and use.* Cambridge, England: Cambridge University Press.

Biber. D., Conrad, S., Reppen, R., Byrd, P., & Helt, M. (2002). Speaking and writing in the university: A multi-dimensional comparison. *TESOL Quarterly, 36*(1), 9–48.

Biber, D., & Finegan, E. (Eds.), (1994). *Sociolinguistic perspectives on register.* Oxford, England: Oxford University Press.

Biber, D., & Hared, M. (Eds.), (1994). Linguistic correlates of the transition to literacy in Somali: Language and adaptation in six press registers. In D. Biber & E. Finnegan (Eds.), *Sociolinguistic perspectives on register* (pp. 182–216). Oxford, England: Oxford University Press.

Biber, D., Johansson, S., Leech. G., Conard, S., & Finnegan, E. (199). *Longman grammar of spoken and written English.* London: Pearson.

Blankenship, J. (1962). A linguistic analysis of oral and written style. *Quarterly Journal of Speech, 48*, 419–422.

Chafe, W. (1982). Integration and involvement in speaking, writing, and oral literature. In D. Tannen (Ed.), *Spoken and written language: Exploring orality and literacy* (pp. 35–54). Norwood, NJ: Ablex.

Cixous, H. (1975). "Sorties" in La Jeune Née, Paris, Union Générale d'Editions, 10/12; English translation in E. Marks & I. de Courtivion (Eds.) (1980). *New French feminisms: An anthology.* Amherst. University of Massachusetts Press.

Conard, S., & Biber, D. (Eds.), (2001). *Variation in English: Multi-dimensional studies.* London: Longman.

Coulmas, F., & Elich, K. (Eds.), (1983). *Writing in focus.* New York: Mouton.

DeVito, J. A. (1967, May). A linguistic analysis of spoken and written language. *Central States Speech Journal,* pp. 81–85

Frawley, W. (Ed.), (1982). *Linguistics and literacy: Proceedings of the Delaware symposium on language studies.* New York: Plenum.

Goody, J., & Watt, J. (1968). The consequences of literacy. In J. Goody (Ed.), *Literacy in traditional societies* (pp. 27–68). Cambridge, England: Cambridge University Press.

Goody, J. (Ed.), (1968). *Literacy in traditional societies.* Cambridge, England: Cambridge University Press.

Goody, J. (1977). *The domestication of the savage mind.* Cambridge, England: Cambridge University Press.

Goody, J. (1986). *The logic of writing and the organisation of society.* Cambridge, England: Cambridge University Press.

Green, G. (1982). Colloquial and literary uses of inversions. In D. Tannen (Ed.), *Spoken and written language: Exploring orality and literacy* (pp. 119–154). Norwood, NJ: Ablex.

Halliday, M. A. K. (1979). Differences between spoken and written language: Some implications for literacy teaching. In G. Page, J. Elkins, & B. O'Connor (Eds.), *Communication through reading; Proceedings of the 4th Australian reading conference* (Vol. 2, pp. 000–000). Adelaide, South Australia: Australian Reading Association.

Heath, S. B. (1982). Protean shapes in literacy events: Ever-shifting oral and literate traditions. In D. Tannen (Ed.), *Spoken and written language: Exploring orality and literacy* (pp. 91–118). Norwood, NJ: Ablex.

Hunston, S. (2002). *Corpora and applied linguistics.* Cambridge, England: Cambridge University Press.

Kay, P. (1977). Language evolution and speech style. In B. G. Blount & M. Sanches (Eds.), *Sociocultural dimensions of language change* (pp. 21–33). New York: Academic Press.

Kennedy, G. (1998). *An introduction to corpus linguistics.* Harlow, England: Addison Wesley Longman.

Kim. Y., & Biber, D. (1990). A corpus-based analysis of register variation in Korean. In D. Biber & E. Finnegan (Eds.), *Sociolinguistic perspectives on register* (pp. 157–181). Oxford, England: Oxford University Press.

Kroll, B. (1977). Ways communicators encode propositions in spoken and written English: A look at subordination and coordination. In E. O. Keenan & T. Bennett (Eds.), *Discourse across time and space* (SCOPIL No. 5) (pp. 69–108). Los Angeles: University of Southern California.

Lakoff, R.T. (1982). Some of my favorite writers are literate: The mingling of oral and literate strategies in written communication. In D. Tannen (Ed.), *Spoken and written language: Exploring orality and literacy* (pp. 239–260). Norwood. NJ: Ablex.

McEnety, A. M., & Wilson, A. (1996). *Corpus linguistics*, Edinburgh, Scotland: Edinburgh University Press.

Meyer, C. (2002). *English corpus linguistics: An introduction.* Cambridge, England: Cambridge University Press.

O'Donnell, R. C. (1974). Syntactic differences between speech and writing. *American Speech, 49,* 102–110.

Olson, D. (1977). From utterance to text: The bias of language in speech and writing. *Harvard Educational Review, 43*(3), 257–281.

Olson, D. (1988). Mind and media: The epistemic functions of literacy. *Journal of Communications, 38*(3), 254–279.

Ong, W. (1967). *The presence of the word.* Minneapolis: University of Minnesota Press.

Ong, W. (1977). *Interfaces of the word.* Ithaca, NY: Cornell University Press.

Ong, W. (1982). *Orality and literacy The technologizing of the word*. London: Methuen.
Poole, M. E., & Field, T. W. (1976). A comparison of oral and written code elaborations. *Language and Speech, 19*, 305–311.
Roberts, C., & Street, B. (1997). Spoken and written language. In F. Coulmas (Ed.), *The handbook of sociolinguistics* (pp. 168–186). Oxford, England: Blackwell.
Scribner, S., & Cole, M. (1981). *The psychology of literacy*. Cambridge, MA: Harvard University Press.
Street, B. (Ed.), (1984). *Literacy in theory and practice*. Cambridge, England: Cambridge University Press.
Street, B. (Ed.), (1993). *Cross-cultural approaches to literacy*. Cambridge, England: Cambridge University Press.
Stubbs, M. (1980). *Language and literacy: The sociolinguistics of reading and writing*. London: Routledge.
Tannen, D. (1982a). The oral/literate continuum in discource. In D. Tannen (Ed.), *Spoken and written language: Exploring orality and literacy* (pp.1–16). Norwood, NJ: Ablex.
Tannen, D. (Ed.), (1982b). *Spoken and written language: Exploring orality and literacy.* Norwood, NJ: Ablex.
Tannen, D. (1985). Relative focus on involvement in oral and written discourse. In D. R. Olson, N. Torrance, & A. Hildyard (Eds). *Literacy, language and learning: The nature and consequences of reading and writing*. Cambridge, England: Cambridge University Press.

8.
SPOKEN AND WRITTEN MODES OF MEANING
M. A. K. Halliday

Spoken Language and Education

It seems to me that one of the most productive areas of discussion between linguists and educators in the past quarter century has been that of speech and the spoken language. Twenty-five years ago, when I launched the "Linguistics and English Teaching" project in London, which produced *Breakthrough to Literacy* and *Language in Use*, it was still rare to find references to the place of spoken language in school, or to the need for children to be articulate as well as literate. Dell Hymes had not yet introduced "communicative competence"; the words *oracy* and *orality* had not yet entered the field (Andrew Wilkinson's *Some Aspects of Oracy* appeared in 1967); David Abercrombie (1963/1965) had only just published his "Conversation and Spoken Prose." Language, in school, as in the community at large, meant written language.

The word *language* itself was hardly used in educational contexts. In the primary school, there was reading and writing; in the secondary school there was English, which meant literature and composition. Not that a classroom was a temple of silence; but the kind of spoken language that had a place, once a pupil had got beyond the infant school, was prepared speech: reading aloud, drama, debating—language that was written in order to be spoken, or at least was closely monitored in the course of its production. Spoken language in its natural form, spontaneous and unselfconscious, was not taken seriously as a medium of learning.

Among linguists, by contrast, the spoken language had pride of place. One learnt in the first year of a linguistics course that speech was logically and historically prior to writing. The somewhat aggressive tone with which linguists often proclaimed this commitment did not endear them to educators, who sensed that it undermined their authority as guardians of literacy and felt threatened by a scale of values they did not understand, according to which English spelling was out of harmony with the facts of the English language—whereas for them it was the pronunciation that was out of step, being a distorted reflection of the reality that lay in writing.

The linguists' professional commitment to the primacy of speech did not, however, arise from or carry with it an awareness of the properties of spoken discourse. It arose from the two sources of diachronic phonology (the study of sound change) and

---

Halliday, M. A. K. "Spoken and Written Modes of Meaning." *Comprehending Oral and Written Language.* Eds. Rosalind Horowitz and S. Jay Samuels. San Diego: Academic Press, 1987. 55–82.

articulatory phonetics (the study of speech production), which came together in twentieth century phonological theory. This was an interpretation of the system of speech sounds and of the phonological properties of the stream of speech; it did not involve any attempt to study the grammar and semantics of spoken as distinct from written language. As early as 1911, in his discussion of functional variation in language, Mathesius (1911/1964) was referring to "how the styles of speech are manifested in the pronunciation of language, in the stock of words, and in syntax" (p. 23), and to "the influence of functional styles on the lexical and semantic aspects of speech" (p. 24); and it is clear that "speech" for him (*parole*) did encompass both spoken and written varieties. But it was not until the 1950s, with the appearance of tape recorders, that natural speech could become the object of systematic study. The notion of "spoken text" is still not easily accepted, as can be seen from the confusion that prevails when spontaneous speech is reduced to writing in order to be analysed.

Spoken language came to figure in educational discussions in the context of language in the classroom: the language used by teachers to structure, direct and monitor their students' progress through the lesson. But the emphasis was on verbal strategies rather than on the text as a document; the investigators of the fifties and early sixties were not concerned with the particular place of spoken language in the learning process. It was assumed, of course, that students learnt by listening; but the expository aspects of the teacher's language were given little attention, while the notion that a student might be using his own talk as a means of learning was nowhere part of the picture. Probably it would have been felt that the principal means of learning through the spoken language was by asking questions; but studies of the early seventies (e.g., the Toronto research reported in *Five to Nine*) revealed that students seldom do ask questions—not, that is, while they are occupying their student role (i.e., in class). It is the teachers that ask the questions; and when they do so, both question and answer may be somewhat removed from the patterns of natural dialogue.

Complexity of Natural Speech

Already half a century earlier Franz Boas (1911/1963) had stressed the unconscious character of language, unique (as he saw it) among the phenomena of human culture. Boas' observation was to be understood in its contemporary context as a characterization of the language system (*langue*); not that, writing in 1911, he could have read Saussure's *Course in General Linguistics,* any more than Mathesius could have done; but the unconscious was in the air, so to speak, and playing a critical role in the conception of systems as regularities underlying human behaviour. But Boas may also have had in mind the unconsciousness of the behaviour itself: the act of speaking (*acte de parole*) as an unconscious act. The lack of conscious awareness of the underlying SYSTEM, and the difficulty that people have in bringing it to consciousness, are things which language shares with other semiotic systems—for example, social systems like that of kinship; what is unusual about language is the extent to which even the MANIFESTATION of the system, the actual process of meaning, remains hidden from observation, by performer and receiver alike. In that respect talking is more like dancing, or even running, than it is like playing chess. Speaker and listeners are of course aware that the speaker is speaking; but they are typically not aware of what he is saying, and if asked to recall it, not only the listeners but also the speaker will ordinarily offer a paraphrase, something that is true to the meaning but not by any means true to the wording. To focus attention on the wording of language is something that has to be learnt—for example if you are studying linguistics; it can be a difficult and somewhat threatening task.

About 30 years ago, as a result of being asked to teach English intonation to foreign students, I began observing natural spontaneous discourse in English; and from the start I was struck by a curious fact. Not only were people unconscious of what they themselves were saying; they would often deny, not just that they HAD said something I had observed them to say, but also that they ever COULD say it. For example, I noticed the utterance *it'll've been going to've been being tested every day for the past fortnight soon*, where the verbal group *will have been going to have been being tested* makes five serial tense choices, present in past in future in past in future, and is also passive. This passed quite unnoticed by both the speaker and the person it was addressed to; yet at the time it was being seriously questioned whether a simple verb form like *has been being tested*, which one can hear about once a week, could ever occur in English. Five-term tense forms are, predictably, very rare—one can in fact make a reasonable guess as to how rare, on the basis of observed frequencies of two- and three-term tense forms together with the constraints of the tense system; but they are provided for within the resources of the spoken language. Another instance I observed was *they said they'd been going to've been paying me all this time, only the funds just kept on not coming through*.

Other things I noted regularly included present in present participial non-finites like *being cooking* in *I never heard you come in—it must have been with being cooking*; marked thematic elements with reprise pronoun, as in *that poor child I couldn't get him out of my mind*; and relatives reaching into dependent clauses, such as *that's the noise which when you say it to a horse the horse goes faster*. These are all systematic features that people are unaware that they incorporate in their speech, and often deny having said even when they are pointed out; or at least reject as unsystematic—after "I didn't say it," the next line of defence is "well it was a mistake." But of course it was not a mistake; it was a regular product of the system of spoken English.

But perhaps the most unexpected feature of those early observations was the complexity of some of the sentence structures. Here are two examples from recordings made at the time:

> (i) *It's very interesting, because it fairly soon is established when you're meeting with somebody what kind of conversation you're having: for example, you may know and tune in pretty quickly to the fact that you're there as the support, perhaps, in the listening capacity—that you're there, in fact, to help the other person sort their ideas; and therefore your remarks, in that particular type of conversation, are aimed at drawing out the other person, or in some way assisting them, by reflecting them, to draw their ideas out, and*

> you may tune in to this, or you may be given this role and refuse it, refuse to accept it, which may again alter the nature of your conversation.
>
> (ii) The other man who kicks is the full-back, who usually receives the ball way behind the rest of his team, either near his line or when somebody's done what the stand-off in the first example was doing, kicked over the defenders; the full-back should be able then to pick it up, and his job is usually to kick for touch—nearly always for touch because he's miles behind the rest of his side, and before he can do anything else with the ball he's got to run up into them, before he can pass it, because he can't pass the ball forward, and if he kicks it forward to another of his side the other man's automatically off-side.
>
> And you get a penalty for that, do you, the other side?
>
> Depending on whether it's kicking or passing forward. Passing forward—no, it's a scrum. If you kick it forward and somebody else picks it up that will be a penalty.
>
> And if not, if the other side picks—
>
> If the other side picks it up that's all right; but the trouble is this is in fact tactics again, because you don't want to put the ball into the hands of the other side if you can avoid it because it's the side that has possession, as in most games of course, is at an advantage.

Examples such as these were noteworthy in two respects. One was that they embodied patterns of parataxis (combining with equal status) and hypotaxis (combining with unequal status) between clauses which could run to considerable length and depth. The other was that they were remarkably well formed: although the speaker seemed to be running through a maze, he did not get lost, but emerged at the end with all brackets closed and all structural promises fulfilled. And this drew attention to a third property which I found interesting: that while the listeners had absorbed these passages quite unconsciously and without effort, they were difficult to follow in writing.

Lexical Density

These two examples have been around for a long time; so let me turn to some recent specimens taken from recordings made by Guenter Plum to whom I am indebted for drawing them to my attention. In these spontaneous narratives Plum regularly finds sequences such as the following:

> 1A *I had to wait, I had to wait till it was born and till it got to about eight or ten weeks of age, then I bought my first dachshund, a black-and-tan bitch puppy, as they told me I should have bought a bitch puppy to start off with, because if she wasn't a hundred percent good I could choose a top champion dog to mate*

> *her to, and then produce something that was good, which would be in my own kennel prefix.*

This displays the same kind of mobility that the earlier observations had suggested was typically associated with natural, unselfconscious speech—which is what it was. I asked myself how I would have expressed this in writing, and came up with two rewordings; the first (1B) was fairly informal, as I might have told it in a letter to a friend:

1B *I had to wait till it was born and had got to about eight or ten weeks of age; that was when I bought my first dachshund, a black-and-tan bitch puppy. By all accounts I should have bought a bitch puppy at the start, because if she wasn't a hundred percent good I could mate her with a top champion dog and produce a good offspring—which would carry my own kennel prefix.*

My second rewording (1C) was a more formal written variant.

1C *Some eight or ten weeks after the birth saw my first acquisition of a dachshund, a black-and-tan bitch puppy. It seems that a bitch puppy would have been the appropriate initial purchase, because of the possibility of mating an imperfect specimen with a top champion dog, the improved offspring then carrying my own kennel prefix.*

The aim was to produce a set of related passages of text differing along this one dimension, which could be recognized as going from "most likely to be spoken" to "most likely to be written." How such variation actually correlates with difference in the medium is of course problematic; the relationship is a complicated one, both because written/spoken is not a simple dichotomy—there are many mixed and intermediate types—and because the whole space taken up by such variation is by now highly coded: in any given instance the wording used is as much the product of stylistic conventions in the language as of choices made by individual speakers and writers. Here I am simply moving along a continuum which anyone familiar with English usage can readily interpret in terms of "spoken" and "written" poles.

The kind of difference that we find among these three variants is one that is often referred to as a difference of "texture," and this familiar rhetorical metaphor is a very appropriate one: it is as if they were the product of a different weave, with fibres of a different yarn. But when we look behind these traditional metaphors, at the forms of language they are describing, we find that much of the difference can be accounted for as the effect of two related lexicosyntactic variables. The written version has a much higher lexical density; at the same time, it has a much simpler sentential structure. Let us examine these concepts in turn.

The *lexical density* is the proportion of lexical items (content words) to the total discourse. It can be measured in various ways: the ratio of lexical items either to total running words or to some higher grammatical unit, most obviously the clause; with or without weighting for relative frequency (in the language) of the lexical items

Table 8.1 Lexical Density of Texts 1A, 1B, and 1C

	(1) Lexical items	(2) Running words	(1:2)	(3) Clauses	(1:3)
1A	23	83	1:3.6	13	1.8:1
1B	26	68	1:2.6	8	3.3:1
1C	25	55	1:2.2	4	6.3:1

themselves. Here we will ignore the relative frequency of the lexical items and refer simply to the total number in each case, providing two measures (Table 8.1): the number of lexical items (1) as a proportion of the number of running words, and (2) as a proportion of the number of clauses. Only non-embedded clauses have been counted (if embedded clauses are also counted, then each lexical item occurring in them is counted twice, since it figures in both the embedded and the matrix clause— i.e., both in the PART, and in the WHOLE of which it is a part). The figures are given to the nearest decimal.

As Jean Ure showed in 1969 (Ure, 1971), the lexical density of a text is a function of its place on a register scale which she characterized as running from most active to most reflective: the nearer to the "language-in-action" end of the scale, the lower the lexical density. Since written language is characteristically reflective rather than active, in a written text the lexical density tends to be higher; and it increases as the text becomes further away from spontaneous speech.

Jean Ure measured lexical density as a proportion of running words; but as is suggested by the figures given above, if it is calculated with reference to the number of clauses the discrepancy stands out more sharply. Thus in the example given above, while the number of lexical items remained fairly constant and the number of running words fell off slightly, the number of clauses fell steeply: from 13, to 8, to 4. In other words, the lexical density increases not because the number of lexical items goes up but because the number of non-lexical items—grammatical words—goes down; and the number of clauses goes down even more.

Let us attempt a similar rewording the other way round, this time beginning with a passage of formal written English taken from *Scientific American*:

> 2A *Private civil actions at law have a special significance in that they provide an outlet for efforts by independent citizens. Such actions offer a means whereby the multiple initiatives of private citizens, individually or in groups, can be brought to bear on technology assessment, the internalization of costs and environmental protection. They constitute a channel through which the diverse interests, outlooks and moods of the general public can be given expression. The current popular concern over the environment has stimulated private civil actions of two main types.*

2B is my attempt at a somewhat less "written" version; while 2C is another step nearer to speech:

2B *Private civil actions at law are especially significant because they can be brought by independent citizens, so enabling them to find an outlet for their efforts. By bringing these actions, either as individuals or in groups, private citizens can regularly take the initiative in assessing technology, internalizing costs and protecting the environment. Through the use of these actions as a channel, the general public are able to express all their various interests, their outlooks, and their moods.*

  Because people are currently concerned about the environment, they have been bringing numerous private civil actions, which have been mainly of two types.

2C *One thing is especially significant, and that is that people should be able to bring private civil actions at law, because by doing this independent citizens can become involved. By bringing these actions, whether they are acting as individuals or in groups, private citizens can keep on taking the initiative; they can help to assess technology, they can help to internalize costs, and they can help to protect the environment. The general public, who want all kinds of different things, and who think and feel in all kinds of different ways, can express all these wants and thoughts and feelings by bringing civil actions at law.*

  At present, people are concerned about the environment; so they have been bringing quite a few private civil actions, which have been mainly of two kinds.

Table 8.2 shows the relative lexical density of the three variants of Text 2. Again, the number of lexical items has remained fairly constant; the variation in lexical density results from the increase in the total number of words—which means, therefore, in the number of grammatical words. This, in turn, is related to the increase in the number of clauses—where, however, the discrepancy is again much more striking.

Grammatical Intricacy

We have characterized the difference in general terms by saying that written language has a higher lexical density than spoken language; this expresses it as a positive feature of written discourse and suggests that writing is more complex, since presumably lexical density is a form of complexity. Could we then turn the formulation around, and express the difference as a positive characteristic of spoken language? To say that spoken discourse has more words in it, or even more clauses, does not seem to convey anything very significant about it. We need to look at how the words and clauses are organized.

Table 8.2 Lexical Density of Texts 2A, 2B, and 2C

	(1) Lexical items	(2) Running words	(1:2)	(3) Clauses	(1:3)
2A	48	87	1:1.8	5	9.6:1
2B	48	101	1:2.1	12	4.0:1
2C	51	132	1:2.6	17	3.0:1

Let us consider a shorter example of a pair of texts related in the same way, one "more written" (Text 3A), the other "more spoken" (Text 3B). I have constructed these so that they resemble the originals of Texts 1 and 2; but they are based on a natural example occurring in two texts in which a person had described the same experience twice over, once in speech and once in writing.

	More "written":		More "spoken":
3A	Every previous visit had left me with a sense of the risk to others in further attempts at action on my part.	3B	Whenever I'd visited there before I'd end up feeling that other people might get hurt if I tried to do anything more.

The first version (3A) is one sentence, consisting of one clause: a "simple sentence" in traditional grammar. The second version (3B) consists of four clauses (assuming that *ended up feeling* and *tried to do* are each single predicators); but these too have to be transcribed as one sentence, since they are related by hypotaxis—only one has independent status. These four clauses form what is called in systemic grammar a *clause complex* (for analysis and notation see Table 8.3):

Whenever I'd visited there before	$^{x}\beta$
I'd end up feeling	$\alpha\ \alpha$
that other people might get hurt	$\alpha\ '\beta\ \alpha$
if I tried to do anything more	$\alpha\ \beta\ ^{x}\beta$

The structural representation of this clause complex is given in Figure 8.1. The lower lexical density of Text 3B again appears clearly as a function of the number of clauses. But the significant factor is not that this text consists of four clauses where Text 3A consists of only one. It is that Text 3B consists of a CLAUSE COMPLEX consisting of four clauses. The clauses are not strung together as one simple sentence after another; they are syntactically related. Looked at from the point of view of the sentence structure, it is the spoken text that appears more complex than the written one. The spoken text has a lower degree of lexical density, but a higher degree of grammatical intricacy.

Let us return to Text 1, in its original spoken form (Text 1A). This consisted of 13 clauses. However, these 13 clauses were not strung out end to end; they were

Table 8.3 Notational Conventions for the Clause Complex[1]

Logical-semantic relations			Interdependencies	
Category		Symbol	Category	Symbol
expansion:	elaborating	=	parataxis	1 2 3 ...
	extending	+	hypotaxis[2]	$\alpha\ \beta\ \gamma$ ...
	enhancing	×		
projection:	idea	'		
	locution	"		

Spoken and Written Modes of Meaning

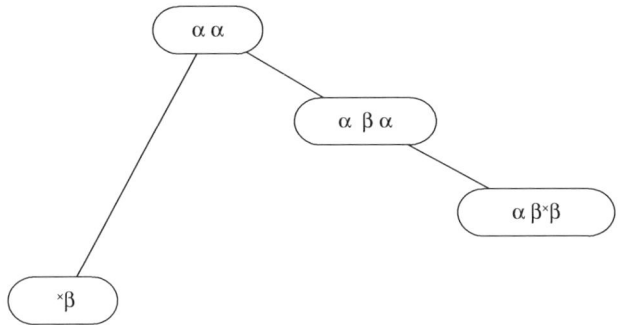

Figure 8.1 Structural representation of Text 3B as clause complex.

constructed into a small number of clause complexes of mixed paratactic and hypotactic construction: arguably just one clause complex throughout. Here is its interpretation as one clause complex:

1 1	*I had to wait*
1 = 2 α	*I had to wait*
1 2 ×β 1	*till it was born*
1 2 β + 2	*and till it got to about eight or ten weeks of age*
×2 α	*then I bought my first dachshund, a black-and-tan bitch puppy*
2 ×β α	*as they told me*
2 β "β α α	*I should've bought a bitch puppy*
2 β β α ×β	*to start off with*
2 β β ×β α 1α	*because . . .*
2 β β β ×β	*if she wasn't 100% good*
	. . . I could choose a top champion dog
2 β β β α 1 ×β	*to mate her to*
2 β β β α ×2 α	*and then produce something that was good*
2 β β β α 2 + β	*which would be in my own kennel prefix*

Sequences of this kind extend to a considerable length and depth in parataxis and hypotaxis. A typical pattern is one in which both these kinds of "taxis," or interdependency, occur, with frequent alternation both between the two and also among their various subcategories, as in the example here. The relationships between successive pairs of clauses in Text 1A are set out in Table 8.4.

Other examples from the same source but from different speakers show similar patterns; there are, obviously, individual differences (including perhaps in the preference for one or other type of interdependency), but the same free-flowing intricacy is noticeable all the time, as in Texts 4–6:

4   *Roy was always interested in dogs and unfortunately he'd never had the opportunity to have a dog of his own, just because of circumstances—where he lived and what not, and so I bought him a Shepherd pup, which was supposedly,*

you know, pure-bred Shepherd, but unfortunately people sold it because it didn't have papers with it, so it was a "pup."

5   Now how I got a German Shepherd was that I worked with a veterinary surgeon, as I've told you before, and there used to be a lady that brought her Shepherds along to the clinic and I used to admire them greatly, and she said, "Well," she said, "if you get married I'll give you one as a wedding present," so immediately I bustled around looking for someone to marry so I could get a Shepherd given to me for a wedding present, you see, so that's how that worked out—well, not quite! However I got my Shepherd and he was my first dog, mainly because I was a youngster I always wanted a dog but I lived with grandparents who wouldn't have dogs or cats and I was a very frustrated animal lover at that stage of the game, so as soon as I got out on my own I sort of went completely berserk!

6   So we rang up the breeder, and she sort of tried to describe the dog to us, which was very hard to do over the phone, so we went over to have a look to see what they were like, and we bought Sheba, because at that stage Bob was away a lot on semitrailers with the army and it used to get quite bad with the exercises—you'd have prowlers and perverts through the married quarters, so if we, you know, got a dog, which we could do because it didn't matter what sort of dog anyone had, it'd bark and they wouldn't bother us.

Types of Complexity

Two distinct points need to be made here, and both of them run counter to received attitudes towards spoken language. One is that speech is not, in any general sense, "simpler" than writing; if anything, it is more complex. There are, of course, many different kinds of complexity, and we have already noted one measure—lexical density—whereby speech will appear as the simpler of the two. But the patterns we

Table 8.4 Clause Complex Relationship in Text 1A

Clause number	Symbol	Type of interdependency	Logical-semantic relation	Marker
1–2	=2	parataxis	elaborating: repetitive	(tone concord)
2–3	ˣβ	hypotaxis	enhancing: temporal	*till*
3–4	+2	parataxis	extending: additive	*and*
4–5	ˣ2	parataxis	enhancing: temporal	*then*
5–6	ˣβ	hypotaxis	enhancing: causal	*as*
6–7	"β	hypotaxis	projecting: locution	—
7–8	ˣβ	hypotaxis	enhancing: purpose	*to*
8–9	ˣβ	hypotaxis	enhancing: causal	*because*
9–10	ˣβ	hypotaxis	enhancing: conditional	*if*
10–11	ˣβ	hypotaxis	enhancing: purpose	*to*
11–12	ˣ2	parataxis	enhancing: temporal	*and then*
12–13	+β	hypotaxis	extending: additive	*which*

have been illustrating, which are the patterns of the organization of the clause complex, referred to above as *grammatical intricacy*, would seem to be at least as central to any conception of complexity; and in this respect, speech appears as the more complex. The "syntactic complexity expected in writing," with which Deborah Tannen (1982) introduces her discussion of oral and literate strategies, does not turn out to be a characteristic of written discourse.

Of course, there are many other variables. Some writers achieve considerable intricacy in the structure of the clause complex; it can be learnt and consciously developed as a style. Some forms of spoken discourse, on the other hand, militate against it: rapid-fire dialogue presents no scope for lengthy interdependencies—complex semantic patterns can be construed BETWEEN interactants, but usually without being realized in syntactic terms. And the categories of "written" and "spoken" are themselves highly indeterminate—they may refer to the medium in which a text was originally produced, or the medium for which it was intended, or in which it is performed in a particular instance; or not to the medium at all, but to other properties of a text which are seen as characteristic of the medium. So it is important to indicate specifically which variable of discourse is being referred to, when one variety is being said to display some distinctive characteristic.

My point here is to question the assumption that written language is syntactically more complex than spoken, and to suggest that, as far as one particular kind of syntactic complexity is concerned—the intricacy (I do not want to call it "structure" because that assumes a particular interpretation) of the sentence or "clause complex"—this is more a characteristic of the most unconscious spontaneous uses of language. The more natural, un-self-monitored the discourse, the more intricate the grammatical patterns that can be woven. Usually, this kind of discourse will be spoken, because writing is in essence a more conscious process than speaking. But there are self-conscious modes of speech, whose output resembles what we think of as written language, and there are relatively spontaneous kinds of writing; spoken and written discourse are the outward forms that are typically associated with the critical variable, which is that of consciousness. We can use the terms spoken and written LANGUAGE, to refer to the idealized types defined by that variable.

Spoken and written language, then, tend to display different KINDS of complexity; each of them is more complex in its own way. Written language tends to be lexically dense, but grammatically simple; spoken language tends to be grammatically intricate, but lexically sparse. But these *buts* should really be *ands*, because the paired properties are complementary, not counterexpective. It is hard to find a form of expression which will show them to be such; I have usually had recourse to metaphors of structure versus movement, saying for example that the complexity of written language is crystalline, whereas the complexity of spoken language is choreographic. The complexity of spoken language is in its flow, the dynamic mobility whereby each figure provides a context for the next one, not only defining its point of departure but also setting the conventions by reference to which it is to be interpreted.

With the sentence of written language, there is solidarity among its parts such that each equally prehends and is prehended by all the others. It is a structure, and is not essentially violated by being represented synoptically, as a structural unit. With the clause complex, of spoken language, there is no such solidarity, no mutual prehension among all its parts. Its mode of being is as process, not as product. But since the study of grammar grew out of writing—it is when language comes to be written down that it becomes an object of study, not before—our grammars are grammars of the written language. We have not yet learnt to write choreographic grammars; so we look at spoken language through the lens of a grammar designed for writing. Spoken discourse thus appears as a distorted variant of written discourse, and not unnaturally it is found wanting.

For example, Chafe (1982) identifies a number of regular differences between speech and writing; writing is marked by more nominalization, more genitive subjects and objects, more participles, more attributive adjectives, more conjoined, serial and sequenced phrases, more complement clauses, and more relative clauses; all of which he summarizes by saying, "Written language tends to have an 'integrated' quality which contrasts with the fragmented quality of spoken language" (p. 38).

The general picture is that of written language as richly endowed, while speech is a poor man's assemblage of shreds and patches. But Chafe has described both speech and writing using a grammar of writing; so it is inevitable that writing comes out with positive checks all round. Not that he has no pluses on the spoken side: speech is said to have more first person references, more speaker mental processes, more *I means* and *you knows*, more emphatic particles, more vagueness like *sort of*, and more direct quotes—all the outward signs of language as interpersonal action. Chafe summarizes them as features of "involvement" as opposed to "detachment"; but they are items of low generality, and negative rather than positive in their social value.

This leads me to the second point that, as I remarked above, runs counter to our received attitudes towards speech. It is not only that speech allows for such a considerable degree of intricacy; when speakers exploit this potential, they seem very rarely to flounder or get lost in it. In the great majority of instances, expectations are met, dependencies resolved, and there are no loose ends. The intricacy of the spoken language is matched by the orderliness of spoken discourse.

The Myth of Structureless Speech

Why then are we led to believe that spoken discourse is a disorganized array of featureless fragments? Here it is not just the lack of an interpretative grammar for spoken language, but the convention of observing spoken discourse that we need to take into account.

Speech, we are told, is marked by hesitations, false starts, anacolutha, slips and trips of the tongue, and a formidable paraphernalia of so-called performance errors; these are regularly, more or less ritually, cited as its main distinguishing feature. There is no disputing the fact that these things occur, although they are much less prevalent than we are asked to believe. They are characteristic of the rather self-conscious, closely self-monitored speech that goes, for example, with academic seminars, where I suspect much of the observation and recording has taken place. If you are consciously planning your speech as it goes along and listening to check the outcome, then you naturally tend to lose your way: to hesitate, back up, cross out, and stumble over the words. But these things are not a particular feature of natural spontaneous discourse, which tends to be fluent, highly organized and grammatically well formed. If you are interacting spontaneously and without self-consciousness, then the clause complexes tend to flow smoothly without you falling down or changing direction in the middle, and neither speaker nor listener is at all aware of what is happening. I recorded this kind of casual discourse many years ago when studying the language spoken to and in the presence of a small child, and was struck by its fluency, well formedness, and richness of grammatical pattern. Interestingly, the same feature is apparent at the phonological level: spontaneous discourse is typically more regular in its patterns of rhythm.

However, while the myth of the scrappiness of speech may have arisen at the start from the kind of discourse that was first recorded, it has been perpetuated in a different way—by the conventions with which it is presented and discussed. Consider, for example, Beattie (1983, p. 33):

> Spontaneous speech is unlike written text. It contains many mistakes, sentences are usually brief and indeed the whole fabric of verbal expression is riddled with hesitations and silences. To take a very simple example: in a seminar which I recorded, an articulate (and well-known) linguist was attempting to say the following:
>
>> No, I'm coming back to the judgements question. Indeterminacy appears to be rife. I don't think it is, if one sorts out which are counterexamples to judgement.
>
> But what he actually said was:
>
> No *I'm saying* I'm coming back to the judgements question (267) *you know there appear to* (200) *ah* indeterminacy (1467) appears to be rife. I don't think it is (200) *if one* (267) if one sorts out which one counterexamples (267) to judgement, *I mean observing*.
>
> Here, the brief silences (unfilled pauses) have been measured in milliseconds and marked (these are numbers in brackets) and all other types of hesitation—false starts, repetitions, filled pauses and parenthetic remarks put in italics. It is these hesitations (both filled and unfilled) which dominate spontaneous speech and give it its distinctive structure and feeling.

In other words: when you speak, you cannot destroy your earlier drafts. If we were to represent written language in a way that is comparable to such representations of spoken language, we should be including in the text every preliminary scrap of manuscript or typescript, with all the crossings out, misspellings, redraftings and periods of silent thought; this would then tell us what the writer actually wrote.

Now, there are undoubtedly research purposes for which it is important to show the planning, trial and error, and revision work that has gone into the production of a piece of discourse: it can have both educational and clinical applications. This is as true of writing as it is of speech: written material of this kind has been used in neuropsychiatry for most of a century. But for many purposes the discarded first attempts are merely trivial; they clutter up the text, making it hard to read, and impart to it a spurious air of quaintness. What is much more serious, however, is that transcribing spoken discourse in this way gives a false account of what it is really like. It may seem a harmless piece of self-gratification for a few academics to present spoken language as a pathological phenomenon; one might argue that they deceive nobody but themselves. But unfortunately this is not the way. Just when we are seeing real collaboration between linguists and educators, and the conception of "language in education" is at last gaining ground as a field of training and research, it seems we are determined to put the clock back to a time when spoken language was not to be taken seriously and could have no place in the theory and practice of education.

Let us recapitulate the argument. Speech and writing as forms of discourse are typically associated with the two modal points on the continuum from most spontaneous to most self-monitored language: spontaneous discourse is usually spoken, self-monitored discourse is usually written. We can therefore conveniently label these two modal points "spoken" and "written" language. Spoken and written language do not differ in their systematicity: each is equally highly organized, regular, and productive of coherent discourse. (This is clearly implied once we recognize them both as "language.")

Discourse in either medium can be characterized by hesitation, revision, change of direction, and other similar features; these tend to arise when attention is being paid to the process of text production. Since highly monitored discourse is typically written, these features are actually more characteristic of writing than of speech; but because most written text becomes public only in its final, edited form, the hesitations and discards are lost and the reader is shielded from seeing the process at work. Where they are likely to remain in is precisely where they occur least, in the more spontaneous kinds of writing such as personal letters. (Not all discourse features that are regarded as pathological, or assigned negative value, are of this self-monitoring kind. One form of discourse that has received a lot of critical attention is casual conversation, where the well-recognized characteristics are those of turn-taking, such as interruptions and overlaps. But the strictly LINGUISTIC "deviations" of casual conversation are mainly systematic features that would not seem deviant if we had a grammar that took into account the specifically "spoken" resources of the linguistic system.)

Spoken and written language do differ, however, in their preferred patterns of lexicogrammatical organization. Neither is more organized than the other, but they are organized in different ways. We have already identified the principal variable. Spoken language tends to accommodate more clauses in the syntagm (to favour greater "grammatical intricacy"), with fewer lexical items in the clause. Written language tends to accommodate more lexical items in the clause (to favour greater "lexical density"), with fewer clauses in the syntagm. (This does not imply, of course, that the AVERAGE number of clauses per clause complex will be greater in spoken language, because there may also be a tendency towards very short ones, especially in dialogue. It would be better to say that the greater the intricacy of a clause complex the more likely it is to be a product of spontaneous speech.) We must now return to this distinction in order to look through and beyond it.

A Closer Look at the Difference

Let us illustrate with another passage of written discourse (Text 7):

> 7   *Thus the sympathetic induction of people into a proper and deep understanding of what Christianity is about should not be bracketed simply with the evangelizing aim to which I referred earlier. It is not absolutely incompatible with that aim, however, for the following reason. What counts as indoctrination and the like depends upon a number of criteria, to do with the degree to which a teacher fails to mention alternative beliefs, the tone of voice used, the lack of sympathy for the criticisms levelled at Christianity or Humanism and so on. A dogmatic teacher or lecturer differs from an open one. The non-dogmatic teacher may be tepid; the open one may be fervent. Fervour and indifference are not functions of closedness and openness.* (Smart, 1968, p. 98)

This has the high lexical density that is typical of written language: 52 lexical items, 8 clauses, density 6.5 (ignoring embedded clauses; if embedded clauses are counted, then 66 lexical items, 19 clauses, density 4.7). Let us make this explicit by setting it out clause by clause:

>   clause complex boundary |||
>   clause boundary ||
>   embedded clause   [ ]
>   lexical items shown in **boldface**

> ||| Thus the **sympathetic induction** of people into a **proper** and **deep understanding** of [what **Christianity** is about] should not be **bracketed simply** with the **evangelizing aim** [to which **I referred earlier**]. ||| It is not absolutely **incompatible** with that **aim**, however, for the **following reason**. ||| [What **counts** as **indoctrination** and the like] **depends** upon a number of **criteria,** || to **do** with the **degree** [to which a **teacher fails** to **mention alternative beliefs**], the **tone** of voice [**used**], the **lack of sympathy** for the **criticism** [**levelled** at **Christianity** or **Humanism**] and so on. ||| A **dogmatic teacher** or **lecturer differs** from an **open** one. ||| The **non-dogmatic** teacher may be **tepid;** || the **open** one may **be fervent.** ||| **Fervour** and **indifference** are not **functions** of **closedness** and **openness.** |||

To see how this lexical density is achieved, we can look at the first clause. After the cohesive *thus,* it begins with a nominal group *the sympathetic induction of people into a proper and deep understanding of what Christianity is about.* The Head is *induction;* the Postmodifier consists of a series of alternating embedded prepositional phrases and nominal groups, mainly one inside the other, and ending with an embedded clause:

> | *the sympathetic induction* [*of* [*people*]] [*into* [*a proper and deep understanding*
> [*of* [[*what*] <*Christianity* | *is*> *about*]]]] |

group or phrase boundary |
embedded group or phrase   [ ]
enclosed elements   < >
(the prepositional phrase *what . . . about* is discontinuous, the items *Christianity* and *is being* enclosed within it)

This nominal group contains a large amount of lexical information; and if we take this passage as a whole we find that out of the 52 lexical items the only ones that do NOT occur in nominal groups are *bracketed, simply, depends, do,* and *differ.* It is a characteristic of written discourse that most of the lexical information is encoded in nominal form: that is, in nominal groups, with their structure potential of Head (typically a noun or adjective), Premodifier (typically adjectives and nouns), and Postmodifier (typically embedded phrases and clauses, which then have further nominal groups inside them).

Not every instance of a nominal group has a complex structure, of course; the remaining ones in this passage range from

| *the lack* [*of* [*sympathy* [*for* [*the criticisms* [*levelled* | *at* [*Christianity or Humanism*]]]]] |

which like the first one involves considerable embedding, to simple nominal groups such as *tepid, the open one, fervour* and *indifference.* But it is the potential for extended structures of this kind which enables the nominal group to take over the main burden of the lexical content of the, discourse.

So while spoken English is marked by intricacy in the clause complex, written English is marked by complexity in the nominal group. Since the lexical items have to go somewhere, lexical density is accompanied by its own characteristic resources within the grammar. The key factor is the structure of the nominal group; and within that, the critical resource is that of embedding, because of its open-endedness—the recursive function which generates sequences like

implicit [*in* [*the argument* [*about* [*the necessity* [*of* [*the parahistorical approach* [*to* [*religious studies*]]]]]]]]

(Smart, 1968, p. 98)

If now we construct a more "spoken" variant of one of the long nominal groups taken from Text 7, we might arrive at something like the following:

||| *people can be sympathetically persuaded* α
|| *so that they understand properly and deeply* $^{\times}\beta\alpha$
|| *what Christianity is about* ||| $\beta'\beta$

where the structure is $\alpha\ ^{\times}\beta\alpha\ \beta'\beta$. In place of the embedding, which is a nominalizing device, we have hypotaxis, which is a form of interdependency between clauses; and this points up the difference between the two variants.

This difference is obscured, on the other hand, if the grammar fails to distinguish between embedding and **hypotaxis.** Traditional grammar lumped them together, under the heading of subordination, and treated them both as **embedding** (noun clause, adjectival clause, adverbial clause). In other words, being a grammar of written language, it recognized only the category that was characteristic of written language. This ambiguity is in fact still present in the concept of embedding, which is why I have often employed the term **rank shift** to refer just to embedding in the strict sense, and so distinguish it from the interdependency relation of hypotaxis, where one element is dependent on another but is not a constituent of it. Hypotaxis is more like parataxis than it is like embedding; and both are characteristic of spoken rather than written language. So in order to do justice to the particular mode of organization of both spoken and written discourse, the grammar needs to distinguish between the constituency relation of embedding, or rank shift, where one element is a structural part of another, and the dependency relation of "taxis," where one element is bound or linked to another but is not a part of it. Either of these relations can be reduced to a form of the other one, but only at the cost of distorting the nature of discourse.

The distinction between embedding and hypotaxis—between, for example, *the conviction* [*that he failed*] / [*of failure*] and *was convinced* || *that he had failed;* or between *the effect* [*of such a decision*] *would be* [*that no further launchings could take place*] and *if they decide that way* || *no further . . .* —is an important one; but it is really an instance, and a symptom, of a more general and fundamental divergence. As always, when we talk about these phenomena, and when we illustrate them, they will appear as dichotomies: either this way or that. As always, however, at least in the present context (but also in most issues that have to do with language), they must be seen as tendencies—more or less continuous variation along a line, but with most actual instances (most texts, in this case) tending towards one pole or the other. The divergent tendency that is manifested in the distinction of hypotaxis and embedding is one that can be expressed in terms of the familiar opposition of process and product. Written language represents phenomena as if they were products. Spoken language represents phenomena as if they were processes (see the discussion in Martin, 1984).

In other words: speaking and writing—each one makes the world look like itself. A written text is an object; so what is represented in writing tends to be given the form of an object. But when one talks, one is doing; so when one talks about something, one tends to say that it happened or was done. So, in Text 3 above, the written variant tells the story in nouns: *visit, sense, risk, attempt, action;* whereas the spoken version tells it in verbs: *visited, ended up feeling, might get hurt, tried to do.*

This is to look at it from the point of view of the writer or speaker. For reader or listener, there is a corresponding difference in the way the discourse is received. To the reader, the text is presented synoptically: it exists, spread out on the page. So the reader is predisposed to take a synoptic view of what it means; behind it is a tableau—like the pictures from which writing originally evolved. But when one is listening, the text reaches one dynamically: it happens, by travelling through the air. So the listener is predisposed to take a dynamic view of what it means; behind it is a film, not a picture.

Grammatical Metaphor

Where then in the linguistic system do spoken and written discourse diverge? A language, if it is not written down, consists of three interrelated subsystems: a semantic system (meanings), coded into a lexico-grammatical system (wordings), recoded into a phonological system (sounds). A language that has a writing system has an alternative form of expression: visual symbols as well as sounds. In such a language, a written text could, in principle, be a spoken text that has been written down ("transcribed"); here the written version is a transcoding of something that has already been coded in sound. Most writing is not like this. Secondly, a written text could be an alternative EXPRESSION of a given wording: in this case meanings are coded as words and structures ("wordings"), which are then expressed EITHER in sound OR in writing. If this was the norm, there would be no systematic difference between spoken and written texts; the medium would not be a significant register variable. But there are such differences; so, to some extent at least, spoken and written discourse must represent alternative WORDINGS. In this case, meanings are coded either as "speakable wordings" or as "writeable wordings," the former appropriate to the dynamic nature of the text process, the latter appropriate to the synoptic nature of the text product. This is the sort of interpretation we have been offering.

But is it the whole story? There is still a fourth possibility—that speech and writing can diverge already at the semantic level, so that spoken and written discourse embody different meanings. Is there any sign that this can happen? It would of course be only a very partial effect; no one has suggested that the two derive from different semantic systems (or even two different lexicogrammatical systems, for that matter). But we should consider the possibility that there is some flowback into the meaning.

Consider the last sentence of Text 2, in its original written form (2A):

The current popular concern over the environment has stimulated private civil actions of two main types.

We "translated" it into something more speechlike as:

At present, people are concerned about the environment; so they have been bringing quite a few private civil actions, which have been mainly of two kinds.

But this could be wrong; it may have meant:

At present, people are concerned about the environment; so there have been mainly two kinds of action being brought by private citizens.

There is no way of deciding: BY REFERENCE TO THE SPOKEN VERSION, the written version is simply ambiguous. Compare the following, also from a written text:

A further complication was the 650-ton creeper cranes poised above the end of each 825-foot arm.

Does this mean

> *Above the end of each 825-foot arm there were poised 650-ton creeper cranes, and they made the work more complicated.*

or does it mean

> *... and this made the work more complicated.*

(i.e., not the cranes, but the fact that they were poised where they were)? Another example is

> *Slavish imitation of models is nowhere implied.*

This could be reworded either as *it is nowhere implied that models have been slavishly imitated,* or as *... that models should be slavishly imitated.*

Examples of this kind could be added to indefinitely; they arise because nominal constructions fail to make explicit many of the semantic relations that are made explicit in clause structure. Written discourse conceals many local ambiguities of this kind, which are revealed when one attempts a more "spoken" paraphrase.

But the final sentence of Text 2 illustrates another significant feature of written language, which can be seen in the wording *popular concern over the environment has stimulated private civil actions.* We reworded this as *people are concerned about the environment, so they have been bringing private civil actions.* The original is one clause with the verb *stimulate* representing the Process; in other words, the thesis is encoded as a single happening, and what happened was that A brought about B. But A and B are themselves nominalized processes. The meaning of *stimulate* here is as in *pruning stimulates growth.* The spoken version represents the thesis as two distinct processes, linked by a relation of cause; cf. *if the tree is pruned, it will grow.*

Here one kind of process has been dressed up by the grammar to look like a process of a different kind—or, in this instance, two processes, one mental and one material, have been dressed up as one which is neither. This coding of a semantic relation BETWEEN two processes as if it was THE single process is very common in writing; the sentence immediately preceding Text 2A contained another example of the same thing, here with the verb *leads to:*

> *A successful tort action leads to a judgment of damages or an injunction against the defendant company.*

But this is just one type of a more general phenomenon, something that I call **grammatical metaphor** (Halliday, 1985, chap. 10). Written language tends to display a high degree of grammatical metaphor, and this is perhaps its single most distinctive characteristic.

Here are three further examples of grammatical metaphor taken from various written sources, together with suggested rewordings which are less metaphorical:

Issue of the specially-coded credit cards will be subject to normal credit checking procedures.
    'Credit cards have been specially coded and will be issued only when credit has been checked in the normal way.'

Strong Christmas sales were vital to the health of the retail industry, particularly in the present depressed climate.
    'Unless many goods were sold at Christmas the retail industry would not be healthy, particularly when the economy is depressed as it is now.'

He also credits his former big size with much of his career success.
    'He also believes that he was successful in his career mainly because he used to be big.'

In all these examples **nominalization** plays a significant part, as it does in many types of grammatical metaphor; so it is perhaps worth stressing that nominalization is well motivated in English. It is not simply a ritual feature that has evolved to make written language more ambiguous or obscure; like the passive, which is another feature whose functions are widely misunderstood, nominalization is an important resource for organizing information. Take the example *youth protest mounted*, which is not a headline but a complete sentence from a feature article. We might reword this as *more and more young people protested*, or *young people protested more and more*; but the only way to get the combination of *youth* and *protest* as the Theme of the clause is by means of a nominalization (not necessarily such a laconic one; it might have been *the protests of the young people*, but this is still a nominalizing of the process). So while there is a price to be paid, in that the information being conveyed may become mildly (and sometimes severely) ambiguous, there is also a payoff: more choice of status in the discourse. In terms of systemic theory, there is a loss of ideational information, but a gain in textual information. This of course favours the specialist: you need to know the register. If you do not know the register you may misinterpret the thesis, so the fact that it is highly coded as a message is not very helpful to you; but if you do know it you will select the right interpretation automatically, and the additional "functional sentence perspective" is all tax-free profit.

Some nominalizations of course cannot be denominalized, like *private civil actions at law* or *an injunction against the defendant company*. These are abstractions that can enter into the structure of a clause—civil actions can be brought, an injunction can be issued—but cannot themselves be coded as finite verbs. Much of our environment today consists of such abstract entities and institutions; their representation in nominal form is no longer metaphorical—if it ever was—and they have become part of our ideology, our way of knowing about the world we live in. Patterns of this kind invade the spoken language and then act as infiltrators, providing cover for other metaphorical nominalizations—which are still functional in speech, but considerably less so, because spoken language has other resources for structuring the message, such as intonation and rhythm.

Grammatical metaphor is not confined to written language: quite apart from its tendency to be borrowed from speech into writing, there are specific instances of it which seem clearly to have originated in speech—most notably the pattern of lexically empty verb with the process expressed as "cognate object" (Range) as in *make a mistake* 'err', *have a bath* 'bathe', *give a smile* 'smile'. But in its principal manifestations it is typically a feature of writing. Writing—that is, using the written medium—puts distance between the act of meaning and its counterpart in the real world; so writing—that is, the written language—achieves this distance symbolically by the use of grammatical metaphor. It is often said that written discourse is not dependent on its environment; but it would be more accurate to say that it creates an environment for itself (see Nystrand, this volume), and this is where it depends on its metaphorical quality. If I say *technology has improved,* this is presented as a message; it is part of what I am telling you. If I say *improvements in technology,* I present it as something I expect you to take for granted. By objectifying it, treating it as if it was a thing, I have backgrounded it; the message is contained in what follows (e.g., ... *are speeding up the writing of business programmes*). Grammatical metaphor performs for the written language a function that is the opposite of foregrounding; it backgrounds, using discourse to create the context for itself. This is why in the world of writing it often happens that all the ideational content is objectified, as background, and the only traces of process are the relations that are set up between these taken-for-granted objects. I recall a sentence from the O.S.T.I. Programme in the Linguistic Properties of Scientific English (Huddleston, Hudson, Winter, & Henrici, 1968) which used to typify for us the structures found in scientific writing:

> *The conversion of hydrogen to helium in the interiors of stars is the source of energy for their immense output of light and heat.*

Ways of Knowing and Learning

In calling the written mode metaphorical we are of course making an assumption; in fact each mode is metaphorical from the standpoint of the other, and the fact that the spoken is developmentally prior—the individual listens and speaks before he reads and writes—while it means that the language of "process" is LEARNT first, does not guarantee that it is in any sense "closer to reality." It might be a hangover from an earlier stage of evolution, like the protolanguage that precedes the mother tongue. But personally I do not think so. I am inclined to think the written language of the future will go back (or rather forward) to being more processlike; not only because the traditional objectlike nature of written discourse is itself changing—our reading matter is typed into a memory and fed to us in a continuous flow as the lines follow each other up the screen—but also because our understanding of the physical world has been moving in that direction, ever since Einstein substituted space-time for space and time. As Bertrand Russell expounded it in 1925 (1977, p. 54),

> We are concerned with *events*, rather than with *bodies*. In the old theory, it was possible to consider a number of bodies all at the same instant, and since the time was the same for all of them it could be ignored. But now we cannot do that if we are to obtain an objective account of physical occurrences. We must mention the date at which a body is to be considered, and thus we arrive at an '*event*', that is to say, something which happens at a given time.

Meanwhile, grammatical analysis shows spoken and written English to be systematically distinct: distinct, that is, in respect of a number of related tendencies, all of which combine to form a single package. But it turns out to be a semantic package: the different features that combine to distinguish spoken and written discourse can be shown to be related and encompassed within a single generalization, only when we express this generalization in semantic terms—or at least in terms of a functional, meaning-oriented interpretation of grammar. Speech and writing will appear, then, as different ways of meaning: speech as spun out, flowing, choreographic, oriented towards events (doing, happening, sensing, saying, being), processlike, intricate, with meanings related serially; writing as dense, structured, crystalline, oriented towards things (entities, objectified processes), productlike, tight, with meanings related as components.

In their discussion of the comprehension and memory of discourse, Hildyard and Olson (1982, p. 20) suggested that meaning is PRESERVED in different ways by speakers and listeners:

> Readers and listeners may tend to extract different kinds of information from oral and written statements. Listeners may tend to recall more of the gist of the story and readers may recall more of the surface structure or verbatim features of the story.

In other words, the listener processes text largely at the level of meaning, the reader more, or at least as much, at the level of wording. But this is specifically a function of the medium in which the text is received, rather than of the linguistic features of the code that lies behind it. The notion of different ways of meaning implies, rather, that there are different ways of knowing, and of learning. Spoken and written language serve as complementary resources for acquiring and organizing knowledge; hence they have different places in the educational process. Teachers often know, by a combination of intuition and experience, that some things are more effectively learnt through talk and others through writing. Official policy usually equates educational knowledge with the written mode and commonsense knowledge with the spoken; but teachers' actual practice goes deeper—educational knowledge demands both, the two often relating to different aspects of the same phenomenon. For example: definitions, and structural relations, are probably best presented in writing; demonstrations of how things work may be more easily followed through speech. The two favourite strategies for describing the layout of an apartment, reported in the well-known study by Linde and Labov (1975), would seem to exemplify spoken and written modes of symbolic exploration. We may assume that speech and writing play different and complementary parts in the construction of ideologies (Hasan, 1986), since each offers a different way of knowing and of reflecting on experience.

Considerations of this kind are an essential element in any linguistic theory of learning. The development of such a theory is perhaps the most urgent task of educational linguistics; and certain components of it can already be recognized: (1) the child's construction of language, from presymbolic communication through protolanguage to the mother tongue; (2) the processing of new meanings into the system; (3) the interaction between learning elements that are ready coded and learning the principles of coding; (4) the relation between system and process in language; (5) the unconscious nature of linguistic categories; (6) the social construction of reality through conversation; (7) linguistic strategies used in learning; (8) the development of functional variation, or registers; (9) the relation between everyday language and technical language; and (10) the development of generalization, abstraction, and metaphor. The absence of any general theory of learning based on language has been a significant gap in educational thinking and practice. This provides an important context for our current concern, since the complementarity of spoken and written language will certainly be a central issue in any learning theory which has language as its primary focus.

Notes

1 For details of analysis see Halliday (1985, pp. 192 ff).
2 Hypotaxis is not equivalent to embedding, which is a constituency (not a "tactic") relation; see Table 8.4.

References

Abercrombie, D. (1963). Conversation and spoken prose. *English Language Teaching, 18*(1). (Reprinted in *Studies in phonetics and linguistics* (Language & Language Learning, Vol. 10, pp. 1–9). London: Oxford University Press, 1965.)

Beattie, G. (1983). *Talk: An analysis of speech and non-verbal behaviour in conversation.* Milton Keynes: Open University Press.

Boas, F. (1911). *Introduction to the Handbook of American Indian Languages* (Bulletin of the Bureau of American Ethnology, Vol. 40, No. 1). Washington, DC: Smithsonian Institution. (Reprinted with Foreword by C. I. J. M. Stuart. Washington DC: Georgetown University Press, 1963.)

Chafe, W. L. (1982). Integration and involvement in speaking, writing and oral literature. In D. Tannen (Ed.), *Spoken and written language: Exploring orality and literacy* (Advances in Discourse Processes, Vol. IX, pp. 35–54). Norwood, NJ: Ablex.

Doughty, P. S., Pearce, J. J., & Thornton, G. M. (1971). *Language in use.* London: Arnold (for the Schools Council).

Halliday, M. A. K. (1985). *Introduction to functional grammar.* London: Arnold.

Hasan, R. (1986). The ontogenesis of ideology: an interpretation of mother child talk. In T. Threadgold *et al.* (Eds.), *Semiotics, ideology, language* (Sydney Studies in Society and Culture, Vol. 3, pp. 125–146). Sydney: Sydney Association for Studies in Society and Culture.

Hildyard, A. & Olson, D. R. (1982). On the comprehension and memory of oral vs. written discourse. In D. Tannen (Ed.), *Spoken and written language: Exploring orality and literacy* (Advances in Discourse Processes, Vol. IX, pp. 19–34). Norwood, NJ: Ablex.

Huddleston, R. D., Hudson, R. A., Winter, E. O., & Henrici, A. (1968). *Sentence and clause in scientific English* (O.S.T.I. Programme in the Linguistic Properties of Scientific English, Final Report). London University College, Communication Research Centre.

Hymes, D. H. (1971). Competence and performance in linguistic theory. In R. Huxley & E. Ingram (Eds.), *Language acquisition: Models and methods*. London & New York: Academic Press.

Linde, C. & Labov, W. (1975). Spatial networks as a site for the study of language and thought. *Language, 51,* 924–939.

Mackay, D., Thompson, B., & Schaub, P. (1970). *Breakthrough to literacy.* London: Longman (for the Schools Council).

Martin, J. R. (1984). Process and text: two aspects of human semiosis. In J. D. Benson & W. S. Greaves (Eds.), *Systemic perspectives on discourse: Selected theoretical papers from the Ninth International Systemic Wokshop.* Norwood, NJ: Ablex.

Mathesius, V. (1911). O potenciálnosti jevů jazykových [On the potentiality of the phenomena of language]. *Proceedings of the Czech Academy of Sciences, Philosophy and History Section.* (English trans. in J. Vachek (Ed.), *A Prague school reader in linguistics* (pp. 1–32). Bloomington, IN: Indiana University Press, 1964.)

Russell, B. (1925). *ABC of relativity.* London: Allen & Unwin. (3rd rev. ed., F. Pirani (Ed.), 1977.)

Smart, N. (1968). *Secular education and the logic of religion.* London: Faber & Faber.

Tannen, D. (1982). Oral and literate strategies in spoken and written narrative. *Language, 58,* 1–21.

Ure, J. N. (1971). Lexical density and register differentiation. In G. E. Perren & J. L. M. Trim (Eds.), *Applications of linguistics: Selected papers of the Second World Congress of Applied Linguistics, Cambridge, 1969* (pp. 443–452). London: Cambridge University Press.

Wilkinson, A. M. (Ed.) (1966). *Some aspects of oracy.* London: National Association for the Teaching of English.

9.
THE SHIFTING RELATIONSHIPS BETWEEN SPEECH AND WRITING
Peter Elbow

> Paradoxes ... beset the relationships between the original spoken word and all its technological transformations.... [I]ntelligence is relentlessly reflexive, so that even the external tools that it uses to implement its workings become "internalized," that is, part of its own reflexive process.
>
> (Ong, *Orality*, 81)[1]

We have seen interesting work in recent years on the nature of speech and writing and the mentalities associated with each. The insights from these investigations are extremely valuable, but a dangerous assumption is sometimes inferred from them: that speech and writing are distinctly characterizable media, each of which has its own inherent features and each of which tends to foster a particular cognitive process, or "mentality."[2] I am interested in the cognitive processes associated with speech and writing, but instead of saying that each medium has a particular tendency, I will argue that each medium can draw on and foster *various* mentalities. This essay is a call for writers and teachers of writing to recognize the enormous choice we have and to learn to take more control over the cognitive effects associated with writing. This essay is in three parts—each showing a different relationship between speech and writing.

I. The Traditional View: Indelible Writing, Ephemeral Speech

Obviously writing is more indelible or permanent than speech. Speech is nothing but wind, waves of temporarily squashed air, waves that begin at once to disperse, that is, to lose their sound. Writing, on the other hand, stays there—"down in black and white." Once we get it on paper it takes on a life of its own, separate from the writer. It "commits us to paper." It can be brought back to haunt us: read in a different context from the one we had in mind—read by any audience, whether or not we know them or want them to see our words.

Where the *intention* to speak usually results automatically in the *act* of speech, writing almost always involves delay and effort. Writing forces us not only to form the letters, spell the words, and follow stricter rules of correctness (than speech); we must also get into the text itself all those cues that readers might need who are not present to

---

Elbow, Peter. "The Shifting Relationships Between Speech and Writing," *College Composition and Communication* 36 (1985): 283–303.

us as we write, who don't know the context for our words, and who don't know us or how we speak. In addition to this "contextualizing," we must capture onto the page some substitute for all those vocal and visual cues for listeners that we give without effort or attention in speaking. We can take nothing for granted in writing; the text has to say it all.

In the effort to do all these things as we write, how can we help but pause and reflect on whether what we are engaged in putting down is really right—or even if it is, whether it is what we really wanted to say? If we are going to take the trouble to write something down, then, we might as well get it right. *Getting it right,* then, feels like an inherent demand in the medium itself of writing.

Research (see Tannen, "Oral and Literate Strategies") shows that speech tends to carry more "phatic" messages than writing—messages about the relationship between the speaker and the listener or between the speaker and his material (e.g., "I know you're my friend"), even when the ostensible function of the spoken words is purely substantive or informational. Thus writing tends to carry a much higher proportion of "content" messages to absent readers—more permanent messages which are judged for validity and adequacy, not just accepted as social interchange.

This feeling that we must get things right in writing because written words are more indelible than speech is confirmed when we look to the *history* of speech and writing. The development of writing as a technology seems to have led to the development of careful and logical thinking—to a greater concern with "trying to get it *really* right" (see Ong, *Orality,* and his other works; Goody, *Domestication;* Havelock, *Plato*). Ong claims that the development of writing gave us a new "noetic economy," that is, a wholly new relationship to words and knowledge—new habits of shaping, storing, retrieving, and communicating what we know.[3]

We see a parallel argument about the teaching of writing. That is, leading theorists tell us that the poor thinking we see in many of our students stems from their not yet having made that great developmental leap from oral language strategies to written or literate language strategies (Lunsford, "Cognitive Development"; Shaughnessy, *Errors.*) Obviously, students can think better when they can examine their thoughts more self-consciously as a string of assertions arranged in space. The technology of indelible writing permits students in a sense to step out of the flux of time: to detach themselves from oral discourse, from the context in which words are uttered and first thought about, and from the tendency in speech to rely on concrete and experiential modes of discourse. As Havelock emphasizes, writing helps to separate the knower from the known.

This contrast between the two media is reinforced when we turn to the story of how we learn to speak and to write as individuals. We learn speech as infants—from parents who love us and naturally reward us for speaking at all. Our first audience works overtime to hear the faintest intention in our every utterance, no matter how hidden or garbled that meaning may be. Children aren't so much criticized for getting something wrong as praised for having anything at all to say—indeed they are often praised even for emitting speech as pure play with no message intended.

What a contrast between that introduction to speech and the introduction to writing which most children get in school. Students can never feel writing as an activity they engage in as freely, frequently, or spontaneously as they do in speech. Indeed, because writing is almost always a requirement set by the teacher, the act of writing takes on a "required" quality, sometimes even the aspect of punishment. I can still hear the ominous cadence in my ears: "Take out your pens." Indeed, in the classic case of school punishment the crime is speech and the punishment is writing ("I will not talk in class. I will not talk in class."). Do some teachers still insist, as some of mine did, that ink must be used? The effect was to heighten our sense of writing as indelible, as the act of making irrevocable choices—as though there were something wrong about changing our minds.

I don't want to imply gradgrindish conditions which may no longer be widespread. But the school setting in which most of us learn to write and have most of our writing experiences till we leave school is just one more reason why we experience writing as more indelible than speech—and why we experience writing as inherently a medium for *getting it right*.[4]

But we need to turn this accustomed picture upside down.

II. *Speech* as Indelible, Writing as Ephemeral

As Roland Barthes says, "it is ephemeral speech which is indelible, not monumental writing.... Speech is irreversible: a [spoken] word cannot be retracted..." ("Death of the Author"). Precisely because speech is nothing but temporary crowdings in air molecules, we can never revise it. If we speak in the hearing of others—and we seldom speak otherwise—our words are heard by listeners who can remember them even (or especially) if we say something we wish they would forget. Once we've said (as a joke), "I've never liked that shirt you gave me," or (in a fight), "Well damn it, that *is* a woman's job," or even (in a seminar, without thinking about what our colleagues might think of us), "I've never been able to understand that poem"—or once Jesse Jackson refers to Jews in public as "hymies"—once any of these words are spoken, none can be undone.

Speech is inherently more indelible than writing also because it is a more vivid medium. When we speak, listeners don't just see our words, they see us—how we hold and move ourselves. Even if we only hear someone over the phone or on the radio—perhaps even someone we've never met—still we experience the texture of her talk: the rhythms, emphases, hesitations, and other tonalities of speech which give us a dramatized sense of her character or personality. And if we *don't* reveal ourselves more through our speech than our writing, that too is taken as a revelation: someone will say, as of Gary Hart, "he seems a bit cool and aloof."

But perhaps you will reply that *casual speech is* more ephemeral than writing. Yet there are plenty of occasions when we are trying as hard as we can to "get it right" in speech—because our speech is "a speech," or an "oral report," or discourse to strangers; or for some reason we feel we are being carefully judged for our speech, as in a job interview. Perhaps casual speech is more common in our culture—or in literate or print cultures—than in others. In oral cultures such as the Homeric Greek, the

Anglo-Saxon, and the Native American, there was scorn for anyone who spoke hasty unplanned words. Perhaps we fall into the assumption that speech is ephemeral because we live in a blabbing culture.

In short, our sense of speech as ephemeral and writing as indelible stems not so much from the nature of speech and writing as media but from how and where they are most often used. (And researched. See Schafer, "Spoken and Written," for a corrective view.) Our paradigm for speech is casual conversation among trusted friends; our paradigm for writing is more formal discourse to a little-known audience or an audience that is likely to judge us on our utterance.

So far from speech being ephemeral, then, the problem with speech is that it isn't ephemeral enough. What we need is a mode of discourse that really *is* ephemeral—we need the luxury of being able to utter everything on our minds and not have anyone hear it until *after* we decide what we really mean or how we want to say it. Interestingly enough, the most indelible medium of all is also the most ephemeral: writing.

However indelible the ink, writing can be completely evanescent and without consequences. We can write in solitude—indeed we seldom write otherwise—we can write whatever we want, we can write as badly as we want, and we can write one thing and then change our mind. No one need know what we've written or how we've written it. In short, writing turns out to be the ideal medium for *getting it wrong*. (This evanescence of writing is enormously enhanced by the new electronic media where words are just electrical or magnetic impulses on a screen or a disk.)

Perhaps there's nothing new in the idea of writing as ephemeral. Perhaps the phrase from Barthes has tempted me into that Gallic weakness for trying to phrase the obvious as a scandal. In the days of parchment people wrote to last, but now we are flooded with ephemeral temporary documents.[5]

But though we float on a rising tide of ephemeral writing, our writing habits and instincts are dominated by the old assumption that writing is indelible. That is, most people, even when they are writing a draft that no one will read, nevertheless write by habit *as though readers were going to see it.* Do I exaggerate? Plenty of people experiment or make a mess as they write. Yet what do most people do when they are writing along and they suddenly wonder whether they really believe what they are about to write, or whether it holds up on examination, or even whether it is well phrased. Most people stop writing and don't resume writing till they have figured out what they want to say. This *feels* like a reasonable and normal way to behave, but notice the assumption it reveals: that the function of writing is to record what we have *already* decided—not to figure out *whether* we believe it. If we were speaking, we would be much more likely to speak the train of thought as it comes to mind even though we're not sure of our final opinion—as a *way* of making up our minds. It is almost as though we fear, as we write, that someone might at any moment swoop down and read what we have just written and see that it is rubbish.

Thus writing for most people is dominated by the experience of not writing: of elaborate planning beforehand to decide what to write and frequent pausing in midcourse to search for the right word or the right path. This non-writing behavior is not surprising since *planning* is probably stressed more than anything else in advice to writers. (This advice is stressed not only in traditional textbooks but in recent ones such as Linda Flower's.) But because of my own difficulties in writing, I have come to notice the enormous cognitive and linguistic leverage that comes from learning to avoid the mentality dominated by the indelibility of writing and learning instead to exploit the ephemeral or "under" side of writing. It feels very different to put down words not as commitment but as trial, or as Barthes and some of the deconstructionists say, as play, *jouissance*, or the free play of language and consciousness. Thinking is enriched. Writing in this mode can produce an *immersion in discourse itself* that doesn't occur when we sit and think—an immersion in language that can entice us into ideas and perceptions we could not get by planning.

Exploiting the ephemeral quality of writing is often a matter of exploiting chaos and incoherence. Often I find I cannot work out what I am trying to say unless I am extremely disorganized, fragmented, and associative, and let myself go down contrary paths to see where they lead. (Note that what one is *trying to say* is more than what one *has in mind*—see Perl on "felt sense" in "Understanding Composing.") I can't be that incoherent when I start off trying to write it right. I can't even be that incoherent in speech. My listeners are too impatient for sense, for my main point. (Now I know why I often close my eyes when talking about something difficult: it is an instinctive attempt to blot out the audience and their implicit demand that I be clear and come to the point.) So when trying to write it right, and even in speaking, I must usually settle for the short run of *some* coherence—making *some* sense—and abandon the thread (only it's not really a thread because it's so broken) of the long-run, incipient, more complex meaning which has been tickling the back of my mind. But when I write in the ephemeral and fully exploratory mode for myself alone, I can usually find that meaning by inviting myself to wander around it and finally stumble into it. Thus whereas the commonsense view is that planning is more appropriate to writing than to speaking, the opposite is also true: we badly need arenas for *nonplanning* in our discourse, and speech is too constricting. For nonplanning we need private writing.

We think of the mind's natural capacity for chaos and disorganization as the *problem* in writing—and before we finish any piece of indelible public writing, of course, that incoherence must be overcome. But what a relief it is to realize that this capacity for ephemeral incoherence is valuable and can be harnessed for insight and growth. The most precious thing in this kind of writing is to find one contradicting oneself. It guarantees that there will be some movement and growth in one's thinking; the writing will not just be a record of past thoughts or prejudices. (Good teachers, in commenting on student papers, have learned to see contradictions in the text as positive opportunities for mental action and growth, not just as problems.)

But even when we have the safety of knowing that our words are private and ephemeral and that we will revise them into coherence, we often feel there is something dangerous about letting ourselves write down what is wrong or doubtful or ungainly, or even just something we are not sure we believe. To do so seems to violate a taboo that derives from a magical sense that writing is indelible even if no one else ever sees the words. We stop and correct our words or crumple up the sheet because it feels as though if we leave the wrong words there, they will somehow pollute us. Words on paper will "take"—debilitate the mind. Yet we cannot exploit the ephemerality of language unless we are willing to take the risk.

But why not use the *mind* for all this ephemeral work? Would God have given us a mind if he'd wanted us to waste all this paper writing down what's wrong or badly put? But that internal thinking process lacks a dimension which writing provides. When we just think inside our heads, the cycle of language is incomplete; we are prey to obsession. The thoughts, sentences, images, or feelings that play in our heads continue to play round and round. But when we write down those thoughts or feelings, the sterile circle is often broken: they have a place on paper now; they evolve into another thought or even fade away. Writing is a way to get what is inside one's head outside, on paper, so there's room for more.[6] (Of course speaking too can have this same function—"getting things out"—but sometimes the presence of a listener is a hindrance.)

I come here to what I most want to emphasize: the *mentalities* related to speech and writing. Ong and the others emphasize how the use of writing enhances logical, abstract, and detached thinking. True enough. But there is a very different kind of good thinking which we can enhance by exploiting the underside of writing as ephemeral. And like the effect Ong speaks of, this kind of thinking is not just an occasional way of considering things but a pervasive mode of cognitive functioning, I'm talking about the mentality that gradually emerges when we learn how to put down what's in mind and invite that putting down to be *not* a committing ourselves to it but the opposite, a letting go of the burden of holding it in mind—a letting go of the burden of having it shape our mind. Having let it go, our mind can take on a different shape and go on to pick up a different thought.

In this way writing can function as a prosthesis for the mind—a surrogate mind instead of just a mouthpiece for the mind. For the mind is a structure of meaning and so too is a piece of writing. The mind, as a structure of meaning, can grow and develop through stages and so too can a piece of writing. Thus writing provides us with two organisms for thinking instead of just one, two containers instead of just one; the thoughts can go back and forth, richen and grow. We think of writing as deriving meaning from the mind that produces it, but when all goes well the *mind* derives meaning from the text it produces. (Organization, or meaning, or negative entropy, can flow in both directions.)

I don't mean to sound too mysterious here. I am just talking about the common phenomenon of people's ideas developing and changing as a result of their thinking. It often happens as people live and talk and write over months and years. But in truth, people tend to stay stuck in their points of view. They are prevented from growing until they get out of or move past the structure of meaning that is their mind. Ong might say that indelible, careful writing enhances such growth. Yes, that's true when all goes well. But the crucial mental event in growth is often the *abandonment* of a position we hold. Ephemeral writing is usually better than careful writing at helping us abandon what we start out thinking. (See Elbow, *Teachers*, Appendix essay.)

Thus the potentiality in writing that I want to highlight here does not just involve generative techniques for getting first drafts written quicker, but rather a genuine change in mentality or consciousness. The original development of writing long ago permitted a new mentality that fostered thinking that was more careful, detached, and logical. But along with it and the indelibility that makes writing valuable came also a mentality that tends to lock us into our views once we have carefully worked them out in writing. In contrast, the cultivation of writing as ephemeral fosters the *opposite* mentality whereby we use discourse (and writing in particular) not so much to express what we think but rather to develop and transform it.

Before going on to Section III, I should emphasize that the opposite claims in the first two sections—that writing is both more and also less indelible than speech—do not really undercut each other. My celebration of writing as ephemeral in no way diminishes the fact that writing is also the best medium for being careful, for getting things right, for "quality." I am unrepentant about insisting that we can have it both ways—if we learn how.

We need writing to help domesticate our minds (the title of Goody's book about the development of literacy is *The Domestication of the Savage Mind*), but we also need writing as a way to unleash some cognitive savagery—which is often lacking in a "literate" world too often lulled into thinking that picking up a pencil means planning and trying to get things right. And speech, being a social medium, seldom leads us to the conceptual wilderness we sometimes need.

For not only is there no theoretical contradiction between the two functions of writing, it turns out that they enhance or reinforce each other. People can be *more* careful and get their final drafts *righter* when they spend some of their time unhooking themselves from the demands of audience and inviting themselves to get it wrong. And contrarily, people can be more fruitful in the mentality of nonsteering when they know they will turn around and shift consciousness—impose care and control and try for indelibility—before their text goes to the real audience.

III. Writing as Similar to Speech

Having indicated two ways in which speech and writing are *different* or *opposite* from each other, finally I want to argue how they are or can be essentially similar. I will proceed by focusing on a series of features characteristic of speech, and argue in each case why we should seek to foster them in writing.

To exploit the speech-like qualities of writing as we teach is a way of teaching to strength: capitalizing on the oral language skills students already possess and helping students apply those skills immediately and effortlessly to writing—a way of helping with the crucial process Ong calls the "internalization of the technology of writing."

(1) In informal speech situations we can utter our words spontaneously—comfortably, naturally, unselfconsciously—with full attention on our meaning and no attention on how we actually *form* the signs or symbols that convey our meaning. We can come close to achieving this situation in writing through the use of

"spontaneous writing" or "freewriting": writing in which we put down whatever words come to mind—without regard to the conventions of forming words and without regard to the quality of the writing. We don't give the writing to an audience—or if we do, the audience merely "listens" to it for the meaning and doesn't respond (see Elbow, *Power*, 13–19). The work of Graves and Calkins shows how much we have tended to overestimate the amount of special knowledge or control of the medium people need for fluent and comfortable writing.

Speech is usually social and communal, writing solitary. But we can make writing communal too by having people write together and to each other in ways that are worth spelling out in more detail below.[7]

(2) Speech usually responds to a particular occasion and fits a particular context. It's not usually meant to last or be recorded—it's for a particular audience which is right there when the discourse is uttered and hears it right away. We can make all this happen in writing if we have students write in class or in small groups—particularly if they write about some issue or situation in which they are involved—and have them immediately share with each other what they write. The audience is right there and known; the writing is part of the context and the interaction of a particular group on a particular day. In speech, when something isn't clear, the audience asks for clarification right away. We can invite this naturally to happen in response to writing.

(3) In speech, the response—immediate, of course—is usually a *reply* to *what* has been said, not an *evaluative comment* on *how* it was said. And the reply is almost invariably an invitation to the speaker to reply to the reply. We can make this happen too in our teaching (though students often need coaching to get out of the assumption that the only way to respond to a text is to criticize it).

For of course the point of speech is often not to be a final or definitive statement but rather to keep the discourse going and produce more discourse in response—to sustain an ongoing dialogue or discussion. We can easily give writing this quality too by making our course a forum for constant writing-in-response-to-each-other's-writing, that is, by stressing the ways in which writing naturally functions as an invitation to future writing or a reply to previous writing—which is how most writing in the world actually occurs. Paradoxically, it turns out that if we invite much of the writing in a course to be more temporary and speech-like (that is, if we relax some of the pretense of chirographic, i.e., formal, definitiveness), students often manage to achieve *higher* levels of text-like definitiveness or indelibility on the fewer pieces where we stress revision and transcendence of local context.

For obviously I am not arguing that we should exploit similarities to speech in *all* the writing we ask of students. Many of our assignments should stress indelibility—stress the need for tight, coherent, final drafts which are statements that could survive outside the context of local author and local audience. We can decide on how much writing to treat in one mode or the other depending on the students we are teaching. For example, if the course is for weak students who are scared or uncomfortable in their writing, I would go quite far in exploiting speech similarities.

Thus the teaching practices I have just described *could* be called condescending strategies: ways to manage the writing context so as to *relax* temporarily some of the inherent difficulties in writing as a medium.[8] But I wish to go on now to stress how writing of the very highest quality—writing as good as any of us could possibly hope to achieve—not only can but should have many of the essential qualities somewhat misguidedly labelled "inherent in speech."

(4) The best writing has *voice*: the life and rhythms of speech. Unless we actively train our students to *speak onto paper,* they will write the kind of dead, limp, nominalized prose we hate—or *say* we hate. We see the difference most clearly in extreme cases: experienced teachers learn that when they get a student who writes prose that is so tied in knots that it is impenetrable they need only ask the student to *say* what she was getting at and the student will almost invariably speak the thought in syntax which is perfectly clear and lively, even if sometimes inelegantly colloquial. If the student had known enough to "speak the thought onto paper" and then simply cleaned up the syntax, the writing would have been much better than her best "essay writing."

(5) Excellent writing conveys some kind of involvement with the audience (though sometimes a quiet non-obtrusive involvement). This audience involvement is most characteristic of oral discourse. The best writing has just this quality of being somehow a piece of two-way communication, not one-way—of seeming to be an invitation to the audience to respond, or even seeming to be a reply to what the audience had earlier thought or said. This ability to connect with the audience and take its needs into account is *not* lacking in most students—contrary to much recent received opinion. Students use this social skill quite spontaneously and well in much of their speech to a present audience, but they naturally enough neglect to use it in much of their writing since the audience is less clear to them. We can easily help students transfer to writing their skill in connecting with an audience by having them write more often in a local context to a limited and physically present audience (as when they talk).

I am speaking here to what I see as a growing misconception about the inability of adolescents to "decenter": a dangerous tendency to make snap judgments about the level of a student's cognitive development on the basis of only a text or two—texts which are anything but accurate embodiments of how the student's mind really operates. Teachers and researchers sometimes describe the weakness of certain student writing as stemming from an inability to move past oral language strategies and a dependence on local audience and context.[9] But in reality the weakness of those pieces of writing should often be given the *opposite* diagnosis: the student has drifted off into writing to *no one in particular.* Often the student need only be encouraged to use *more* of the strategies of oral discourse and the discourse snaps back into good focus, and along with it usually comes much more clarity and even better thinking.

(6) Commentators like to distinguish speech from writing by saying that speech is reticent: it invites listeners to fill in meanings from their involvement in the context and their knowledge of the speaker. Good writing, on the other hand (so this story goes), must make all the meanings explicit, must "lexicalize" or "decontextualize" all the

meanings, and not require readers to fill in. But here too, this talk about the inherent nature of speech and writing is misguided. It is precisely a quality that distinguishes certain kinds of good writing that it makes readers *contribute to* or *participate in* the meanings, not just sit back and receive meanings that are entirely spelled out.

Deborah Tannen, a speech researcher, illuminates this confusion ("Oral and Literate," 89):

> If one thinks at first that written and spoken language are very different, one may think as well that written literature—short stories, poems, and novels—are the most different from casual conversation of all. Quite the contrary, imaginative literature has more in common with spontaneous conversation than with the typical written genre, expository prose.
>
> If expository prose is minimally contextualized—that is, the writer demands the least from the reader in terms of filling in background information and crucial premises—imaginative literature is maximally contextualized. The best work of art is the one that suggests the most to the reader with the fewest words.... The goal of creative writers is to encourage their readers to fill in as much as possible. The more the readers supply, the more they will believe and care about the message in the work.

Although we can *maximize* the unstated only in imaginative literature, nevertheless, I believe it is unhelpful to go along with Tannen's oversimple contrast between imaginative and expository writing. Surely it is the mark of really good essays or expository writing, too, that they bring the reader *in* and get him or her to fill in and participate in the meanings, and thereby make those written meanings seem more real and believable. (I think of the expository writing of writers like Wayne Booth, Stephen Gould, or Lewis Thomas.) And even to the degree that imaginative literature is different from expository prose, we must not run away from it as a model for what gives goodness to good expository prose.

If we accept uncritically the assumption that "cognitive development" or "psychological growth" consists of movement from concrete "oral" modes to abstract "literate" modes, we are left with the implication that most of the imaginative literature we study is at a lower developmental and cognitive level than most of the expository writing turned in by students. I'm frightened at the tendency to label students cognitively retarded who tend to exploit those oral or concrete strategies that characterize so much good literature, namely narration, description, invested detail, and expression of feeling. I'm not trying to deny the burden of Piaget, Bruner, etc., etc., namely, that it is an important and necessary struggle to learn abstract reasoning, nor to deny that teaching it is *part* of our job as teachers of writing. Again I claim both positions. But there is danger in *over*emphasizing writing as abstract and nonspeech-like. (Even Bruner makes a similar warning in his recent work "Language, Mind.")

(7) Commentators on orality and literacy tend to stress how speech works in time and writing in space. Ong is eloquent on the evanescence of speech because it exists only as sound and thus is lost in the unstoppable flow of time. In speech, past and future words *do not exist* (as they would do if they were part of a text): the only thing that exists is that fleeting present syllable that pauses on the tongue in its journey to disappearance. Speech and oral cultures are associated with narration—which takes

time as its medium. Writing and literate cultures are associated with logic—which exists outside of time.

This is an important distinction and people like Ong are right to exploit its remarkably wide ramifications, but there is a danger here, too. In truth, writing is also essentially time-bound. Readers are immersed in time as they read just as listeners are when they hear. We cannot take in a text all at once as we can a picture or a diagram. We see only a few written words at a time. It is true that if we pause in our reading, we can *in a sense* step outside the flow of time and look back to earlier sections of the text, or look forward to later sections; I don't mean to underestimate the enormous contrast here with speech where such "back-" or "forward-scanning" is impossible. Nevertheless the essential process of reading a text is more like listening than looking: the essential phenomenology involves being trapped in time and thus unable to take in more than a few words at a time.

This point is not just theoretical. The problem with much poor or needlessly difficult writing is the way it pretends to exist as it were in space rather than in time. Such writing is hard to read because it demands that we have access all at once to the many elements that the writer struggled to get into the text. The writer forces us repeatedly to stop and work at finding explanations or definitions or connections which he *gave*, it is true, or *will* give in a few pages, but which he does not bring to our minds now when we need them. (It often feels to the writer as though he's *already* given us the material we need when we are reading page two—even though we don't get it till page six—because he's *already* written page six when he rewrites page two.) Poor writers often assume that because they are making a document rather than a talk, they are *giving us a thing in space* rather than *leading us on a journey through time*, and that therefore they can pretend that we can "look at the whole thing."[10]

One of the marks of good writers, on the other hand, is their recognition that readers, like listeners, are indeed trapped in the flow of time and can take in only a few words at a time. Good writers takes this as an opportunity, not just a problem. The drama of movement through time can be embodied in thinking and exposition as naturally as in stories. And the ability to engage the reader's time sense is not a matter of developing some wholly new skill or strategy, it is a matter of developing for writing that time-bound faculty we've all used in all speaking.

(8) By reflecting on how writing, though apparently existing in space, is essentially speech-like in that it works on readers in the dimension of time, we can throw important light on the peculiar *difficulties of organizing or structuring a piece of writing.*

In thinking about organization in writing we are tempted to use models from the spatial realm. Indeed our very conception of organization or structure tends to be spatial. Our *sense*, then, of what it means to be well organized or well structured tends to involve those features which give coherence to space—features such as neatness, symmetry, and non-redundancy. Giving good organization to something in time, however, is a different business because it means giving organization or structure to something of which we can grasp only one tiny fraction at any moment.

A thought experiment. Imagine a large painting or photograph that looks well organized. Imagine next an ant crawling along its surface. How would we have to modify that picture to make it "well organized" for the ant? Since he cannot see the picture all at once, we would have to embed some tiny, simplified reductions or capsule "overviews" of the whole picture at periodic points in his path—especially where he starts and finishes. Otherwise he could never make sense of the barrage of close-up details he gets as he crawls along; he would have no overall "big picture" or gestalt into which to integrate these details. But if we should make such modifications we would make the picture much "messier" from a visual point of view.

The plight of our ant points to the interesting work in composition theory and cognitive science about "chunking" and short- and long-term memory and the magic number seven. (In effect, the ant needs the visual information "chunked" for him.) Because language is time-bound, its meanings cannot actually enter our minds through our eyes—its meanings must detour through memory. If eyes were enough, "chunking" would be much easier, for as gestalt psychology has shown, vision as a cognitive process involves the making of gestalts, i.e., automatic chunking. (See G. A. Miller's classic essay, "The Magical Number Seven.")

Thus the test of good organization in writing—as in speech—is not whether the text *looks* neat when diagrammed in an outline or some other visual scheme, but whether it produces an *experience* of structure and coherence for the audience in time. But how is this effect achieved? The issue is complex, but I would suggest that certain common features of speech help discourse function as coherent in time—and thus are helpful for creating the sense of good structure in a text. We are more likely in speaking than in writing to give the quick forward- and backward-looking structural aids that readers need when they are trapped in the flow of time. When we are speaking we are less likely to put our heads down and forget about the structural needs of our audience because our audience is right there before us.

Discourse is sometimes given coherence by the use of cyclical or spiral patterns characteristic of speech—or a kind of wave-like repetition in which new material is introduced only after some allusion (however brief) to the past material needed for understanding the new material. This is the archetypal back-and-forth movement of waves on a beach which Auerbach (*Mimesis*) relates to the rhythm of Old Testament poetry—or the homely "mowing long grass" pattern of movement where repeatedly you push the mower forward four feet and back two feet, so each piece of ground is covered twice: there is always a quick summary before going forward.[11]

Oddly enough, *lists* (that feature of oral and epic poetry) are remarkably effective ways to give structure to discourse in time. As researchers into document design have noticed, written texts are often much more coherent to readers when a connected chain of statements is reshaped into a main statement and a *list* of supporting or following items. Lists have an interesting cognitive characteristic: as we take in each item we tacitly rehearse our sense of what that item is an instance *of*. Thus, a list is a way of increasing unity and also giving readers a reiterated sense of the main point without having to repeat it explicitly for them.

Discourse is sometimes given coherence in time by the use of recurring phrases, metaphors, images, or resonant examples (not merely decorative or illustrative but structural) which "chunk" or function as micro-summaries. Such recurring miniature units are characteristic of oral discourse (and music). A phrase can continue to ring in the reader's ear or an image continue to appear in the mind's eye while trapped in the underbrush of prose, and thus give structure or coherence to an experience in time.

The big picture problem is really a problem of how to get readers to hold in mind a *pattern* or *relationship* among elements while having to focus attention on only one of those elements. Imagine an essay with three major points or sections (as with the present essay). If we think of it "structurally" or "from above"—that is, spatially—we see three emphases or focuses of attention, as so many paintings and photographs are organized triangularly. But what holds the picture together is the fact that in the realm of vision we can focus on one of the three main areas yet simultaneously retain our view of the other two and our sense of how they relate to the one we are looking at. With an essay, on the other hand, we can read *only* one small part at a time, and so it is hard to experience the *relationship* or *interaction* of the three parts.

Thus the problem of structure in a temporal medium is really the problem of how to *bind time*. Whereas symmetry and pattern bind space (and also bind smaller units of time—in the form of rhythm), they don't manage very well to hold larger units of time together. What binds larger units of time? Usually it is the experience of anticipation or tension which then builds to some resolution or satisfaction. In well-structured discourse, music, and films (temporal media) we almost invariably see a pattern of alternating dissonance-and-consonance or itching-and-scratching. Narrative is probably the most common and natural way to set up a structure of anticipation and resolution in discourse.

But how do we bind time with patterns of anticipation and resolution in *essays or expositiory writing*?[12] Here the tension or itch that binds the words is almost always the experience of some *problem* or *uncertainty,* that is somehow conveyed to the reader. Unless there is a felt question—a tension, a palpable itch—the time remains unbound. The most common reason why weak essays don't hang together is that the writing is all statement, all consonance, all answer: the reader is not made to experience any cognitive dissonance to serve as a "net" or "set" to catch all these statements or answers. Without an itch or a sense of felt problem, nothing holds the reader's experience together—however well the text itself might summarize the parts. (This is a common problem in the essays of students since they so often suppose that essays are only for telling, not for wondering.) I wish workers on coherence and cohesion would focus more on the ways in which writers convey a sense of felt problem or itch. Surely that does more to hold texts together than repeated words or phrases.

If it seems as though I'm trying to fiddle with our sense of structure in texts, I must plead guilty. For I think that we often call texts well structured when they are merely "neat" or symmetrical, but really don't *hold* together: we "look through" our temporal experience of the text to a projected outline of the meanings. Particularly as academics, we are trained to read this way. Other readers—"popular" or informal readers—often do not notice that atemporal neatness and so feel such texts as incoherent. Yet on the other hand such readers are sometimes *satisfied* with the structure of texts that are less "neat"—we would call them sprawling—because the writer has been able to string those sprawling elements together experientially in time.

Have I gone too far? Obviously this is a tangled matter. For we yearn for neatness, economy, and spatial structure in our texts: poor writing is often poor because of the lack of these features. The problems of structure in writing are subtly difficult. Because of the confusion introduced into our very notion of structure by the pervasive metaphor of space, I suspect that we are still waiting for the help we need in showing us simple and valid models of good structure in time. If we want to explain the structure of well-ordered expository writing, we probably would do well to look to studies of the structure of music and film and poetry. (See, for example, Meyer and Zuckerkandl on music.)

Yet we mustn't plead ignorance too fast. As speakers, everyone has had extensive experience organizing discourse in time to make it coherent to listeners. (I admit that coherent speech is rare—but not as rare as coherent writing. And it is true that we speak in dialogue more often than in monologue—but we have had more experience with monologue than with writing.) Thus, continual experience with speaking of all sorts—even experience in not being understood and then clarifying our meaning—has built up for all speakers extensive intuitive skill at organizing discourse in time.

Thus we do well to exploit these intuitive, time-oriented speech skills when we try to organize our writing (particularly expository or conceptual writing where organizational problems are most difficult). When we tell ourselves to "be careful about organization" or to "give good structure" to our text, we tend to think in terms of building blocks laid out in space, and thus we often fail to give our readers an experience of coherence and clarity (however neatly we pattern our blocks). If, on the other hand, we think of our structural problem as that of trying to speak a long monologue so it is coherent to listeners in time, we are more likely to invoke crucial temporal organizational skills at two levels:

(a) In the large, overall structure of our text, we are more likely to "tell the story" as it were of our thinking. This doesn't usually mean turning it into actual narrative (although that needn't be ruled out as the most natural and effective structure for thinking), but rather saying, "Where does this thinking *start*? Where is it *going*? And where is it trying to *get to*?" Our attempt to speak a monologue will get us to find the larger *movement* of thought and help us intuitively to appeal to the faculty of hearing and memory, not visual schematics.

(b) In the smaller structures of our text, we are even more likely to appeal directly to hearing if we think of ourselves as speaking a monologue, and this will help us naturally chunk shorter sequences of information or thinking (from one to several paragraphs) into "heard" units which will cohere and thus be more easily understood and remembered.

So here again my point is that in order to make writing good we should try to make it like speech. When we structure speech we naturally exploit our time sense, our hearing, and our memory; and we naturally build in patterns of tension and resolution, not just arrangement of parts.

(9) A final reason why writing needs to be like speech. Perhaps it is fanciful to talk of speech having a magic that writing lacks—call it presence, voice, or *pneuma*—but the truth is that we tend to experience meaning somehow more in spoken words than written ones. (Socrates and Husserl make this point: See Searle, "The Word Turned Upside Down.")

This vividness of speech is illustrated in academic conferences where people speak written papers out loud. Because we are listening to *writing* presented orally, we may notice in a curiously striking way how it seldom seems as semantically "inhabited" or "presenced" as speech.

Of course most of us can convey *more* meaning by reading a written essay out loud than by trying to give a speech from notes—more precisely, clearly, and quickly too. Yet the moment-to-moment language of a recited essay (even if more precise) is almost invariably less "full of meaning" than the language of our actual live speech (even if that speech has some stumbling and lack of precision). In short, writing seems to permit us to get *more* meaning into words (get more said more quickly), but speech helps get our meanings integrated more *into* our words.

But why should it be that we seem to experience the meaning more in spoken words than written words? Is it just because spoken words are *performed* for us and so we get all those extra cues from seeing the speaker, hearing how she speaks—all those rhythms and tonalities? That is important, but there's something else that goes deeper: in listening to speech we are hearing mental activity going on—live; in reading a text we are only encountering the record of completed mental events. It's not that the audience has to *receive* the words while the mental activity is going on, but that the language has to be *created* while the mental activity is going on: the language must embody or grow out of live mental events. The important simultaneity is not between meaning-making and hearing, but between meaning-making and the production or emergence of language. The crucial question for determining whether discourse achieves "presence" is whether the words produced are *an expression of something going on* or *a record of something having gone on.*

To speak is (usually) to give spontaneous verbal substance to mental events occurring right at that moment in the mind. Even when we are stuck or tongue-tied we seldom remain silent for long: Billy Budd is the exception. Usually we say something about our inability to figure out what to say. To write, however, is usually to *rehearse* mental events inside our heads before putting them down. (Someone's speech usually sounds peculiar if he rehearses his words in his head before speaking them.)

My hypothesis then, is that when people produce language *as* they are engaged in the mental event it expresses, they produce language with particular features—features which make an audience feel the meanings very much *in* those words. Here then is an important research agenda for discourse analysis: what are the language features that correlate with what people experience as the semantic liveness of speech? (See Halpern, "Differences," for a start at this job.)

Such research would have very practical benefits for writing theory, since of course writing *can* be as alive as speech. What characterizes much excellent writing is precisely this special quality of lively or heightened semantic presence. It's as though the writer's mental activity is somehow there in the words on the page—as though the silent words are somehow alive with her meaning.

When a writer is particularly fluent, she has the gift of doing less internal rehearsal. The acts of figuring out what she wants to say, finding the words, and putting them down somehow coalesce into one act—into that integrative meaning-making/language-finding act which is characteristic of speech. But even beginners (or writing teachers) can achieve this liveliness and presence when they engage in freewriting or spontaneous writing. It is this semantic presence which often makes freewriting seem peculiarly lively to read. One of the best directions for coaching freewriting is to tell oneself or one's students to "talk onto the paper."

Of course we cannot usually produce a carefully-pondered and well-ordered piece of writing by talking onto paper. In any piece of writing that has been a struggle to produce, there is often a certain smell of stale sweat. And freewriting or spontaneous speech may be careless or shallow (the meaning is *in* the words but the *amount* of meaning is very small). But if we learn to talk onto paper and exploit the speech-like quality possible in writing, we can have the experience of writing words with presence, and thereby learn what such writing *feels* like—in the fingers, in the mouth, and in the ear. This experience increases our chances of getting desirable speech qualities into the writing we revise and think through more carefully.

IV. Conclusion

I have argued three contrary claims: writing is essentially unlike speech because it is more indelible; writing is essentially unlike speech because it is more ephemeral; and writing is essentially *like* speech. My goal is to stop people from talking so much about the inherent nature of these media and start them talking more about the different ways we can *use* them. In particular I seek to celebrate the flexibility of writing as a medium, and to show that we need to develop more control over ourselves as we write so that we can *manage* our writing process more judiciously and flexibly. Let me end with three images for the writer (one to match each claim)—and with each image a mentality.

First, I see the writer clenched over her text, writing very slowly—indeed pondering more than writing—trying to achieve something permanent and definitive: questioning everything, first in her mind before she writes the phrase, then after she sees it on paper. She is intensely self-critical, she tries to see every potential flaw—even the flaws that some unknown future reader might find who is reading in an entirely different context from that of her present audience. She is using the "new" technology of indelible writing that Ong and others speak of and thereby enhancing her capacity for careful abstract thinking by learning to separate the knower from the known. She is learning the mentality of detachment.

Second, I see the writer in a fine frenzy: scribbling fast, caught up in her words, in the grip of language and creation. She is writing late at night—not because of a deadline but because the words have taken over: she wants to go to bed but too much is going on for her to stop. She has learned to relinquish some control. She has also learned to let herself write things she would never show to anyone—at first anyway. By exploiting the ephemeral underside of writing, she learns to promote the mentality of wildness with words-the mentality of discourse as play. And perhaps most important, she has learned to promote the mentality of involvement in her words rather than of detachment or separation. But because that involvement is so totally *of the moment,* she knows she may well write a refutation tomorrow night of what she is writing tonight. She writes to explore and develop her ideas, not just express them.

Third, I see the writer at her desk conjuring up her audience before her in her mind's eye as she writes. She is looking at them, speaking *to* them—more aware of the sound of her spoken words in her ear than the sight of her written words on paper. She is the writer as raconteur, the writer with the gift of gab. She is not "composing" a text or "constructing" a document in space—she is "uttering" discourse in time; she is not "giving things" to her readers, she is leading readers on a mental journey. She is a bit of a dramatist, using discourse as a way to *do* things to people. She is involved with her discourse through being involved with her audience. Often her audience is a genuine community and her writing grows out of her sense of membership in it.

Is one of these modes of writing better? I don't believe so. Yet in the end I think there *is* a single best way to write: to move back and forth among them. And I believe there is a particular mentality which the technology of writing is peculiarly suited to enhance (as speech is not), namely *the play of mentalities.* We can learn to *be* all three writers imaged above. Writing can show us how to move back and forth between cognitive processes and mentalities which at first may seem contradictory, but which if exploited will heighten and reinforce each other.

Notes

1. For quotations and references I give an abbreviated title and page number for works listed in the bibliography at the end [not printed here]. I am grateful for feedback by colleagues here at Stony Brook, the Breadloaf School of English, and the Penn State Conference on Rhetoric and Composition—where I read earlier drafts of this paper.
2. See Walter Ong, *Orality and Literacy*, 1982, for a powerful summary of his extensive work in this area and his wide-ranging citations to others working in it. For welcome warnings about stereotyping the mentalities associated with orality and literacy, see Cooper and Odell, "Sound in Composing"; Harste, "Assumptions"; Scribner and Cole, *Psychology of Literacy*; Heath, "Oral and Literate Traditions"; and Robinson, "Literacy." A number of the essays in Kroll and Vann, *Exploring Speaking-Writing Relationships,* e.g. O'Keefe, also warn against oversimplifying the contrast between speech and writing as media.
3. Ong focuses on the development of writing, but it is important to stand back and take a longer perspective. That is, the biggest boost to careful thinking came earlier with the birth of *language itself*—original spoken language. "As long as we carry intuitive belief without a symbolic representation, we are one with it and cannot criticize it. But once we have formulated it, we can look at it objectively and learn from it, even from its rejection." (Karl Popper, cited in Kroll and Vann, *Exploring Speaking-Writing Relationships,* p. 151.) See also Vygotsky, *Thought and Language,* on the effect of language itself as a "second signalling system."
4. It may be, however, that many of the effects we are tempted to ascribe to literacy are really effects of schooling. See Gere, "Cultural Perspectives"; Olson, "Languages of Instruction"; and Scribner and Cole, *Psychology of Literacy*.

5 Literate people like to complain that the telephone and other electronic media have almost destroyed writing by permitting people to do most of their business orally and refrain from writing unless there is some pressing need for "hard" (i.e. indelible) copy. But I suspect that more people write more now than ever before. Engineers are estimated to spend from a quarter to a third of their working time involved in some kind of writing. See Faigley et al, "Writing After College." The spread of radios and phonographs raised fears that people would no longer go to concerts or play musical instruments: the opposite has occurred.

6 This somatic perspective heightens the paradoxes. Writing is the external indelible medium—yet is the most easily changed. Thinking is the most internal and changeable medium—yet from another point of view it is the most intractable to change: try removing or changing a thought you don't like. Speech, chameleon-like, is in the middle.

7 In enumerating these characteristics of speech I am drawing on Tannen, "Oral and Literate"; see also Emig, "Writing as a Mode of Learning." In describing some ways to provide speech conditions in a writing class I am drawing on a discussion with members of the fall 1983 teaching practicum at Stony Brook—for whose help I am grateful.

8 I don't really grant this point, however. Though these procedures are particularly suitable for basic students, they are also the kinds of writing that occur in many workplace settings (for example with a research team, an investigative committee, or any other working group whose members communicate to each other in letters, queries, and rough position papers). Sometimes people who talk about the "inherent difference" between speaking and writing get carried away and ignore the brute fact that much of the writing in the world—perhaps even most of it—takes place in a strongly social or communal context: the writing is in response to an earlier discourse and gives rise to subsequent discourse and is asked for and read by particular people whom the writer knows—people who share a common context and set of assumptions with the writer.

9 See Lunsford, "Cognitive Development," and Shaughnessy, *Errors,* Instead of just talking about "oral interference" as a problem, I would also use the term in the positive sense: oral skills and habits can "run interference" for writing—knocking down some of the obstacles that make writing difficult.

10 This is particularly a problem in certain technical documents and reports, and it is interesting to see how canny readers of such genres have learned to accommodate to the bad treatment they receive: they "read" such documents as though they were looking at a diagram rather than reading a text—namely, by quickly scanning through it, perhaps more than once, trying to develop an overview and a sense of perspective which they know the writer does not provide. Being trained and consenting to read in this way, in a sense they perpetuate the problem.

11 Theorists of style in general and of cohesion and coherence in particular talk about this phenomenon at the sentence or syntactic level (see Joseph Williams, *Style*), but I'm not sure that there's enough recognition of it at the level of the whole. See, however, the reference to beginning work on the "macrotheme-rheme" problem in Witte and Faigley's "Coherence, Cohesion."

12 We should recognize how often good essays or books are actually held together by being stories: "here is the story of my thinking," or "here is a ride on the train of my thought," or even just, "this and this and this, and here is the moral."

Works Cited

Note: For two rich bibliographies on the relation between speech and writing, see the Kroll and Vann volume noted below, and the annotated bibliography by Sarah Liggett in the recent *CCC*: 35 (October, 1984), 334–44.

Auerbach, Erich. *Mimesis.* Tr. W. Traske, Berne, 1946.
Barthes, Roland, "Death of the Author." In *Image, Music, Text.* New York: Hill and Wang, 1977.
Bruner, Jerome. *Studies in Cognitive Growth.* Cambridge, MA: Harvard University Press, 1966.

———. "Language, Mind, and Reading." In *Awakening Literacy,* Ed. Hillel Goelman, Antoinette Obeng, and Frank Smith. Exeter NH: Heineman Educational Books, 1984.

Calkins, Lucy. *Lessons from a Child on the Teaching and Learning of Writing.* Exeter, NH: Heinemann Educational Books, 1983.

Cooper, Charles and Lee Odell. "Considerations of Sound in the Composing Process of Published Writers." *RTE,* 10 (Fall, 1976), 103–115.

Elbow, Peter. *Writing Without Teachers,* New York: Oxford University Press, 1973.

———. *Writing With Power,* New York: Oxford University Press, 1981.

Emig, Janet. "Writing as a Mode of Learning." *CCC,* 28 (May, 1977), 122–128. Reprinted in *The Writing Teacher's Sourcebook,* Ed. Gary Tate and Edward P. J. Corbett. New York: Oxford University Press, 1981.

Faigley, L. et al. "Writing After College: A Stratified Survey of the Writing of College-Trained People," Writing Program Assessment Technical Report No. 1, University of Texas, Austin, 1981.

Gere, Anne Ruggles. "A Cultural Perspective on Talking and Writing." In Kroll and Vann, *Exploring Speaking-Writing Relationships.*

Goody, Jack. *The Domestication of the Savage Mind.* Cambridge, England: Cambridge University Press, 1977.

Graves, Donald. *Writing: Teachers and Children at Work.* Exeter, NH: Heinemann Educational Books, 1983.

Halpern, Jeanne, "Differences Between Speaking and Writing and Their Implications for Teaching," *CCC,* 35 (October, 1984), 345–357.

Harste, Jerome C., Virginia A. Woodward, Carolyn L. Burke, "Examining our Assumptions: A Transactional View of Literacy and Learning," *RTE,* 18 (February, 1984), 84–108.

Havelock, Eric A. *Preface to Plato.* Cambridge, MA: Belknap Press of Harvard University Press, 1963.

Heath, Shirley Brice. "Oral and Literate Traditions." *International Social Science Journal*, 36 (1984), 41–57.

Kroll, Barry M., and Roberta J. Vann (ed.) *Exploring Speaking-Writing Relationships.* Urbana, IL: National Council of Teachers of English, 1981.

Lunsford, Andrea. "Cognitive Development and the Basic Writer." *CE,* 41 (September, 1979), 38–46.

Meyer, Leonard B. *Emotion and Meaning in Music.* Chicago: University of Chicago Press, 1956.

Miller, George. "The Magical Number Seven Plus or Minus Two: Some Limits on our Capacity for Processing Information." *Psychological Review,* 63 (March, 1956), 81–97.

Olson, D. R. "The Languages of Instruction: The Literate Bias of Schooling." In R. C. Anderson, R. J. Siro, and W. E. Montague (ed.), *Schooling and the Acquisition of Knowledge. Hillsdale,* NJ: Lawrence Erlbaum, 1977.

Ong, Walter J. *Orality and Literary.* New York: Methuen, 1982.

Perl, Sondra: "Understanding Composing." *CCC,* 31 (December 1980), 363–369.

Robinson, Jay L. "The Users and Uses of Literacy." In *Literacy of Life: The Demand for Reading and Writing.* Ed. Richard W. Bailey and Robin Melanie Fosheim. New York: Modern Language Association, 1983.

Schafer, John C. "The Linguistic Analysis of Spoken and Written Texts." In Kroll and Vann, *Exploring Speaking-Writing Relationships.*

Scribner, Sylvia, and Michael Cole. *The Psychology of Literacy.* Cambridge, MA: Harvard University, Press, 1981.

———. "Unpackaging Literacy." In *Variations in Writing: Functional and Linguistic-Cultural Differences*. Ed. Marcia Farr Whiteman. Hillsdale, NJ: Lawrence Erlbaum Assocs, 1981, 71–87.

Searle, John. "The Word Turned Upside Down." *The New York Review of Books*, 27 October 1983, 74–79.

Shaughnessy, Mina P. *Errors and Expectations: A Guide for the Teacher of Basic Writing*. New York: Oxford University Press, 1977.

Tannen, Deborah. "Oral and Literate Strategies in Spoken and Written Discourse." In *Literacy for Life: The Demand far Reading and Writing*. Ed. Richard W. Bailey and Robin Melanie Fosheim. New York: Modern Language Association, 1983.

Vygotsky, Lev. *Thought and Language*. Cambridge, MA: MIT Press, 1962.

Williams, Joseph M. *Style: Ten Lessons in Clarity and Grace*. Glenview, IL: Scott Foresman and Co, 1981.

Williams, Joseph M. and Rosemary L. Hake. "Style and Its Consequences: Do as I Do, Not as I Say." *College English*, 43 (September, 1981), 433–451.

Witte, Stephen and Lester Faigley. "Coherence, Cohesion, and Writing Quality." *CCC*, 32 (May, 1981), 189–204.

Zuckerkandl, Victor. *Sound and Symbol: Music and the External World*. New York: Pantheon Press, 1956, reprinted 1976.

10.
PUNCTUATION AND THE PROSODY OF WRITTEN LANGUAGE
Wallace Chafe

When we speak, we produce a variety of consonant and vowel sounds that are more or less well represented by the letters of our writing system. In spite of the inconsistencies of English spelling, there is at least a rough correspondence between the sounds we make in speaking and the letters of the alphabet we use in writing. But there are other aspects of speaking that are not as well represented in writing: the rises and falls in pitch, the accents, the pauses, the rhythm, the variations in voice quality—all of them features of sound that contribute significantly to speaking but that writing shows haphazardly if at all. As a well-known introductory linguistic textbook puts it, "Writing never really got around to providing a regular way of marking accent . . ., and it has virtually disregarded rhythm and intonation" (Bolinger, 1975, p. 472).

But to say that written language falls short in representing these "prosodic" aspects of language is not to say that it is an impoverished form of language from which prosody is simply absent, as if it were composed of "words without song." As the same textbook remarks, "We monitor our writing sub-vocally, reading in an intonation, and the fact that the intonation is not actually shown and our reader is going to have to guess at it is as likely as not to escape our attention" (Bolinger, 1975, p. 602).

Eudora Welty, in her autobiographical book *One Writer's Beginnings* (1983), describes the following kind of experience:

> Ever since I was first read to, then started reading to myself, there has never been a line read that I didn't *hear*. As my eyes followed the sentence, a voice was saying it silently to me. It isn't my mother's voice, or the voice of any person I can identify, certainly not my own. It is human, but inward, and it is inwardly that I listen to it. It is to me the voice of the story or the poem itself. The cadence, whatever it is that asks you to believe, the feeling that resides in the printed word, reaches me through the reader-voice. I have supposed, but never found out, that this is the case with all readers—to read as listeners—and with all writers, to write as listeners. It may be part of the desire to write. The sound of what falls on the page begins the process of testing it for truth, for me. Whether I am right to trust so far I don't know. By now I don't know whether I could do either one, reading or writing, without the other.

Chafe, Wallace L. "Punctuation and the Prosody of Written Language." *Written Communication* Vol. 5 No. 4. (October 1988): 395–426.

> My own words, when I am at work on a story, I hear too as they go, in the same voice that I hear when I read in books. When I write and the sound of it comes back to my ears, then I act to make my changes. I have always trusted this voice.
>
> (pp. 12–13)

Russell Long (n.d.) has made a similar observation, pointing out a relation between writing and reading aloud:

> While some of my colleagues object to my use of the ward *hearing* to describe the mental activity that goes on as we write, I am convinced that, at least metaphorically, it is the most accurate term to choose. As I write these sentences, even though my lips are not moving, I am quite conscious of the sound the words I am writing would make *if they were read aloud*. To extend this recognition one step further, I am convinced that the competent writer writes in the same way he reads aloud, using preceding syntactic and semantic context to project meaning, word choice, and punctuation that will follow.
>
> (p. 15)

These quotes from Bolinger, Welty, and Long show that I am not alone in believing that writers when they write, and readers when they read, experience auditory imagery of specific intonations, accents, pauses, rhythms, and voice qualities, even though the writing itself may show these features poorly if at all. This "covert prosody" of written language is evidently something that is quite apparent to a reflective writer or reader.[1]

What follows is an initial attempt to explore the relationship between the covert prosody of writing and one device—in fact the principal device—that writers use in order to make it at least partially overt. That device is punctuation. Although punctuation certainly fails to represent the total range of prosodic phenomena a writer or reader may assign to a piece of written language, it does capture some major aspects of a writer's prosodic intent, to the extent that the quality and impact of a piece of writing may be greatly affected by the author's skill (or lack of it) in punctuating. Furthermore, a skillful author will use punctuation as a resource to enhance the effectiveness of his or her writing, just as a skillful speaker will manipulate pitch and hesitations to enhance the effectiveness of his or her speech.

At this point some readers may object that the signaling of prosody is only one of the functions of punctuation, and perhaps not the primary one. Although that is a common belief, and although certainly there are instances of punctuation that do not serve prosodic ends, I will defend the position here that those instances are departures from its main function, which is to tell us something about a writer's intentions with regard to the prosody of that inner voice.

Punctuation Units and Intonation Units

My own interest in this question has come especially from an interest in seeing how written language compares with spoken. In making such a comparison I have been struck by a relation between certain prosodic units already known to be present in spoken language and certain units of written language that are defined by punctuation. Before going any further I need to say something more about this.

Spoken language exhibits important prosodic units of a kind that I have been calling "intonation units" (Chafe, 1980, 1987). These intonation units occur as spurts of vocalization that typically contain one or more intonation peaks, that end in any one of a variety of terminal pitch contours, and that usually but not always are separated from each other by pauses. Their grammatical form is variable, but the majority are single clauses. In the following illustration I have written each intonation unit on a separate line. The sequences of two and three dots indicate shorter and longer pauses, respectively, and the commas and question marks show terminal pitch contours of different types:

>...But a...a friend of mine,
>this um...guy I've been going out with,
>...he...he had a student,
>...he teaches flute,
>...and
>...did you meet him at my house?
>...The flute player?
>...Got a blond beard,
>looks like my friend Sam?

It is natural to wonder whether and in what way something comparable to these intonation units might be represented in writing, and the answer that immediately suggests itself is that writers show the boundaries of their privately heard intonation units with marks of punctuation. We can compare the intonation units illustrated just above with the following illustration of what we can call "punctuation units" (the stretches of language between two punctuation marks). The example is from Chapter 10 of Thoreau's *Walden* (1854):

> Sometimes I rambled to pine groves, standing like temples, or like fleets at sea, full-rigged, with wavy boughs, and rippling with light, so soft and green and shady that the Druids would have forsaken their oaks to worship in them.
>
> (p. 137)

The reader of these lines will, I hope, notice a tendency to "hear" a terminal pitch contour and a pause at each place where there is a punctuation mark. Perhaps this effect is more obvious if the punctuation units are written on separate lines:

> Sometimes I rambled to pine groves,
> standing like temples,
> or like fleets at sea,
> full-rigged,
> with wavy boughs,

and rippling with light,
so soft and green and shady that the Druids would have forsaken their oaks to worship in them.

The careful reader may also notice certain differences between the spoken and written illustrations. For example, the written punctuation units are more variable in length than the spoken ones, ranging from one word ("full-rigged") to eighteen words ("so soft and green and shady that the Druids would have forsaken their oaks to worship in them"). If we pursued further this attempt to relate intonation units and punctuation units we would find other differences, stemming from at least three sources: (1) a particular writer's lack of skill in punctuating, (2) varying styles of punctuating, and (3) punctuation that is determined by factors other than prosody.

Lack of Skill in Punctuating

Evidently a writer's ability to use punctuation to mark the boundaries of something comparable to spoken intonation units is an acquired skill. This is one of the most obvious areas in which inexperienced writers do poorly. Writing teachers are familiar with examples such as the following (taken from Danielewicz & Chafe, 1985, p. 220):

> Lucy never was able to form whole, and completely new sentences whereas Helen was able to start conversations and express her ideas.

If this had been spoken language, it is quite possible that there would have been an intonational break after the word "whole," a possibility that probably led the writer to introduce a comma at that point. But certainly it is even more likely that a speaker would have produced an intonation unit boundary after the word "sentences," and this writer failed to mark that break with punctuation. Inexperienced writers may often fail to be guided consistently by their inner voice.

Varying Styles of Punctuating

Even with professional writers, however, we find extensive variation in punctuation use. Much of this variation is associated with different punctuating styles that are popular in different periods, while some of it can be attributed to the habits of individual authors.

During most of the nineteenth century, the fashion was to create punctuation units that were very much like the intonation units of speech. Thus, for example, Melville's (1851) description of the last moments of Ahab:

> The harpoon was darted;
> the stricken whale flew forward;
> with igniting velocity the line ran through the groove;
> —ran foul.

> Ahab stooped to clear it;
> he did clear it;
> but the flying turn caught him round the neck,
> and voicelessly as Turkish mutes bowstring their victim,
> he was shot out of the boat,
> ere the crew knew he was gone.
> (p. 535)

But even when writing had separated itself from such a close relation to speech, it still showed clear analogies to spoken intonation units, however lengthened, elaborated, and interwoven they may have become. The following example is typical:

> Though there was already talk of the erection,
> in remote metropolitan distances "above the Forties,"
> of a new Opera House which should compete in costliness and splendor with those
> of the great European capitals,
> the world of fashion was still content to reassemble every winter in the shabby red
> and gold boxes of the sociable old Academy. (Wharton, 1978, p. 5)

Here the second punctuation unit interrupts the long and complex unit made up of the first and third together, while the last punctuation unit, though uninterrupted, is longer and more complex than anything one would find in normal speech.

In what might be called the Hemingway style, however, the possibility of a relation between punctuation units and intonation units came to be deliberately ignored. The following example is from Hemingway himself:

> Earlier in the evening he had taken the ax and gone outside of the cave and walked through the new snow to the edge of the clearing and cut down a small spruce tree.
> (Hemingway, 1940, p. 258)

For physiological and cognitive reasons it would be impossible for a speaker under normal circumstances to produce a single intonation unit as long as this one.

Nonprosodic Uses of Punctuation

The third source of difficulty in equating punctuation units with intonation units is the fact that grammarians, editors, educators, and whoever else contributes to the establishment of written usage have developed a variety of rules for punctuating, not all of which are prosodically motivated. As a result, a piece of writing is likely to contain at least some punctuation marks that were inserted for reasons other than to guide the reader in following the prosodic intentions of the writer. Some may have been placed at grammatical boundaries that were not at the same time prosodic ones, and there may be others that were dictated by completely arbitrary conventions.

The earliest grammars of English emphasized the prosodic function of punctuation, above all its role as an indicator of pauses. Thus Robert Lowth, in his *A Short*

Introduction to English Grammar, published in 1762, implicitly recognized the tie between writing and the way language sounds:

> Punctuation is the art of marking in writing the several pauses, or rests, between sentences, and the parts of sentences, according to their proper quantity or proportion, as they are expressed in a just and accurate pronunciation. As the several articulate sounds, the syllables and words, of which sentences consist, are marked by letters; so the rests and pauses between sentences and their parts are marked by points.
>
> (Lowth, 1967, p. 154)

Although one doubts that he ever made the appropriate measurements, Lowth believed that the period marked a pause twice as long as that marked by a colon, the colon a pause twice as long as that marked by a semicolon, and the semicolon a pause twice as long as that marked by a comma. But there were other marks that had more to do with intonation:

> Beside the points which mark the pauses in discourse, there are others which denote a different modulation of the voice in correspondence with the sense.... The interrogation and exclamation points... mark an elevation of the voice. The parenthesis... marks a moderate depression of the voice.
>
> (pp. 171–172)

However, the compendious up-to-date successor to Lowth's grammar, Quirk, Greenbaum, Leech, and Svartvik's *A Comprehensive Grammar of the English Language* (1985), takes the point of view that most punctuation is dictated by grammatical conventions and not by prosody:[2]

> Punctuation practice is governed primarily by grammatical considerations and is related to grammatical distinctions. Sometimes it is linked to intonation, stress, rhythm, pause, or any other of the prosodic features which convey distinctions in speech, but the link is neither simple nor systematic.... Punctuation marks tend, therefore, to be used according to fairly strict conventions and even in the peripheral areas where universal convention does not obtain, each individual publishing house imposes one for all materials that it puts forth in print.
>
> (p. 1611)

It is not clear whether this statement rests on systematic observation (any more than Lowth's statement regarding the relative lengths of pauses), or whether it simply reflects a folk opinion. It is interesting that immediately following this passage the same authors remark:

> There are two important qualifications to the foregoing generalizations. In the first place, there is, as we shall see, a great deal of flexibility possible in the use of the comma: in its presence or absence, or in its replacement by other marks. The comma in fact provides considerable opportunity for personal taste and for implying fine degrees of cohesion and separation. Secondly, the conventions as a whole are not followed as rigorously in

manuscript use (especially personal material, such as private letters), where there may be inconsistencies in their application that would not be permitted in most printed material.

That commas show more flexibility of use than other marks is interesting in view of the fact that the same authors found, in a varied 72,000-word sample from the "Brown corpus" (Francis & Kuçera, 1982), that fully 47% of the punctuation marks were commas (Quirk et al., 1985, p. 1613). About half of the marks, then, belonged to this "flexible" category. Beyond that, 45% were periods. We will see presently that there is good reason to suppose that, in all but a few special cases, periods represent falling pitch. If, then, 92% of the punctuation marks in a representative body of written English are either overwhelmingly prosodic (the periods) or at least subject to "personal taste" (the commas), the statement that "punctuation practice is governed primarily by grammatical considerations" leads to a certain amount of puzzlement.

The second qualification in the above quote is also worth pondering. If "manuscript use" such as private letter writing shows a less consistent adherence to grammatical punctuating conventions, does this mean that writers who are not the victims of copyediting are able to be guided more consistently by prosody? It is too bad to imply that writers who use prosody-based punctuation are exhibiting a sloppiness "that would not be permitted in most printed material." It would seem that the question should not be put in terms of sloppiness versus care, but in terms of extent to which writers are guided by their inner voices—by auditory imagery—versus the extent to which they are guided by imposed rules.

But the fact that there are such rules, and that they do exert a significant influence on punctuation, can hardly be doubted. As an example we can consider the two possible rules that govern the placement of commas between items in a series. One of these rules arbitrarily inserts commas between all the items in the series, regardless of whether intonation breaks are intended. Thus commas are prescribed as rigidly in the unitary phrase "red, white, and blue," which would normally be spoken without any prosodic breaks, as they are in the prosodically separated clauses "I came, I saw, I conquered."

Any series must have these commas, regardless of the author's prosodic intentions. The arbitrariness of this rule is made even clearer by the existence of the two well-known conventions: one that dictates a comma before the "and" in an example such as "red, white, and blue," another that omits such a comma—"red, white and blue." Whatever governs the choice between these two conventions, it is certainly not prosody.

As mentioned above and demonstrated below, periods are typically associated with an auditory image of falling pitch. That image is in turn typically associated with the end of a sentence. We see, then, that in many cases there may be no point in asking whether some instance of punctuation is determined by prosody or grammar. So long as prosody and grammar coincide, the only proper answer is "both."

Question marks, on the other hand, provide a good example of punctuation that is at least ambiguous with respect to prosody. Functionally there are two major types of questions: "yes-no" questions and "question-word" questions. Yes-no questions generally exhibit a final rising pitch; question-word questions, a falling pitch. (For a fuller discussion, including cases in which these pitches are reversed, see Chafe, 1970, pp. 309–345.) That both of the following examples are written with question marks, in spite of the fact that the first ends with a rising pitch and the second with a falling one, shows that function can override prosody in some cases:

(a) Did you buy some artichokes?
(b) What did you buy?

But what may be the clearest example of conflict between grammar and prosody is a negative one: the dictate that a comma must *not* be used between a subject and a predicate. Quirk et al. (1985, p. 1619) discuss the following example:

The man over there in the corner, is obviously drunk.

They mention that in speech this sentence "might have a tone unit break where the unacceptable comma has been inserted and we are sometimes tempted to match this with a comma in writing, an error particularly likely to arise with lengthy subjects. . . . The rule, however, is clear enough and is strictly observed in print" (p. 1619).

Its observance in print, however, is something that developed only recently. We find Melville, for example, frequently writing sentences such as the following:

But this august dignity I treat of, is not the dignity of kings and robes.
Only the most unprejudiced of men like Stubb, nowadays partake of cooked whales.

similar examples:

Two cups of Quaker 100% Natural Cereal mixed with a little of this and a little of that, make the best cookies you've tasted in years.

Or in a student paper:

Those who are in disagreement, hold that babbling is essential to language development.

Or in a department memo:

Not asking me, will give me time to post things as they come.

Or in a fortune cookie:

Those who place all their hopes in money, usually get short changed.[3]

Or in a department memo:

Evidently unconstrained writers still have an inclination to place a comma after a long or heavy subject, thus marking a natural intonation break. Older writers such as Melville did this without hesitation, and it is apparently only the fear of rules, or of copy editors, that keeps modern writers from doing the same.

The discussion that follows will try to throw a little more light on the role punctuation plays in making overt the covert prosody of written language. It grapples with the question, To what extent, and in what ways, does punctuation function to signal the prosody of that inner voice? It would be much easier to answer this question if there were some direct and independent way of knowing what the covert prosody of a piece of writing was—the prosody intended by the author, and that assigned by a reader. We could then simply compare those prosodies with the punctuation, documenting the places where it coincides and where it does not. Unfortunately, there is no such direct independent manifestation of the inner voice, and we will have to approach it in more indirect ways.

Reading Aloud

It may be remembered that Russell Long equated the prosody that is "heard" in one's auditory imagery with the prosody that would be present if a piece of writing were read aloud. To repeat part of what he said:

> As I write these sentences, even though my lips are not moving, I am quite conscious of the sound the words I am writing would make *if they were read aloud*. To extend this recognition one step further, I am convinced that the competent writer writes in the same way he reads aloud, using preceding syntactic and semantic context to project meaning, word choice, and punctuation that will follow.

If the auditory imagery we are concerned with could always be made overt by reading aloud, we would have a simple and direct way to submit it to public view. To capture the prosodic intentions of writers, we could ask them to read their own works aloud (whenever that was possible). To capture the auditory imagery of readers, we could ask them to read aloud the works of others. The reasoning might be as follows. Reading aloud converts written language into spoken language, spoken language necessarily has a prosody, and from that prosody we can see (or, better, hear) the prosody that is hidden in the writing. If we are interested in the relation between prosody and punctuation, we can then go on to compare the read-aloud prosody with the written punctuation to see where the two do or do not coincide.

But of course things are not that simple. Reading aloud, when it is examined in any detail, turns out to be a highly peculiar activity. It is neither spoken language nor written language, but both and neither at the same time. Although it is spoken language in the sense that it is, quite literally, spoken, there are very few people whose oral reading would be mistaken for speech. A tape recording of someone reading aloud will almost always be recognizable as such, for two reasons. First of all, the form of the language itself—its lexical, grammatical, and rhetorical properties—will be of a written rather than a spoken nature. We know written language when we hear it. Second, the prosody used by oral readers—the intonation, hesitations, even the voice quality—will be different from that used by a speaker. People simply do not read aloud the way they talk.

In early 1986 I asked twenty members of an undergraduate class at the University of California at Berkeley to take home with them six brief written passages and read them into a tape recorder. Since their mean age was about 20, I will refer to this first group of oral readers as the "younger subjects" in order to differentiate them from a second group to be mentioned presently. The passages were intended to be diverse in style and punctuation, and included excerpts from an automobile advertisement in *Time*, from Thoreau's *Walden*, from James's *The Turn of the Screw*, from a news report in the *San Francisco Chronicle*, from Hemingway's *For Whom the Bell Tolls*, and from an article in the *American Anthropologist*. The mean length of these excerpts was 227 words.

Not wishing to limit this study to college undergraduates, in the fall of 1986 I asked eight people in an adult education class in Santa Barbara to tape-record their readings of a set of similar passages. The mean age of these readers was about 64, and I will refer to them as the "older subjects." Educated two generations earlier and with decades of reading and writing behind them, these older subjects might have been expected to show markedly different prosodic habits from the 20-year-olds, but in fact the differences were minor.

The excerpts that were read by this second group were chosen to be parallel to those read by the college students. I did not use the same passages for both groups, since this was an exploratory study and I wanted to introduce some variety among the readings as well. Again there was an excerpt from *Walden*. To parallel the James passage there was a passage from Wharton's *The Age of Innocence*. There was another news report, this time from the *Santa Barbara News-Press*. Instead of an automobile advertisement, I chose a software advertisement in *Time*, and a different article from the *American Anthropologist*. Instead of Hemingway, I used an excerpt from Agee's *A Death in the Family*. The mean length of these excerpts was 220 words.[4]

These tape recordings were transcribed like any other samples of spoken language, special attention being given to the boundaries of intonation units. A distinction was made between terminal pitch contours showing falling pitch, as at the end of a sentence, and any other, nonfalling terminal pitch contours. Contours of the falling pitch type were transcribed with a period, those of the nonfalling pitch type with a comma.

The intonation units of ordinary spoken language show a relatively constant length in terms of the number of words they contain. This length varies from language to language depending on the language's morphological type, since some languages pack more information into a word than others. In English the mean length of an intonation unit is between 5 and 6 words. It is interesting, then, that the mean length of the intonation units produced by the younger subjects in oral reading was 5.7 words, and that produced by the older subjects was 5.2 words, both within the typical range of ordinary spoken language. This figure can be compared with the length of the punctuation units in the excerpts these people were reading from, where the mean was 8.9 words for the passages read by the younger subjects and 9.4 words for the passages read by the older subjects. The oral readers obviously introduced many more prosodic boundaries than were signaled by the punctuation in the passages before them. Evidently they went beyond the punctuation in order to make what they were saying coincide

Table 10.1 Comparison of Lengths of Punctuation and Intonation Units: Younger Subjects

	Mean Words per Punctuation Unit in Original Passage	Mean Words per Intonation Unit in Read-Aloud Versions
Advertisement	5.4	4.5
Thoreau	6.9	5.2
James	9.6	6.5
Newspaper	11.9	6.2
Hemingway	12.1	6.6
Academic	13.3	5.7
Overall	8.9	5.7

with the norm for spoken language. From this evidence it would seem that all spoken language—including oral reading—adheres to a strong constraint on intonation unit length. If a written passage fails in its punctuation to allow for that constraint, oral readers will introduce their own prosodic boundaries in order to bring their reading into line with what seem to be unavoidable requirements of speaking.

There were real differences among the six passages in the extent to which their punctuation reflected this spoken language constraint. (The passages were chosen with such differences in mind.) Table 10.1 shows, in the left-hand column, the mean number of words per punctuation unit for each of the six passages, increasing from a low of 5.4 words for the advertisement in *Time* to a high of 13.3 words for the article in the *American Anthropologist*. The right-hand column shows the mean number of words per intonation unit in the orally read versions of these passages. The range here was much smaller: from 4.5 to 6.6 words, a range that might be found in spoken language. The reading aloud was closest to the punctuation in the advertisement, with 4.5 words per intonation unit reflecting the 5.4 words per punctuation unit of the original. It diverged the most from the punctuation in the academic article, with 5.7 words per intonation unit reflecting the 13.3 words per punctuation unit of the original.

Table 10.2 gives the same information for the older subjects. It can be seen that the results are similar. Whereas the punctuation units of the original passages increased

Table 10.2 Comparison of Lengths of Punctuation and Intonation Units: Older Subjects

	Mean Words per Punctuation Unit in Original Passage	Mean Words per Intonation Unit in Read-Aloud Versions
Thoreau	6.5	5.2
Wharton	8.8	6.0
Newspaper	10.0	4.7
Advertisement	10.0	5.5
Academic	10.8	4.8
Agee	12.5	5.4
Overall	9.4	5.2

in length from 6.5 words for Thoreau to 12.5 for Agee, the intonation units ranged from 4.7 to 6.0, evidently just as constrained by the requirements of speaking as they were for the younger subjects. (The ordering of the genres was somewhat different in this respect. Especially noticeable is the fact that the software advertisement here contained punctuation units almost twice as long as the automobile advertisement in the earlier data.)

Since speaking of any kind evidently imposes a strong constraint on intonation unit length, we have here a measure of the degree to which the punctuation of a particular piece of writing accords with the prosody of spoken language. Thus we can say that the automobile advertisement as well as the Thoreau passages were quite spokenlike in this respect, whereas the academic articles and the Agee passage were especially unspokenlike in their punctuation.

The oral readers obviously introduced many prosodic boundaries that were not signaled by punctuation marks in the writing. The percentages that follow are based on the oral reading of the younger subjects only; percentages for the older subjects were similar. Of the total number of prosodic boundaries in the versions read aloud by the younger subjects, about 60% reflected punctuation marks in the written passages, while 40% did not. In total, 91% of the added boundaries were nonfalling pitches and only 9% falling. Thus when these oral readers added prosodic boundaries over and above those indicated by the punctuation, they nearly always added boundaries that were not of the sentence-final type.

The punctuation marks that the written passages did contain were almost always read as prosodic boundaries. In only 6% of the possible cases was a punctuation mark not read aloud as a boundary. Furthermore, in most cases the kind of punctuation determined the kind of prosody. That was especially true of periods, which constituted 37% of the punctuation marks in the written passages. Of these periods, 94% were read aloud as falling pitches. More common than periods were commas, constituting 52% of the punctuation marks in these passages. Commas were not quite as strong a determinant of a particular read-aloud intonation: 66% were read as nonfalling pitches, while 25% were read as falling. These proportions were, however, skewed by the Thoreau passage, where 44% of the commas were read as if they were periods. (The passage itself contained only two periods.) If we left the Thoreau passage out of account and looked only at the 5 other passages, 72% of the commas were read as nonfalling pitches and 16% as falling. To summarize, periods were almost always read aloud as falling pitches, while commas were usually read aloud as nonfalling pitches, though the proportions in the latter case were not quite as overwhelming.

Although periods and commas together constituted 89% of the punctuation marks in the original passages, it is of some interest to see how other punctuation marks were read aloud. There were some that were usually read aloud as falling pitches. For example, semicolons were read as falling pitches 89% of the time. Colons, of which there were only two examples, were read as falling pitches 95% of the time. The one question mark was read as a falling pitch 90% of the time. This question mark occurred at the end of a question-word question ("How was this . . . accomplished . . .?"), where a falling pitch is normal. The only marks beside commas that were usually read aloud as nonfalling pitches were parentheses. The three open parentheses were preceded by nonfalling pitches in oral reading 80% of the time, and the one close parenthesis that was not immediately followed by a comma was read aloud as a nonfalling pitch 95% of the time. The four dashes, all of which occurred in the Henry James selection, were prosodically ambiguous. When the dash could be interpreted as the end of a sentence (regardless of the following context), it was usually read as a falling pitch. When, on the other hand, it functioned to set off a parenthetical remark ("She wished, of course—small blame to her!—to sink the whole subject;") it was usually read as a nonfalling pitch. Thus the dash, like the question mark, apparently has no consistent pitch interpretation, but receives such an interpretation from its context.

Repunctuating

We can by no means be certain that reading aloud captures completely the auditory imagery that is in a writer's or reader's mind during the silent processing of written language. Reading aloud is useful in showing that there is a correspondence between punctuation marks and their prosodic interpretation. Not only do oral readers interpret punctuation marks as signals of prosodic boundaries, they also interpret specific marks as signals of specific kinds of boundaries. But what of the many boundaries oral readers introduce that are not signaled by any punctuation? Are such boundaries also present for silent readers, or are they introduced only because of the requirements of spoken language production? If spoken language is locked into a format in which intonation units contain about 5 or 6 words, that accounts for the 40% of the read-aloud prosodic boundaries that were not triggered by any punctuation. But why would the auditory imagery that accompanies silent writing or reading be subject to the same spoken-language constraint? Why should either writers or readers be locked into the same 5- or 6-word format?

Writers have the leisure to construct longer units and, since they can peruse a segment of language repeatedly, they are not subject to the same short-term memory limitations as speakers. Time is less pressing for writers than for speakers. But what of silent readers? The relation between reading and listening is a curious one. Of necessity we can listen only as fast as we are spoken to. In listening to a speaker whose pace is too slow, our minds may try to leap ahead, but if we are really listening we have no choice but to follow the tempo of what is being presented to us. In reading, on the other hand, we are free of any tempo constraint that might be imposed by the producer of the language. We can follow whatever pace is comfortable, speeding up and slowing down as we wish. There is nothing to prevent us from exceeding the approximately 180-words-per-minute pace that governs speaking, and therefore listening. If readers of written language are able to assimilate chunks of language that are larger than speakers of spoken language are able to produce, then the 5- or 6-word ceiling of spoken language need not be a restriction that applies to silent auditory imagery. To find out more about this, we need to look at written language prosody in ways that are free of the constraints inevitably placed on spoken language production.

One possible way is to ask people to provide their own punctuation for written passages from which the original punctuation has been removed. To the extent that these "repunctuators" are guided by their auditory imagery, their punctuation may give us some idea of what that imagery is. As with any assignment of punctuation, the disturbing factors listed earlier may be present. People may be more or less skilled in using punctuation to represent their prosodic imagery. They may be influenced by current fashions in punctuating. And they may also be influenced by nonprosodic rules of punctuating. For these reasons we cannot take repunctuation as an unambiguous indicator of prosodic imagery. In spite of these reservations it does appear that repunctuation may give us some useful insights into that imagery.

At the same time that I collected the first set of oral readings discussed above, I also asked 20 other undergraduates to repunctuate the same passages. I gave them doctored versions that lacked all punctuation, and asked them to insert punctuation as they thought appropriate. Later I did the same with another group of eight older subjects, using the passages that had been read aloud by the older subjects discussed above.

So far as the length of the resulting punctuation units is concerned, with both groups of subjects there was a closer correspondence between the repunctuators and the original authors than there was between the oral readers and the original authors. It will be recalled that the mean length of intonation units in the younger subjects' reading aloud was 5.7 words, compared with 8.9 words in the punctuation units of the original passages. The mean length of the punctuation units created by the younger repunctuators was 9.4 words. And, whereas the mean length of intonation units in the older subjects' reading aloud was 5.2 words, compared with 9.4 words in the punctuation units of the original passages, the mean length of the punctuation units created by the older repunctuators was 10.6 words. In other words, for both sets of repunctuators the punctuation units tended to be even somewhat longer than those of the originals, but closer in length to the originals than were the intonation units of the oral readers.

More interesting is the fact that the introduced punctuation units showed no ceiling effect of the type that kept the oral readers from producing intonation units that averaged between 5 and 6 words in length. Table 10.3 shows how, in general, as the punctuation units of the originals increased in length, from the automobile adver-

Table 10.3 Comparison of Original and Repunctuated Units: Younger Subjects

	Mean Words per Punctuation Unit in Original Passage	*Mean Words per Punctuation Unit in Repunctuated Passage*
Advertisement	5.4	5.6
Thoreau	6.9	10.0
James	9.6	9.7
Hemingway	11.9	11.2
Newspaper	12.1	13.2
Academic	13.3	11.1
Overall	8.9	9.4

Table 10.4 Comparison of Original and Repunctuated Units: Older Subjects

	Mean Words per Punctuation Unit in Original Passage	Mean Words per Punctuation Unit in Repunctuated Passage
Thoreau	6.5	8.7
Wharton	8.8	10.9
Newspaper	10.0	11.7
Advertisement	10.0	11.2
Academic	10.8	10.9
Agee	12.5	10.7
Overall	9.4	10.6

tisement at one extreme to the academic article at the other, the punctuation units of the younger repunctuators also increased in length. In the advertisement and the James, the introduced punctuation units were almost identical in length to those of the original. They differed by about one word in the Hemingway and the newspaper article. The difference was somewhat greater in the case of the academic article and especially the Thoreau.

Table 10.4 shows the pattern for the older repunctuators. Here the introduced punctuation units were almost identical in length to those of the original in the academic passage. They were about one word longer for the advertisement, and about two words longer for the Thoreau, Wharton, and newspaper excerpts. For the Agee passage, on the other hand, they were about two words shorter. Again there appears to have been no limit on the length of the punctuation units, but their correspondences to the original punctuation units were quite diverse.

To what extent did this punctuation agree with that of the original authors? For the younger subjects 80% of their punctuation marks, and for the older subjects 83%, corresponded to some kind of punctuation in the original passages. These figures can be compared with those for reading aloud, where for the younger subjects 60% of their prosodic boundaries reflected original punctuation, and for the older subjects 53%.

However, while the repunctuators tended more than the oral readers to punctuate in just those places where the authors had punctuated, there was less agreement with respect to specific kinds of punctuation. For the younger subjects 67% of the original periods (for the older subjects 76%) were mirrored by periods in the repunctuated versions, compared with the falling pitches used in reading periods by 94% and 95% of the younger and older oral readers, respectively. For the younger subjects 54% of the original commas (for the older subjects 49%) were mirrored by commas in the repunctuated versions, compared with the nonfalling pitches used in reading commas by 66% and 65% of the younger and older oral readers. The oral readers, of course, saw the authors' punctuation marks, while the repunctuators did not. Furthermore, the repunctuators were free to use marks other than periods and commas, whereas the oral readers were transcribed as having only falling or nonfalling pitch contours. This freedom to use other punctuation marks contributed to the distance between the originals and the repunctuated versions. For example, 17% of the original periods were repunctuated by the younger subjects as neither periods nor commas.

If oral reading can suggest the degree to which the punctuation of a particular piece of writing is spokenlike, repunctuating, by showing us the punctuation that a consensus of readers would assign to a piece of writing, can suggest the degree to which a piece of writing captures the auditory imagery of ordinary readers. In that light we can say that in the first set of readings the automobile advertisement and the James captured the readers' auditory imagery very well, while in the second set the same was true for the academic article. The greatest discrepancy, in either set, perhaps surprisingly, was with Thoreau, who used much shorter punctuation units than the repunctuators did.

Why Are Punctuation Units Longer than Intonation Units?

One finding that is clear from a comparison of Tables 10.1–4 is that, for a given piece of writing, the mean length of punctuation units is always greater than the mean length of the intonation units produced by oral readers. This is true whether the punctuation units were those produced by the original authors or whether they were those produced by the repunctuators. The difference between the punctuation and intonation units is greater for some pieces of writing than for others, but the difference is always there. Why should there be this consistent difference?

Two possibilities suggest themselves. One is that both writers and silent readers are able to process larger chunks of information at a time. For writers, their freedom from a speaker's need to create language on the run may provide the leisure to create punctuation units that exceed the length of what a speaker is capable of. For silent readers, unconstrained by the necessity to follow the pace set by a speaker, it may be possible to assimilate more information in a single gulp of comprehension (assuming that comprehension also takes place as a series of brief acts).

An alternative possibility is that written language signals prosodic boundaries in other ways, in addition to punctuation. Perhaps a writer's or reader's prosodic interpretation of a piece of writing is not dependent on punctuation alone. More specifically, perhaps learning to deal with written language involves learning to give prosodic interpretations to specific syntactic patterns, even when punctuation is not involved.

There may be no point in trying to choose between these two alternatives, for it is likely that both are correct. It is likely that the syntax of written language does provide clues to prosodic boundaries, but also that these boundaries can be, and often are, extended beyond what would be natural in spoken language. It is likely in addition that both writers and readers have flexibility, creating syntax and interpreting syntax prosodically in ways they find most comfortable under their own individual conditions of expression and understanding. A writer's omission of punctuation maximizes such flexibility. Instead of locking the reader into a single prosodic interpretation a writer may leave possibilities open.

To make this more concrete, it is instructive to look at cases where the original authors and the repunctuators inserted approximately the same number of punctuation marks, but where the oral readers inserted more. Such was true of the selection from James, where the mean number of words per punctuation unit in the original was 9.6 and for the repunctuators 9.7, but the mean number of words per intonation unit of the oral readers was 6.5.

James wrote, for example:

We were to keep our heads if we should keep nothing else—

A total of 16 of the repunctuators agreed with James in preserving this sequence as an unpunctuated unit, only 4 of them inserting a comma after "heads." Among the oral readers, on the other hand, 17 of them inserted a nonfalling international break after "heads," only 3 of them pronouncing the entire sequence as a single intonation unit. Most of the oral readers thus quite characteristically divided these 12 words into two 6-word units. Why did James write all this as a single unit, and why did the repunctuators agree with him? In spoken language there is a constraint that limits the amount of information in a single intonation unit to one "new" idea—new in the sense that it is being newly activated for the hearer (Chafe, 1987). Such information contrasts with that which is "given," or already activated. There is, however, a gray area of information that is inferable from the context. Rather than being completely new, such information can be regarded as in some way already "accessible." The first clause of the above example, "we were to keep our heads," expresses information that is accessible from the immediately preceding clause:

we were of a common mind about the duty of resistance to extravagant fancies.

"Keeping our heads" is essentially a paraphrase of "resisting extravagant fancies." In this context, the sequence "we were to keep our heads if we should keep nothing else" does not really express two new ideas but one, the idea contained in the second clause. Beginning with the accessible idea "we were to keep our heads," it adds the new idea "if we were to keep nothing else." That new idea itself, furthermore, does not carry forward the development of ideas in the narrative, but serves only as a reinforcement of the preceding idea.

The point is that, whereas this example may appear superficially to convey two clauses worth of new information, and thus to be too much to process in a single gulp of comprehension, in fact the first clause conveys information that is already accessible from the immediately preceding context, while the second clause conveys new information that does nothing more than to emphasize what preceded. A reader's cognitive capacities are not, then, severely taxed by the need to interpret this sequence as a single unit. Furthermore, if a reader did need to interpret it in two separate acts of comprehension, the word "if" can be almost as good a signal for a break as a comma would be. By not using a comma after "heads" James showed his understanding of the light cognitive load exacted by this sequence in the context given. But in addition, the clause structure, clearly signaled by the word "if," makes it easy for the reader to direct either one or two focuses of attention on these words, whichever seems most comfortable.

Close Versus Open Punctuating

If punctuation serves to make a writer's prosodic intentions explicit, but if at the same time there are other cues that, in the absence of punctuation, enable readers to assign their own prosody, then writers can enjoy a certain amount of freedom in this respect. While few of them are likely to deviate from using periods at the ends of declarative sentences, in the use of commas they may be entirely explicit, or they may leave prosody in part to the imagination.

Such flexibility opens the doors to fashion. Where choices can be governed by taste rather than inevitable rules, the tastes will vary with the times and the creativity of individuals. The continuum of possibilities in the use of commas has come to be identified in terms of "close" or "open" punctuating. At the present time it is fashionable to prefer a relatively open style. As stated in *The Chicago Manual of Style* (1982):

> The tendency to use all the punctuation that the grammatical structure of the material suggests is referred to as close punctuation. It is a practice that was more common in the past, and though it may be helpful when the writing is elaborate, it can, when misused, produce an uninviting choppiness. There is a tendency today, on the other hand, to punctuate only when necessary to prevent misreading. Most contemporary writers and editors lean toward this open style of punctuation yet preserve a measure of subjectivity and discretion.
>
> (p. 132)

We have seen that the close punctuating favored in the past was more in accord with the prosody of speech. Probably this fact was related to the widespread habit of reading aloud, as described, for example, by Walter Ong (1982):

> The famous *McGuffey's Readers,* published in the United States in some 120 million copies between 1836 and 1920, were designed as remedial readers to improve not the reading for comprehension that we idealize today, but oral, declamatory reading. The *McGuffey's* specialized in passages from "sound-conscious" literature concerned with great heroes ("heavy" oral characters). They provided endless oral pronunciation and breathing drills.
>
> (pp. 115–116)

The constraints on information flow that are responsible for the intonation units of spoken language were, then, during the nineteenth and early twentieth centuries, applied as well to the punctuation of written language. The trend toward open punctuation seems to have gained momentum at the same time that the popularity of oral reading declined. As is customary when rules are legislated, this change was validated with appeals to logic (one should not "separate inseparables"), or aesthetics (one should avoid "uninviting choppiness"), or the ease with which a rule can be stated ("the rule is clear enough"). But in the end all such appeals simply rationalize the results of a decline in the habit of reading aloud, the most powerful of the ties between writing and speaking.

Thoreau provides an interesting case study of what might now be regarded as exaggerated close punctuation, although, as we shall see, the choices may not always have been those of Thoreau himself. In reading the following passage aloud, virtually 100% of our subjects inserted prosodic breaks just where Thoreau had shown them, and few of them inserted breaks anywhere else, except that 70% also introduced a break after "shady" in the last line. Thus Thoreau's frequent use of commas seems to have accorded well with the requirements of speaking:

> Sometimes I rambled to pine groves,
> standing like temples,
> or like fleets at sea,
> full-rigged,
> with wavy boughs,
> and rippling with light,
> so soft and green and shady that the Druids would have forsaken their oaks to worship in them.

The repunctuators, on the other hand, were very conservative in punctuating this passage. There was only one comma that was inserted by more than half (75%) of them:

> Sometimes I rambled to pine groves standing like temples or like fleets at sea,
> full-rigged with wavy boughs and rippling with light so soft and green and shady that the Druids would have forsaken their oaks to worship in them.

It is interesting that Thoreau's original intentions for this passage fell between these extremes. In the draft of the manuscript sent to the printer he punctuated as follows:

> Sometimes I rambled to pine groves standing like temples, for like fleets at sea,
> full-rigged with wavy boughs and rippling with light,
> so soft and green and shady,
> that the druids would have forsaken their oaks to worship in them.

Printers at that time took many liberties with an author's punctuation, many believing that their own skill was superior to that of the author. Shillingsburg (1986) mentions C. H. Timperley's *The Printers' Manual* published in London in 1838, "a book which also laments the ignorance of most writers in the art of punctuation and fantasizes about a world in which authors turn in manuscripts with no punctuation at all, leaving that chore to the professional competence of the compositors." Thoreau received a proof that contained a maximum degree of close punctuation:

> Sometimes I rambled to pine groves,
> standing like temples,
> or like fleets at sea,
> full-rigged,
> with wavy boughs,
> and rippling with light,

so soft,
and green,
and shady that the druids would have forsaken their oaks to worship in them.

He then deleted the commas after "soft" and "green," leaving the published punctuation with which we began.[5] The effect was to treat "soft and green and shady" as a unitary quality of the pine groves, not as a series of three separate qualities.

The example shows us something of how punctuation was negotiated by an author and a printer during the heyday of close punctuation. It also shows how the data from oral reading and repunctuating can be useful in identifying punctuation styles. In the typical case of close punctuation we find agreement between the author and oral readers, but disagreement between the author and modern repunctuators, whose commas are apparently influenced by their experience with more open styles.

At the other extreme, an exaggerated form of open punctuating became a trademark of certain twentieth-century writers, among whom in America were Hemingway and Agee. The following passage from the Agee excerpt (the book was published posthumously in 1957) provides an example:

> He has been dead all night while I was asleep and now it is morning and I am awake but he is still dead and he will stay right on being dead all afternoon and all night and all tomorrow while I am asleep again and wake up again and go to sleep again and he can't come back home again ever any more but I will see him once more before he is taken away.
>
> (pp. 263–264)

Oral readers divided this passage into as many as 16 intonation units. In the following version the square brackets show the percentage of oral readers who introduced a break at that point:

He has been dead all night, [100%]
while I was asleep, [100%]
and now it is morning, [88%]
and I am awake, [100%]
but he is still dead, [100%]
and he will stay right on being dead, [75%]
all afternoon, [88%]
and all night, [88%]
and all tomorrow, [75%]
while I am asleep again, [100%]
and wake up again, [100%]
and he can't come back home again, [63%]
ever any more. [100%]
But I will see him once more, [88%]
before he is taken away. [100%]

Most or all segmented the passage before a conjunction—before "and," "but," "while," and "before"—thus helping to confirm the notion that conjunctions signal prosodic breaks when punctuation is absent. More than half also introduced a prosodic boundary at a potential sentence closure—a place where a sentence could have ended but did not—even when no conjunction followed: "and he will stay right on being dead, all afternoon" and "and he can't come back home again, ever any more."

The repunctuators were, as usual, much less liberal than the oral readers in segmenting this passage. The following version shows a break wherever at least half of the repunctuators introduced one:

> He has been dead all night while I was asleep and now it is morning and I am awake but he is still dead, [50%]
> and he will stay right on being dead all afternoon and all night and all tomorrow while I am asleep again, [63%]
> and wake up again, [63%]
> and go to sleep again, [50%]
> and he can't come back home again ever any more. [100%]
> But I will see him once more before he is taken away. [100%]

These breaks were always triggered by the presence of a conjunction, but not every conjunction had this effect.

The oral readers showed what a close punctuator might have done with this passage, and the repunctuators what an open punctuator might have done. Agee's own version, however, was more extreme. It has been thought that writing without commas reproduces somehow a narrator's "stream of consciousness," but that notion is ironic if it is correct to view intonation units as the verbal representations of focuses of consciousness (Chafe, 1980). Consciousness probably flows in spurts rather than in a steady stream, and commas help to capture this spurtlike quality.

Suppressing commas has two other effects. First, it forces the reader to rely wholly on syntax for prosodic divisions. Through a liberal use of "and" (as in the Agee example) it can make that task an easy one, for "and" alone may be almost as good a marker of an intonational boundary as a comma. Second, through its deviation from accustomed usage it calls attention to the language itself. Other writers may use punctuation to increase the transparency of their language. By signaling the boundaries of normal processing units, they relieve readers of the necessity of creating those boundaries for themselves, and thus allow the ideas behind the language to show through without interposing the language as something else to pay attention to. Agee forces his readers to create their own processing units, and in so doing makes his language a separate object of attention. Reading his sentence makes one as aware of the sentence itself as of the ideas behind it. This tactic, of course, can have its own aesthetic value.[6]

Points of Dispute

There are specific places in the grammar of English where the presence or absence of a punctuation mark is likely to cause anxiety. These may be places where an inexperienced writer will use punctuation in a way that is considered "wrong," or they may be places where even experienced writers will disagree. Typical of such cases is the presence of a mismatch between one's prosodic imagery and a punctuation rule. I will discuss only two examples here, but the list could easily be multiplied (see also Danielewicz & Chafe, 1985).

Cases Where a "Heard" Prosodic Boundary May Need to Be Suppressed

In certain places in our data, we found neither the original authors nor the repunctuators using punctuation, but most of the oral readers inserting a prosodic break. In such cases, particularly where an explicit rule of punctuation is involved, we can infer that the boundary inserted by the oral readers did reflect a covertly "heard" break that was suppressed in writing because of a rule. This inference is confirmed when we find the same rule being ignored by casual or inexperienced writers, or by writers of other periods.

A good example, already discussed and illustrated, is the boundary between a subject and a predicate. Quirk et al. (1985) were quoted earlier as describing a common punctuation "error" based on the fact that in speech a sentence "might have a tone unit break where the unacceptable comma has been inserted and we are sometimes tempted to match this with a comma in writing, an error particularly likely to arise with lengthy subjects" (p. 1619). In the current data there were a number of cases where the original author and the repunctuators dutifully omitted punctuation between a subject and a predicate, but where oral readers did introduce such a boundary. In the following examples the read-aloud prosodic boundary is shown with a comma that was, of course, not present in the writing, and the percentage of oral readers who introduced a prosodic break is given in square brackets:

> The car ahead with the "I brake for squirrels" bumper sticker, [85%]
> really does brake for squirrels.
> One of the long-standing puzzles of Pacific prehistory, [85%]
> is how the seafaring lineage of Austronesians . . .

The subjects of the above clauses may have qualified as "lengthy," but the subject need not be a lengthy one if it conveys information that is completely new, as in the following example where the judge had not been mentioned before:

> Writing the court's opinion,
> Judge Skelly Wright, [90%]
> said he disagreed with the government's argument that the time for justice has passed.

It is very tempting in these cases to recommend that the prohibition be relaxed, so that contemporary authors would be free to follow the practice of their nineteenth-century predecessors. The rule, however, is by now so entrenched that it would be difficult to repeal. For writing teachers, the best practice may be to teach it as an arbitrary rule, while at the same time allowing students to recognize the discrepancy for what it is. There should at least be respect for the sensitivity of student writers who, like accomplished writers of the past, follow their inner voices in this regard. There might even be admiration for the special courage of anyone who went so far as to separate a verb from its *object*, in the rare cases where the verb and object express independent new ideas. The author of the following did not do that, but if he had he would have captured the prosody that was "heard" and expressed by 75% of the people who read this passage aloud:

> it is now possible to track archaeologically,
> the major part of this migration.

Cases Where Punctuation May Need to Be Imposed

There are cases of the opposite sort in which an author obeyed a rule dictating the presence—not the absence—of a comma, but where that comma may not have captured a "heard" prosodic boundary. Contrary to what we might expect, the evidence for such cases does not come from reading aloud. Oral readers, who prefer intonation units that are as short as they can be, seize any excuse to introduce a prosodic boundary. With few exceptions, if a comma is there, an oral reader will respect it. The evidence for the cases I have in mind comes rather from the repunctuators. Where the author used a punctuation mark but most of the repunctuators did not, we can suspect a failure of most silent readers to "hear" a prosodic break. We may wonder why the repunctuators did not respect the rule, but it seems that rules for inserting punctuation are less rigidly adhered to than those forbidding it.

The Chicago Manual of Style (1982) recommends that "commas should be used to set off interjections, transitional adverbs, and similar elements that effect a distinct break in the continuity of thought" (p. 140). Transitional adverbs are illustrated with "indeed," "after all," "on the other hand," "therefore," "perhaps," "however," and "consequently." Usually such adverbs express some logical relation between a sentence and the preceding context, like switches that control the progress or sidetracking of a train of thought. Because of this function, they are likely to occur at the beginnings of sentences or clauses. In the following examples, the figures in square brackets show the percentage of repunctuators who duplicated the comma that was present in the original passage. Noteworthy is the fact that it was a minority of the repunctuators who did so:

> Yet, [15% of younger subjects]
> recent archaeological research confirms the conventional wisdom ...
> In fact, [25% of older subjects]
> a few recent publications argue that the type of paleodemographic study thought to be
>   most secure ...

A transitional adverb may also occur within a clause, in which case the rule dictates a comma on both sides of it (the percentages are from the younger subjects):

> The appeals court ruled that the seven-year statue of limitations did not [30%]
> in fact, [30%]
> begin until 1980.
> Disc brakes on all four wheels are, [40%]
> of course, [40%]
> an old story.

The oral readers, being more inclined to introduce boundaries in general, were fairly consistent in doing so after transitional adverbs:

> Yet, [60% of younger subjects]
> recent archaeological research confirms the conventional wisdom . . .
> In fact, [75% of older subjects]
> a few recent publications argue that the type of paleodemographic study thought to be most secure . . .

What the oral readers did with the transitional adverbs located within a clause has some additional interest. Even though at least half of them respected the author's punctuation, more of them introduced a break after the adverb than before it. Thus there may be a tendency to "hear" such passages in the following way, where I have omitted the first of the two commas. The percentages are for the younger oral readers.

> The appeals court ruled that the seven-year statute of limitations
> did not [55%] in fact, [75%]
> begin until 1980.
> Disc brakes on all four wheels are [50%] of course, [80%] an old story.

Transitional adverbs, then, illustrate boundaries that may be "heard" less often than they are obliged to appear in writing. Again, it would be wise to teach punctuation with this fact in mind, retaining a tolerance or even respect for writers who are sensitive enough to follow what their inner voices "say."

Conclusion

I began by pointing to introspective evidence that both writers and readers experience auditory imagery of intonations, accents, and hesitations in written language. I suggested that some aspects of this "written language prosody"—in particular the boundaries of imaged intonation units as well as the terminal contours of these units—are made partially overt through punctuation. If one is to study the degree to which punctuation succeeds in performing this function, one would like to discover some independent ways of uncovering written language prosody. I explored two such ways: asking people to read passages aloud and asking them to repunctuate (insert punctuation marks in passages from which punctuation has been removed). Each of these devices can provide some insights, but each also has its limitations.

People who read aloud nearly always produce intonation units whose length lies within the normal range for ordinary spoken language. The degree to which their segmentations match the punctuation units of a piece of writing provides an index of the degree to which that writing is prosaically spokenlike. Oral reading is also useful in showing how different punctuation marks are prosodically interpreted; for example, periods are almost interpreted as falling pitches, and commas are usually interpreted as nonfalling pitches.

There is no reason to believe that either writers or readers are governed by exactly the same temporal processing constraints that are responsible for the relatively brief intonation units of spoken language. One way of obtaining information on constraints that are more specific to written language may be repunctuation. On the whole, repunctuators come closer than oral readers to matching the punctuation of the original authors, at least so far as the location of punctuation is concerned. They may, at the same time, provide a way of measuring the degree to which a piece of writing captures the auditory imagery that is "heard" by ordinary readers.

I raised the question of why punctuation units, whether of the original authors or of repunctuators, are consistently longer than the intonation units produced by oral readers. I suggested both (1) that writers and (silent) readers are able to process larger chunks of information at a time, and (2) that written language provides syntactic as well as punctuational clues to prosodic boundaries. I discussed an example from James that suggested how an author might be sensitive to the cognitive "accessibility" of a considerable amount of information packed into single punctuation unit. The same example also suggested how, in the absence of punctuation, the presence of a conjunction might provide a reader with a due to a prosodic boundary if the reader's cognitive load required such a boundary.

The distinction between "close" and "open" punctuation was discussed in this light. The effects of open punctuation were seen as (1) forcing a reader to rely on syntax alone for prosodic segmentation, and (2) calling the reader's attention to the language itself, removing some of its "transparency." Passages from Thoreau and Agee were discussed as extreme examples of close and open punctuation, respectively.

Finally, I discussed two examples of specific grammatical sites at which there is a discrepancy between punctuation and auditory imagery. One was a case in which a "heard" (and read-aloud) boundary must be suppressed because of a punctuation rule. The other was the opposite, a case in which punctuation is inserted by a rule but no segmentation is "heard," as suggested by the failure of repunctuators to insert the prescribed comma. It was suggested that arbitrary rules for omission and insertion of punctuation should be taught with an appreciation of the fact that they do conflict with auditory imagery.

In spite of these occasional prescribed deviations from the inner voice, and in spite of certain styles of writing that deliberately disregard that voice, the most broadly applicable finding of this study is that most writing most of the time does use punctuation in a way that respects the prosody of written language. Reading aloud and repunctuating are limited ways of making that prosody reveal itself. In the end, however, the most satisfying guidance comes from listening to the inner voice itself. Nurturing that listening can only improve the quality of written language.

Notes

1 It is possible, however, that fast reading or skimming tends to degrade this prosody, which evidently comes closest to the prosody of speech when the reader maintains a tempo close to that of speech.
2 The question of whether, or in what centuries, punctuation has been governed by "grammatical" or "rhetorical" considerations has been inconclusively debated for a long time. Deneau (1986) provides a useful summary of this literature. Unfortunately, no detailed history of punctuation practices has yet been written.
3 For the last four examples I am indebted to Sandra Thompson.
4 I am grateful to Loretta Kane and Adelfa Hain for help in processing, respectively, the materials from the younger and the older subjects.
5 For information on the punctuation history of *Walden* I am indebted to Elizabeth Witherell.
6 Deborah Tannen has brought to my attention a curiosity that is quoted in Walker (1985). Lavery (1923) believed that close punctuating was feminine: "Instead of a rugged and bold reliance on words to convey meaning, which would be the masculine way of doing things, the habit has grown up of dressing up a sentence with the lace and ruffles of punctuation." One wonders whether the extremes of open punctuation found in Hemingway and his followers have anything to do with this belief.

References

Agee, J. (1957). *A death in the family.* New York: Putnam.
Bolinger, D. (1975). *Aspects of language* (2nd ed.). New York: Harcourt Brace Jovanovich.
Chafe, W. (1970). *Meaning and the structure of language.* Chicago: University of Chicago Press.
Chafe, W. (1980). The deployment of consciousness in the production of a narrative. In W. Chafe (Ed.), *The pear stories: Cognitive, cultural, and linguistics aspects of narrative production of a narrative production.* Norwood, NJ: Ablex.
Chafe, W. (1987). Cognitive constraints on information flow. In R. Tomlin (Ed.), *Coherence and grounding in discourse.* Amsterdam: John Benjamins.
The Chicago Manual of Style (13th ed). (1982). Chicago: University of Chicago Press.
Danielewicz, J., &. Chafe, W. (1985). Now "normal" speaking leads to "erroneous" punctuating. In S. Freedman (Ed.), *The acquisition of written language: Response and revision.* Notwood, NJ: Ablex.
Deneau, D. P. (1986). Pointing theory and some Victorian practices. In *Yearbook of research in English and American literature.* New York: Modern Language Association.
Francis, W. N., & Kuçera, H. (1982). *Frequency analysis of English usage: Lexicon and grammar.* Boston: Houghton Mifflin.
Hemingway, E. (1940). *For whom the bell tolls.* New York: Scribner's.
Lavery, U. A. (1923). Punctuation in the law. *American Bar Association Journal, 9,* 225–228.
Long, R. (n.d.). *Common features of writing and oral reading: Implications and applications.* ERIC Document ED 196012.
Lowth, R. (1967). *A short introduction to English grammar* (facsimile ed.). Menston, England: Scolar. (Original work published 1762)
Melville, H. (1851). *Moby Dick or The white whale.* New York: New American Library.
Ong, W. (1982). *Orality and literacy: The technologizing of the word.* London: Methuen.

Quirk, R., Greenbaum, S., Leech, G., & Svartvik, J. (1985). *A comprehensive grammar of the English language.* London: Longman.

Shillingsburg, P. L. (1986). *Scholarly editing in the computer age: Theory and practice,* Athens: University of Georgia Press.

Thoreau, H. D. (1854). *Walden, or Life in the woods.* New York: New American Library.

Walker, A. G. (1985). *From oral to written: The "verbatim" transcription of legal proceedings.* Unpublished doctoral dissertation, Georgetown University.

Welty, E. (1983). *One writer's beginnings.* New York: Warner.

Wharton, E. (1978). *The age of innocence.* In *The Edith Wharton omnibus.* New York: Scribner's. (Original work published 1920)

11.
RELATIVE FOCUS ON INVOLVEMENT IN ORAL AND WRITTEN DISCOURSE
Deborah Tannen

Introduction

Most research on spoken versus written language has analyzed casual conversation as spoken language and expository prose, or what Olson (1977) calls "essayist literacy," as written. This is not by chance. There is something typically spoken about face-to-face conversation and something typically written about expository prose. These genres typify but do not exhaustively characterize spoken and written discourse. In recent writings (Tannen, 1982a, 1982b, 1983) I have demonstrated that both spoken discourse and written discourse exhibit combinations of features that have been identified with spoken and written language, respectively, or, more generally, with an oral and a literate tradition. I have previously called these features *oral and literate strategies*.

I have suggested, furthermore, that these features do not reflect orality versus literacy per se. Rather, what I was calling oral strategies and others have called features of orality or of spoken language in fact are the result of relative focus on interpersonal involvement. And what I was calling literate strategies and others have called features of literacy or of written language are actually the result of relatively less focus on interpersonal involvement, with consequently more focus on the information conveyed. Thus, the terms *oral strategies* and *literate strategies* are misnomers. For this reason, I would like now to move away from them and refer instead to features reflecting relative focus on interpersonal involvement.

The significance of relative focus on involvement is not an arbitrary or trivial notion, nor is it limited to issues of orality and literacy. One of the reasons it is appealing as an explanatory hypothesis is that it accounts for variation in all forms of discourse, including conversation. The framework of relative focus on interpersonal involvement is related to a framework that runs through the recent work of many scholars on interaction—the universal simultaneous but conflicting human needs to be connected to others and to be independent. This has been discussed in linguistics under the rubric of universal politeness phenomena (R. Lakoff, 1973, 1979; Brown

---

Tannen, Deborah. "Relative Focus on Involvement in Oral and Written Discourse." *Literacy, Language, and Learning: The Nature and Consequences of Reading and Writing.*" Eds. David R. Olson, Nancy Torrance, and Angela Hildyard. NY: Cambridge UP, 1985. 125–47.

& Levinson, 1978) and as the cline of person (Becker & Oka, 1976) and in sociology as deference (Goffman, 1967).

The concept of relative focus on involvement is related to what Bateson (1972) describes as the double bind in communication—a phenomenon that he introduced to account for pathology but that, Scollon (1982) demonstrates, characterizes all human communication. As rephrased by Becker (1982), humans continually subject each other to simultaneous conflicting messages to the effect that "You are like me," and "You are not me," or, put another way, "I want to be close to you" and "I want to be separate from you." These two conflicting messages necessarily grow out of the conflicting human needs to be connected to other people and to be distant from them—that is, not to be engulfed by closeness.

Indeed, humans are not the only creatures caught in this double bind. Bettelheim (1979) cites the example of porcupines who seek shelter in a cave during a cold winter. They huddle together for warmth, but their quills prick each other, so they pull away. Then they get cold again. They must continually adjust their closeness and distance in order to balance their simultaneous but conflicting needs to be close to each other and not to get pricked.[1]

The need to serve these conflicting goals motivates linguistic choices. For example, indirectness is used in conversation to avoid imposing one's wants or opinions on others; and much of casual conversation has little significant information to impart but is important because it shows connection. In Bateson's terms, it carries a metamessage of rapport: The fact that it is said communicates that the speaker wants to be involved with the addressee.

In this chapter I first outline the evolution of my own thinking about oral and written discourse, then describe and further discuss the features that grow out of relative focus on involvement (previously called "oral strategies" and "literate strategies"), explain how they grow out of relative focus on involvement, and demonstrate that they cut across spoken and written modes, using examples from my own and others' research. Finally, I suggest that the features reflecting relative focus on involvement seem to underlie successful production and comprehension of discourse in both spoken and written modes.

From Oral/Literate Tradition to Involvement

My use of terms has evolved from *oral and literate tradition* (Tannen, 1980a) to an *oral/literate continuum* (Tannen, 1980b, 1982b), to *oral and literate strategies* (Tannen, 1982a, 1983), to *features of involvement focus versus content focus*,[2] to my present notion of *features reflecting relative focus on involvement*.

In the process of analyzing narratives told in English and Greek about the same film I found myself faced with a "So what?" problem. I had identified certain differences between Greek and American narratives—for example, the Greeks tended to approach the narrative as a storytelling task whereas the Americans tended to approach it as a memory task, with complex discourse consequences in both cases—but I could not figure out the significance of these differences. John Gumperz suggested that I turn to research on oral versus literate tradition and directed me to Goody and Watt (1963). Eureka! This seemed to explain the differences I had found. One after another of the discourse phenomena in the Greek and American narratives could be explained by the hypothesis that the Greeks were using narrative strategies associated with oral tradition—for example, selecting an overall theme of the film, including only those details that contributed to the theme, making use of culturally familiar explanations, personalizing, and philosophizing—whereas Americans were using strategies associated with literate tradition—for example, listing details for correctness, fussing over temporal accuracy, critiquing the filmmaker's skill, and analyzing the film as an artifact (Tannen, 1980b).

Soon I had immersed myself in the literature on this topic (for example, Olson, 1977; Goody, 1977; Ong, 1967, 1977; Havelock, 1963; Kay, 1977; Cook-Gumperz & Gumperz, 1981). The oral/literate dichotomy had the power and fascination of a revelation.

Looking back on research I had done on conversational discourse, I saw that this too could be explained by the oral/literate dichotomy. Analyzing taped, transcribed spontaneous conversation among friends, I had discovered that certain speakers tended to use such conversational strategies as cooperative overlap, that is, talking at the same time without interrupting; exaggerated paralinguistic features such as dramatic changes in rate of speech, loudness, and pitch; and frequent storytelling in which the point of the story is dramatized rather than stated and tends to be about personal feelings. These and other conversational strategies could be seen as sacrificing the explicit and clear statement of information for the demonstration of interpersonal involvement. (This phenomenon will be illustrated presently. See also Tannen, 1981, 1984.) Thus I began to think in terms of an oral/literate continuum.

It occurred to me, then, that the broad perspective of research on oral and literate tradition went far to account for features that had been identified as associated with spoken versus written (Chafe, 1982; see also Chapter 6) and unplanned versus planned discourse (Ochs, 1979). However, as my students and I systematically looked for these features in spoken and written narratives, it became clear that some written genres—for example, literary prose—combined features of spoken with features of written discourse (Tannen, 1980b, 1982b).

For example, the analysis of a personal narrative first told and then written by the same narrator suggested that written literary narrative combined what Chafe calls features of integration expected in writing with features of involvement expected in speaking. Therefore, it seemed preferable to refer to oral and literate strategies that could be used either in speaking or writing (Tannen, 1982a, 1983).

In all these discussions, I stressed that the key differences motivating discourse are not orality versus literacy per se but rather relative focus on interpersonal involvement and relative focus on content or information conveyed. In a sense, my use of *oral* and *literate* in referring to these features reflected my own heuristic process—it was through research on oral and literate tradition and spoken and written language that I had come to identify the significance of relative focus on interpersonal involvement. However, terminology tends to reify concepts. Since what is really significant is not the distinction between orality and literacy per se but rather relative focus on involvement, I would now like to adopt terminology that places that key dimension in the foreground.

Two Features of Relative Focus on Involvement

Two hypotheses have been advanced to account for differences that have been observed between spoken and written discourse. I will refer to them as the contextualization hypothesis and the cohesion hypothesis. I will consider each in turn, determining whether it is in fact descriptive of spoken versus written discourse and considering it in terms of relative focus on involvement.

The Contextualization Hypothesis

Many scholars have characterized spoken discourse as highly context-bound and written discourse as decontextualized. Thus, a speaker can refer to the context of immediate surroundings visible to both speaker and hearer who are copresent in time and place. For example, I could say, "Look at this!" relying on hearers to see what *this* refers to. Second, speakers are free to be minimally explicit because if the hearer(s) are confused, they can ask for clarification on the spot. Finally, speakers frequently share social background and hence many assumptions about the world, their mutual or respective histories, and so on.

In contrast, according to the contextualization hypothesis, a writer and reader are generally separated in time and place, so immediate context is lost. Second, the reader cannot ask for clarification when confused, so the writer must anticipate all likely confusion and preclude it by filling in needed background information and as many as possible of the steps of a logical argument. Third, because the writer and reader are likely to share minimal social context, the writer can make fewer assumptions about shared attitudes and beliefs.

Clearly, in such a schema, what is thought of as spoken discourse is spontaneous face-to-face conversation, and what is thought of as written discourse is expository prose. For these genres it is informative to point out that spoken language is highly context-bound, while written appears to be less so. Of course, the notion that written discourse—or any discourse—is actually decontextualized is at best an exaggeration. Many scholars, including Fillmore (1979a), Nystrand (1982), and Rader (1982), have demonstrated that no piece of discourse can be understood without prior knowledge of many kinds of contexts. Hymes (personal communication) points out that to verify this one need only read a scholarly article in a discipline other than one's own. Hence, I suggest that the features described grow out of the respective genres and their own contexts rather than out of the spoken and written modes per se.

In face-to-face spontaneous conversation such as that which occurs at a dinner table, the fact of speaking to each other is often more important than the information or messages conveyed. Moreover, most of what is said in social settings is relatively insignificant, as teenagers are quick to notice in their parents' conversations. But that is not to say that the utterances are not important. Quite the contrary: They communicate what Bateson (1972) calls metamessages—statements about the relationship between interactants. Far from being unimportant, metamessages are the necessary basis for any interaction. Typical are such metamessages as "I am [or am not] well disposed toward you," "I'm teasing you," and the like.

Expository prose is a special genre in which the message (as distinguished from the metamessage) is relatively important. Thus Kay (1977) points out that what has been associated with writing, what he calls "autonomous language," has come with technological advancement. A complex technological society has need for much communication, typically among strangers, in which interpersonal involvement is ostensibly beside the point and communication is more efficiently carried out if such involvement is conventionally ignored. When carried over to face-to-face communication, however, such conventional ignoring of interpersonal involvement may be seen as peculiarly American or Western. It tends to create misunderstandings when American businessmen and diplomats try to ignore personal involvement and get right down to business with their Japanese, Arab, or Greek counterparts, for whom the establishment of personal relationships must lay the groundwork for any business or diplomatic dealings.

It is not a coincidence that the genres of casual conversation on the one hand and expository prose on the other have been associated with spoken and written language, respectively. There is something typically written about message-focused communication, for it is the innovation of print that made it common to communicate on a large scale with others who are not in one's immediate context. And there is something typically oral about interpersonal involvement. In communication with others with whom one has a close social or personal relationship, it is hard to focus on information exclusively, because the importance of the relationship is too keenly felt to be ignored. This involvement is reflected in the conventional wisdom that one should not take driving lessons from a spouse or parent, or by the fact that any comment can touch off a fight between speakers or any comment can seem particularly charming, depending on the place of the interaction in the history of the relationship between participants.

Nonetheless these two genres, conversation and expository prose, are by no means exclusive. It is possible and indeed common to have written communication in which it hardly matters what the content is; the fact of communication is paramount—for example, in some personal letters, where it is just as possible to write a lot of nothing as it is to whisper sweet nothings, with just as much satisfaction for all concerned. Note-passing in school and at lectures can fall into this category as well. Similarly, it is possible, indeed common, to have communication that is message-focused in an oral mode, as in lectures and radio or television broadcasts (though contemporary radio and television broadcasts, including the news, seem to be getting more involvement-focused and less message-focused). It seems, moreover, that ritual language in traditional society has some of the features usually associated with written texts: The speaker performs a chant or ceremony that was composed long ago by authors far away, addressed to a large and impersonal audience (Chafe, 1982).

A key dimension distinguishing discourse types, then, is whether it is one-way or two-way communication, and this dimension is closely associated with relative focus on involvement, as contrasted with relative focus on information (in Bateson's terms, the metamessage and message, respectively).

One more observation is in order about the close connection between interpersonal involvement and speaking, on the one hand, and focus on information and writing, on the other. The slowness of writing makes it an ill-formed medium for the communication of nonsignificant messages. I have experienced this in communicating with deaf people, wherein writing is the only medium available for communication. Straightaway, I find myself choosing not to communicate all sorts of relatively unimportant asides because they do not seem worth the trouble of writing.[3] Yet it is just such seemingly meaningless interchange that creates social relationships. That is precisely why deafness is such a terrible handicap: It is socially isolating.

Cohesion in Spoken and Written Discourse

A second major observation that has been made about spoken and written discourse—one that indeed seems to be an outgrowth of spoken versus written modes and that accounts for the second major strategy difference I refer to—is the observation that in spoken discourse, cohesion is accomplished through paralinguistic and prosodic cues, whereas in written discourse cohesion must be lexicalized (Chafe, 1982; Cook-Gumperz & Gumperz, 1981; Gumperz, Kaltman, & O'Connor, 1984; Ochs, 1979).

In speaking, everything that is said must be said in some way: at some pitch, in some tone of voice, at some speed, with some expression or lack of expression in the voice and on the face of the speaker. All these nonverbal and paralinguistic features reveal the speaker's attitude toward the message—what Labov (1972) identified as "evaluation" in narrative—and establish cohesion, that is, show relationships among ideas, highlight relative importance, foreground or background certain information, and so on. Just as in a social setting one cannot not communicate—the act of keeping silent within the frame of interaction communicates something (Bateson 1972)—one cannot speak without showing one's attitude toward the message and the speech activity.

In writing, on the other hand, the nonverbal and paralinguistic channels are not available. You may wrinkle your brow until it cracks while you write, but this will not show up on the written page. You may yell or whisper or sing as you compose sentences, but the words as they fall on the page will not reflect this. Print, and to a lesser extent handwriting, is a great leveler; it reduces or inflates all utterances to lines of equivalent evaluative status on a page. Writers try to overcome this limitation by using such devices as capitalization, underlining, italics, exclamation points, and the like.

Therefore, in writing, the relationships between ideas, and the writer's attitude toward them, must be lexicalized. This can be done in a number of ways, including (1) explicit statement (for example, the contrast between smiling, smirking, or chuckling while speaking, as opposed to writing, "In a humorous vein . . ."; or winking while speaking as opposed to writing, "I don't mean this literally"); (2) careful choice of words with just the right connotations; or (3) complex syntactic constructions and transitional phrases. Thus a number of linguists have found that in spoken narrative—and here the genre is important—ideas are strung together with no conjunctions at all or the minimal conjunction *and* (Chafe, 1982; Kroll, 1977; Ochs,. 1979). In contrast, written narrative uses conjunctions such as *so* and *because,* which express the relationship between ideas and subordinate constructions that foreground and background information as is done paralinguistically in speaking.

Thus we may think of discourse in which meaning and attitudes are expressed paralinguistically, nonverbally, or indirectly as being typically spoken, that is, using strategies that are basic to face-to-face conversation and possible only in spoken discourse. These strategies, furthermore, build on interpersonal involvement, since filling in unstated information and relationships between propositions, as well as deducing evaluation from voice quality and other paralinguistic features, requires the hearer to share prior communicative experience and background knowledge and to do some of the work of sense making, all of which create a feeling of involvement. In contrast, discourse that relies on lexicalization of meaning and relationships between propositions either is written or uses strategies that are frequently found in written discourse. And note that lexicalization is message-focused; it draws less on the reader's shared social knowledge and makes the reader do less of the work of sense making. However, written discourse may try to create the effect of face-to-face interaction as novelists do when they add to dialogue such comments as "She said with a wink."

Involvement Focus and Information Focus in Discourse

The observation that spoken discourse can exhibit strategies generally associated with either an oral or a literate mode can be traced back to what Bernstein (1964) calls restricted and elaborated codes. Bernstein found that children's discourse, as elicited by experimental tasks, fell into two stylistic types, which he identified as different "codes." For example, in describing a picture, a child using restricted code might say, "They hit it through there and he got mad." A child using elaborated code might say, "The children were playing ball and hit the ball through the window. The man who lived in the house got mad at them." The second version is easier to understand, but only when the picture is not in view, that is, when the immediate context is not shared. To speak an "elaborated code," that is, to fill in referents and contextual information when it is provided by the immediate context, may be perceived as a denial of shared context and might elicit an offended protest: "I've got eyes. I can see that." It would be perceived as appropriate only in contexts that require such otherwise redundant information, as for example some school or school-like tasks.

Bernstein did not associate these two codes with orality and literacy, but this correspondence is pointed out by Cook-Gumperz and Gumperz (1981), Hill and Varenne (1981), Kay (1977), and Olson (1977).

I would now like to cite some of my own and others' work to demonstrate that both written and spoken discourse can reflect both features typically associated with speaking and those typically associated with writing—that is, features of relative focus on involvement. I will show examples of such features first in spoken and then in written discourse.

Focus on Involvement in Conversation

Let us assume that involvement is marked by discourse that is highly context-bound, that requires maximal contribution from the audience in supplying background information and doing interpretive work, and that depends upon paralinguistic and nonverbal channels rather than lexicalization for cohesion and evaluation. Message-focused discourse relies less on immediate context, it requires less audience contribution in supplying necessary information and connections, and it achieves cohesion through lexicalization.

In my own research on conversation I have identified systematic differences in features I refer to, collectively, as conversational style. These can be understood as different ways of observing relative focus on interpersonal involvement.

In one extended study, I tape-recorded and transcribed two-and-a-half hours of naturally occurring conversation at Thanksgiving dinner among six friends of various ethnic and geographic backgrounds. I identified the linguistic and paralinguistic features that made up participants' speaking styles in this setting, focusing on such features as pacing, rate of speech, overlap and interruption, intonation, pitch, loudness, syntactic structures, topic, storytelling, irony, humor, and so on (Tannen, 1984). I found that many of these features clustered in the styles of participants such that three of the participants seemed to share what might be called one style. (This, of course, is an idealization; each person's style is a unique cluster of devices used in particular ways.) In contrast, the other three clearly did not share this style (that is, they did not use the features identified in the ways the others did, and they did not interpret those features in the way the others intended them). I have called this identifiable style high-involvement, since many of the features that characterize it can be understood as placing emphasis on interpersonal involvement, or the interpersonal dynamic of the interaction. Those who did not share this style expected strategies that may be seen as more message-focused (some would say literate-like) in the sense that they placed more emphasis on the information conveyed.

One way this pattern emerged was in attitude toward and tendency to use overlapped or simultaneous speech. Three of the participants in the conversation I studied were "cooperative overlappers." That is, two or more of them often talked at the same time, but this did not mean that they weren't listening to each other, and it did not mean that they wanted to grab the floor—that is, to interrupt. Often, a listener talked at the same time as a speaker to show encouragement, or showed understanding by uttering "response cries" (Goffman, 1981), or told mini-stories to demonstrate understanding, or finished the speaker's sentences to demonstrate that the listener knew where the sentence was headed. All of this overlapping gives the speaker the assurance that he or she isn't in the conversation alone. In addition, the active listeners often asked questions eliciting information the speaker obviously would have told anyway, not to indicate that they thought the speaker wasn't going to tell, but to assure the speaker that the information was eagerly awaited.

The preference for overlapping talk in some settings has been reported among at least some members of numerous ethnic groups: Armenian, Italian-American, black American, West Indian, Cape Verdean, to name just a few. The preference for overlapping talk sacrifices the clear relay of information for the sake of showing conversational involvement. In that sense, it is typically interactive, valuing the need for interpersonal involvement more highly than the need for the information conveyed. The speakers who exhibit overlapping speech in a casual setting probably do not use it, or use less of it, in such settings as interviews or receiving instructions in which information is relatively more important. But when speakers use this device with others who do not expect or understand its use in this way, the effect is quite the opposite. The other speaker feels interrupted and stops talking. An ironic aspect of this style clash is that the interruption is actually created by the one who stops talking when he or she was expected to continue.

Another aspect of effects of differing focus on involvement that emerged in this study of conversational style is the way speakers got to the point of their personal narratives and what the points of their stories were likely to be. In the conversation of speakers whose style I have characterized as involvement-focused (1) more stories were told; (2) the stories were more likely to be about personal experiences; (3) the point of the story was more likely to concern feelings about those experiences; and (4) perhaps most important, the point of the story was generally not lexicalized but was dramatized by replaying the speaker's reaction or creating a similar reaction in the audience by mimicry of the characters in the narrative.

These differences in storytelling styles left all participants feeling a bit dissatisfied with the narratives told in the style other than their own. All participants tended to react to stories told by different-style speakers with a variant of "What's the point?"—the rejoinder Labov (1972) has aptly called "withering."

The following is an example of a story told during Thanksgiving dinner by Steve:

(1) Steve: I have a little seven-year-old student . . . a little
girl who wears those. . . . . . . She is <u>too</u> much.
p
(2) Deborah: She wears those? [*chuckle*]
Steve: Can you imagine? She's seven years old, and she
acc
sits in her chair and she goes . . . . [*squeals*
acc--------]
and squirms in his seat]
(3) Deborah: Oh:: Go:: d. . . . She's only SEVen?
(4) Steve: And I say, well . . . hów about let's do sò-and-so.
And she says . . . Okay: :. . . . just like thát.
acc--------] [*squealing*]
(5) Deborah: Oh : : : : :
p
(6) David: What does it méan.
p, acc

(7) Steve: It's just so . . . she's acting like such a little girl already.
                p

where

/	indicates primary stress
\	indicates secondary stress
	underline indicates emphatic stress
	CAPITALIZATION indicates most emphatic stress
.	(period) indicates sentence-final falling intonation
?	(question mark) indicates rising intonation
⌈	indicates high pitch on phrase
⌈⌈	indicates very high pitch on phrase
acc	indicates accelerando (speeding up)
p	indicates pianissimo (spoken softly)
:	indicates elongation of vowel sound
. . .	indicates half-second pause (each extra dot = another half-second pause)
[	brackets on two lines indicate simultaneous speech: two speakers talking at once

It is clear from the transcript that the two listeners, David and I, have different reactions to the story. In (3) and (5) *I* show, through paralinguistically exaggerated responses, that I have appreciated the story. In contrast, David states in (6) that he doesn't understand what the story is supposed to mean—or at least that he is not satisfied with the way Steve told it. When I played this segment of the taped conversation to David later, he said that Steve hadn't said what it was about the girl's behavior that he was trying to point out. Moreover, when Steve answered David's question in (7), he didn't explain at all; David observed that "such a little girl" to him means "such a grownup," whereas Steve meant "such a coquette." David seemed to feel that Steve wasn't telling the story right; he should have said what he meant. To Steve, the point was obvious, having been dramatized, and should not be stated.

Elsewhere in the transcript David relates his experiences, and there the reactions of Steve and the other overlap-favoring stylists indicate that they feel David is stating the obvious and not getting to the point quickly enough.

By expecting the point of a story to be made explicit, and by finding events more important than characters' feelings, some of the participants in this conversation were exhibiting expectations that speech make use of strategies typically associated with writing, that is, strategies that focus more on information and less on involvement. By expecting the point of a story to be dramatized by the speaker and inferred by the hearer, and by finding personal feelings more interesting than events, the other speakers were exhibiting typically oral or involvement-focused strategies.

It is particularly significant that the speakers in my study who used involvement-focused strategies are highly literate. Many of the studies that have distinguished between oral and literate strategies in spoken style (including Cook-Gumperz and Gumperz, 1981; Michaels and Cook-Gumperz, 1979; and Michaels and Collins, 1984) have done so to explain the failure of children of certain ethnic groups, often black, to learn to write and read well. The speakers I have found using involvement-focused strategies in speaking are New Yorkers of Eastern European Jewish background, a cultural group that has been documented as having (like black cultural groups) a highly developed oral tradition (Kirshenblatt-Gimblett, 1974), but also a highly developed literate one—in fact, one of the longest literate traditions of any cultural group. And far from having a history of failure in school, children from this community have traditionally performed successfully at literate tasks. Thus, individuals and groups are not either oral or literate. Rather, people have at their disposal and are inclined to use, in speech or in writing, combinations of strategies that have been associated with oral or written modes but that are more accurately understood as reflecting relative focus on involvement.

A final example of how both involvement- and information-focused strategies surface in spoken discourse comes from an analysis of fluency. Fillmore (1979b) distinguishes four types of oral fluency, characterized by the abilities to do the following:

1. Talk at length with few pauses
2. Have appropriate things to say in a wide range of contexts
3. Talk in semantically coherent, reasoned, and dense sentences
4. Be creative and imaginative with language.

I suggest that the first two of these types of fluency are associated with involvement-focused strategies. That is, they grow out of interactive or social goals, when the message conveyed is less important than the metamessage conveyed by the fact and manner of talk. In contrast, the last two are message-focused types of fluency; the third depends on intratextual relationships, and the fourth builds on words as carrying meaning in themselves rather than triggering social meaning.

Focus on Involvement in Written Discourse

If one thinks at first that written language and spoken language are very different, one may think as well that written literary discourse—short stories, poems, novels—are the most different from casual conversation. On the contrary, imaginative literature has more in common with spontaneous conversation than with the typical written genre, expository prose.

If expository prose is minimally dependent on immediate context and maximally dependent on lexicalization—that is, the writer demands the least from the reader in terms of filling in referents, background information, crucial premises, cohesive relationships, and evaluation, then literary discourse is also maximally contextualized, not in the sense of depending on immediate context but by requiring the reader (or hearer) to fill in maximal background and other elided information. The best literary work is the one that suggests the most to readers with the fewest words. Rader (1982) demonstrates this, suggesting that maximal contextualization is not incidental to the nature of literature but rather is basic to it. The goal of the creative writer is to encourage readers to do as much filling in as possible. The more the reader supplies, the more she or he will believe and care about the message in the work. As Rader puts it, "The reader of a novel creates a world according to the instructions given" (p. 195).

The features thought of as quintessentially literary are, moreover, basic to spontaneous conversation and less developed in written expository prose. A few such features are repetition of sounds (alliteration and assonance), repetition of words, recurrent metaphors and other figures of speech, parallel syntactic constructions, and compelling rhythm. (This hypothesis is suggested in Tannen, 1982a, and elaborated in Tannen, 1984. See also Friedrich, 1979.)

Analyzing a transcript of ordinary conversation among family members, Sacks (1971) shows that in determining why a speaker chose a particular variant of a word—for example, *because, cause,* or *cuz*—an analyst should look to see if the variant chosen is "sound coordinated with things in its environment." In the case Sacks presents, a speaker said (referring to fish being eaten), "cause it comes from cold water." A few moments later, the same speaker said, "You better eat something because you're gonna be hungry before we get there." In considering why the speaker chose *cause* in the first instance and *because* in the second, Sacks notes that *cause* appears in the environment of repeated /k/ sounds in *comes* and *cold*, whereas *because* is coordinated with /bi/ (i.e., "bee") in *be hungry* and *before.*

Sacks goes on to suggest that another speaker chose a rather stilted expression, "Will you be good enough to empty this in there," because at that point in the talk there are a number of measure terms (i.e., an extended metaphor) being used, seen in this expression in *empty* and in nearby sentences in the words *more* and *missing.* Hence the choice of *good enough,* in which the measure term *enough* is metaphoric. (Sacks's lecture notes are rich with examples of poetic processes in ordinary conversation.)

Examples of parallel constructions in natural conversation are also ubiquitous. Speakers frequently set up a syntactic construction and repeat it for several sentences. A brief example will be taken from a narrative I have analyzed elsewhere, comparing spoken and written versions of the same story (Tannen, 1982a). In a spontaneous casual conversation, the speaker emphasized the linguistic ability of a coworker by saying, "And he knows Spanish, and he knows French, and he knows English, and he knows German. And *he* is a *gen*tleman." The rhythm of the repeated constructions sweeps the hearers along, creating the effect of a long list, suggesting that he knows even more than the four languages named. (Such parallel constructions are probably also an aid to speech production, since the repeated construction can be uttered automatically while the speaker plans new information to insert in the variable slot. It is a technique public speakers use frequently.) Furthermore, the speaker can use the established rhythm of the repeated construction to play off against, as in the phrase that follows the parallelism: "And *he* is a *gen*tleman." Contrast this with the way the same narrator conveyed the same idea when she wrote the story down: "He knows at least four languages fluently—Spanish, French, English, and something else." This sentence is orallike, or involvement-focused, in its use of the phrase *something else* in place of the name of a fourth language, creating a feeling of immediate narration. The writer could have taken as much time as she needed to think of the fourth language and add it, or choose an alternative grammatical structure and revise the text to read— for example, "including...." But with regard to rhythmicity created by parallel constructions, the written statement exhibits the feature Chafe (Chapter 6) calls "integration," which he finds typical of expository prose, conflating the parallel constructions by eliminating the repeated parts. The result is a sentence that is more word-efficient but rhythmically less involving (and, one might say, less moving).

Rhythm, then, is a fundamental feature of the oral strategy of parallel constructions. Erickson and his collaborators (Erickson & Shultz, 1982) and Scollon (1982) have demonstrated that rhythm is basic to participation in face-to-face conversation. Erickson has shown that ordinary conversation can be set to a metronome, and verbal and nonverbal participation takes place on the beat. In order to show listenership and to know when to talk, one must be able to pick up the beat. In conversation with speakers of different cultural backgrounds, or speakers who tend to take turns more slowly or quickly than one is used to, one cannot tell when others are finished and therefore cannot judge when to start or stop speaking. The effect is like trying to enter a line of dancers who are going just a bit faster or slower than one expects; one has to either drop back or break in, spoiling everyone's rhythm.

Thus rhythm is basic to conversational involvement in the most mechanical sense. It contributes in conversation, as it does in music, poetry, and oratory, to the impact of the discourse on the audience. The rhythm sweeps the audience along and convinces them by moving them emotionally. Saville-Troike (1982) quotes Duncan (1962) to the effect that Hitler, in his preface to *Mein Kampf*, apologizes for writing a book, since he believes that people are moved not by writing but by the spoken word, and that "every great movement owed its growth to great orators, not to great writers."

Why is it that literary language builds on and perfects features of mundane conversation? I believe it is because literary language, like ordinary conversation, is dependent for its effect on interpersonal involvement. It fosters and builds on involvement between speaker and hearer rather than focusing on information or message. It also depends for its impact on the emotional involvement of the hearer. In contrast, expository prose, associated with literate tradition in the way we have seen, depends for its impact on impressing the audience with the strength and completeness of its argument, that is, with aspects of the lexicalized message. In fact, responses to all discourse are probably emotional, just as Olson (1977) points out that most people cannot distinguish between logical arguments and arguments with which they agree. But in justifying their responses to expository prose, most American readers are likely to maintain that they find the argument logical, not that they like the way it sounds. Nonetheless, some awareness of the power of rhythm and sound play can be seen in the observation "It has a nice ring to it," sometimes used to suggest that "it" must therefore be right.

Reading and Writing as Involvement-Focused Skills

A particularly fascinating aspect of the notion of involvement- and information-focused strategies is the possibility that the former, which have been associated with spoken language, may be the most efficient for both writing and reading. Successful writing, which seeks to lexicalize necessary background and cohesive relationships, requires not production of discourse with no sense of audience but rather the positing of a hypothetical audience in order to fulfill its needs. This is the sense in which writing is decontextualized: The context must be posited rather than being found in the actual setting. A better term would be *recontextualized.* The ability to imagine what a hypothetical reader needs to know is an interactive skill. Similarly, reading is a matter of decoding written words—a message-focused skill. But the act of reading efficiently is a matter not so much of accurate decoding, though this is part of it, but of discerning a familiar text structure and hypothesizing what information will be presented, so that it can be efficiently processed when it comes. By making maximum use of the context of prior texts, to use Becker's term, good readers use highly context-sensitive skills, strategies that I am suggesting are interactive or involvement-focused.

Preparation for Literacy in Oral Discourse in School

Cook-Gumperz and Gumperz (1981) suggest that children make a "transition to literacy" when they go to school. Michaels and Cook-Gumperz (1979) analyze in detail an oral discourse activity in a first-grade classroom that prepares children for a literate approach to information: "sharing time." Here children are expected to address the entire class and tell about one thing that is very important. Although the children are communicating face to face and share context in many ways, the teacher encourages them to express known information in order to give a "complete" discourse appropriate to sharing time. Michaels and Collins (1984) give the example of a child who brought to class two candles she had made in day camp and began to talk about them "using highly context-bound expressions and gestures." She said, for example, "This one came out blue and I don't know what this color is." The teacher encouraged the child to produce a more literate-style discourse: "Tell the kids how you do it from the very start. Pretend we don't know a thing about candles." The teacher's use of "from the very start" and "Pretend..." emphasizes the counterintuitive nature of such elaborated-style discourse in face-to-face interaction. The injunction to "pretend we don't know a thing about candles" sets up the reader-as-blank-slate idealization that underlies much expository writing.

Michaels and Cook-Gumperz found that children in the class they observed fell into two groups with respect to how well they performed during sharing time, how much reinforcement they received from the teacher, and consequently how much practice in literate-style discourse they received. Some children were more likely to lexicalize connections in order to focus on the main point, whereas others were more likely to accomplish this cohesion by special intonation patterns that, tragically, the teacher was not able to recognize, since she and these students came from different cultural backgrounds.

In order to document these differences better, Michaels and her coworkers showed the children a short film (as it happens, the same film used to elicit the narratives analyzed in my previously mentioned comparison of Greek and American discourse) and had them tell what they saw in the film. These experimentally elicited narratives also exhibit what Michaels and Collins (1984) call oral-based and literate-based strategies in spoken narratives. In the film a man is shown picking pears. A boy comes along, takes a basket of pears away on his bike, and later falls off his bike. Three other boys help him, and he gives them three pears. At the end, the three boys, eating their pears, walk past the man who was picking them in the first scene. These scenes were designed to set up an encoding problem: In describing the last scene, narrators must identify the man as the same one who appeared in the first scene.

Michaels and Collins characterize one group of children as literate-style speakers (I will call them message-focused), who used complex syntactic constructions and lexicalization to identify the man. A second group, characterized as oral-style speakers (in my terms, involvement-focused ones) used special intonation patterns. Thus, a message-focused speaker says, "there was a man that was picking some pears." Notice that the speaker introduces the man by using an independent clause, "there was . . .," and then identifies him by using a relative clause, "that was picking some pears." In contrast, an involvement-focused speaker introduces the same character by using two independent clauses: "It was about this man. He was, um . . . um . . . takes some, um . . . peach—. . . some . . . pears off the tree." (Readers will notice that the second child is less fluent, but that is not significant for the phenomenon under discussion.)

Even more striking than the use of two independent clauses as opposed to an independent and a subordinate clause is the way these two speakers identify the man when he reappears in the last scene. The message-focused speaker uses a restrictive appositive, a relative clause beginning with "who": ". . . and then . . . they . . . walked by the man who gave . . . wh-who was picking the pears." In contrast, the involvement-focused speaker again uses two independent clauses, identifying the man as the same one previously mentioned by using a special intonational contour on the word *man*: ". . . and when that . . . when he pa:ssed, by that ma:n, . . . the man . . . the ma:n came out the tree." It is the special intonational contour on *man* that signals "You know which man I mean—the one I mentioned before."[4]

Although prosodic cues cannot specify which other man is intended, they can indicate that some particular other man is meant, and this is sufficient to lead a listener to infer which other man that is. (In this case, only one other man has been mentioned.) Thus the two children use different strategies to establish cohesion. Their spoken styles reflect relative reliance on context and paralinguistic cues (hence audience involvement) or on lexicalization (hence message focus).

Finally, these spoken styles have important consequences for written competence. Michaels and Collins compared fourth-grade children's speech styles with their writing styles by having them watch the same film and then both tell and write a narrative account of it. Style differences appeared in the oral narratives of the fourth graders, very much like those described for first graders; furthermore, the children who lexicalized cohesion in speaking also wrote unambiguous prose, whereas the children who relied on paralinguistic channels in speaking were more likely to write a text that was ambiguous. In other words, these children neglected to compensate for the loss of the paralinguistic channel in writing by lexicalizing connections that were signaled paralinguistically in speaking.

For example, a fourth grader who uses complex syntactic constructions and other message-focused devices in speaking uses similar devices in writing, resulting in unambiguous prose. In reintroducing the pear picker, this child begins a new paragraph and writes. "The man collecting fruits noticed. . . ." In contrast, a fourth grader who uses paralinguistic signaling rather than lexicalization to establish cohesion in speaking produces, in writing, prose that is ambiguous concerning which character he is referring to. He writes, "This man was picking pears and this boy was riding by on his bike and he saw the pears. . . ." There is nothing in the text to disambiguate *he:* Does it refer to the man or the boy? (Of course, the reader can make a good guess based on prior contextual knowledge, but that is another matter.) Thus the children's spoken discourse styles have significant consequences for their acquisition of literacy.

Conclusion

I have suggested that previous work on oral and literate tradition and spoken versus written language has led to two hypotheses. The first, that written language is decontextualized whereas spoken is context-bound, seems to grow out of the types of spoken and written discourse that were examined: face-to-face conversation on the one hand and expository prose on the other. I suggest that the identified differences result not so much from the spoken and written modes as from relative focus on interpersonal involvement typically found in conversation and relative lack of focus on involvement in favor of a focus on information or message typically found in expository prose.

The second hypothesis that had been previously put forth is that spoken language establishes cohesion by use of paralinguistic and nonverbal signals, whereas written language depends more upon lexicalization. This is indeed an outgrowth of spoken versus written modes of discourse. Nonetheless, various uses of contextualization and relative reliance on lexicalization can be manipulated both in speaking and in writing in order to produce discourse that is maximally or minimally involving of the audience. Finally, I have suggested that oral strategies may underlie successful discourse production and comprehension in the written as well as the oral mode, insofar as it requires drawing on prior experience, which in the case of written discourse includes the experience of prior written texts. All of these phenomena have implications for interpersonal communication, an understanding of discourse production and comprehension, and the acquisition of literacy.

Notes

1 I am grateful to Pamela Gerloff for calling my attention to this reference. Bettelheim cites Schopenhauer as the source of the simile.
2 Becker helped me to see that relative focus on content is an artifact of relative focus on involvement and that the notion of "content" invokes the conduit metaphor in communication (i.e., messages are placed in a container and sent by conduit to a receiver who extracts them from the container; cf. Lakoff & Johnson, 1980), the connotations of which I wish to avoid.

3 This is true of any situation in which there is an impediment to effortless communication—for example, when someone has laryngitis, is in another room, or is not fluent in the language spoken. Since I am hearing-impaired, I am frequently reminded of this when a request for repetition elicits the maddening "It wasn't important."
4 Not only am I substituting my terms *involvement focused style* and *message-focused style* in place of Michaels and Collins's terms, but I am also substituting my own simplified transcription system for theirs, since theirs contains more information than is needed for the argument I am making here.

References

Bateson, G. *Steps to an ecology of mind.* New York: Ballantine, 1972.

Becker, A. L. Beyond translation: Esthetics and language description. In H Byrnes (Ed.), *Contemporary perceptions of language: Interdisciplinary dimensions* (Georgetown University Round Table on Languages and Linguistics, 1982). Washington, D.C.: Georgetown University Press, 1982.

Becker, A. L., & I Gusti Ngurah Oka. Person in Kawi: Exploration of an elementary semantic dimension. *Oceanic Linguistics,* 1976, *13,* 229–255.

Bernstein, B. Elaborated and restricted codes: Their social origins and some consequences. *American Anthropologist,* 1964, *66*(6), Pt. 2, 55–69.

Bettelheim, B. *Surviving.* New York: Knopf, 1979.

Brown, P., & Levinson, S. Universals in language usage: Politeness phenomena. In E. Goody (Ed.), *Questions and politeness.* Cambridge: Cambridge, University Press, 1978.

Chafe, W. Integration and involvement in speaking, writing, and oral literature. In D. Tannen (Ed.), *Spoken and written language: Exploring orality and literacy.* Norwood, N.J.: Ablex, 1982.

Gook-Gumperz, J., & Gumperz, J. J. From oral to written: The transition to literacy. In M. F. Whiteman (Ed.), *Variation in writing.* Hillsdale, N.J.: Erlbaum, 1981.

Duncan, H. D. *Communication and the social order.* London: Oxford University Press, 1962.

Erickson, F., & Shultz, J. *Gatekeeping in counseling interviews.* New York: Academic Press, 1982.

Fillmore, C. J. Innocence: A second idealization for linguistics. *Proceedings of the Fifth Annual Meeting of the Berkeley Linguistics Society,* 1979a.

———. On fluency. In C. J. Fillmore, D. Kempler, & W. S.-Y. Wang (Eds.), *Individual differences in language ability and language behavior.* New York: Academic Press, 1979b.

Friedrich, P. Poetic language and the imagination: A reformulation of the Sapir hypothesis. In *Language, context, and the imagination: Essays by Paul Friedrich* (selected and introduced by A. S. Dil). Stanford, Calif.: Stanford University Press, 1979.

Goffman, E. *Interaction ritual.* Garden City, N.Y.: Doubleday, 1967. Response cries. In *Forms of talk.* Philadelphia: University of Pennsylvania Press, 1981.

Goody, J. *The domestication of the savage mind.* Cambridge: Cambridge University Press, 1977.

Goody, J., & Watt, I. The consequences of literacy. *Comparative Studies in Society and History,* 1963, 5, 304–345.

Gumperz, J., Kaltman, H., & O'Connor, M. C. Cohesion in spoken and written discourse. In D. Tannen (Ed.), *Coherence in spoken and written discourse.* Norwood, N.J.: Ablex, 1984.

Havelock, E. *Preface to Plato.* Cambridge: Harvard University Press, 1963.

Hill, C., & Varenne, H. Family language and education: The sociolinguistic model of restricted and elaborated codes. *Social Science Information,* 1981, *20*(1), 187–227.

Kay, P. Language evolution and speech style. In B. Blount & M. Sanches (Eds.), *Sociocultural dimensions of language change.* New York: Academic Press, 1977.

Kirshenblatt-Gimblett, B. The concept and varieties of narrative performance in East European Jewish Culture. In R. Bauman & J. Sherzer (Eds.), *Explorations in the ethnography of speaking.* Cambridge: Cambridge University Press, 1974.

Kroll, B. Combining ideas in written and spoken English. In E. O. Keenan & T. Bennett (Eds.), *Discourse across time and space. Southern California Occasional Papers in Linguistics,* 1977, 5, 69–108.

Labov, W. *Language in the inner city.* Philadelphia: University of Pennsylvania Press, 1972.

Lakoff, G., & Johnson, M. *Metaphors we live by.* Chicago: University of Chicago Press, 1980.

Lakoff, R. The logic of politeness, or minding your p's and q's. *Papers from the Ninth Regional Meeting of the Chicago Linguistics Society,* 1973, 292–305

——. Stylistic strategies within a grammar of style. In J. Orasanu, M. Slater, & L. L. Adler (Eds.), *Language, sex, and gender. Annals of the New York Academy of Science,* 1979, *327,* 53–78.

Michaels, S., & Collins, J. Oral discourse style: Classroom interaction and the acquisition of literacy. In D. Tannen (Ed.), *Coherence in spoken and written discourse.* Norwood, NJ.: Ablex, 1984.

Michaels, S., & Cook-Gumperz, J. A study of sharing time with first grade students: Discourse narratives in the classroom. *Proceedings of the Fifth Annual Meeting of the Berkeley Linguistics Society,* 1979, 51–80.

Nystrand, M. Rhetoric's "audience" and linguistics' "speech community": Implications for understanding writing and text. In M. Nystrand (Ed.), *What writers know: The language, process, and structure of written discourse.* New York: Academic Press, 1982.

Ochs, E. Planned and unplanned discourse. In T. Givon (Ed.), *Discourse and syntax.* New York: Academic Press, 1979.

Olson, D. From utterance to text: The bias of language in speech and writing. *Harvard Educational Review,* 1977, *47*(3), 257–281.

Ong, W. J. *The presence of the word.* New Haven: Yale University Press, 1967.

——. *Interfaces of the word.* Ithaca, N.Y.: Cornell University Press, 1977.

Rader, M. Context in written language: The case of imaginative fiction. In D. Tannen (Ed.), *Spoken and written language: Exploring orality and literacy.* Norwood, N.J.: Ablex, 1982.

Sacks, H. Mimeographed lecture notes, March 11, 1971.

Saville-Troike, M. *The ethnography of communication.* London: Blackwell, 1982.

Scollon, R. The rhythmic integration of ordinary talk. In D. Tannen (Ed.), *Analyzing discourse: Text and talk* (Georgetown University Round Table on Languages and Linguistics, 1981). Washington, D.C.: Georgetown University Press, 1982.

Tannen, D. A comparative analysis of oral narrative strategies. In W. Chafe (Ed.), *The pear stories.* Norwood, N.J.: Ablex, 1980a.

——. Implications of the oral/literate continuum for cross-cultural communication. In J. Alatis (Ed.), *Current issues in bilingualism* (Georgetown University Round Table on Languages and Linguistics, 1980). Washington D.C.: Georgetown University Press, 1980b.

——. New York Jewish conversational style. *International Journal of the Sociology of Language,* 1981, *30,* 133–139

——. Oral and literate strategies in spoken and written narratives. *Language* 1982a, *58,* 1–21.

——. The oral/literate continuum in discourse. In D. Tannen (Ed.), *Spoken and written language: Exploring orality and literacy.* Norwood, N.J.: Ablex 1982b.

——. Oral and literate strategies in spoken and written discourse. In R. W. Bailey & R. M. Fosheim (Eds.), *Literacy for life: The demand for reading and writing.* New York: Modern Language Association, 1983.

——. *Conversational style: Analyzing talk among friends.* Norwood, NJ.: Ablex, 1984.

12.
"THE BLACKER THE BERRY, THE SWEETER THE JUICE"
Geneva Smitherman

Written literacy among African American students continues to be of major concern to educators, policy makers, researchers, and the lay community. African American students have consistently scored lower than their European American counterparts in all rounds of the National Assessment of Educational Progress (NAEP) since its inception in 1969 (NAEP 1980; Applebee, Langer, and Mullis 1985). And even in that decade of remarkable progress for African American student writers, 1969 to 1979, where 1979 NAEP results indicated that they had improved *twice* as much as their white counterparts, African American students still were not writing on a par with white students, as the 1979 NAEP results also indicated.

The upward surge first evidenced in 1979 continued in the 1980s, though not with the same dramatic level of improvement. According to NAEP, from 1984 to 1988, "Black and Hispanic students appeared to show consistent improvements at all three grade levels, although the changes were not statistically significant" (Applebee *et al.* 1990, p. 9). Although black students' scores still do not parallel those of whites, there is some slight encouragement in NAEP's finding, particularly in light of their conclusion that generally in 1988 the nation's students "continued to perform at minimal levels on the . . . writing assessment tasks, and relatively few performed at adequate or better levels" (Applebee *et al.,* 1990, 6).

The topic of the African American Verbal Tradition—both its discourse modalities and its grammar—is frequently at the heart of discussion and concern about African American student writing. Of particular significance is the extent to which Black English Vernacular (BEV) patterns of syntax and discourse are reproduced in writing. A significant related issue concerns the potential correlation between a student's use of such BEV patterns and evaluation of his or her essay by writing instructors. This aspect of the study addresses both issues by focusing on BEV *discourse* patterns.

Issues in the Study

Work by researchers such as Whiteman (1976), Scott (1981), Wright (1984), Chaplin (1987), and my own earlier work on NAEP (Smitherman, 1985 NCTE Research Report)

Smitherman, Geneva. "'The Blacker the Berry, the Sweeter the Juice': African American Student Writers and the NAEP." Chapter 10, *Talkin that Talk*. New York: Routledge, 1999. 163–195.

raised issues concerning comparisons of African American and European American student writers, methodological concerns about differential topics, audiences, task conditions for speech and writing, the importance of BEV discourse over BEV syntax in writing, and the relationship between the "students' right to their own language" and teacher ratings of student writing. The following crucial questions are examined here:

1 Can black student writing be characterized by an identifiable discourse style rooted in the African American Verbal Tradition?
2 If so, does use of this discourse style correlate with use of patterns of BEV grammar?
3 What effect, if any, does use of an African American discourse style have on teacher ratings of black student writing?
4 Given writing with *both* BEV discourse and BEV grammar, does one dimension have greater effect on teacher ratings than the other?

Some responses to these questions emerged from the research of Scott (1981) and Chaplin (1987). Scott controlled for the methodological shortcomings in earlier studies (for example, unequivalent topics, modalities, and audiences) by using African American college freshmen's speeches and essays on identical topics, produced under identical conditions. The essays were edited by freshman composition instructors for BEV, mechanics, spelling, and punctuation. Scott then asked the writing instructors to evaluate edited and unedited versions of the students' essays. When she compared the ratings of edited essays with ratings of corresponding unedited essays, no significant difference was found. Scott concluded that other factors such as discourse patterns were probably influencing the ratings.

Chaplin used 1984 NAEP essays for her work. (Hers is believed to be the only other research on African American student writing in NAEP.) She compared African American and European American eighth- and ninth-grade students in NAEP and African American students in the 1986 New Jersey High School Proficiency Test in an attempt to identify discourse patterns differentiating black and white students. She focused on the construct of field dependency-independency, that is, the thinker's-writer's relationship to the event, idea, phenomenon, or "field" under discussion. The field dependent thinker's-writer's style demands involvement with and a lack of distancing from the phenomenon being studied, analyzed, or communicated about. There is a tendency to see things whole, rather than segmented. The field independent thinker's-writer's style demands distance from and a lack of involvement with the field. There is a tendency to view things in parts or segments.

African American psychologists have long theorized that African Americans employ a field dependent style and European Americans a field independent style (e.g., Wilson 1971; Williams 1972; Simpkins, Holt, and Simpkins 1976). Cooper (1979) did the pioneering research on linguistic correlates of field dependency, bringing together the insights of African American psychologists and communication scholars. While the notion of differing cognitive styles, varied along racial-cultural lines, has caused controversy, it is imperative to understand that we are not talking about cognitive style in the "genetic inferiority" sense used by Bereiter and Engleman (1966) or Jensen (1980). Rather, field dependency-independency emanates from different cultural orientations and world views, a view in concert with the theoretical frameworks of Von Humboldt (1841), Sapir (1929), Vološinov ([1923] 1973), Whorf (1956), Vygotsky (1962), and more recently Hymes (1974). It can be argued that we may not sufficiently understand the exact nature of the field dependency-independency constructs, yet a great deal of research substantiates that these constructs are reliable indicators of differing cultural experiences and cosmologies. Critically, and futuristically as US society becomes increasingly diverse, we must arrive at a genuine acceptance of the fact that difference does not mean deficiency.

Chaplin used black and white teacher raters to assess the African American and European American students' use of field dependency-independency as a discourse style in their essays. Her analysis led to the following observation: "[F]or more of the Black than White student writers, there was an identifiable field dependent style" (Chaplin, 1987, p. 26). Without being given an imposed structure or racial identification of the student writers, Chaplin's readers identified two discourse features in the black student writing that marked field dependency: cultural vocabulary-influence and conversational tone. According to Chaplin, cultural vocabulary-influence represented culture-specific words, idioms, and phrases, the language that has "helped them to shape reality" and thus "become a part of their writing" (p. 48). Conversational tone she defined as producing an essay that reads like "recorded oral language or a conversation" (p. 37). Although Chaplin states that there were more similarities than differences in the black and white students' writing, she does conclude that "conversational tone, cultural vocabulary and Black Vernacular English were used more often by Black ... students" (1990, p. 18).

In terms of implications for writing instruction, Chaplin advises that, since "Black students ... seemed ... less able to distance themselves from cultural influences," such instruction "should be conceived within the context of an understanding and appreciation of the Black experience" if we are to "maximize the potential that Black students have for writing development" (1990, p. 21). Chaplin's work has buttressed my own claims about a discernible African American discourse style of writing which I began to explore in analyzing the 1969 and 1979 NAEP essays. Those explorations were extended and developed, and the use of a black discourse style became the focal point in the present study.

Sample and Methods

In developing the methodology for this study, I felt it critical to compare African American student writers with one another, rather than with European American student writers. The research literature is quite definitive about the existence of an African American Verbal Tradition, with varying degrees of survival within the race (see e.g., Herskovits 1941; Dillard 1972; Lincoln 1990; Thompson 1983; Labov 1972; Asante 1990; Smitherman [1977] 1986; Gates 1988b). Our focus here was to analyze the degree to which this tradition survives in the writing of black students across a generational time span, rather than to assess the degree of borrowing from this tradition by European American students. Further, although black students are often disproportionately represented in "basic" writing courses, I felt it imperative to analyze a variety of black student writers, not just those deemed "basic" or "remedial." Because there is diversity of performance within race, writing norms can be derived from African American student performance.

In our study of 1969 and 1979 NAEP essays, we analyzed black discourse, using holistic scoring for field dependency. The discourse analysis involved only the sample of imaginative-narrative essays and employed general, impressionistic ratings of field involvement by a social psychologist, a graduate student in English, and me. We rated the essays holistically using a "field involvement score" based on the rater's assessment of the degree of distance of the writer from his or her subject matter. Some of the stylistic-linguistic features that this measurement involved were the presence of interaction between the writer and others, dialog in the essay that clearly involved the writer, the attribution of human qualities to nonhuman things, and other signals that the writer was in the environment of the communication context he or she created.

For the present work, using 1984 and 1988/89 NAEP essays, we extended and refined that earlier methodology. Several writing instructors experienced in teaching African American students and one other sociolinguist, who specializes in Black English Vernacular studies, worked with me to construct a model of African American discourse to use in analyzing the essays. First, all became conversant with work on field dependency-independency, including Cooper's and Chaplin's studies and my 1985 NAEP study. Then each instructor independently read the same 25 essays, noting any features that struck him or her as discernibly African American. Next, the group members came together to discuss and compare our lists. We repeated this same procedure twice, thus ending up with a model based on independent assessment, discussion, and 85 percent agreement about the black discourse features in 75 essays in the NAEP sample. Each time we came together for discussion, we found ourselves coming up with similar concepts, different labels and terminology to be sure, but essentially the same characteristic conceptual features. We established the following set of criteria for African American discourse in black student writing:

1. Rhythmic, dramatic, evocative language. *Example:* "Darkness is like a cage in black around me, shutting me off from the rest of the world."
2. Reference to color-race-ethnicity (that is, when topic does not call for it). *Example:* "I dont get in trouble at school or have any problems with people picking on me I am nice to every one no matter what color or sex."
3. Use of proverbs, aphorisms, Biblical verses. *Example:* "People might have shut me off from the world cause of a mistake, crime, or a sin . . . Judge not others, for you to will have your day to be judge"
4. Sermonic tone reminiscent of traditional Black Church rhetoric, especially in vocabulary, imagery, metaphor. *Example:* "I feel like I'm suffering from being with world. There no lights, food, water, bed and clothes for me to

put on. Im fighten, scared of what might happened if no one finds me. But I pray and pray until they do find me."
5. Direct address-conversational tone. *Example:* "I think you should use the money for the railroad track ... it could fall off the tracks and kill someone on the train And that is very dangerius. Don't you think so. Please change your mind and pick the railroad tracks. For the People safety O.K." [From letter-writing, persuasive task]
6. Cultural references. *Example:* "How about slipping me some chitterlings in tonite"
7. Ethnolinguistic idioms. *Example:* "... a fight has broke loose"; "It would run me crazy..."
8. Verbal inventiveness, unique nomenclature. *Example:* "[The settlers] were pioneerific"; "[The box] has an eye look-out"
9. Cultural values-community consciousness. Expressions of concern for development of African Americans; concern for welfare of entire community, not just individuals, as for example several essays in which students expressed the view that recreational facilities would have to be for everybody, "young and old, and the homeless among Blacks"
10. Field dependency. Involvement with and immersion in events and situations; personalizing phenomena; lack of distance from topics and subjects.

The research team used holistic scoring to rank each essay in terms of the degree of African American discourse in the essay. We used a 4-point Likert-type scale, from 1 ("highly discernible African American style") to 4 ("not discernible African American style"). Each of the 1984 imaginative essays ($N=432$) and a subsample ($N=435$) of the 1984 and 1988 persuasive essays were coded independently by two members of our research team. In the case of a discrepancy in coding, a third member coded the essay. The total number of essays coded was 867. For 780 of the essays, or in 90 percent of the discourse sample, the two raters agreed independently on the discourse score assigned to the essay.

Each of the essays had also been given a primary trait score or a holistic score, or both by NAEP teachers—raters trained and experienced in holistic scoring and general writing assessment. A holistic score is an assessment of overall writing competency, what NAEP describes as "a global view of the ideas, language facility, organization, mechanics, and syntax of each paper taken as whole" (Applebee *et al.* 1990, p. 84). Further, with holistic scoring, papers are evaluated relative to one another, rather than against specific criteria, as is the case with primary trait scoring. In 1969 and 1979, NAEP raters used a 4-point scale for both types of scoring. In 1984 and 1988, NAEP rates used a 6-point scale for holistic and a 4 point scale for primary trait scoring.

In primary trait assessment, papers are evaluated according to features of specific writing tasks. This score reflects the measure of student success in accomplishing the assigned purpose of the writing (Applebee *et al.* 1990, p. 6). Here, matters of mechanics, grammar, and syntax are subordinated to fluency and execution of the writing task.

For analysis, our team's discourse scores and NAEP's rater scores were compared to ascertain the degree of correlation, if any, between use of an African American discourse style and the primary trait and holistic scores assigned to an essay by raters.

Next, the discourse scores were analyzed to examine the correlation, if any, between the production of BEV syntax and the use of a black oral discourse style. BEV syntax was measured by the percentage of realization of patterns established in the literature as BEV grammatical patterns.

Results

Let us begin with a summary of the findings relative to discourse analysis and primary trait and holistic scores in NAEP 1969 and 1979. Analysis indicated the following:

1   There was no statistically significantly decline in field dependency from 1969 to 1979. This finding contrasted with the significant decline in BEV syntax in the narrative mode over the decade (Smitherman and Wright, 1983a).
2   There was no correlation between use of BEV syntax and field dependency; that is, high users of BEV syntax do not necessarily use field dependent style, nor are those writers who use low BEV syntax predictably field independent.
3   There was no correlation between rater score and field dependency. By contrast, BEV syntax correlated significantly and negatively with rater score for both primary trait and holistic scoring. Even when all variables (sex, year, essay type, field dependency score) were factored into equation, BEV syntax remained the most significant predictor of rater score.

(...) As detailed above, our present NAEP study used a fully developed, explicit set of criteria for identifying varying degrees of black discourse in the 1984 imaginative essays and the 1984 and 1988/89 persuasive essays. Correlations were run between (1) the discourse score and BEV syntax, and (2) the discourse score and holistic and primary trait scores.

In the case of the first relationship, results tend to support the tendency we observed in 1969 and 1979, namely, that BEV syntax and BEV discourse are *not* co-occurring variables. No correlation was found between a discernibly African American discourse style and the production of BEV syntax. In fact, of the three sets of essay data subjected to discourse analysis, *correlations were found between BEV grammar and non-African American discourse style*. Although only one of these analyses reached statistical significance, it is interesting to note that the correlations are all positive. That is, when overall BEV syntax was high, the discourse scores tended to be high also. A high discourse score on our rating scale indicated an essay that *did not have a discernibly African American discourse style,* thus suggesting that the production of BEV grammar goes up as the writing becomes less "black" rhetorically. Although we must propose this as an observed trend, not a conclusion (see Table 12.1), it is interesting to note that this observation coincides with that of researchers who posit that "talking black" does not have to encompass features of BEV grammar (e.g., Taylor, 1992; Hoover, 1978; Smitherman, 1986).

In the second possible relationship—between discourse score and holistic and primary trait scores—results for 1984 and 1988/89 were highly significant, in contrast to the 1969 and 1979 findings. In the 1980s, *the more discernibly African American the discourse, the higher the primary trait and holistic scores; the less discernibly African American the discourse, the lower the primary trait and holistic scores.* This finding was statistically significant for all three data sets and for both holistic and primary trait scoring (see Table 12.2). What the negative correlations in Table 12.2 indicate is that the higher the discourse score, the lower the rater's score. As mentioned, a high discourse score indicates an essay written in a non-African American discourse style. As it turns out, these essays were assigned lower rater scores, whether assessed by using primary trait of holistic scoring criteria. This finding held regardless of the degree of BEV grammar in a given essay, at least with primary trait scoring.

As an illustration of this finding, note the opening sentences in the two essays below. The writers are responding to NAEP's 1984 imaginative essay prompt, a picture of a box with a hole in it and an eye looking out, requiring the writers to "imagine" themselves in the picture and to describe the scene and their feelings in a "lively and interesting" way. Essay 582200 begins this way (see Sample essays for entire essay):

> Well, a boy is in a box outside, may be in his or her back and looking through a square hole. He or she look like hear she is hiding from someone. Maybe he or she is 5 year old and some one is trying to find him/her to beat him or her up.

In terms of its degree of African American discourse, we rated this essay a 4, that is, distinctly non-black style. NAEP raters gave the essay a primary trait score of 1, and a holistic score of 2, both low scores. By contrast, essay 590877 begins this way (refer to Sample essays, p. 189 for entire essay):

> I see little kids playing around me some on the swings, and some on the sliding bord. The kids are enjoying themselfs. As for me I'm in this box because I'm afraid of all of the other kids in the park.

We gave this essay a black discourse score of 1, that is, distinctly black style. NAEP raters gave the essay a primary trait score of 3 and a holistic score of 5, both high scores.

Table 12.1 Correlations between BEV syntax and discourse style, 1984 and 1988

Essay year and type	R-value	P-value
1984 Imaginative	.0361	.45*
1984 Persuasive	.1436	.05**
1988 Persuasive	.0044	.95*

*=Not statistically significant.
**=Statistically significant at .05 or less.

Table 12.2 Correlations between BEV discourse and holistic and primary trait scores, 1984 and 1988

Essay year and type	Scoring method	R-value	P-value
1984 Imaginative*	P	−.1660	.001**
	H	−.1783	.000**
1984 Persuasive	H	−.3260	.009**
1988 Persuasive	P	−.1967	.002**
	H	−.3924	.000**

P=Primary trait.
H=Holistic.
*=Imaginative task not given in 1988.
**=Statistically significant at .05 or lower.

Now, clearly both of the above essays begin with departures from Edited American English. Yet the latter essay exhibits greater fluency and power, and it is clear that this writer is on her or his way somewhere towards a product that will be rhetorically effective. In sum, what our analysis of essays by several hundred African American student writers indicates is this: given a paper with both BEV grammar and BEV discourse, the greater the degree of black discourse, irrespective of the degree-amount of BEV grammar, the higher will be the rating in primary trait scoring, that is, scoring for fluency-accomplishment of the rhetorical task.

Finally, the imaginative-narrative essay continues to be black students' strong suit. These essays were consistently assessed higher by NAEP raters than were the 1984 or 1988 persuasives. Further, the imaginatives also exhibited higher levels of African American Verbal Tradition style, as indicated by the fact that greater numbers of these essays received discourse scores of 1 or 2 by our research team than was the case with our discourse rating of persuasives.

Conclusions and Implications

The title of this essay contains an age-old black proverb whose message speaks to the power of blackness in skin color, rhetorical fluency, and cultural affinity. For 1984 imaginative and 1984 and 1988 persuasive NAEP essays, a team of experienced writing instructors was able to identify a discernible black discourse style and establish criteria for rating the "blackness" of student essays. The team achieved a 90 percent agreement for 867 essays. Results indicated that students who employed a black expressive discourse style received higher NAEP scores than those who did not. In the case of primary trait scores, this finding held regardless of the frequency of BEV syntax (fairly low anyway, and continuing to decline over time; see Smitherman, 1992d).

There are several clear implications here for writing instructors and others concerned about African American students' written literacy. First, capitalize on the strengths of African American cultural discourse; it is a rich reservoir which students can and should tap. Second, encourage students toward the field dependency style, which enables them to produce more powerful, meaningful, and highly rated essays. Third, design strategies for incorporating the black imaginative, storytelling style into student production of other essay modalities. Fourth, de-emphasize your and your students' concerns about BEV grammar; overconcentration on these forms frequently suppresses the production of African American discourse and its rich, expressive style.

As cultural norms shift focus from "book" English to "human" English, the narrativizing, dynamic quality of the African American Verbal Tradition will help students produce lively, image-filled, concrete, readable essays, regardless of rhetorical modality—persuasive, informative, comparison-contrast, and so forth. I am often asked "how far" does the teacher go with this kind of writing pedagogy. My answer: as far as you can. Once you have pushed your students to rewrite, revise; rewrite, revise; rewrite, revise; and once they have produced the most powerful essay possible, then and only then should you have them turn their attention to BEV grammar and matters of punctuation, spelling, and mechanics.

Finally, if you are worried about preparing your students for the next level ("Well, that might be okay in *my* classroom, but then what about when they pass on to Mrs. X's class..."), consider the NAEP results reported here from the perspective of the teacher-raters of the 1980s and beyond. They contrast sharply with those teacher-raters in the 1969 and 1979 NAEP, where African American discourse style had no effect on rater scores. The fact that rater scores in 1984 and 1988 *positively correlated with black discourse styles* speaks favorably for the social and educational efforts of groups such as the Center for Applied Linguistics, the National Council of Teachers of English, the Conference on College Composition and Communication, and others who, over the past twenty years, have worked to sensitize teachers to the linguistic-cultural norms of the African American speech community. Many people now appear to be receptive to and subliminally aware of the rhetorical power of the African American Verbal Tradition, and in some quarters they even consciously celebrate it. Public schools and college teachers, too, now appear to understand that "the blacker the berry, the sweeter the juice."

SECTION 3

EXPLORATIONS OF SOME FEATURES OF SPEECH WITH A SPECIAL RELEVANCE TO WRITING

13.
HISTORICAL DESCRIPTION AND THE IDEOLOGY OF THE STANDARD LANGUAGE
Jim Milroy

The essay that follows is from an important book, The Development of Standard English 1300–1800: Theories, Descriptions, Conflicts, *edited by Laura Wright. The authors successfully undermine the standard historical theory of how we got our version of English, namely, that when London became the political and economic center of a country that had never had such a center, it also became the linguistic center. That is, the speech of Londoners has always been alleged to have become the standard for the nation. This story sounds reasonable but it turns out to be false—while, interestingly, the more accurate story sounds peculiar. It turns out that the early modern English that emerged in the 14th century was an artificial, abstract, idealized dialect: it was never spoken by anyone—Londoners or any other group. This is the historical theory that convincingly emerges from the historical linguists in this book.*

In the essay that follows, Milroy explores what is involved in creating a standardized dialect or language, and in particular the ideology of a standard language–an ideology that has permeated not just the wider culture on the many continents where English is spoken, but the thinking of linguists themselves.

1 Introduction

It has been observed (Coulmas 1992: 175) that "traditionally most languages have been studied and described as if they were standard languages". This is largely true of historical descriptions of English, and I am concerned in this paper with the effects of the ideology of standardisation (Milroy and Milroy 1991: 22–3) on scholars who have worked on the history of English. It seems to me that these effects have been so powerful in the past that the picture of language history that has been handed down to us is a partly false picture—one in which the history of the language as a whole is very largely the story of the development of modern Standard English and not of its manifold varieties. This tendency has been so strong that traditional histories of English can themselves be seen as constituting part of the standard ideology—that part of the ideology that confers legitimacy and historical depth on a language, or—more precisely—on what is held at some particular time to be the most important variety of a language.

Milroy, Jim. "Historical Description and the Ideology of the Standard Language." Wright, Laura ed. *The Development of Standard English 1300–1800: Theories, Descriptions, Conflicts.* Cambridge UP, 2000. 11–28.

In the present account, the standard language will not be treated as a definable variety of a language on a par with other varieties. The standard is not seen as part of the speech community in precisely the same sense that vernaculars can be said to exist in communities. Following Haugen (1966), standardisation is viewed as a *process* that is in some sense always in progress. From this perspective, standard "varieties" appear as idealisations that exist at a high level of abstraction. Further, these idealisations are finite-state and internally almost invariant, and they do not conform exactly to the usage of any particular speaker. Indeed the most palpable manifestation of the standard is not in the speech community at all, but in the writing system. It seems that if we take this process-based view of standardisation, we can gain some insights that are not accessible if we view the standard language as merely a variety. The overarching paradox that we need to bear in mind throughout the discussion is that, despite the effects of the principle of invariance on language description, languages in reality incorporate extensive variability and are in a constant state of change.

It is of course frequently assumed that it is the general public, and not expert linguistic scholars, who are most affected by the ideology of the standard, and, further, that awareness of the standard "variety" is inculcated through a doctrine of correctness in language. In recent years some linguistic scholars have protested at the narrowness of the doctrine of correctness in so far as it affects the educational system and the welfare of children within it. However, I shall argue in this paper that this ideology has also had its effects on descriptive linguists and historians of English—sometimes quite subtle effects—and it seems that these have their origins in the treatment of language states as uniform and self-contained, rather than variable and open-ended. If the ideology of standardisation is involved in these effects, we need to inquire more closely into this in order to determine more precisely what its role has been. In sections 2 and 3, I shall first consider briefly some of the more obvious effects of the standard ideology on recent linguistic theorising before turning to a brief summary of the characteristics of language standardisation.

2 Standardisation and the Database of Theoretical Linguistics

In the development of linguistic theory over the past thirty years, the database has been profoundly affected by the fact that modern English (unlike some other languages in the world) is a language that can be said to exist in a standard form. The sentences cited in early transformational grammar were virtually always sentences of a kind acceptable in more careful styles (and hence conforming to the norms of the standard), and the sequences cited as "ungrammatical" in these studies were frequently perfectly acceptable in vernacular varieties and casual styles. Sometimes the norms of the standard as constituting "English" were appealed to quite directly. One example of a direct appeal is that of Chomsky and Halle (1968) who state that the grammar of English that they are assuming is a "Kenyon-Knott" grammar (this being a pedagogical account of standard English used in American high schools). This grammar is claimed to be perfectly adequate. Generally, however, the appeal has been less direct and couched in terms of the native speaker's intuition. Radford (1981) points out that in practice the intuition appealed to has to be that of the linguistic scholar who is carrying out the analysis. Yet few such scholars seem to have had any expertise in varying forms of English, and it is obvious to the variationist that they are in practice affected by their own personal experience of using educated and formal styles. I have called attention elsewhere (Milroy 1992) to examples of alleged ungrammatical sentences cited by such scholars where there seems to be no basis for calling them ungrammatical other than a constraint invented by a linguist, and no way of proving that they are indeed ungrammatical.

A fairly recent example in which the influence of the standard ideology may be suspected is Creider (1986), who discusses double embedded relatives with resumptive pronouns of the type: "It went down over by that river that we don't know where it goes." An example from our Belfast data is: "These are the houses that we didn't know what they were like inside." The embedded *wh*-clause contains a "shadow" or resumptive pronoun, and what is clear is that it would certainly be ungrammatical if it did not (consider "*These are the houses that we didn't know what were like inside"). Shadow pronoun sequences are commonly found in quite formal styles and can be heard, for example, in high-level discussions of politics and social affairs in the media (one of Creider's examples is an utterance of a US presidential candidate on television). He describes them, however, as "hopelessly and irretrievably ungrammatical" in English. He then comments (1986: 415) that "such sentences may be found in serious literature in Spanish and Norwegian where there can be no question of their grammaticality". This gives us the clue to their grammaticality: it seems that the important criterion is the occurrence of these sentences in serious literature, rather than the intuitions of the native speaker, and it is pointed out further that they exist as named classes ("knot sentences") in Danish and Norwegian grammar books. Thus, they are legitimised by grammarians in Danish and Norwegian, but not—as yet—in English. However, we do not actually know whether the native speaker regards them as ungrammatical in English, and if he does, it may well be because they do not occur in formal written styles. In general, however, the formal literary—even erudite—air of the example sentences used in early textbooks on generative grammar is well known (consider: "The fact that Hannibal crossed the Alps was surprising to John"), and it can perhaps be fairly readily accepted that the assumption of a standard language has often influenced the notion of grammaticality. In the remainder of this paper I shall attempt to show that historians of English long before Chomsky have been influenced in their judgements by a number of issues that arise from the fact of language standardisation. Before proceeding to this, I will now briefly summarise some of the main characteristics of standardisation.

3 The Characteristics of Language Standardisation

We can observe three interrelated characteristics of standardisation. First, *the chief linguistic consequence of successful standardisation is a high degree of uniformity of structure.* This is achieved by suppression of "optional" (generally socially functional) variation. For example, when two equivalent structures have a salient existence in the speech community, such as *you were* and *you was* or *I saw* and *I seen*, one is accepted and the other rejected—on grounds that are linguistically arbitrary, but socially non-arbitrary. Thus, standard languages are high-level idealisations, in which uniformity or invariance is valued above all things. One consequence of this is that no one actually speaks a standard language. People speak vernaculars which in some cases may approximate quite closely to the idealised standard; in other cases the vernacular may be quite distant. A further implication of this, of course, is that to the extent that non-standard varieties are maintained, there must be norms in society that differ from the norms of the standard (for example when the dialect of some British city is an [h]-dropping dialect). These must be in some way enforced in social groupings, and in standard language cultures they are effectively in opposition to the norms of the standard. This vernacular maintenance also implies competing ideologies that are in opposition to the standard (or more generally, institutionalised) ideology.

Second, *standardisation is implemented and promoted primarily through written forms of language*. It is in this channel that uniformity of structure is most obviously functional. In spoken language, uniformity is in certain respects dysfunctional, mainly in the sense that it inhibits the functional use of stylistic variation. Until quite recently, linguistic theorists have not in the main used data from spoken interaction as their database. A well-known history of English, for example (Strang 1970), uses dialogue from published novels and plays to exemplify the norms of spoken conversational English. I presume I need not point out in detail how unsatisfactory this is. Thus, the grammars of languages that have been written define formal, literary or written-language sequences as "grammatical" or well-formed and have few reliable criteria for determining the grammaticality or otherwise of spoken sequences (the discipline of "conversational analysis" has much to say about this: see for example Schegloff, 1979). Similarly, despite the prominent insistence of Henry Cecil Wyld that our aim must be to write histories of spoken English, the canonical account of the history of English is—arguably—still not as far removed as it ought to be from a history of written English.

Third, *standardisation inhibits linguistic change and variability*. Changes in progress tend to be resisted until they have spread so widely that the written and public media have to accept them. Even in the highly standardised areas of English spelling and punctuation, some changes have been slowly accepted in the last thirty years. For example, in textbooks used in English composition classes around 1960, the spelling *all right* was required, and *alright* (on the analogy of *already*) was an "error". It was also required that a colon should be followed by a lower-case letter: the "erroneous" use of a capital letter after a colon is, however, now accepted and sometimes required. These changes had taken place in some usages before standard written practice accepted them. Standardisation inhibits linguistic change, but it does not prevent it totally: there is a constant tension between the forces of language maintenance and the acceptance of change. Thus, to borrow a term from Edward Sapir, standardisation "leaks". In historical interpretation it is necessary to bear in mind this slow acceptance of change into the written language in particular, because even when the written forms are not fully standardised, they are still less variable than speech is. Changes arising in speech communities may thus have been current for long periods before they appeared in written texts. As for standardisation, however, there should be no illusion as to what its aim actually is: it is to fix and "embalm" (Samuel Johnson's term) the structural properties of the language in a uniform state and *prevent* all structural change. No one who is informed about the history of the standard ideology can seriously doubt this. The intention is to prevent change: the effect is to inhibit it.

In what follows we shall chiefly bear in mind the points about uniformity of structure and the transmission of standardisation through written forms of language—these being the most uniform. We shall first turn to the work of the scholars who have built up the tradition of descriptive historical accounts of English. I have elsewhere (Milroy 1996) pointed out the continuing intellectual importance of this tradition and its ideological underpinnings (see further Crowley 1989). What is clearest in the tradition is the equation of the standard language with the *prestige* language.

4 The Standard Ideology and the Descriptive Tradition

The groundwork of comparative (and to a great extent, structural) linguistics was laid down in the nineteenth century, and English philology was effectively a sub-branch of this, applying its principles to the description of the history of English. The ideological underpinnings of much of this are quite apparent in retrospect, and one important ideological stance arose from the development of strong nationalism in certain northern European states and the promotion of the national language as a symbol of national unity and national pride. One side-effect of this ideology was a strong Germanic purist movement in England and other northern European countries and an insistence on the lineage of English as a Germanic language with a continuous history as a single entity (for relevant discussions see Leith 1996, Milroy 1977, 1996). This in itself can be seen as a late stage in establishing the *legitimacy* of a national standard language and is conveniently described as *historicisation*. One consequence of this is that, despite the massive structural differences between Anglo-Saxon and Present-day English, historical accounts generally extend the language backward to 500 AD in a continuous line. Indeed, some older histories devote more than half the account to Old English and Germanic. Toller (1900), for example, in a history of English extending to 284 pages, does not arrive at the Norman Conquest until page 203. This ancient pedigree is repeatedly emphasised, and I give here two examples with over a century between them:

> Taking a particular language to mean what has always borne the same name, or been spoken by the same nation or race ... English may claim to be older than the majority of the tongues in use throughout Europe.
>
> (G. L. Craik in 1861, cited by Crowley 1989)

> The story of the life and times of English, from perhaps eight thousand years ago to the present, is both a long and fascinating one.
>
> (Claiborne 1983)

Craik was a distinguished scholar in his time, but one has to wonder whether Claiborne believes that Proto-Indo-European was actually English. It should be noted also that another effect of the historicisation of English is the tendency to describe structural changes in English as internally induced rather than externally triggered. In this ideology it is extremely important that the history of the language should be unilinear and, as far as possible, pure. For many scholars, it was a matter of regret that English has sometimes been (embarrassingly but considerably) influenced by other languages.

Apart from the nationalism common to all nation states, there was an additional powerful ideological influence on English studies, and this was of course the movement to establish and legitimise standard English (the Queen's English) as the language of a great empire—a world language. To cite Dean Alford:

> It [the Queen's English] is, so to speak, this land's great highway of thought and speech and seeing that the Sovereign in this realm is the person round whom all our common interests gather, the source of our civil duties and centre of our civil rights, the Queen's English is not a meaningless phrase, but one which may serve to teach us profitable lessons with regard to our language, its use and abuse.
>
> (Alford 1889: 2)

It would be wrong to suppose that these Victorian sentiments have been entirely superseded, and the distinction between "use" and "abuse" has powerful reverberations not only in Alford's work (his accounts of [h]-dropping—"this unfortunate habit", "the worst of all faults"—and intrusive [r]—"a worse fault even than dropping the aspirate"—leave us in little doubt: Alford 1889: 30–6), but also in many of his successors until very recently. These are "abuses"—and this means that they are *morally* reprehensible. Those who speak in this way are committing offences against the integrity of the language.

Victorian scholarship actually broke into two streams that on the face of it appear to be divergent. On the one hand there was a tremendous interest in rural dialects of English largely because these were thought to preserve forms and structures that could be used to help in reconstructing the history of the language (a Germanic language) on broadly neogrammarian principles (i.e., emphasising the regularity and gradual nature of internal changes) and extend its pedigree backwards in time. On the other there was a continuing drive to codify and legitimise the standard form of the language, and this is especially apparent in the dictionaries, handbooks and language histories of the period. Among the eminent scholars of the time there were many who advocated both Anglo-Saxon purism and dialect study, and the advocates of the superiority of Standard English could also subscribe to this purism (for a partial account of this see Milroy 1977: 70–98). An important example is T. Kington Oliphant, whose account of the sources of Standard English (Oliphant 1873) includes many lamentations at the damage done to English by the influence of French. In a chapter entitled "Inroad of French into England", he speaks of the thirteenth century as a "baleful" century, during which the "good old masonry" of Anglo-Saxon was thrown down and replaced by "meaner ware borrowed from France . . . We may put up with the building as it now stands, but we cannot help sighing when we think what we have lost." But he is also highly critical of Victorian "corruptions", which threaten the integrity of the modern language. Henry Sweet, writing in 1899, advocated that schoolchildren should not be taught Latin and

Greek until late in their schooling if at all and that they should be taught Anglo-Saxon early. "The only dead languages that children ought to have anything to do with are the earlier stages of their own language.... I think children ought to begin with Old English" (1964: 244–5). In such a context it now seems slightly surprising that Sweet was also a strong defender of Standard English and an opponent of dialect study. For him the dialects of English were degenerate forms.

> Most of the present English dialects are so isolated in their development and so given over to disintegrating influences as to be, on the whole, less conservative than and generally inferior to the standard dialect. They throw little light on the development of English, which is profitably dealt with by a combined study of the literary documents and the educated colloquial speech of each period in so far as it is accessible to us.
>
> (Sweet 1971:12)

I do not have space here to tease out the manifold implications of this important passage, which is echoed by Wyld a generation later (1927: 16), and I need hardly comment that to the variationist it seems extraordinarily wrong-headed. The ideological stance is, however, clear, and the resulting history of English has been a history of "educated speech". It is as if the millions of people who spoke non-standard dialects over the centuries have no part in the history of English. The diachronic distinction (implicit in Sweet's views) between "legitimate" linguistic change and "corruption" or "decay" is often very clearly stated in the nineteenth century and later, as, for example, by the distinguished American scholar, George Perkins Marsh:

> In studying the history of successive changes in a language, it is by no means easy to discriminate ... between positive corruptions, which tend to the deterioration of a tongue ... and changes which belong to the character of speech, as a living semi-organism con-natural with man or constitutive of him, and so participating in his mutations ... Mere corruptions ... which arise from extraneous or accidental causes, may be detected ... and prevented from spreading beyond their source and affecting a whole nation. To pillory such offences ... to detect the moral obliquity which too often lurks beneath them, is the sacred duty of every scholar.
>
> (Marsh 1865:458)

Similar views had been expressed by Dr Johnson a century before, but without the moralism, and some of the Victorian "corruptions" (including "Americanisms") complained of by Marsh and others have long since become linguistic changes. Most of the authoritative histories of English since Sweet's time until quite recently have in effect been retrospective histories of one élite variety spoken by a minority of the population. From about 1550, the story is very largely a historicisation of the development of what is called Standard English (often ambiguously conceived of as a socially élite variety as well as a standard language), and dialectal developments are neglected, confined to footnotes or dismissed as "vulgar" and "provincial". To describe the development of the standard language is of course an entirely legitimate undertaking—and much excellent work has been carried out on the origins of the standard—but it is not a full history of

English. The rejection of some varieties as illegitimate and of some changes as corruptions is part of the standard ideology and an intellectual impoverishment of the historiography of the language as a whole.

A very influential scholar in this tradition was Henry Cecil Wyld, whose work has recently come under scrutiny by Crowley (1989, 1991). Wyld's (1927) comments on the irrelevance of the language of "illiterate peasants" and the importance of the language of "the Oxford Common Room and the Officers' Mess" are now notorious. Wyld's concept of "Received Standard" included not only the grammar and vocabulary, but pronunciation (now known as "Received Pronunciation" or RP), and the effect of this was to restrict the standard language to a very small élite class of speakers, probably never numbering more than 5 per cent of the population. Otherwise it was "dialect" or the "Modified Standard" of "city vulgarians" (these must have been the majority of the population by 1920). Wyld was a very great historian of English and a leader in the field of Middle English dialect study. It now seems paradoxical that he could set such a high value on variation in Middle English and make such an original contribution to the study of variation in Early Modern English (he was a pioneer in the social history of language), while at the same time despising the modern dialects of English. It is interesting to note that a competing tradition of rural dialectology had been represented at Oxford by Joseph Wright, who rose from the status of an illiterate woollen mill worker to become the Professor of Anglo-Saxon, and that Wright was appointed to that Chair in preference to Henry Sweet. However, the ideological bias is clear, and the close association of the standard language with the idea of grades of social prestige appears in Wyld's work, as it also does in American scholarship of the same period (e.g., Sturtevant 1917: 26). The concept of the speech community that underlies this is one in which an élite class sets the standard (the word "standard" here being used in the sense of a desirable level of usage that all should aspire to achieve), and in which the lower middle classes constantly strive to imitate the speech of their "betters". Original as Labov's (1966) approaches have been, his famous graph of the "hypercorrection" pattern of the Lower Middle Class and his focus on the class system as the scenario in which change is enacted, had certainly been anticipated.

What these earlier scholars did was to equate a standard language with a prestige language used by a minority of speakers and thereby introduce an unanalysed social category—prestige—as part of the definition of what in theory should be an abstract linguistic object characterised especially by uniformity of internal structure. As Crowley (1989, 1991) has recently shown, Wyld was especially important in the legitimisation of the Received Standard as the prestige language in that he gave "scientific" status (Crowley 1991: 207–9) to what he thought was the *intrinsic* superiority of that variety (Wyld 1934). He did this by citing phonetic reasons. According to him RP has "maximum sonority or resonance" and the "clearest possible differentiation between sounds".

> If it were possible to compare systematically every vowel sound in R[eceived] S[tandard] with the corresponding sounds in a number of provincial and other dialects, I believe no unbiased listener would hesitate in preferring RS as the most pleasing and sonorous form, and the best suited to the medium of poetry and oratory.
>
> (Wyld 1934)

What Wyld is describing here is an idealisation and not a reality. It is extremely unlikely that his views could be confirmed by quantitative analysis of the output of large numbers of speakers, and these would have to be pre-defined as speakers of the variety in question: a partly social judgement as to whether they were RP speakers would already have been made. However, it is the question of stylistic levels that is crucial here. In empirical studies it has generally been found that in casual conversational styles there is close approximation and overlap between realisations of different phonemes (see for example Milroy 1981, 1992), and there is no reason to suppose that the *casual* styles of RP would be much different in this respect. People do not pay attention to pronunciation in their casual styles. Thus, we have a third strand in the definition of the standard. The standard language is uniform, it has prestige, and it is also "careful". Wyld's idealisation is not merely a uniform state idealisation: it is social and communicative also, and it depends on ideologies of social status and what is desired in public and formal non-conversational language—carefulness and clarity of enunciation. Wyld's 1934 essay was one of the tracts issued by the Society for Pure English, which included in its membership such luminaries as Robert Bridges and George Bernard Shaw, and which was influential in the early development of sound broadcasting. The broadcasters' preference for careful enunciation of RP is clearly relevant. In order to speak this variety you must have a good microphone manner and wear a dinner suit even when you cannot be seen. Although a non-standard variety can be spoken in careful style as well as a casual style, it is much more doubtful whether Wyld's idealised Received Standard can be spoken in anything other than a careful style, preferably in non-conversational modes—poetry, oratory and broadcasting. Yet, if there is such a thing as a spoken standard variety that can function in varying social situations, it cannot be monostylistic.

What is, I think, clear from the tradition is that the focus on uniformity (although implicit in the whole undertaking) was less salient in these scholars' minds than the idea of social prestige and social exclusiveness. References to "good English" are in fact quite routine in mid-twentieth-century histories of English even if they are sometimes more liberal in tone than Wyld's comments had been. Wyld's focus was on the spoken "standard" as an élite variety. Its alleged superiority was attributed partly to its supposed clarity of enunciation and widespread comprehensibility, but much more to its use by the higher social classes who had been educated at the English public (i.e. private boarding) schools and/or the Universities of Oxford and Cambridge. The variety described as spoken standard English was in reality a supra-regional class dialect that was not used by the vast majority of the population and aspired to only by a few. It was overtly used in gate-keeping functions in order to exclude the majority of the population from upward social and professional mobility—so much so that Abercrombie (1963), in an excellent and prescient essay first published in 1951, could speak of an "accent bar" as parallel to the "colour bar". Ironically, in its conservative form it is now recessive and avoided by younger speakers, and the strong defence by Wyld could well be an indication that it was already felt to have passed its heyday. It is very doubtful whether this élite supra-regional variety now retains the sociopolitical niche that it once occupied, and it can be plausibly claimed that for this reason it no longer exists.

. . .

5 Concluding Comments

I have attempted to show that, although linguists do not concur with popular attitudes to correctness, they are themselves in some respects affected by the ideology that conditions these popular views—the ideology of language standardisation with its emphasis on formal and written styles and neglect of the variable structure of spoken language. This ideology has arguably strengthened the tendency to think of languages as wholly separate pre-defined entities, consisting of sequences that can be defined as "grammatical". It has also strengthened the desire to describe the history of English as a unilinear uniform-state set of developments—as far as possible—and to reject variation as unstructured.

In a different essay from the same book, Jonathan Hope offers intriguing and concrete linguistic evidence for the larger argument: that the standard English that we inherit from "Early Modern Standard" is an abstract idealized language not derived from any single spoken dialect. He points to various features of standard English grammar to show that they "can be characterised as the least likely to have been selected (if 'naturalness' or frequency is a criterion) from a pool of variation" (2000, 52). Here are his examples:

- *The rule against double negatives. He shows that double negatives are ubiquitous in most dialects of English—and indeed in most languages of the world, n'est pas?*
- *The rule against wh as a relativiser. That is, starting in the fourteenth century people were supposed to stop saying "She gave me the money what she borrowed from me"—despite the fact that this grammatical form was ubiquitous in all dialects of English.*
- *The surprising lack of a distinction in second person pronouns between singular and plural. "Middle English, Early Modern English, and most present-day dialects have a six-person system retaining or reinventing singular and plural second person reference, e.g. thou/you, you/youse, you/you-all (52)." It's hard to believe that some group of English speakers suddenly dropped this distinction.*
- *Using third-person s in present tense verbs. This is "typologically the least likely slot to be morphologically marked—even highly synthetic languages often have this slot unmarked (52)." Note, of course, the absence of third person s in Black English (he run) and many other dialects of English.*

The larger argument of these essays is that the development of the English that we inherit is the story of multiple dialects, not a single dialect.

But how could this uniquely abstract and idealized dialect have come to exist and become accepted? Hope suggests that "the 'selection' process of standardisation is not the selection of a single dialect, but the selection of single linguistic features from a range of dialects" (51). This selection process took place "when language users encounter formal written texts, and become unconsciously sensitive to linguistic variation. This awareness triggers natural processes of competition . . . which operate independently for each linguistic variable, producing the hybrid features of Standard English" (52). In other words, the development of this odd dialect is not a product linguistic processes (for example the kind of historical linguistic process that led to the simplification of noun endings in English). The effect of this more social and psychological selection process is the ideology we all notice most in our culture, namely an ideology that implies, in effect, that everyone speaks wrong.

References

Abercrombie, D. 1963. "RP and local accent", in *Studies in Phonetics and Linguistics*. Oxford: Oxford University Press.

Alford, H. 1889. *The Queens English*, 8th edn. London: George Bell (first published 1864).

Chomsky, N. and Halle, M. 1968. *The Sound Pattern of English*, New York: Harper Row.

Claiborne, R. 1983. *Our Marvelous Native Tongue: the Life and Times of the English Language*, New York: Times Books.

Coulmas, F. 1992. *Language and Economy*, Oxford: Blackwell.

Creider, C. 1986. "Constituent-gap dependencies in Norwegian: an acceptability study", in Sankoff, D. (ed.), *Diversity and Diachrony*. Amsterdam: John Benjamin, 415–24.

Crowley, T. 1989. *Standard English and the Politics of Language*, Urbana and Chicago: University of Illinois Press.

1991. *Proper English? Readings in Language, History and Cultural Identity*, London: Routledge.

Haugen, E. 1966. "Dialect, language, nation", *American Anthropologist* 68, 922–35.

Hope, Jonathan. "Rats, Bats, Sparrows, and Dogs: Biology, Linguistics and the Nature of Standard English," in Wright, Laura (ed.) *The Development of Standard English 1300–1800: Theories, Descriptions, Conflicts*. London: Cambridge University Press, 2000, pp. 49–56.

Labov, W. 1966. *The Social Stratification of English in New York City*, Washington DC: Center for Applied Linguistics.

Leith, D. 1996. "The origins of English", in Graddol, D., Leith, D, and Swann, J., *English: History, Diversity and Change*, London: Routledge.

Marsh, G. P. 1865. *Lectures on the English Language*, London: John Murray.

Milroy, J. 1977. *The Language of Gerard Manley Hopkins*. London: Deutsch.

1981. *Regional Accents of English: Belfast*, Belfast: Blackstatt.

1992. *Linguistic Variation and Change*, Oxford: Blackwell.

1996. "Linguistic ideology and the Anglo-Saxon lineage of English", in Klemola, J., Kytö, M. and Rissanen, M. *Speech Past and Present: Studies in English Dialectology in Memory of Ossi Ihalainen*, Frankfurt: Peter Lang, pp. 169–86.

Milroy, J. and Milroy, L. 1991. *Authority in Language*, 2nd edn, London: Routledge.

Oliphant, T. K. 1873. *Sources of Standard English*, London: Macmillan.

Radford, A. 1981. *Transformational Syntax*, Cambridge: Cambridge University Press.

Schegloff, E. 1979. "The relevancœ of repair to syntax for conversation", in Givon, T. (ed.) *Discourse and Syntax*, New York: Academic Press, pp. 261–86.

Strang, B. M. H. 1970. *History of English*, London: Methuen.

Sturtevant, E. M. 1917. *Linguistic Change*, Chicago: University of Chicago Press.

Sweet, H. 1964. *The Practical Study of Languages*, Oxford: Oxford University Press.

1971. *The Indispensable Foundation*, ed. Eugenie Henderson. Oxford: Oxford University Press.

Toller, T. N. 1900. *History of the English Language*, Cambridge: Cambridge University Press.

Wyld, H. C. 1927. *A Short History of English*, London: John Murray.

1934. "The best English", *Proceedings of the Society for Pure English* 4 (Tract xxxix 603–21).

14.
INTONATION: A VIRTUE FOR WRITING AT THE ROOT OF EVERYDAY SPEECH
Peter Elbow

Intonation is a virtue in speech that may provide a bigger payoff for writing than any of the nine virtues I described in the last chapter. Intonation is the rich music everyone uses to sing almost every word they speak. I like to illustrate intonation for students with a mini-workshop. I ask everyone in class to say the single word, "Hello," but in each case to try to send a slightly different message. After each "performance" we see what listeners heard. Besides the various obvious seductive forms of "hello," there is the Sherlock Holmes' "hellll-o" that says "Here's an interesting fact." And the "helloo-*ooo*" that says, "Wake up, dummy." Other words work well for this mini workshop: "no," "maybe," "yes." It's amazing how many messages human speakers can send with the *sound* of just one word—a word that is *silent* on the written page.

    Virtually everyone is a master of intonation, yet consider how complex this musical instrument is that we can all play unconsciously. There is pitch (low, high); volume (soft, loud); speed (slow, fast); accent (stress, no stress); intensity (relaxed, tense); timbre (breathy, shrill, nasal, and many more); pausing (long, short). Note that these are not binary items, for in each case there is a full continuum between extremes (e.g., between low and high, slow and fast, loud and soft). There are glides and jumps. Also, there are patterned sequences. For example, tune is a *pattern* of pitches; rhythm is a *pattern* of speed and accent. Combinations of all of these elements create a rich music for conveying subtle (and not so subtle) meanings.

    Very small children who are learning to talk seem preoccupied with intonation. They continually practice and often exaggerate the vocal music that goes with speech. I remember a very small child saying, "*Actually*, I don't think I *want* to go to bed right now"—not angry or even recalcitrant, just firm. His whole sentence—especially his "actually" and "want"—created a richly musical performance that was far more dramatic and expressive than anything I'd ever heard come out of his parents' mouths. There is reason to suspect that intonation is a favored doorway for children into the mastery of syntax. ("It is well known that young children are more sensitive to tone and context of an utterance than to its precise verbal form" Olson *World on Paper* 92).

Elbow, Peter. "Intonation: A Virtue for Writing at the Root of Everyday Speech." Chapter Five, *Vernacular Eloquence: What Speech Can Bring to Writing*. NY: Oxford UP, 2012. 104–21

It's rare for people to speak without intonation; even *no-intonation* or monotone is a kind of intonation that usually sends its own message. I notice that faculty meetings are often dominated by monotone where people often take all the music out of their speech. It's a sign of being on guard. (*Don't let anyone get a glimpse of how you really feel. This is a dangerous place.*) Bakhtin was fascinated with intonation and speaks of how we lose it if we don't have "choral support" from our listeners. The "stiffness" of stiff adults often brings restricted intonation. Wooden politicians like Al Gore and John Kerry spend a good deal of time with coaches who try to teach them to be even half as intonationally expressive as they were at age five. When we can't understand someone who speaks a different language or dialect, we often understand their intonation just fine. In his extended and remarkably clear treatment of intonation, Bolinger notes that even speakers of tonal languages like Chinese use plenty of additional intonation.

About terminology. Linguists sometimes use the word "intonation" in a strict and narrow sense—limiting it to mean pitch or melody alone. In that sense it's a subcategory of the larger concept of "prosody": the complete range of all audible features that speakers can use with spoken words, such as varying the speed, lengthening syllables, accent, and silent pausing. I've opted to use the term "intonation" rather than prosody because it's a more familiar and less technical term. Besides, in literary theory, "prosody" has a different meaning altogether, describing features of poetic versification like meter and rhythm. Besides, I see people like Bolinger and Chafe sometimes letting "intonation" cover a wide range of audible effects. Bakhtin too prefers the term and starts off an important essay ("Discourse in Life") by exploring the rich complex messages conveyed in a single empty word, "well." (For this book, I have no need for a technical investigation of the difference between intonation and prosody, narrowly defined.)

About monotone or the avoidance of intonation. I've always been struck with how T. S. Eliot reads his poetry. Alan Bennett speaks of

> sitting on winter afternoons in the nave of Ely or Lincoln [cathedrals] and hearing from the (so-called) loudspeaker a dry, reedy, unfleshed voice taking evensong. And one was grateful that the voice was without feeling—no more emotion than from an announcer giving the times of the departure of trains: the words themselves so powerful that they do not need feeling injected into them, any more than poetry does. Or, as T. S. Eliot said, who had that style of delivery himself, 'Speak the word, speak the word only.'
>
> (544)

Eliot's "liturgical" style of reading seeks to remove any sense of a particular *person*—or even a particular interpretation—between his actual words and the listener. He was a champion of "impersonality" in poetry.

Catherine Madsen writes a fascinating study of language written for liturgy. The goal, she says, is language that bears listening again and again over decades or more—language that will yield constantly changing meanings that are deep and lasting. She writes of the use of a "liturgical monotone" that "allow[s] several readings without comment—without 'privileging' any one over the others. . . . In liturgy, intimate secrets can be simultaneously spoken and concealed." (157)

Intonation and Meaning

People most commonly associate intonation with what is expressive, interpersonal, or emotional—revealing, for example, whether the speaker feels happy or lonely—or whether the person is characteristically peppy or depressed. It's notable how often our intonation betrays our real feeling or character even when we try to sound otherwise.

But in this book, my interest is in how intonation relates not so much to feeling as to grammatical, syntactical, semantic, and connotational meaning. As just one example, consider how this sentence has different meanings—depending on mere emphasis:

> The prime minister <u>wasn't</u> selected [as opposed to expectations that he would be]
> The <u>prime minister</u> wasn't selected [as opposed to someone else who was elected]
> The prime minister wasn't <u>selected</u> [as opposed to some other process of choosing him]

That is, intonational stress causes an (often unstated) meaning to light up in the mind of the listener. Meaning shifts as intonation shifts. The sound of irony or sarcasm causes a particularly strong shift: it turns a positive meaning into a negative one. We embed quiet subtle meanings into sound at every instant of natural speech.

The different stresses in the sentence about the prime minister are crude compared to all the possible subtleties of meaning that intonation can create. So when we hear natural appropriate intonation, we get the gift of *hearing meaning* as opposed to having to *construct* meaning: the music of intonation enacts a rhythm and melody of meaning. As listeners, we often feel as though the speaker and the language are doing the work of getting the meanings into our heads.

As *readers*, however—stuck with a silent *text*—we often feel that *we* have to do the work of extracting the meaning. That's why people tend to understand naturally spoken language more easily than they understand silent writing. Consider the sentences in this book that you've had to read twice. If I or someone else had given even a decent reading of them out loud, the meanings would have jumped right into your head on the first hearing. Shakespeare is often difficult on the page but clear when spoken well.

Poor sad writing. The cat has its tongue. How can silent text on the page carry any of this rich audible intonation that's so helpful for communicating meaning? Of course we *could* send a recording with every text we write; readers could get all these audible aids to comprehension—and pleasure. That's why so many people like books on tape. But my goal in this book is to get the best of *both* speaking and writing. If we insist that readers listen to a recording, we lose two central virtues of writing that are lacking in books on tape—speed and flexibility: readers of silent text can go fast, skip passages, and jump around to read sections in any order. But I'll argue below that we *can* get some of the benefits of intonation even onto the silent page.

Intonation and Voice

Intonation doesn't just give us the sound of *meaning*; it also gives us the sound of *people*. When we listen to talk, we tend to *hear* a kind of person: eager? sarcastic? hesitant? guarded? We tend to *hear* personal traits like honesty, untrustworthiness, arrogance, open mindedness. Many people have been struck with the words that Eudora Welty used to start off her memoir:

> Ever since I was first read to, then started reading to myself, there has never been a line read that I didn't *hear*. As my eyes followed the sentence, a voice was saying it silently to me. It isn't my mother's voice, or the voice of any person I can identify, certainly not my own. It is human, but inward, and it is inwardly that I listen to it. It is to me the voice of the story or the poem itself. The cadence, whatever it is that asks you to believe, the feeling that resides in the printed word, reaches me through the reader-voice.

Some sophisticated scholars want us to stop hearing that way—stop reading that way.

> *No, we <u>don't hear</u> a voice or an attitude or a personality—we <u>infer</u> it. And we should stop doing that because we are so often wrong. Don't pay attention to anything but the <u>meaning</u>.*

True. Strictly speaking, we *don't* hear attitude or personality in words. But if we take that line of reasoning, we have to realize that we don't even hear *meaning* in words—we have to infer it too—read it in. We hear the sound *dear*, but the sound itself doesn't tell us if it means "dear" or "deer." We read it in. When a German hears the same sound, he hears "you" ("dir"). Meanings are not in words, they are in people.

So it's hopeless to tell people to stop "hearing" attitude and character on the page. The only sensible goal is to help people hear better—which means helping them be more aware of the attitude or personality or tone of voice that those words tempt them to read in—and to question themselves about what's genuinely implied by the words and what they are temperamentally prone to hear. When purists pay attention to meaning alone, they tend not to notice how strongly influenced they are by the voice they are "not hearing." Teachers, for example, often find more mistakes and weaknesses in student essays where the voice unconsciously irritates them or turns them off. Their only hope of fairness comes from learning to notice how they have been reacting (perhaps unawarely) to the voice.

Voice is a complex and controversial topic. (I've recently tried to sum up conflicting issues and opinions in my "Voice Again"). But the bottom line for writers is pretty obvious. Readers tend to enjoy texts better and keep reading longer when they hear a voice or a person in a text—as long as it's not the wrong voice for the job. An effective voice can pull readers through difficult or unwelcome ideas. The voice is a matter of all those "silent sounds" that intonation can put into silent writing.

But even though I'm an enthusiast for voice, I must end with an important warning for enthusiasts who are tempted to think it's the main thing. Intonational phrasing and sound and voice are big pluses for writing, but they aren't enough in themselves to make writing *good*. Some of the emptiest, wrongest, and most dangerous writing is full of intonational phrasing, sound, and voice.

> By the way, in a review of linguistic research about intonation and gender, Sally McConnell-Genet found evidence that women used somewhat more intonation in their speaking than men. The differences were not extreme, but women used a wider range of ups and downs. She related that to her hypothesis that women show themselves more aware of status. She made some other interesting observations or claims about how people perceive intonation. "[T]he group heard as effeminate used a significantly wider range of speaking pitches and changed pitch more frequently." One- and 2-way glides on single syllables tended to be perceived as nonmasculine. Interestingly, "[a]dult males whose speech was heard as effeminate by judges had, on the average, slightly lower-pitched voices than a matched group of males whom judges heard as nonremarkably masculine in their speech" (549).

Intonation Units

If we are interested in writing, the most fruitful way to look at intonation is to look at the little packages it comes in. For it turns out that when humans speak, whether casually or carefully or even reading aloud, they tend to chunk their speech into little musical spurts of sound that are commonly called intonation units. (Crystal calls them "tone units"; Halliday calls them "tone units or information units.")

Here is a passage of spontaneous speech. (It's part of the longer excerpt that I printed in Chapter 1 from an interview in a retirement community.) As with much transcription by linguists, each intonation unit is given its own line.

>   NEAL
>   the last time we talked
>   you said you were a world traveler.
>   you've been all over the [place] [overlapping speech in brackets]
>   ALBERTINE
>   [oh yes] yes yes
>   that was after I married.
>   and we decided—
>   I wanted to know
>   the great question that was on my mind—
>   I'll never forget—
>   that's folk curiosity.
>   I wanted to know
>   what makes people tick.
>   and so ah . . .
>   my husband loved to travel.
>   so ah . . .
>   the same I
>   so we went out to find—

Intonation

> what makes people tick. [chuckles]
> and of all our travels
> we all came back home after many many years.
> that there was just one answer
> everybody ticks alike. [chuckling]
> There's no difference.

Chafe writes that intonation units

> occur as spurts of vocalization that typically contain one or more intonation peaks, that end in any one of a variety of terminal pitch contours, and that usually but not always are separated from each other by pauses".
>
> (397 "Punctuation")

Chafe is particularly interested in how widespread this feature of language seems to be:

> In spite of problematic cases, intonation units emerge from the stream of speech with a high degree of satisfying consistency, not just in English, but in all languages I have been able to observe and in fact in all styles of speaking, whether conversation, storytelling, oration, the performance of rituals, or even (or especially) reading aloud. That fact suggests that they play an important functional role in the production and comprehension of language.
>
> (*Discourse* 62)

Here's another illustrative passage from Chafe. It records an academic speaking at a conference. First she stands off to the side because she's shorter than the podium—and she speaks in a casual extemporaneous way. Then as she starts reading her paper, she moves back behind the podium. Yet the intonational pausing persist across these two forms of speech. (He uses initial periods to represent tenths of a second of pause.)

> ... I'm standing over here to talk to you,
> because,
> (laugh) I'm too short to be seen,
> (laugh) you know over the podium.
> ... (laugh)
> ... You—
> most people have,
> ... uh,
> ... an image of me,
> ... mainly cowlick and eyebrows,
> ... and,
> ... so this,
> ... this is a ... good compromise.
> [then moving behind the podium, she starts to read]
> ... Now most students,

... of human development,
... seek to discover.
... what is universal,
... in the developmental process.
... no matter what aspect of human development,
... they happen to be investigating.
... They assume that the course of development,
... to one extent or another,
... is largely shaped.
... by biological dis-predispositions.

In this passage, "the intonation units in both the spoken and read-aloud portions were almost identical in length, in each case averaging 1.9 seconds, a figure that is typical of spoken English in general, regardless of how it is produced." (Chafe, "Reading Aloud" 9) Even when speech is coherent and flowing, we still see intonation units of more or less the same duration.

Chafe argues that this intonational habit reflects cognitive limitations for both speakers and listeners. Intonational pausing reflects "in a gross way a strong constraint on the capacity of active consciousness" (*Discourse* 65). Thus speakers focus their full attention or active consciousness on one piece of meaning as they articulate it, but then it takes cognitive effort to shift their focus of attention to another bit of meaning and create another unit—usually but not always with a tiny pause or gap between them. Sometimes the whole intonational "phrase" is no more than "uhhh" or "well," but speakers create this kind of "place-holder" intonation unit when they are giving their limited attention to the problem of figuring out what they want to say next.

> Intonation units represent the amount of information to which a person can devote his central attention at any one time.
>
> ("Cognitive Constraints" 180)

We encounter this limitation every day when we ask someone for their phone number. It's very hard to speak or hear or remember a phone number without breaking it into intonation units. Even if it's just seven digits, we seem to need two pieces of intonational grammar. European phone numbers are often laid out all in a row with no breaks, and that makes them hard even to take in.

> Chafe has studied intonation units extensively. See Chapter Five in his *Discourse, Consciousness, and Time* for a clear and extended treatment. Chafe notes that there can sometimes be some ambiguity in identifying the beginning and end of a unit; some are fragments. But he argues that they are usually clear to an attentive listener of recorded speech who considers the variety of factors that usually characterize a unit. Usually a brief pause at the end; almost always a kind of closure "tune" ("terminal pitch contour"); usually an accent or pitch prominence—occasionally more than one; often they start with a bit of speed up and then gradually slow down; they often move from a higher pitch towards a lowering; often they end with a change in voice *quality* like a tiny creak. About sixty percent of the units that Chafe has looked at among large

samples represent a clause. He hypothesizes that we tend to start out with the intention of building a clause into an intonation unit—but very often we get derailed. He notes that intonation units can be substantive ("but isn't she healthy?"), or regulatory ("well"), or fragmentary ("I mean she").

Still the linguistics of intonation units or "tone units" is complex (as Chafe implies when he says that identification can be ambiguous). Halliday and Greaves have studied intonation in even finer technical detail than Chafe and they disagree about pausing: "[T]here are typically no pauses between tone units; the melodic contour of spoken discourse is continuous, and a pause is much more likely to occur in the middle of a tone unit—for example before a rare or unexpected word—than at the point where the tone unit ends" (58). I confess I find Chafe easier to understand.

To illustrate how speakers don't always manage to shift their focus of attention so smoothly from one bit of meaning to the next, I'll reprint the fragment of dinner table conversation that I printed in from Chafe in Chapter 1. He notes pauses in fractions of a second—and also strong and weak stresses:

   ... (0.3) Some élephants and these
   ... (0.1) they
   ... (0.7) there
   these gáls were in a Vólkswagen,
   ... (0.4) and uh,
   ... (0.3) they uh kept hónkin' the hórn,
   ... (0.2) hóotin' the hóoter,
   ... (0.6) and uh,
   ... (0.4) and the .. élephant was in frónt of em,
   so he jùst procèeded to sìt dòwn on the V̌W.

But it's not just speakers who have limited attention. Listeners also have limits on how much information *they* can focus full attention on during any one instant. So even if speakers do manage to get their minds around a big chunk of meaning and language that they *could* rattle off nonstop for much longer than two seconds (or can read the words off a page), they mostly don't rattle on nonstop. Experience has taught them, for the most part unconsciously, that listeners tune out or don't understand if they speak too long without any pauses or changes of pitch or accents. A stream of language with none of that intonational architecture is hard to understand and deadening in its effect. Consider our sample astronomy sentence from the previous chapter:

The conversion of hydrogen to helium in the interiors of stars is the source of energy for their immense output of light and heat.

For a written text, it's far from awful, but people don't *say* sentences like this in everyday conversation—and it doesn't carry much implicit intonational chunking to help silent readers. If an academic wanted to read it outloud in a conference paper, she *could* make it clear if she "read with careful expression"—which would probably mean making a brief pauses where I've inserted slashes:

The conversion of hydrogen to helium / in the interiors of stars / is the source of energy for their immense output of light and heat.

But this reading is a bit clunky; it's creating some intonational music that's not actually built into the silent written sentence. (Academics in many areas of the humanities and social sciences often jettison the intonational wisdom they have in their bones and read papers nonstop out loud at academic conferences. Scientists, interestingly, often use a more "human" language modality at their conferences and *talk* from slides and notes—rather than read papers. They are often amazed to hear about the unhuman linguistic practices at conferences in other fields.)

Whether or not Chafe is right in his ambitious hypothesis that intonational chunking has been favored by evolution, he has the psychological and philosophical wisdom to stand back and notice that it's actually a miracle that one speaker can get a piece of meaning almost instantaneously from his mind into someone else's mind where it didn't exist. Intonational chunking increases the likelihood of this miracle.

The title of Chafe's book on this topic shows his interest in time: *Discourse, Consciousness, and Time: The Flow and Displacement of Conscious Experience in Speaking and Writing*. He points out the obvious fact that speech happens *in time*—"on line," as the jargon has it. Time won't pause while we speak and listen, so *we* must pause and chunk our language into intonational music because of the limits on how much information we and our listeners can process at any instant.

> *Consciousness* is another key word in his title. By focusing on cognitive constraints in speakers' minds, Chafe is of course building part of his theory on what is not observable—what's inside speakers' heads. He understands the dangers of this kind of hypothesizing, but still he gently chides most linguists and social scientists for a timid form of empiricism that limits them to observable language. He argues that we cannot have an adequate theory of speech without making hypotheses about the consciousness of speakers. (See his eloquent methodological introduction.)
>
> He hypothesizes three limitations on people as they speak to each other: (a) It takes mental effort to get a new idea into consciousness (calling this *activation cost*). (b) Thus it's hard it is to start off an intonation unit except with what's already in mind (calling this the *light subject constraint*). (c) And there's only so much information we can focus on at one moment (calling this the *one-new idea* constraint). He says that these three constraints "involve the expenditure of a minimum amount of mental effort in the activation of subject referents." (*Consciousness* 289)

Intonation Units and Writing

But things are different, notes Chafe, when we move from speech to writing. Writers and readers work "off line" and therefore don't need this chunking. Writers can take as much time as they want to pack meanings into their clauses and sentences, and readers can take as much time as they need to unpack and swallow and digest the contents of those rich unchunked stretches of language. Chafe's view here is common—almost universal—and it has two obvious arguments to support it. First, writers and readers *can* take as much time as they want. Second, most writing—or at least most essayist expository writing—*does* have longer more complex sentences and clauses than we find in speech.

Linguists, teachers, and copy editors tend to smile benignly on this difference between speech and expository writing. But I don't smile. They affirm a kind of wall between speaking and writing that I want to knock down. I say that writers should *exploit* this gift for intonational chunking that we've learned all our lives from the pressures of time and listener presence. For reading is *not* immune to time. The text may be laid out in space, but readers are wholly constrained by time. Since they can take in only a few words at once, the reading process is a temporal process: really, it's more like listening to speech than what people unconsciously think of as "reading"—more like listening to music than looking at a picture (more about this in Chapter 15 and my "Music of Form"). Do readers really have all the time in the world? They're usually in a hurry. Often enough they stop reading if have to reread sentences to figure out the meaning. They appreciate language they can understand first time around—which means language sculpted into intonational units. Most writers want readers to keep reading.

Besides it's no good saying that writers should emulate an *average* of *all* expository writing. Our goal ought to be *good* expository writing. I think I see *good* writers making their writing clearer by using more of the intonational instincts they learn from speaking. Why shouldn't writing heed the "strong constraints" imposed by human consciousness? Of course the intonation units in writing can be longer than the two second needs of speech, but good writing needs units short enough so that readers don't have to take extra time to extract the meaning.

This sounds like an argument for simple plain writing. It is. Simpler would be lovely, even for academic writing. Note the short intonation units in the preceding three sentences. For most of my writing, I allow myself longer ones—but I hope I'm right in thinking that intonational phrasing makes the writing easier to understand.

But calling on the intonational wisdom in our bones does not mean we have to write simple prose. *Highly* complex prose, when it's effective, harnesses intonational architecture and the constraints of consciousness. The pauses in complex prose can even grow out of self-interruptions—a feature characteristic of speech. Look again at the remarkably complex sentence from late Henry James with all its intonational pausing (I quoted it in the last chapter to illustrate left-branching and right-branching syntax). I've underlined separate intonational units and put slashes at points of greatest implied pause:

> But she saved herself in time, / conscious above all that she was in the presence of still deeper things than she had yet dared to fear, / that there was "more in it" than any admission she had made represented—/ and she had held herself familiar with admissions: / so that, not to seem to understand where she couldn't accept, / and not to seem to accept where she couldn't approve, / and could still less / with precipitation, advise, / she invoked the mere appearance of casting no weight whatever into the scales of her young friend's consistency.
>
> (*Golden Bowl* 184)

He builds astounding intricacy out of a deeply *spoken* habit of intonational pausing and chunking. In much seventeenth and eighteenth century prose too (for example, in Hume or Gibbon), we see a similar complexity of syntax that nevertheless builds elegantly on the intonational chunking characteristic of speech. And by the same token, we see it in good contemporary writers who favor rich flexible syntax. Note Geertz:

> The recent tsunami in southern Asia, in which perhaps a quarter-million people of all ages and conditions were swept indifferently away by a blind cataclysm, has, at least for the moment—perhaps only for the moment—concentrated our minds.
>
> (5)

In short, the goal for writers is to do what speakers do: chunk language into intonational units.

A written intonational unit is a phrase that's comfortably sayable in one nonstop piece of rhythm: a phrase with a bit of musical shape or intonational rhythm to it, and a phrase that probably ends with at least a tiny natural pause. It might be as short as *still less* (James), or as long as *perhaps a quarter-million people of all ages and conditions* (Geertz). But of course readers have full choice about how to read or hear a sentence. So we might decide that there are *two* intonation units in that Geertz phrase: *perhaps a quarter-million people [/] of all ages and conditions*—or this one: *swept indifferently away [/] by a blind cataclysm*. For strictly considered, intonation is a purely *audible* matter and doesn't exist in silent writing—or it exists only in oral performance of writing (outwardly or in the inner ear).

So even though intonation in writing is a matter of hypothesis or estimation, nevertheless there is a huge practical payoff for writers: syntax can strongly *suggest* how it wants to be performed—and thus suggest the shape of units; written words can be shaped so that they *invite* helpful intonational shaping and pausing in readers' ears, even without punctuation marks. Writing that lacks this kind of intonational shaping is harder on readers—clunky, less comfortable to say, harder to process.

Intonation Units and Syntactic Glue

Look again look at this bit from Albertine's talk about why she likes to travel. It shows why people so often badmouth speech. The syntax is strained and broken:

> that was after I married.
> and we decided—
> I wanted to know
> the great question that was on my mind—
> I'll never forget—
> that's folk curiosity.
> I wanted to know

People do speak that way, often enough. (But don't forget the research by Labov and Halliday [P X] showing that spoken language is not as much of a syntactic mess as it's often accused of being. This messy patch is only a small part of her monologue.) I certainly produce lots of this messy syntax. Often after we've just started to say one thing, we break off and start something new because we have a new thought or a qualification or a little story. The connections between phrases are often weak or faulty.

However, what's important to notice is that most of these bad connections come *between* intonation units—where there's often a pause—when the speaker is shifting attention from one bit of meaning to another. Weak glue. Grammar crime.

But look at the strong glue *within* the intonation units. Strong connections: the words inside the intonation unit follow each other with smooth natural syntax. So look again at that "broken illiterate speech" from Albertine in the retirement community. Notice this time how *unbroken* the links are within each intonation unit:

> that was after I married.
> and we decided—
> I wanted to know
> the great question that was on my mind—
> I'll never forget—
> that's folk curiosity.
> I wanted to know

Lines of poetry are often highly indebted to intonational chunking. John Ashbery has won just about every poetry prize on earth for poems that often give the effect of seemingly random strings of very spoken intonation units. Here is the opening stanza of a poem called "The Virgin King":

> They know so much more, and so much less
> "innocent details" and other. It was time to
> put up or shut up. Claymation is so over,
> the king thought. The watercolor virus
> sidetracked tens.

Why is the syntactic glue so strong between words inside intonational phrases? The answer is a little startling at first: because of nonplanning. The words came in a "spurt," to use Chafe's word. We give birth to the whole phrase as a unit and utter the words more or less without choosing them. Of course we might have consciously chosen the new piece of meaning and even a key word or two, but once we launch ourselves into an intonation unit the words tend to unroll on their own. Often enough, we don't even have any awareness of the words we are in the act of not choosing. When we utter one word, the next word is pulled along or just pops out—no effort or forethought. The unplanned words in an intonational phrase usually blend syntactic and semantic meaning at a finer level than we see in planned or monitored or "constructed" language. The sequence feels natural and unplanned because it *was* natural and unplanned. The syntactic glue is so strong because we did so little work.

In other words, intonation units help readers not just because of the pausing that I celebrated in the previous section—the pausing that helps listeners and readers catch their syntactic and semantic breath. In addition intonational chunking generates powerful glue between words within the units. So if we want to talk about the syntactic coherence in unplanned spoken language, we can't just complain about weak "ungrammatical" glue *between* the phrases; we have to celebrate the strong glue *within* the phrases.

> Some words are even more tightly glued because they come in ready-made clumps like "paying attention" or "as we speak." In recent years, linguists have become more and more interested in these "lexical bundles" or "familiar collocations" as basic building blocks in a language. But these clumps explain only a small part of the glue in intonation units.

What's so good about the well glued words within an intonation unit? I'll put my answer crudely: if words *came out* of one mind easily all together, then they'll *go into* another other mind easily too. Or at least they will if the speaker and listener share the same language or dialect or speech community—that is, if the listener has a mind that's organized by the same syntactic structures as the speaker's mind. For example, unplanned intonational language by computer geeks won't sound so natural and easy to computer-phobes—even when they are brother and sister.

Because Halliday is a highly technical linguist, he doesn't settle for a crude answer. He shows how the many patterns of intonation are really reflections of *grammar* or *syntax*. He works this out in great detail by mapping different patterns of stress and pitch contour onto different syntactic structures.

> Intonation is not phonetic icing on the real lexicogrammatical cake. There are such icings, for example the quality of voice which expresses anger or sorrow or whatever. But intonation doesn't work that way. It is a system of [lexicogrammatical] choices which you can and must choose from whenever you speak.
> (Email to me, 1/10, from William Greaves, co-author with Halliday of *Intonation in the Grammar of English*)

(The Halliday model of intonation is fascinating but highly complex—a bit more technically detailed than I can comfortably master. See the co-authored book length analysis. Also Halliday/Matthiessen, pp 87–94. David Crystal argues, by the way, that Halliday goes a bit too far in linking intonation so very deeply to grammar.)

In short, the grammatical links *between intonation units* may be highly problematic, but the grammatical links *within intonation units* are strong and basic to the syntax of the language. It's this strong glue that helps written language attain the ideal that some writers since Aristotle have set: to sound natural and not carefully planned.

SponTax

So if we want *written* words to be clearest and easiest for readers to understand, then here's another virtue of intonation chunking: Writing is clearer and stronger when we have that unplanned connection between word A and word B that we find inside intonation units—those natural, almost unsplittable links. Consider Henry James' phrase *"still deeper things than she had yet dared to fear"*; or Geertz's *"perhaps only for a moment."* They might have well labored over the wording, but if so, they were laboring to replicate the linguistic virtue of a natural intonational phrase. And that virtue is clarity and ease of comprehension.

The syntactic quality I'm interested in here is like something we see in graceful human walking, or good running by a dog, or good lying down by a cat. Each submovement follows the one before *efficiently*: unplanned and without rehearsal or control. So by the same token, the sequence of unplanned words in an intonation unit is "syntactically efficient" for both the human *production* of language and human *reception.*

This quality that's so helpful in writing, then, is *spontaneous syntax.* It's this sinewy bond between individual words in unplanned speech that helps both writers and readers. Let's bottle it!

SponTax.
Spontaneous Syntactic Glue. Extract of Speech. Available in liquid or tablet form. Consult your doctor to see what SponTax can do for you. Possible side effects include clichés, logorrhea, and bored listeners. If writing persists for more than thirty-six hours, consult your physician.

With a few well placed bribes, perhaps we could get the Language and Drug Administration to approve it. The demographic is brilliant: it works for all ages and populations. We could get rich!

But damn! We have a problem. It's free. All humans from the age of three or four already have an infinite supply of SponTax coursing through their veins. People never run out. In truth, the bureaucrats have been pushing the other way. Long ago, some group bribed the Language and Drug Administration into *discouraging* the use of SponTax—the taint of speech—in all "serious writing." A good deal of money has been made getting people to fear the strong clear effective syntax they get for free. Everyone has been subjected to a campaign that says, "Writing means conscious vigilance. Never use an unplanned unchosen word. Never just let words come."

I can illustrate the deep cultural prejudice against spontaneous syntax from first hand experience. Here are two phrases that I used in my writing that were changed by copy editors in such a way as to destroy SponTax. I wrote *always comes with* and it was changed to *is always accompanied by.* I wrote *who has a strong sense of* and it was changed to *who retains a deep conviction that.* There was no *mistake* for the copy editor to root out (I'm always grateful when they do). He or she was rooting out SponTax—or what I like to call (in a phrase that's best said with a wrinkled nose) "the *taint* of speech." Academic copy editors sometimes say they are fighting "too much informality" or "low register." And SponTax is often strong in casual or slangy speech. But my offending phrases were not low or slangy—except for those people who call *all* natural speech low by definition. In fact, plenty of SponTax is available in noncasual, nonslangy language.

Hand-crafted SponTax

Some readers will charge me with romantic sentimentality for my praise of spontaneity—and I cannot deny the charge. Yet I can turn around and insist on my equal love for conscious sophisticated craft. There's no conflict between my two loves. The fact is that good writers down through the ages have been using careful conscious craft to *synthesize* SponTax in their home laboratories. In Chapter 3 [of the original volume], I quoted even Aristotle on the goal of working hard and consciously to create language that sounds genuinely spontaneous and natural.

Good writers sometimes use SponTax in an interestingly oblique way. That is, they try for language that is obviously *not* spontaneous or unplanned while at the same time having the *feel* of unplanned syntax. Look at this poem by Robert Hass:

> Mouth Slightly Open
> The body a yellow brilliance and a head
> Some orange color from a Chinese painting
> Dipped in sunset by the summer gods
> Who are also producing that twitchy shiver
> In the cottonwoods, less wind than river,
> Where the bird you thought you saw
> Was, whether you believe what you thought
> You saw or not, and then was not, had
> Absconded, leaving behind the emptiness
> That hums a little in you now, and is not bad
> Or sad, and only just resembles awe or fear.
> The bird is elsewhere now, and you are here.

The poem is largely made of well shaped intonation units within which the words are well glued. But look at some of those phrases: *dipped in sunset* and *twitchy shiver* and *less wind than river* and *the emptiness that hums a little in you now*. They are intonation units that give the *feeling* of "naturalness" and even spontaneity—that kind of rhythm and audible architecture—and yet they also give us the pleasure of the unexpected that's created by conscious elegant craft. They use the same glue that makes cliches work—but they are as far away as you can get from cliches. Hass's language is not speech, but he crafts his written elegance out of the *resources* or *features* of everyday speech. Spontaneous syntax follows well used grooves, but writers can consciously choose unexpected words to lay down in well used syntactic grooves.

Clichés are built out of spontax, but that's not their problem; their problem is in being overused as total word-packages. The actual syntax in cliches is precious for writing. (In many or even most other cultures, people welcome cliches or sayings in serious writing. See Fox.)

As a poet, Hass exploits even the *weak* glue that speakers so often use between intonation units—the weak glue that creates the "bad grammar" that grows like weeds in careless speech:

> Where the bird you thought you saw
> Was, whether you believe what you thought
> You saw or not, and then was not, had
> Absconded

Understandably, we aren't allowed to write that kind of grammar for most purposes and I've tried to avoid it in this book. Hass purposely confuses us into a breakdown or misunderstanding in our first reading—and in this way he makes us go back and *say* and *hear* the words because speaking/hearing is the only way to understand the syntax. (We wouldn't have been much confused if we heard it spoken in a good performance—with full intonational stress, rhythm, and melody.) I love how he puts the rhythm and syntax of careless speech in a highly wrought poem. He exploits the *intricacy* of casual spoken grammar—a grammar that highlights the music of intonation. And his larger strategy is to insist that we *hear* his poem, not just take it in conceptually. In this way, he builds pleasure in the counterpoint between the spoken rhythm and his line breaks.

The Goal for Writers of Prose?

It's the same as I stated earlier: create intonation units. But now I can be more specific. *Inside* your phrases, use strong glue—like that found in unplanned spoken language. But *between* your phrases, use better, stronger glue than we find in lots of unplanned speaking. This last point, crudely translated, means "Use good grammar," but I hope my analysis in terms of intonation units can show scared or inexperienced writers that they can get correct grammar and still not be stuck with simplistic "Dick and Jane" grammar.

In short, SponTax comes to us free when we speak, but it disappears when we are struggling to work out a difficult train of thought in writing. If I'm trying to be clear about an idea that is buried or tangled in a draft—for example if I'm trying to figure out why X seems true and Y seems true but X and Y contradict each other—I find I often have to choose individual words, slowly and painfully, one word, then the next; then sometimes discover I need to stick another word between those two. I have to change words, change the order of words, and try to muscle words into saying some idea or distinction that I'm struggling to understand. This process kills SponTax every time. It's what must have happened to the writer of this sentence:

> My own research shows that in a model simultaneously accounting for both House and presidential on-year voting in terms of voters' issue preferences, partisanship, economic evaluations, assessments of the presidential candidates' personal qualities, and demographic characteristics, the electoral value of being an incumbent rather than an open-seat candidate fell to 16 percent, on average, from 1980–88 to 1992–2000.

So I'm not arguing against conscious choosing and deciding. In the end, as we revise and edit, we are doing nothing *but* making conscious decisions. (See Chapter 10 on Care.) My argument is against the powerful forces that tell writers *never* to use unplanned syntax. Indeed, the reason skilled writers are good at careful revising is *because* they learned the feel of *unplanned* syntax in their mouths and ears.

We therefore need a later stage of revising to harness a different kind of conscious planning to make language sound as though it came naturally and easily to the mouth as an uttering human—even if that language is making some thought or distinction that we struggled hard to untangle. In Part Three of this book, I'll explore that precious later stage of writing.

Final warning (to be printed on the labels of SponTax bottles). The strong syntactic glue found inside spoken intonation units will give clarity and energy to writing, but it will not create good writing. There may still be terrible links *between* intonation units—and besides, clear energetic writing may be expressing nonsense.

Summary Illustration of the Virtues of Speech

I'll try to illustrate the virtues of speech that I've described in this and the preceding chapter by recasting three sentences from Chafe's book. He's a good academic writer whom I admire not just for his insights and research but for his writing. He's not one of those who are painful and frustrating to read. But I'll try to make some of his sentences even clearer and stronger by calling on the virtues of speech.

> CHAFE: [E]ach intonation unit verbalizes the information active in the speaker's mind at its onset. Let us hypothesize that an intonation unit verbalizes the speaker's focus of consciousness at that moment.
>
> SPEECH GEAR REVISION: When speakers create intonation units, they are finding words for the meanings that are active in their minds at that moment.
>
> CHAFE: At the completion of an intonation unit the speaker must intend that a reasonable facsimile of his or her focus of consciousness will have become active in one or more other minds.
>
> SPEECH GEAR REVISION: At the end of an intonation unit, the speaker hopes to have gotten his or her focus of consciousness into the active consciousness of a listener.
>
> CHAFE: It is through this dynamic process of successive activations, first for the speaker and then, through the utterance of an intonation unit, for the listener, that language is able to provide an imperfect bridge between one mind and another.
>
> SPEECH GEAR REVISION: When speakers shape their words into intonation units, each unit represents a speaker's focus of attention, and each does what it can to help the listener to create the same focus of attention. This dynamic way of structuring speech increases the chances that one mind will understand another.

It's surely obvious that I didn't get these revisions by just blithely speaking onto the page—just as I didn't rewrite that astronomy sentence in the previous chapter except by conscious effort and deliberation. In both cases, I had to try phrasing after phrasing in my mind's ear (or out loud). It took conscious work. Often it wasn't quick. But my goal in this work was to reproduce the syntactic *quality* that I've learned to value by paying attention to what comes free in casual conversation. If we speak our words onto the page using our nonplanning speaking gear, we will get language with lots of intonation units, but that language won't work for careful writing. In Chapters 11 and 12 I'll explore more concretely and practically how to harvest intonation—and the other virtues described in the previous chapter—for careful effective writing.

> I think I might be able to teach a meta-lesson based on my revisions of Chafe. It strikes me (only at a late stage of revising this book) that Chafe's third sentence is better than my "improvement." It's effectively elegant and his syntax carries his meaning well—and my revision is a bit clunky and deaf. I speak in Chapter 12 of the dangers when stylists are too governed by a theory and not enough by their ear.

APPENDIX
WRITERS TRYING TO CREATE THE ILLUSION OF SPEECH: A SELECTION OF BRIEF PASSAGES

[C]hattiness, slanginess, in-your-face-ness, and any other features of writing that are conventionally characterized as "like speech" are usually the results of laborious experimentation, revision, calibration, walks around the block, unnecessary phone calls, and recalibration."

(Menand "Bad Comma" 104)

Introduction
Robert Burns, from "To A Mouse. On Turning Her Up in Her Nest with the Plough" (1785)
Mark Twain, from *Adventures of Huckleberry Finn* (1885)
Robert Frost, from "The Death of the Hired Man" (1917)
Zora Neale Hurston, from *Their Eyes Were Watching God* (1937)
Jozuf Hadley (bradajo), "chaloookyu eensai" (1972/2002)
Juliet Kono, from "A Scolding from My Father" (1995)
David Mamet, a link to a passage from *Glengarry Glen Ross* (1984)
Louise Bennett, from "Aunt Roachy Seh" (1993)
James Kelman, from *How Late It Was, How Late* (1998)
Alan Bennett, from *Talking Heads* (2008)
Laura Wright, from "Medieval Business English" (2001)

Introduction

We all look at writing, but few of us try to analyze it *as writing*; we all listen to speech, but only linguists can analyze it *as speech*. But if we look at *representations of speech* by writers, we get an intriguing perspective on the relationship between speech and writing.

As long as humans have had the technology of writing, careful writers have tried to create silent texts that give readers the illusion of speech. Interestingly, transcribed recordings of *actual* speech often fail to give that illusion. Few readers *hear* speech, for example, when they read the Nixon tapes. Sometimes recorded speech is so tangled that we can't even hear meaning.

Here I will finesse two almost impossible questions—what is speech and what does it sound like—and just give some samples that show an assortment of writers trying to solve the problem in different ways. Many of my examples will be in nonstandardized or even stigmatized versions of English. I'm not saying that such versions of English have any advantage in giving the illusion of speech—and indeed they are at a disadvantage with many readers who don't have that version of English in their ears. But I have an ulterior motive: I want to highlight the under-appreciated fact that there is lots of published writing in these versions of English that mainstream cultures have called "illiterate" (literally without letters). And indeed, the Burns and Hurston have become canonized as classics in the canon of English literature despite being written in stigmatized versions of English. The Twain and Frost are also canonized, as examples of more or less "White" vernacular on the page.

Robert Burns, from "To A Mouse. On Turning Her Up in Her Nest with the Plough." (1785)

In this poem, as with some of the others, Burns uses the tradition of the monologue, not conversation, as in the Frost passage that follows. Shakespeare and Browning made the genre particularly familiar as a genre. In monologue, the words are often addressed to someone—or sometimes only to self—but that someone is often not there or not answering. Nevertheless, the genre seeks to make us hear the words as genuinely spoken. By the way, Browning's Scots dialect was every bit as stigmatized in English society, and often Scots society, as African American English has been in our culture.

To A Mouse

Wee, sleekit, cowrin, tim'rous beastie,	*sleek (also sly)*
O, what a panic's in thy breastie!	
Thou need na start awa sae hasty,	
Wi' bickering brattle!	*chatter*
I wad be laith to rin an' chase thee	
Wi' murd'ring pattle!	*spade/plow blade*

I'm truly sorry man's dominion,
Has broken nature's social union,
An' justifies that ill opinion,
What makes thee startle
At me, thy poor, earth-born companion,
An' fellow-mortal!

I doubt na, whiles, but thou may thieve;	*not sometimes*
What then? poor beastie, thou maun live!	*must*
A daimen icker in a thrave	*occasional ear 24 sheaves*
'S a sma' request;	
I'll get a blessin wi' the lave,	*leavings*
An' never miss't!	

But Mousie, thou art no thy lane,	*not alone*
In proving foresight may be vain;	

The best-laid schemes o' mice an' men
Gang aft agley,   *awry*
An' lea'e us nought but grief an' pain,
For promis'd joy!

Still thou art blest, compar'd wi' me;
The present only toucheth thee:
But och! I backward cast my e'e,
On prospects dreaer!
An' forward, tho' I canna see,
I guess an' fear!

"To a Mouse, on Turning Her Up in Her Nest with the Plough." 1785. *The Poems and Songs of Robert Burns. The Harvard Classics.* Ed. Charles W. Eliot. New York: P. F. Collier & Son, 1909–14. Vol. 6, of 51.

Mark Twain, from *Adventures of Huckleberry Finn*. First three paragraphs. (1885)

You don't know about me without you have read a book by the name of The Adventures of Tom Sawyer; but that ain't no matter. That book was made by Mr. Mark Twain, and he told the truth, mainly. There was things which he stretched, but mainly he told the truth. That is nothing. I never seen anybody but lied one time or another, without it was Aunt Polly, or the widow, or maybe Mary. Aunt Polly—Tom's Aunt Polly, she is—and Mary, and the Widow Douglas is all told about in that book, which is mostly a true book, with some stretchers, as I said before.

    Now the way that the book winds up is this: Tom and me found the money that the robbers hid in the cave, and it made us rich. We got six thousand dollars apiece—all gold. It was an awful sight of money when it was piled up. Well, Judge Thatcher he took it and put it out at interest, and it fetched us a dollar a day apiece all the year round—more than a body could tell what to do with. The Widow Douglas she took me for her son, and allowed she would sivilize me; but it was rough living in the house all the time, considering how dismal regular and decent the widow was in all her ways; and so when I couldn't stand it no longer I lit out. I got into my old rags and my sugar-hogshead again, and was free and satisfied. But Tom Sawyer he hunted me up and said he was going to start a band of robbers, and I might join if I would go back to the widow and be respectable. So I went back.

Adventures of Huckleberry Finn. London: Penguin Classics, 2002, p. 3.

Robert Frost, from "The Death of the Hired Man." Lines 7–30. (1917)

        "Be kind," she said.
She took the market things from Warren's arms
And set them on the porch, then drew him down
To sit beside her on the wooden steps.

"When was I ever anything but kind to him?
But I'll not have the fellow back," he said.
"I told him so last haying, didn't I?
'If he left then,' I said, 'that ended it.'
What good is he? Who else will harbour him
At his age for the little he can do?
What help he is there's no depending on.
Off he goes always when I need him most.
'He thinks he ought to earn a little pay,
Enough at least to buy tobacco with,
So he won't have to beg and be beholden.'
'All right,' I say, 'I can't afford to pay
Any fixed wages, though I wish I could.'
'Someone else can.' 'Then someone else will have to.'
I shouldn't mind his bettering himself
If that was what it was. You can be certain,
When he begins like that, there's someone at him
Trying to coax him off with pocket-money,—
In haying time, when any help is scarce.
In winter he comes back to us. I'm done."

"Sh! not so loud: he'll hear you," Mary said.

"I want him to: he'll have to soon or late."

Robert Frost. Lines 7–30, "The Death of the Hired Man."
North of Boston. New York: Henry Holt & Co., 1917.

Zora Neale Hurston, from *Their Eyes Were Watching God.* (1937)

> Alice Walker's [Celie] . . . <u>writes</u> herself to a personal freedom and to a remarkable level of articulation in the dialect voice in which Hurston's protagonist <u>speaks</u>.
>
> (Gates, 169, his emphasis)

"Hey, dere, y'all! Don't dump dem bodies in the hole lak dat! Examine every last one of 'em and find out if they's white or black."

"Us got tuh handle 'em slow lak dat? God have mussy! In de condition they's in got tuh examine 'em? Whut difference do it make 'bout de color? Dey all needs buryin' in uh hurry."

"Got orders from headquarters. They makin' coffins fuh all de white folks. 'Tain't nothin' but cheap pine, but dat's better'n nothin'. Don't dump no white folks in de hole jus' so."

"What tuh do 'bout de colored folks? Got boxes fuh dem too?"

"Nope. They cain't find enough of 'em tuh go 'round. Jus' sprinkle plenty quicklime over 'em and cover 'em up."

"Shucks! Nobody can't tell nothin' 'bout some uh dese bodies, de shape dey's in. Can't tell whether dey's white or black."

..."They's mighty particular how dese dead folks goes tuh judgment," Tea Cake observed to the man working next to him. "Look lak dey think God don't know nothin' 'bout de Jim Crow law."

Tea Cake had been working several hours when the thought of Janie worrying about him made him desperate. So when a truck drove up to be unloaded he bolted and ran. He was ordered to halt on pain of being shot at, but he kept right on and got away. He found Janie sad and crying just as he had thought. They calmed each other about his absence then Tea Cake brought up another matter.

"Janie, us got tuh git outa dis house and outa dis man's town. Ah don't mean tuh work lak dat no mo'."

"Naw, naw, Tea Cake. Less stay right in heah until it's all over. If dey can't see yuh, dey can't bother yuh."

"Aw naw. S'posin' dey come round searchin'? Less git out hea tuhnight."

"Where us goin', Tea Cake?"

"De quickest place is de 'Glades. Less make on back down dere. Dis town is full uh trouble and compellment."

"But Tea Cake, de hurricane wuz down in de 'Glade too. It'll be dead folks tuh be buried down dere too."

"Yeah, Ah know, Janie, but it couldn't never be lak it 'tis heah. In de first place dey been bringin' bodies out outa dere all day so it can't be but so many mo' tuh find. And then again it never wuz as many dere as it wuz heah. And then too, Janie, de white folks down dere knows us. It's bad bein' strange niggers wid white folks. Everybody is against yuh."

"Dat sho is de truth. De ones de white man know is nice colored folks. De ones he don't know is bad niggers." Janie said this and laughed and Tea Cake laughed with her.

"Janie, Ah done watched it time and again; each and every white man think he know all de GOOD darkies already. He don't need tuh know no mo'. So far as he's concerned, all dem he don't know oughta be tried and sentenced tuh six months behind the United States privy house at hard smellin'."

    Zora Neale Hurston. *Their Eyes Were Watching God.* New York: J. B. Lippincott, Inc., 1937; New York: Harper and Row, 1990.

Joe Hadley, from "Chaloookyu Eensai" From *Three Poems in Pidgin English*. (1972/2002)

In this poem, Hadley wants to represent the sound of someone saying these words in Hawaiian "Pidgin." The words are addressed to a "you," but of course he's not trying to give the illusion of everyday conversation. It's in the tradition of monologue (as canonized by Shakespeare and Browning).

* Hadley's poem illustrates how there are seldom official orthographies for nonstandardized versions of English. In 1972, bradajo seemed to want to highlight the differences between Pidgin and standardized English—not caring that his poem was hard for non-local readers. Later writers of Pidgin went the other direction, no doubt wanting to make their work available*

to more readers. (Possibly, Pidgin itself had slightly "de-creolized" and drifted slightly toward the dominant version of English.)

From "chaloookyu eensai"	**"Try look You — inside!"**
	bradajo (Jozuf Hadley)
yuno smollkeedtime	You know small kid time?
sooo machmo preedee no	So much more pretty, no?
damounten	The mountain!
wy yu falla	Why you fellows like (to)
like scrape damounten laidat	scrape (bulldoze) the mountain like that?
waystime	Waste-time!
chaloook wansanset	Try look one sunset!
howyugoin	How you going (to)?
wasetime	waste time,
so mach beeldeen	so much building!
yuteenk yumo nathol	You think you more natural
eensai dabox	Inside the box?
chaloookyu eensai	Try look You inside!
yunokan teenkstrate	You no can think straight
weedoll deeskine contrapshenz	with all these kind (of) contraptions!
hod fobreed yuno	Hard to breathe, you know!
yuno wy	You know why get
get somanee axident	so many accidents?
yumekom	You make 'um,
aswy	that's why!
chaloookyu eensai	Try look You inside!
howmach peepols now	How much people now!
mebe asdachrabol	Maybe that's the trouble!
mobeta osstop	More better us stop
makeenbaby	making baby!
bime by dahouse broke	By and by the house broke!
chaloookyu outsai	Try look You outside!
da toorees	The tourists?
deywanfoget	They went (and) forget!
nokan fine paradise outsai	No can find paradise outside!
outsai weah	Outside where?
outsai yu	Outside you?
howkan	How can?
aveyteen eensai	Everything's inside!
asjalike srrrfeenah	That's just like surfing, yuh?
wanyugatwan	When you get

gooooodride	one good ride.
asleeveenah	That's living, yuh?
aswatyucol eensai	That's what you call inside!
yuwan foget lauv owat	You went (and) forget love? Or what?
asakine yuno	That's the kind, you know!
watkine	What kind?
chaloookyu eensai	Try look You, inside!

From *chaloookyu eensai*, three lyrical compositions in Hawaii folk talk by bradajo (2002)

> yumo
> smallkeedtime
> sooomachmo
> preedee no
> damounten
>
> wy yufalla
> like scrape
> damounten
> laidat
>
> waystime

> chalooook
> wansanset
> howyugoin
>
> wasetime
> somach
> beeldeen
>
> yuteenk
> yumo
> natchol
> eensai
> dabox
>
> chaloookyu
> eensai

A note on the text. The poem was originally published in 1972 in Three Poems in Pidgin English *by Joe Hadley, Sandwich Islands Publishing, Inc. But in 2002, the author printed his own new edition. He listed himself as bradajo and printed in the handwritten form you see in the illustration—and with the spellings you see here (whereas the 1972 edition had slightly different spellings).*

In the "eenchro" to this 2002 edition, bradajo writes, "I have long wished to present those originals as they appear here. Isn't it true that the marks made while embracing a particular vision transmit the energy of that moment?"

bradajo has a website titled Jozuf Hadley: http://www.jozufhadley.com/, where you can order the small book with all three poems—which comes with an audio CD of him reading the poems in Hawaiian Pidgin.

Juliet Kono, from "A Scolding from My Father." (1995)

The orthography in this poem is more typical of later poets writing in Hawai'ian Pidgin.

What kind Japanee you?
Nothing more worse in this world

than one Japanee
who like be something
he not.
No matter how much you like—
no can!

No can *be* haole.
Who the girl? You know, the Michael girl.
The doctor's daughta, good-looking,
live in the big house Wailuku Drive.
Big eyes, nice car, blonde hair.
You like talk like one haole?
You like big eyes?
You try live their house.

No can be Chinee.
Rich. Wong-family-rich.
Daughta go Honolulu, dorm at Punahou.
We no more their kind money.
Me? I only one mechanic.
Your mother, Baker II
at Waiakea Waena Elementary School Cafeteria.

And no can be Hawaiian.
Like Keli`i family daughta.
You know which one—the smart one.
Good hula dancer, fast swimmer, going mainland.
You like dance like her?
Nice nose too she get—some tall.
You like one nose like her?
You dreaming girl.
Come from her mother side.
You one flat nose Japanee
because your mother get flat nose.
So why you like ack different for?
Why you like be something you not?

  Juliet Kono. *Tsunami Years.* Honolulu, HI: Bamboo Ridge Press, 1995, pp. 124–125.

But there's one linguistic wrinkle here: The speaker is presumably a first-generation Japanese man (like Kono's father) whose native tongue is Japanese and whose "Pidgin English" is a true incomplete pidgin—not the genuine creole of most speakers of Hawaiian "Pidgin." Second-generation speakers like Kono grew up hearing an incomplete pidgin but—given the amazing powers of a child's linguistic capacity—came to speak the creole version as a native language: a fully developed complex language with all the linguistic bells and whistles of, say, English or French or German. *The orthography here is typical of the remarkable renaissance of Hawaiian "Pidgin" writing starting in the 1970s.*

A link to a Passage from David Mamet's *Glengarry Glen Ross*, (1984)

Instead of reproducing a small portion of the play here, you can follow this link to an extended passage from this play that any reader can go to on the web: http://www.dailyscript.com/scripts/glengarry.html.

Louise Bennett, from "Aunt Roachy Seh." (1993)

So yuh a de man me hear bout!	
Ah yuh dem seh dah teck	*say take*
Whole heap a English out seh dat	*say that*
You gwine kill dialec!	
Meck me get it straight, Mas Charlie,	
For me no quite understand—	
Yuh gwine kill All English dialec	
Or just Jamaica one?	
Ef yuh dah equal up wid English	
Language, den wha meck	
Yuh gwine go feel inferior when	
It come to dialec?	
Ef yuh cyann sing "Linstead Market"	*can't*
An "Water come a me yeye"	
Yuh wi haffi tap sing "Auld Lang Syne"	*stop*
And "Comin through de rye."	
Dah language wey yuh proud a,	*which*
Weh yuh honour and respect—	
Po Mas Charlie, yuh no know seh	*see*
Dat it spring from dialec!	
Dat dem start fi try tun language	
From de fourteen century—	
Five hundred years gawn an dem got	
More dialec dan we!	
Yuh wi haffi kill the Lancashire,	
De Yorkshire, de Cockney,	

De broad Scotch and de Irish brogue
Before yuh start kill me!

Yuh wi haffi get de Oxford Book
A English Verse, an tear
Out Chaucer, Burns, Lady Grizelle
An plenty a Shakespeare!

. . .

An mine how yuh read dem English *mind*
Book deh pon yuh shelf,
For ef yuh drop a "h" yuh mighta
Haffi kill yuhself!

Louise Bennett. *Aunt Roachy Seh*. Kingston, Jamaica:
Sangster's Book Stores Ltd., 1993.

James Kelman, From *How Late It Was, How Late.* (1998)

This short passage is from a novel in which Kelman uses the Glaswegian dialect. It's not an external monologue but an internal one. It illustrates the nonstop talking to ourselves that typically goes on inside our heads. The speaker, Sammy, has gotten drunk, been beat up, passed out, and now finds himself blind as he tries to make his way along the street to a pub.

Kelman does an interesting experiment with voice. The language is mostly in first person—inside Sammy's head. But continually the voice drifts into wisps of third person syntax—allegedly from a narrator—but really the third person words convey the voice and consciousness of Sammy. In effect, the allegedly third person narrator takes on the identity of the character. *Wayne Booth analyzes this hybrid technique of indirect discourse in his* Rhetoric of Fiction. *He points out how common it is, but often unnoticed—especially in small, almost inadvertent phrases. Kelman's novel, controversially, won the Man Booker Prize in 1994.*

The feet were fucking killing him too, these bastard stupit fucking trainers. Somebody brushed past him, he turned to try and tap him for the bus-fare, whoever it was, but stopped. Stupit. How do you know who ye're talking to it might have been somebody worked in the pub, then they'd get him huckled in the name of christ it could even be a sodjer ye were putting the bite on. The way his luck was going he would lose his fucking legs man know what I'm talking about.

So okay. So that was that. Ye just took it from here, ye pushed ahead.

And a bit of practicality for christ sake man sober up, relax, it's like a mental arithmatic problem; 2 times 2 equals 4.

He felt like sitting down. Sharing a drink with somebody. Just telling them the score. Fucking hell man. No that he had ever liked *The Blazer* much. Some guys he knew drank there; at least they used to, a couple of the auld squad. But he didnay really want to see them, no unless you needed something. Even then ye had to be wary. Ye pay for everything in this life. Once upon a time.

But no now. Sammy was past that. That was one thing man, the auld mental days, they were finished. Helen was wrong about that; totally.

Still, ye could imagine it, sitting down with a frothy big pint, a packet of tobacco.

Ah, fucking fairy tales. Mind you but getting blootered, it would be one way of making it home. Weans [*wee ones*] and drunks man [*must*] know what I'm saying, the ould god fellow, the central authority, that's who he looks after. Sometimes that was what the bevy [*beverage*] was like but a magic carpet Othertimes it wasnay.

Okay, take yer time. Ye go left. Ye go left. Jesus christ! Come on. Okay: ye go left, ye just turn left. Sammy took a step forwards, his hands on the building, patting his way along till he reached a point he forgot what he was doing and he was just getting there christ he was used to that I mean he was used to walking long distances, skint and fucking starving, cold and fucking with naywhere to go man all that kind of deprivation shite. Fuck all new in this game.

So think of a song. Nay songs Nay fucking songs. This was it and that was that.

Past tense.

Ach it was his own fault anyway.

James Kelman. *How Late It Was, How Late*. New York: Vintage, 1998. 62 lines from pp. 44–46.

Alan Bennett, from "Mrs Fozzard Finds Her Feet". In *Talking Heads* (Vol. 2). (2008)

> *Dante wrote a short book called* De Vulgare Eloquentia. *At the time, "vulgar" meant simply "of the people." It's interesting that a term that was neutral has come to mean "low" and "crude." I had originally intended to call my book* Vulgar Eloquence *but was persuaded that this raised too many problems, and instead I titled it* Vernacular Eloquence.
>
> *Given some of the preceding examples that I chose from writers trying to represent vernacular speech, it might be thought that I've gotten mixed up and considered "vernacular" to mean vulgar. I hope the following selection will dispel that idea. Alan Bennett shows here his gift for portraying the speech and even the inner thoughts of English people who care deeply about propriety. And he uses yet another convention for rendering speech (and thinking), and gives a kind of pretense that the speaker is addressing an intimate listener—or perhaps just the self as listener. Indeed, Bennett wrote these for live performance. They were brilliantly performed by some of England's best actors. BBC has published both paper and audio versions of the work.*

Bit of a bombshell today. I'm just pegging up my stocking when Mr Suddaby says, "I'm afraid, Miss Fozzard, this is going to have to be our last encounter." Apparently this latest burglary has put the tin hat on things and what with Mrs Suddaby's mother finally going into a house and their TV reception always being so poor there's not much to keep them in Leeds so they're making a bolt for it and heading off to Scarborough. Added to which Tina, their chow, has a touch of arthritis, so the sands may help and the upshot is they've gone in for a little semi near Peasholme Park.

"But," Mr Suddaby says, "none of that is of any consequence. What is important, Miss Fozzard, is what are we going to do about your feet? You've been coming to me for so long I don't like to think of your feet falling into the wrong hands."

I said, "Well, Mr Suddaby, I shall count myself very lucky if I find someone as accomplished as yourself and, if I may say so, with your sense of humour." Because it's very seldom we have a session in which laughter doesn't figure somewhere.

He said, "Well, Miss Fozzard, chiropody is a small world and I've taken the liberty of making a few phone calls and come up with two possibilities. One is a young lady over in Roundhay, who, I understand is very reasonable."

"A woman?" I said, "In chiropody? Isn't that unusual?" "No," he said, "not nowadays. The barriers are coming down in chiropody as in everything else. It's progress, Miss Fozzard, the march of, and Cindy Bickerton has her own salon." I said, "Cindy? That doesn't inspire confidence. She sounds as if she should be painting nails, not cutting them."

"Well," he said, "in that case the alternative might be more up your street. I don't know him personally but Mr Dunderdale has got all the right letters after his name. He's actually retired but still likes to take on a few selected clients, just to keep his hand in. However he does live out at Lawnswood and unless I'm very much mistaken you're not motorized?" I said, "No problem. I can just bob on the 17. It's a bus I like. No, if it's all the same to you and the Equal Opportunities Board I'll opt for Mr Dunderdale." He said, "I think it's a wise decision. Allow me" (and he winked) "Allow me," he said, "to shake hands with your feet."

I've been going to Mr Suddaby for years. I think it's an investment particularly if you're like me and go in for slim-fitting court shoes (squeeze, squeeze). Mr Suddaby reads me the riot act, of course, but as he says, "It's a free country, Miss Fozzard. If you want to open the door on a lifetime of hard skin, I can't stop you." What view this Mr Dunderdale will take remains to be seen.

When I get back Mrs Beevers has her hat and coat on, can't wait to get off. Says Bernard has been propped up in a chair staring at the TV all evening. She helps me get him upstairs and then I sit by the bed and, as per the recovery programme, give him a run-down on my day.

Mr Clarkson-Hall down at the Unit says that when somebody has had a cerebral accident, "In lay terms, a stroke, Miss Fozzard, we must take care not to treat them like a child. If your brother is going to recover his faculties, dear lady, the more language one can throw at him the better."

I was just recounting my conversation with Mr Suddaby and how they're decamping to Scarborough when Bernard suddenly throws back his head and yawns.

I rang Mr Clarkson-Hall this morning. He says that's progress.

Alan Bennett. *Talking Heads (Vol. 2)*. London: BBC Books, Ebury Books, 2008, pp. 34–35.

Laura Wright, Medieval Business Writing. (2001)

There are no more examples of "written speech" in this tiny appendix. For this last selection I have chosen a passage where the writer was trying explicitly to avoid *speech. I include it nevertheless because it's such a startling picture of how speech and writing can relate to each other. The writer jumps around between Medieval Latin and fourteenth-century English (creating a kind of artificial "written code switching or code meshing"). Here's the last item in this book, and it might be said to fit Roy Harris's argument that I quickly summarized in the first paragraph of the book (in the Introduction). Here we see the power and benefit of writing when it abandons any attempt to represent speech.*

It's "non-standard" but it's hardly a "dialect." And yet you'll see Wright arguing with scholarly authority that the "dialect" is remarkably standardized. I include it also because I suspect it's as unknown to many of my readers as it was to me.

First, here, comes a short passage from Wright's introductory article; and after the selection, I've included some of her commentary.

From "The Role of International and National Trade in the Standardisation of English."

From the Norman Conquest until the rise of Standard English there was a business writing system which was used all over Britain and which did not, in its fundamental structure, vary regionally. Such business writing incorporated Medieval Latin and Anglo-Norman with Middle English in a non-random, orderly way.

Keeping accounts is crucial for anybody in business, both to keep track of monies in and out and for public demonstration. Accounts are written for the present owners of the business, for the auditors a year or so later, and then kept as a matter of record for ever after. This is why such a large number remain in archives from the medieval period. The following data [passage] is of the Medieval Latin plus English variety and comes from the archive of London Bridge . . . 1460–1461. [Translations provided by Wright.]

1. *Reman j vile & Serra* (left margin)
1. There remains 1 file and 1 saw
2. *It P j vyle P acuacoe de ley Tide sawes empt & reman xijd It P j noua serra empt*
2. And for 1 file for sharpening of the tidesaws bought and remaining, 12d. And for 1 new saw bought
3. *P le Tideman & reman in stauro pont iijs iiijd It pro quinque pailes & iiijor*
3. for the tideman and remaining in the Bridge's store, 3s 4d. And for five pails and 4
4. *scovpes empt xxd It P j skeyne de Pakthrede empt per Custod batellaO vijd It P j*
4. scoops bought, 20d. And for 1 skein of pachthread bought by the custodian of the boats, 7d. And for 1
5. *shodeshouell empt iiijd It P iij shouell treis empt vjd It P xiiija polles de frax . . .*
5. shod shovel bought, 4d. And for 3 shovel trays bought, 6d. And for 14 poles of ash
6. *empt P bedehokes inde fact xijd It P vj doS ix lb candelaO hoc anno empt &*
6. bought for making beadhooks therefrom, 12d. And for 6 dozen nine-pound candles this year bought and

Appendix

[From Wright] The two languages are not randomly distributed. English is variably used for the content words (nouns, adjectives, stems of verbs, *-ing* forms), and Medieval Latin is compulsorily used for the function words, and variably for all other parts of speech.

... The scribe did know how to write in monolingual Medieval Latin, but used both languages because that is the custom of the text type.

... The business text-type written in Medieval Latin plus English described here is characterised by its multiplicity of options in both languages. This all points to a highly-developed, sophisticated writing system. It even functioned if the English-speaking reader had only a very small grasp of Medieval Latin. Variation enables the rules of both systems (English and Medieval Latin) to function at once, and the text can be read (partially, but potentially optimally: that is, a trader could glean whatever he needed to know) as Medieval Latin or as English. This text type is helped by variable spelling and by the use of the medieval abbreviation and suspension system. If words had a single spelling, and could not have their inflexional endings rendered by a symbol, then the text-type could not function quite so elastically as it did, visually stretching the boundaries of each language. The radical thing about the newly emerging Standard form of written English was its decreasing tolerance of variation, so that twenty-first-century Standard written English is as invariant as it has ever been. As demonstrated, it is not the case that variation equals a lack of structure or free-for-all. On the contrary, what we see is an application of three sets of principles: those that govern English, those that govern Medieval Latin, and those that govern the mixed variety.

From "The Role of International and National Trade in the Standardisation of English." Isabel Moskowich-Spiegel Fandino, Begona Crespo Garcia, Emma Lezcano Gonzalez, and Begona Simal Gonzalez (eds.) *Re-interpretations of English. Essays on Language, Linguistics and Philology* (I). A Coruna: Universidade da Coruna, 2001, pp. 189–207.

Works Cited

Booth, Wayne. *The Rhetoric of Fiction*. Chicago: University of Chicago Press, 1961.

Gates, Henry Louis, Jr. *The Signifying Monkey: A Theory of African-American Literary Criticism.* New York: Oxford UP, 1988.

Menand, Louis. "Bad Comma: Lynne Truss's Strange Grammar." *New Yorker*, 28 June 2004: 102–04.

INDEX

Note: 'N' after a page number indicates a note; 'f' indicates a figure; 't' indicates a table.

Abercrombie, David 157, 265
abjads, as type of writing system 19
abstract thought: in creation of writing systems 8, 22, 182; and distanciation of writing 92; and Greek philosophers 64–66; and literacy 51, 58, 99. *See also* logic
academic discourse 14n3, 276
academic learning, vs. wisdom 91
academic prose. *See* informational prose
activation cost 276
activity theory 114
administration 90
African Americans: and field dependency/independency 247–248, 253–254; Heath's study of language among 101; literacy among 246; and orality/literacy binary 100; study on black discourse style among 246–258. *See also* black discourse style; Black English Vernacular (BEV)
afterlife 23
Agee, James 220–221
Age of Innocence (Wharton) 205
ahistoricism, of oral tradition 67
Akinnaso, F. 142
Akinnaso, Niyi 101
Akkadians 29, 53
Al-Aynati, M. M. 133
Alcuin 7
Alford, H. 262
alienation 68
alphabet: advantages of, over other systems 30, 54–55; Greek 34, 35, 56, 58–59; invention of 8–10, 24–25; Roman 31, 54; as type of writing system 9–10, 19; use of term 77n20

ambiguity: of spoken language 175; of written language 176
analytic thought: literacy as origin of 84, 99; oral traditions as incapable of 84, 92–93. *See also* orality/literacy binary
Anaximander 60
anthropology 46, 73, 75
anti-logoi 36, 41
Apache people 101
Aristophanes 57
Aristotle 64–66, 74
ars dictaminis 117–118, 120
art: origins of 19–20; and origins of written language 7–8, 20–21
Ashbery, John, "The Virgin King" 279
Ashurbanipal 53
Australian aborigine people 48
authenticity, and voice 13
authors. *See* writers
authorship: attitudes toward 130–131; collaborative 116–117, 119, 130–131; individual 120–121, 130
autonomous model. *See* orality/literacy binary
Azande people 58

Babylonian culture 53
Bakhtin, Mikhail 269
Barnes, J. A. 50
Baron, N. S. 121, 128, 132
Barthes, Roland 121, 130, 183
Basso, Keith 101
Bateson, G. 229, 232
Beaman, K. 142
Beattie, G. 169
Becker, A. L. 229

Index

Becker, Alton 37
Bennett, Alan 269
Bennett, William 98
Bernstein, B. 234
Berthoff, Ann 98–99, 104–105
Bettelheim, Bruno 229
BEV. *See* Black English Vernacular (BEV)
bias, toward writing, as standard language 11
Biber, Douglas 5, 148
Bizzell, Patricia 98, 100, 104, 105
black discourse style: Black English Vernacular (BEV) 246–247, 251–254; and black student texts 246–247; and field dependency/independency 247–248; study conclusions 253–254; study on 246–258; study results for 251–253; study sample and methodology 248–251. *See also* African Americans
Black English Vernacular (BEV). *See* black discourse style
Bloom, Allan 98
Boas, Franz 51, 158
Bolinger, D. 201, 269
Bolter, J. D 127–128
Bonaventura da Bagnoregio 119
boustrophedon 38
the brain: and Chinese language 92; and voice recognition 133–134
Brandt, Deborah 106, 109–110
Bridges, Robert 265
Brodkey, Linda 106
Bronze Age 36
Burnyeat, M. F. 135n3

calendrical function, of writing systems 26
Calkins, Lucy 188
Carruthers, M. J. 117, 119
cartouches 36
Cassidorius 116
Cassirer, Ernst 57, 58
Catholicism 105
cell phones 129, 132
Cervantes, Miguel 71
Chadwick, John 29, 37–38
Chafe, Wallace 5, 168, 230, 240, 269, 273–276, 284
Champollion, Jean Francois 28–29
Charlemagne 7
Chaytor, H. J. 6
Chicago Manual of Style 218, 223

children 234, 241–243, 268
China, origins of written language in 20, 25–26
Chinese language: and the brain 92; Granet on 70; as logographic writing system 10, 52–53; technological challenges of 30; as tonal language 269
Chomsky, N. 258
Chorneyko, K. A. 133
"chunking" 192, 194. *See also* intonation units
Cicero 115, 117, 134n2
Claiborne, R. 261
Clanchy, M. T. 117
class issues: and dictation 122; and literacy 53–54, 68–69, 102, 107, 109; and silent writing 122; and standard language 264–265
clause complex 164–165, 166t, 167, 168, 169, 172
cline of person 229
close punctuation 218–221, 225, 226n6. *See also* punctuation
cognition: and orality/literacy binary 99, 142, 182; and pre-writing 185–186. *See also* abstract thought
cognitive load 217, 225, 274–276
cohesion hypothesis 233–234
Cole, Michael 101, 114, 142
Collins, J. 241–242
colons 212
commas 206–208, 212, 215, 223; and consciousness 221
communality: of speech 188; of written language 188, 198n8
communication: double bind in 229; Greek vs. American styles of 229–230
composition. *See* writing process
composition and rhetoric studies: *I-thou* relation in 105, 108; and literacy as liberation 102–104; speech in 12
Comprehensive Grammar of the English Language (Quirk, Greenbaum, Leech, and Svartvik) 206–207, 208, 222
computers 30–31, 84–85, 94; and gender 126; and voice-recognition dictation software 127, 128–129. *See also* technology
Conrad, S. 148
consciousness: and commas 221; and intonation units 276; and private writing 185–187; and silent writing 120; transformation of, as

result of written language 87–88, 94–95. *See also* abstract thought; cognition
conservatism, of oral tradition 84
"content" messages 182
contextualization 190, 234, 238–239, 241
contextualization hypothesis 231–233
conversation: common grammatical features of 146, 147–148t; dimensions of 152–153; vs. informational prose 144; interpersonal involvement as focus of 231–232, 235–238; linguistic features of 145–148; multidimensional (MD) analysis of 151–153; and overlapping talk 235–236; rhythm in 240; as spontaneous discourse 170; strategies of 230; as typical speech 144. *See also* speech
Cook-Gumperz, J. 234, 241
Cornelius, Janet 109
Cornford, Francis M. 59
corpus-based analysis 145. *See also* multidimensional (MD) analysis
Coulmas, Florian 28
Craik, G. L. 261
Cree Indian language, as syllabic writing system 10–11
Creider, C. 259
Crowley, S. 120–121, 126
Crowley, T. 264
Crystal, David 272, 280
cult of Noble Savage 70–71
cultural literacy 98
culture: influence of, on technology use 114; and literacy 107–110; transmission of, in non-literate societies 47–51. *See also* literate tradition; oral tradition
cuneiform script 24, 29, 53
cup marks 20

dashes 213
deafness 233
A Death in the Family (Agee) 220–221
decipherment 28–29
deference 229
democracy 66–67
Demosthenes 40
Derrida, Jacques 14n3
DeVito, J. A. 141
Dictaphones 124–125, 126–127

dictation 3, 6–7, 14n2; and cell phones 129; and class issues 122; as collaborative 126; and future of communication 126–134; history of 114–122; in late antiquity 115–116; and memory aids 119; in Middle Ages 116–119; modern 123–124; and silent literacy 119, 122–124; voice-recognition dictation software 113, 127–129, 131, 132–134. *See also* technology; voice-recognition dictation software; writing process
dictionaries 90, 92, 93
Dionysius 60
directions of writing 38
Diringer, David 54–55, 78n26
dissoi logoi 41–42; definition of 36
distanciation: and naming 94–95; of written language 88–92, 177, 231
Donehower, Kim 106
Dorsey-Gaines, Catherine 109
double bind 229
double negatives 266
Dow, Sterling 37
Durkheim, Émile 47–48, 71

early modern English 2, 257, 266. *See also* standard language
economic function: as divorced from writing 23; of writing systems 20–21
Ede, L. 130
Edel, L. 123
education: effects of literacy as due to schooling 197n4; preparation for literacy in oral discourse 241–243; and public vs. private literate traditions 69–70; and speech 157–158, 178–179; and writing as punishment 183; and written language 178–179. *See also* teaching practices
Egypt: cartouches as precursor to paragraph 36; origins of written language in 24
elaborated code 234
Eliot, T. S. 14n4, 269
e-mail 132
embedding 173
emoticons 31
Empedocles 42
English language: as alphabetic writing system 10; development of modern 257–267; dialects of 263; historicisation of 257–258,

261–266; London as linguistic center of 257. *See also* language
Enos, Richard 38, 100
ephemerality: of speech 181–182; of written language 183–187
Epi-Olmec Hieroglyphic 29
Erard, Michael 7, 8, 9
E. Remington & Sons 128
Eskimo people 51
ethics, of literacy research 109
ethnographic studies 101, 106
Evans, Arthur 36–37
Evans-Pritchard, E. E. 58
expository prose. *See* informational prose

Faigley, Lester 97, 109
Farrell, Thomas J. 100
field dependency/independency 247–248, 253–254
Fillmore, C. J. 231, 238
Fishman, Andrea 106
Flowers, Linda 185
fluency 238
formality, of written language 3, 5
For Whom the Bell Tolls (Hemingway) 205
Foucault, M. 121, 130
Frawley, William 101
"freewriting" 188, 196
Freire, Paulo 102–105
Fuery, Patrick 99–100, 102–103, 108
funeral rites, and writing systems 23

Gandz, Solomon 55
Gardner, Howard 127
Gavrilov, A. K. 135n3
Geertz, Clifford 277, 281
Gelb, I. J. 27, 38; on Greek alphabet 34; on language and writing 43
gender: and clerical work 125–126; and intonation 272; and punctuation 226n6
genealogies 49–51, 77n10
Gere, Anne 106, 108
glyphs 26–27
Gonja people 50
Goody, Jack 12, 28, 29, 90, 99, 101; on Milton's dictation practice 123; on written mode 144
Gore, Al 269
Gorgias 42

grammar: embedding vs. hypotaxis 173; of spoken language 5–6, 11; and written language 168. *See also* punctuation
grammatical metaphor 174–177
grammatology 27
Granet, Marcel 70
grapholects 92
Graves, Donald 188
great leap theory. *See* orality/literacy binary
Greaves, William 274, 280
Greek civilization: alphabet in 34, 35, 56, 58–59; and democracy 66–67; dictation 115; directions of writing in 38; literacy of 12, 56–66; myth vs. history in 58–61; oral and literate rhetoric as linked in 34–35; paragraph's evolution in 43; techniques of oral rhetoric in 35–36. *See also* rhetoric
Greenberg, Karen 100
Grusin, R. 127–128
Gumperz, John 229–230, 234, 241

Haas, C. 114
Halbwachs, Maurice 48
Halle, M. 258
Halliday, M. A. K. 3, 5–6, 11, 272, 274, 277, 280
Halverson, C. 127, 128
Halverson, John 102
Harris, Roy 1–2, 13
Hart, Gary 183
Hartwell, Patrick 100
Hass, Robert, "Mouth Slightly Open" 282–283
Haugen, E. 258
Havelock, Eric 12, 27, 34, 38, 84, 88, 92, 93, 98, 99, 102, 182. *See also* orality/literacy binary
Heath, Shirley Brice 101, 102
Hebrew 8
Hecataeus 60
Hellanicus 60
Hemingway, Ernest 205, 226n6
Heraclitus 59, 93
Herodotus 60
hieroglyphs 9, 28–29, 52, 78n26
Hildyard, A. 178
Hill, C. 234
Hilligoss, Susan 109
Hirsch, E. D. 98
historicisation 261

history, vs. myths 58–61
Hitler, Adolph 240
Holzman, Michael 105
Homer 115
hooks, bell 105
Hope, Jonathan 266
Hopi people 73
Horn, D. 127, 128
Horsman, Jennifer 106
Howard, Tharon 109
human evolution, and language 46
Hymes, Dell 157, 231
Hyperides 40
hypotaxis 160, 164–165, 172–173

identity, and literacy 106
ideology: and descriptive tradition 261–266; effects of, on linguists 258–259, 261–266; of standard language 257–266
illiteracy: as deviant 83. *See also* literacy
individualism 72, 77n7, 121
informality, of speech 3, 5
informational prose: common grammatical features of 146–147, 149–150t; vs. conversation 144; dimensions of 152–153; expression of problem as key to 193; integration in 240; vs. interpersonal involvement 232; linguistic features of 145–148; multidimensional (MD) analysis of 150–153; as typical writing 144–145. *See also* texts; written language
integration 240
interpersonal involvement: cohesion hypothesis 233–234; contextualization hypothesis 231–233; and conversation 230, 231–232, 235–238; and double bind 229; features of focus on 231–234; and orality/literacy binary 228–231; and prosody 242; and reading 241; and spoken vs. written language 231–232; and writing process 241; and written language 238–241
interpretation, vs. data 89
intonation 268–285; elements of 268; functions of 269; and gender 272; and meaning 270; use of term 269; and voice 271–272; and written vs. spoken language 270
intonation units: and cognitive constraints 274–276; in *A Death in the Family* (Agee) 220–221; definition of 272–273; length of 216–217, 274; and listeners 275; and poetry 279; and punctuation units 202–209, 216–217; and reading aloud 225; and reading silently 225; role of 273; and speakers 273–275; in speech 203; and spontaneous syntax ("SponTax") 281–283; and syntactic glue 277–280; and written language 275–278; of written vs. spoken language 210–211. *See also* prosody
Introduction to English Grammar (Lowth) 205–206
involvement. *See* interpersonal involvement
Isocrates 40
I-thou relation 105, 108

Jackson, Jesse 183
Jacoby, Felix 60, 80n73
Jaeger, Werner 57, 58
Jakpa, Ndewura 50, 77n14
James, Henry 123–124, 217, 277, 281
Japanese language 54
Jaszi, P. 130
Jefferson, Thomas 67
Justeson, John S. 29

Kapitzke, Cushla 106
Karat, C. 127, 128
Karat, J. 127, 128
Kay, P. 141, 232, 234
Kennedy, George 34, 42
Kenyon-Knott grammar 258
Kerry, John 269
Killingsworth, Jimmie 107
Kintgen, Eugene 101
Kirsch, Gesa 109
Knox, B. M. W. 135n3
Knox, Sanka 34
Korean language 152
Kroll, Barry 101

Labov, W. 179, 233, 236, 264, 277
language: "high" vs. "low" 91–92; and human evolution 46; sex-linked 91; spoken 5–6; spontaneous vs. careful 3, 5–6, 169–170; subsystems of 174; variation within 258, 266. *See also* English language; speech; standard language
language, history of, as ideological 257–258, 261–266

Latour, Bruno 29–30
Lee, Dorothy D. 73
Lentz, Tony M. 38
Lesu island 48
"letteraturizzazione" 42
letter writing 117, 170
Lewis, J. 134
lexical bundles 280
lexical density 160–164, 162t, 163t, 167, 170–172
lexicalization 233–234, 242–243
lexico-grammatical systems 174
liberation narrative: contributions of 107–108; as leftist 108–109; of literacy 102–104
libraries 66
light subject constraint 276
Linde, C. 179
Linear A 29, 36
Linear B 29, 36, 37
linguistic features: of conversation vs. informational prose 145–148; of written vs. spoken language 141–142
linguistic products: speech as 4–5; writing as 4–5
linguistics, and speech 157–158
linguists, ideology's effects on 258–259, 261–266
listeners: and intonation units 275; and speakers 182, 183
listening: and conversational strategies 235–236; vs. reading 173–174, 178–179, 191, 213
lists 192
literacy: and abstract thinking 51, 58, 99; among African Americans 246; among Greek and Roman slaves 7; and analytic thought 84, 99; and awareness of time 51, 67; and children's oral discourse 241–243; in Chinese 10, 53; and class issues 53–54, 68–69, 102, 107, 109; conditional 78n22; as contextual 106; cultural 98; and culture 107–110; and democracy 66–67; effects of 61–64; effects of, as due to schooling 197n4; and Greek civilization 12, 56–66; and historical accretion 67–68; and identity 106; as ideological 101, 106; and invention of alphabet 24; liberation narrative of 102–104; and logic 58, 64–66; in Middle Ages 117; narratives of 97–110; as normative 83; and religion 106; spread of 55–56; and

technology 109, 114. *See also* illiteracy; orality/literacy binary
literacy research, ethics of 109
literate tradition: and American narrative strategies 230; evolution of 46–47; vs. oral tradition 69–70; public vs. private 69–70. *See also* abstract thought; literacy; orality/literacy binary
liturgy 269
Locke, John 74, 99
LoDagaa people 48
logic: and literacy 58, 64–66; vs. rhetoric 90–91; and written language 92–93, 191. *See also* abstract thought
logographic symbols 9–10, 52–53
logosyllabaries, as type of writing system 19
London, England, as linguistic center of English language 257
Long, Russell 202, 209
Longman Grammar of Spoken Written English 145
Longman Spoken Written English (LSWE) Corpus 145
Lowth, Robert 205–206
LSWE. *See* Longman Spoken Written English (LSWE) Corpus
Lubar, S. 125
Lunsford, A. 130
Lupton, E. 125, 126
Luria, A. R. 93
Lyotard, Jean-Francois 97, 105

Madsen, Catherine 269
Malinowsky, Bronislaw 48, 58
Mansfield, Nick 99–100, 103, 108
Marsh, George Perkins 263
Marxist theory 102, 107
mass media 69
materialist explanation 29–30
mathematics, and written vs. spoken language 2
Mathesius, V. 158
Maya writing system 26–27
McConnell-Genet, Sally 272
McLuhan, Marshall 12, 27, 29
MD analysis. *See* multidimensional (MD) analysis
Mead, Margaret 69

meaning: and intonation 270; for listeners vs. readers 173–174, 178–179; in spoken vs. written language 195–196
medical profession 132–133
Melville, Herman 204–205, 208
memoria 119–122, 131
memory: limitations of, for speakers 213; in oral tradition 48–50, 62; and organization of written language 192; social function of 48–51; writing as destructive to 80n73, 85
memory aids: and dictation 119; mnemonic techniques 119; in oral tradition 49–50, 84; paragraphs as 39, 41, 42; written language as 55
Mencius 70
mental actions: speech as 3; writing as 3
Meskalamdug 23
Mesoamerica, origins of written language in 20, 26–27
Mesopotamia, origins of written language in 7, 20–25
metamessages, vs. messages 232–233
metaphor, grammatical 174–177
Michaels, S. 241–242
Middle Ages: dictation in 116–119; literacy in 117; speech and writing in 6–7
Mill, James 67
Mill, John Stuart 67
Milroy, Jim 11
Milton, John 123
Minoan writing 37
mnemonic techniques. *See* memory aids
Moby Dick (Melville) 204–205, 208–209
modernism 120–121
monotone 269
Mortensen, Peter 109
Moss, Beverly 106
Mullen, Mark 98
multidimensional (MD) analysis, of registers in speech and writing 143, 148, 150–153
Murphy, J. J. 115, 116, 135n4
music 2
myths, vs. history 58–61

NAEP. *See* National Assessment of Educational Progress (NAEP)
National Assessment of Educational Progress (NAEP) 246
nationalism, and standard language 262–263
Neolithic Revolution 21
nominalization 176–177
non-literate culture. *See* oral tradition
numerals, creation of 22
Nystrand, M. 231

objectivity 88
office work, division of labor in 124–126
Oliphant, T. Kington 262
Olsen, J. 133
Olson, D. 228, 234, 240
Olson, David 28, 29, 99, 141
Olson, D. R. 178
one-new idea constraint 276
One Writer's Beginnings (Welty) 201–202
Ong, Walter 12, 27–28, 29, 34, 98, 101–102; on development of writing 182; on literacy 141; on reading aloud 218; on secondary orality 132; on silent writing 120; on sound-sight split 118; on speech 190; on writing and thinking 186. *See also* orality/literacy binary
open punctuation 218–221, 225, 226n6. *See also* punctuation
oral fluency 238
orality: secondary 131–134; temporality of 83–84. *See also* dictation
orality/literacy binary 27–28, 48; and African Americans 100; and anthropology 73, 75; and cognition 99, 142, 182; contributions of 107; as controversial 100; danger of 190; as elitist 108–109; and interpersonal involvement 229–231; Olson on 141; Ong on 141; overview of 98–100; refutations of 101–102; as scholarly argument 12. *See also* interpersonal involvement
oral tradition: and African American culture 100; ahistoricism of 67; as conservative 84; and genealogies 49–51; and Greek narrative strategies 230; idealization of 70–71; as incapable of linear analysis 85, 92–93; vs. individualism 77n7; and interpretation 89; vs. literate tradition 69–70; and memory 48–50, 62; memory aids in 49–50, 84; and myth vs. history 58–61; and non-verbal meaning 90, 93; past vs. present in 90; Plato as defender of 62–64; symbol-referent relationships in 47–48; and transmission of culture 47–51. *See also* orality/literacy binary

organization: "chunking" 192, 194; lists 192; problems of 193–194; recurring units 192–193; of written language 191–192
origins: of art 19–20; of art vs. written language 20–21; of writing systems 7–11, 20–29
orthography. *See* writing systems
overlapping talk 235–236

Paradise Lost (Milton) 3
paragraph: definition of 35; earliest forms of 36–39; evolution of, in Greek rhetoric 43; as legal term 40–41; as memory aid 39, 41, 42; "scratch marks" 36–40; as theatre cue 40; as tool for structuring meaning 35–37, 41–42; as vocal segregate 39–40, 41. *See also* rhetoric
paralinguistic cues 233–234, 242–243
parallel constructions 239
parataxis 160, 165, 173
parentheses 213
Parmenides 93
Parry, Milman 134n1
periods 207, 212, 215
permanence: of speech 183–187; of written language 181–182, 184
Perry, Milman 27
Petrucci, A. 119
Phaistos Disk 29, 36
"phatic" messages 182
Phillpotts, Bertha 70
philosophy, and written language 92–93
phonemes, and alphabetic writing systems 9, 24, 55
phonetic writing systems 53–54
phonograms, creation of 22–23
phonological systems 174
physical actions: speech as 3; writing as 3
physical products: speech as 4; writing as 4
pictography 22–23, 51–53
Piggott, Stuart 78n22
Pindar 60
Pinker, Stephen 6
pitch. *See* intonation units; prosody
Pitman, I. 134n2
Plato 56, 61–66, 67, 70, 84–85
Plum, Guenter 160
Plutarch 115
poetry 279
Pohl, M. 27
politeness. *See* universal politeness phenomena

Pope, K. 27
Popper, Karl 197n3
Powers, Richard 14n2
pre-writing 184–186
print 92, 99, 121–122
Printers' Manual (Timperley) 219
printing press 121
private writing 185–187
prosody: and interpersonal involvement 242; intonation units 203; and punctuation 202, 209–213; and reading aloud 209–213, 225–226; study on, of reading aloud 210–213, 211t; of written language 201–226. *See also* intonation units; punctuation; punctuation units
protoliteracy 77–78n22
proto-writing 7
punctuation: in *Age of Innocence* (Wharton) 205; close 225, 226n6; close vs. open 218–221; and cognitive load 217, 225; colons 212; commas 206–208, 212, 215, 223–224; dashes 213; in *A Death in the Family* (Agee) 220–221; disagreements regarding 221–224; and gender 226n6; in James's work 217; in *Moby Dick* (Melville) 204–205, 208–209; nonprosodic uses of 205–209; open punctuation 218–221, 225, 226n6; parentheses 213; periods 207, 212, 215; and prosody 202, 209–213; question marks 207–208, 212; and reading aloud 213, 222–224; and reading silently 223–224; repunctuation 213–216, 219, 221, 223–224, 225; rules of 207–209, 222, 225; semicolons 212; skill in 204; in study of prosody 210–213; and transitional adverbs 223–224; varying styles of 204–205; in *Walden* (Thoreau) 203–204, 219–220; in *For Whom the Bell Tolls* (Hemingway) 205
punctuation units: and intonation units 202–209, 216–217; length of 216–217; of written vs. spoken language 210–212. *See also* prosody

question marks 207–208, 212
Quintilian 115–116, 124

Rader, M. 231, 239
Radford, A. 258–259
Radway, Janice 106

Ramus, Peter 120
rank shift 173
Rawlinson, Henry Creswicke 29
readers: engagement of 189–190, 197; and writers 182
reading: and interpersonal involvement 241; vs. listening 173–174, 178–179, 191, 213
reading aloud: and close punctuation 218–220; and intonation units 225; and prosody 209–213, 225–226; and punctuation 213, 222–224; study on, of prosody 210–213, 211t; and writing process 201–202
reading silently 34, 39, 113; in antiquity 135n3; effect of, on authors 118–119; and intonation units 225; and open punctuation 220–221; pace of 213; and printing press 122; and punctuation 223–224; vs. secondary orality 131–134; skimming 226n1
rebus 8, 22
"Received Pronunciation" (RP) 264–265
Redfield, Robert 68
registers: and corpus-based analysis 145; definition of 142; dimensions of 152–153; multidimensional (MD) analysis of 143, 148, 150–153; variation within 142–143. *See also* conversation; informational prose
religion, and literacy 106
repunctuation 213–216, 214t, 215t, 219, 221, 223–224, 225
restricted code 234
retrograde direction 38
Rhapsodes 35
rhetoric: anti-logoi 36, 41; ars dictaminis 117–118, 120; compositional features of 36–42; dissoi logoi 36, 41–42; invention and structure 41–42; linearity and syntax 36–39; vs. logic 90–91; memory and dissociation 40–41; paragraphs as vocal segregates 39–40, 41; techniques of, in ancient Greece 35–36. *See also* paragraph
rhythm 2, 240
Ricoeur, Paul 88
Robinson, Andrew 9–10
Roeper, Tom 12
Rogers, Henry 28
romance novels 106
Roman civilization, dictation in 115–116
Rongo Rongo 29
Rose, Mike 98, 100, 101

Rosetta stone 28–29
Russell, Bertrand 178

Sacks, H. 239
Saenger, P. 116, 117–118, 122, 135n3
Sapir, Edward 260
Saville-Troike, M. 240
Schlangenschrift 38
Schmandt-Besserat, Denise 7, 8, 9
scholarship: on orality vs. literacy 12, 27–28; on spoken and written language 11–13; on voice 12–13
Scollon, R. 229
Scribner, Sylvia 101, 142
script. *See* writing systems
second person pronouns 266
the self, and voice 13
Selfe, Cynthia 109
semantic ratification 47–48
semantic systems 174
semicolons 212
sentence structure: complexity of spoken 159–168; of written vs. spoken language 161–162, 164–166
Sequoya 10
Shaw, George Bernard 265
Shillingsburg, P. L. 219
Shneiderman, B. 133–134
Sholes, Christopher 128
sign language 4
silent reading. *See* reading silently
silent writing: and class issues 122; and dictation 119, 122–124; effect of, on authors 118–119; Ong on 120; vs. secondary orality 131–134
Sioux people 48
Skeat, T. C. 115
slaves, literacy among 7
"snake-writing" 38
social change, and literacy as liberation 103–104
social class. *See* class issues
social function: of memory 48–51; of written language 51–57
Society of Pure English 265
sociology 46
Socrates 63–64
Somali language 152–153
Soviet Union 93

Index

spatial mode. *See* visual/spatial mode
speakers: and intonation units 273–275; and listeners 182, 183; short-term memory limitations of 213
speaking. *See* speech
speech: ambiguity of 167, 175; and clause complex 164–165, 166t, 167, 169, 172; cohesion in 233; as communal 188; complexity of natural 158–168; in composition and rhetoric departments 12; as contextual 231; definitions of 3–7; as different from written language 1–2, 5, 86–95, 167–168, 170, 174–175, 178, 181–182; as different from written texts 161; and education 157–158, 178–179; as ephemeral 181–182; grammar of 5–6, 11; grammatical intricacy of 163–167; and grammatical metaphor 177; as informal 3, 5–6; interpersonal involvement in 231–232; intonation units in 203, 210–211; lexical density of 160–164, 162t, 163t, 167, 170; linguistic features of 141–142; and linguistics 157–158; as mental action 3; in Middle Ages 6–7; pace of 213; as permanent 183–187; as physical action 3; preparation for literacy in oral discourse 241–243; punctuation units in 210–212; scholarly views of 11–13, 28, 141–142; as similar to written language 5, 143, 170, 187–196; sound of, emulated 22–23; spontaneous vs. careful 169–170; as temporal/audible 1–2, 4, 83–84; temporality of 1–2, 4, 83–84, 190–191, 276; typical 5–6, 144; as unconscious act 158–159; virtues of 284–285; voice in 195–196; and writing systems 10. *See also* conversation; intonation units; writing
Spengler, Oswald 65, 66
spoken language. *See* speech
"SponTax" 281–283
Spooner, M. 127
Sreberny-Mohammadi, Annabelle 107
standardisation: characteristics of 259–261; and database of theoretical linguistics 258–259; development of 266–267; as implemented through written language 260; as inhibiting variation 260–261; as process 258
standard language: as idealisations 258, 260, 265, 266; ideology of 257–266; legitimisation of 262; as prestige language 261, 263–265; and "Received Pronunciation" (RP) 264–265; and social class 264–265; and writing systems 258. *See also* English language; ideology; language
stoichedon 38
storytelling, as conversational strategy 230
Stratton, R. E. 100
Street, Brian 99, 101–102, 144
structural amnesia 50, 67
structure. *See* organization
Stubbs, M. 144
Stuckey, Elspeth 102
students: and black discourse style 246–247; and punctuation 204
style, vs. voice 12–13
Sullivan Patricia 42
Sumerians 52, 53
Swearingen, Jan 100
Sweet, Henry 262–263, 264
Swift, Jonathan 67
syllabaries: development of 52; Semitic 54–55; as type of writing system 9–11, 19
syntactic glue 277–280

tablets 129
Tannen, Deborah 101, 142, 167, 190, 226n6
taxonomy 64
Taylor, Denny 109
teaching practices: and reader engagement 189–190, 197; and voice 189; and writing as akin to speech 188; writing as punishment 183. *See also* education; organization
Tebeaux, E. 121, 127
technical writing 121, 127, 198n10
technology: and authorship as collaborative 130–131; cell phones 129, 132; and Chinese language 30; for communication 31; and consciousness 87–88; cultural influences on uses of 114; Dictaphones 124–125, 126–127; e-mail 132; and literacy 109, 114; and persistence of written language 198n5; printing press 121; tablets 129; texting 31; typewriters 123–125, 128; Unicode 30–31; voice-recognition dictation software 113, 127–129, 131, 132–134; written language as 83–95, 182. *See also* specific items
technology of writing, interiorization of 83–84

temporality: and oral tradition 90; of spoken language 1–2, 4, 83–84, 190–191, 276; of written language 191–193, 277
texting 31
texts: as intermediary between author and reader 94; resources provided by, as non-obvious 144–145; as unresponsive 85. *See also* writing
Theodoric 116
thinking. *See* cognition
Thomas Aquinas 119
Thoreau, Henry David 203–204, 219–220
Thucydides 60–61
time, awareness of 51, 67
Timperley, C. H. 219
Tiro 115
Tiv people 49–51
Tóibín, Colm 14n4
token system 21
Toller, T. N. 261
Trajan 39
transcription 124, 125, 126, 128, 129, 131, 133. *See also* dictation
transitional adverbs 223–224
Trimbur, John 110
Trobrianders 48, 73
two-dimensional signs 21–22
typewriters 123–125, 128
Tzeng, O. J. L. 92

Unicode 31
universal politeness phenomena 228–229
Universal Scripts Initiative 31
Ure, Jean 162

Vai people 101
Varenne, H. 234
variation: within language 258–259, 266; within registers 142–143; standardisation as inhibiting 260–261
Vásquez, Camilla 5
Ventris, Michael 29, 34, 37–38
visual/spatial mode: and paragraph 39–40; of written language 1–2, 4, 190–191
visual symbols. *See* art; writing systems
vocabulary, as reflective of societal interests 48
voice: and authenticity 13; definition of 189; examples of 14n4; and intonation 271–272; scholarly arguments on 12–13; and the self 13; in spoken vs. written language 195–196; vs. style 12–13; and teaching practices 189; types of, in text 14n3
voice-recognition dictation software 113, 127–129, 131, 132–134
von Nagy, C. 27
Vygotsky, L. S. 114

Waiters, Keith 102
Walden (Thoreau) 203–204
Wang, W. S.-Y. 92
Watt, Ian 12, 99
Weber, J. 133
Weber, Max 74
Welch, Kathleen 100, 120
Welty, Eudora 201–202, 271
West, Cornel 105
Wharton, Edith 205
whites, and field dependency/independency 247–248
Whorf, Benjamin Lee 73
Wilkinson, Andrew 157
Williams, Tennessee 14n4
wisdom, vs. academic learning 91
women: as clerical workers 125–126; ethnographic studies by and about 106
Woodhead, A. G. 38
Woodmansee, M. 119, 130
Wright, Joseph 264
writers: and readers 182; and silent reading/writing 118–119; types of 119; visual representation of 113. *See also* authorship
writing: definition of 4–8. *See also* written language
writing process: and consciousness 87–88, 94–95; and interpersonal involvement 241; as mental action 4–5; in Middle Ages 7–8, 116–119; modern division of labor in 124–126; as physical action 4; and pre-writing 184–186; as punishment 183; and reading aloud 201–202. *See also* authorship; dictation
writing systems: and abstract thinking 182; alphabetic 9–10, 54–57; calendrical function of 26; as cultural inventions 8; definition of 19; economic function of 20–21, 23; and funeral rites 23; hieroglyphs 9, 28–29, 52, 78n26; logographic 9–10, 52–53;

non-phonetic 52–53; origins of 7–11, 20–29; phonetic 53–54; pictography 22–23, 51–53; sentences in 23; and speech 10; spread of 23–24; and standard language 258; as subsystem of language 174; syllabic 9–11; token system 21; types of 9, 19. *See also* specific systems

written language: ambiguity of 167, 176; bias toward, as standard language 12; as communal 188, 198n8; and contextualization 190, 238–239; as different from speech 2–3, 5–6, 86–95, 167–168, 170, 174–175, 178, 181–182; distanciation of 88–92, 177, 231; and education 178–179; as ephemeral 183–187; formality of 4, 6; future of 30–31; and grammar 168; and grammatical metaphor 175–177; guidelines for improving 284–285; interpersonal involvement in 232, 238–241; and intonation 270; and intonation units 210–211, 275–278; lexical density of 161–164, 162t, 163t, 167, 170–172; lexicalization of 233–234; linguistic features of 141–142; and logic 191; materialist explanation for 29–30; and memory 80n73; as memory aid 55; organization of 191–192; as permanent 181–182, 184; persistence of 198n5; Plato's condemnation of 62–63, 84–85; prosody of 201–226; punctuation units in 203–204, 210–212; and reader engagement 189–190, 197; scholarly views of 12–14, 28, 141–142; as similar to speech 6, 143, 170, 187–196; social function of 51–57; vs. spoken language 160–164; and spontaneous syntax ("SponTax") 281–283; spread of 29–30, 55–56; standardisation as implemented through 260; as technology 83–95, 182; temporality of 191–193, 277; types of 51–57; typical 6–7, 144–145; as visual/spatial product 2–3, 5, 190–191; voice in 195–196. *See also* informational prose; speech; texts

Wyckoff, William 128
Wyld, Henry Cecil 260, 263, 264–265

Xenophanes 59
Xenophon 64
Xu Shen 25

Yates, J. 124, 125
Yeats, W. B. 59, 70
Yoruba people 101
Young, Richard 37, 42

Zick, R. G. 133
zoology 46
Zuni people 48